At the Kremlin Gates

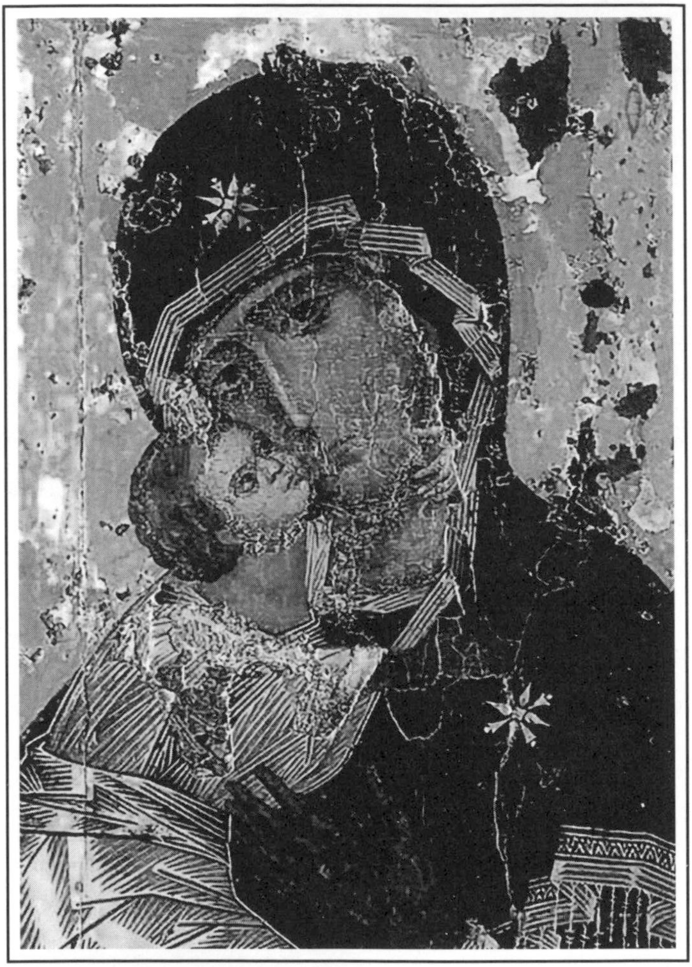

Vladimir Mother of God, Holy Protectress of Russia. Created in Constantinople and brought to Russia in the twelfth century. Divine intercession is reputed to have saved Russia and Moscow several times, against Tamurlane in 1395 and against the Mongols in 1451 and 1480. Some believe that her presence was felt in 1812 and in 1941, both times when Moscow was again threatened with extinction.

At the Kremlin Gates

A Historical Portrait of Moscow

Gerald R. Skinner

Signal

First published in the UK in 2011 by
Signal Books Limited
36 Minster Road
Oxford OX4 1LY
www.signalbooks.co.uk

A catalogue record for this book is available from the British Library

ISBN 978-1-904955-81-8
Cover, illustration mastering and text design: Claire Reika Wright
Typesetting and layout: Claire Reika Wright
Cover image and motifs (c) Claire Reika Wright
Back cover image: Wikipedia Commons File: Aristarkh Lentulov 'St Basil's Cathedral'; Illustrations to chapter openings: Ch1: Shchusev State Museum of Architecture; all others courtesy of Wikipedia Commons Files

Printed in India

Contents

Acknowledgments

Many have contributed to this book, and I am grateful to all, especially to those Muscovites who have confided in me, but would prefer that their names be witheld.

Professor Emeritus Archie Brown of St. Antony's College of the University of Oxford was a constant source of encouragement. The staff of the Schweizerische Osteuropabibliothek of the University of Berne were generous in offering the research facilities of its Sager collection.

Moscow City itself was a major contributor, through its publications and the willingness of its specialists to guide me through the mountains of material on the city. I am particularly grateful to Irina Vasilevna Smagina of the Museum of the History of Moscow.

The views as well as any the errors are of course mine alone.

Gerald R. Skinner

Introduction

This book has several origins. Firstly, it is a very personal pilgrimage to a city which has shaped a good part of my adult life. I belong to the 1960s generation, and shared that generation's hopes and fears. We lived with the unpredictable possibility of nuclear war, either inadvertent or planned. Moscow was far away, its exoticism matched by its menace. I heard Moscow before I saw it, via a German-manufacture short-wave receiver owned by my Russian-language teacher. I believed (or wanted to believe) that he was a former British intelligence officer whose cover had been blown and who had been sent to Canada with a new identity. Radio Moscow used a simplified language designed for its International Service. Simplified or not, the language was dauntingly difficult. It took me many years before children in the Moscow streets stopped asking me where I was from. Even then, it turned out I could still be identified as a foreigner. I was once addressed in English in an open-air market by a man wanting to sell me something. How did he know I was not Russian? 'Easy', he said, 'your teeth. No Russian has teeth like that at your age.'

My fellow graduate students at Moscow University's Law Faculty made no distinction between me and anyone else. We were in it together. The only 'others' were Komsomol activists, and the various state-appointed monitors whose task was to keep the student body in line. In the mid 1960s, at the height of the Vietnam War and the Sino–Soviet ideological dispute, the student body was regularly called upon to demonstrate against the war or to throw ink at the Chinese Embassy, located conveniently close to the main university building. The obligation to participate, which many regarded as a kind of tax for the privilege of attending the university, was managed in such a way as to reduce disruption to our schedule of lectures and social life to a minimum. There was a kind of roster, and all knew well in advance when their turn was up.

In contrast to Western students of the 1960s generation who went on the streets demanding change, their Russian counterparts stood aside. In 1968 the *jours de mai* student riots in Paris and the Prague Spring held little resonance despite the concerns of the Soviet leadership. Russia, and Moscow in particular, seemed isolated, impassive and immutable. Yet less than a generation later Moscow became the epicentre of a geopolitical collapse whose aftershocks still reverberate. A good number of my student contemporaries were direct participants.

By tradition, Moscow is the Easternmost bastion of Western civilization. It shows most of the characteristics of any large urban community. The city has an identifiable centre and a well-developed infrastructure with an array of officials to run it. It meets the requirements and functions of any other city as a place where people gather for mutual benefit, to conduct business, and are provided with reasonable levels of security. It is the focal point of a complex communications network that extends well beyond its own boundaries. Like many other great cities, it also holds something of the sacred in its buildings. The collective memory of its citizens sets it apart from being merely a large settlement occupied with trade and commercial transaction. But the massive tower-blocks of post-Soviet Moscow do not erase a sense of remoteness from the Western urban experience.

A diffracted image of their city is held by Muscovites themselves. In a manner sometimes puzzling to outsiders, a number of opponents of the August 1991 coup attempt by conservative representatives of Soviet power came from the senior ranks of the security apparatus who had revolted against the erstwhile political authorities within the Communist Party.

This did not mean that they were pro-Gorbachev, or even in favour of his reforms. In the KGB, the army and other organs of state security, very few were. They were pro-Russia and had a belief in the Russianness of Russia's capital that transcended its Soviet overlay. As the drama of the coup unfolded, the focus of confrontation was in Moscow. That drama had a physical dimension. It was between the White House, seat of the Russian government, and the Kremlin. Many Muscovites regarded the Kremlin as the headquarters of an internal occupation.

Moscow is one of a handful of cities which like Troy have risen out of their own ruins. More than once, it has reinvented itself through a near-miraculous combination of physical circumstance, history and sheer human will, sometimes assisted by overwhelming faith. Indeed, the central theme of Moscow's narrative is survival.

This begins with its founding myths through its development into a metropolis with a global outreach. Adopting a 'theme-park' approach, guide books tend to describe Moscow in terms of its architectural features, the dimensions of rooms and the weights of bells. In the process the tragedy, drama and triumph lying just behind its modern steel-and-glass curtains are lost. At the other end of the scale are barely accessible and dense academic texts. There is little in between.*

This book is a portrait of a city over time, an interpretation of its origins, the influences upon its development and character. Several dominant themes run through Moscow's narrative, together defining the city and its meaning. The first theme is the city's self-perception, from its original purpose as a citadel of defence and then of domination—at one point the largest fortress in Europe—to a city of transcendent aspiration, originally as the Third Rome and later as headquarters of a world revolutionary movement which held that history was on its side. The second theme relates to Moscow's organic pattern of growth and decline from which a new Moscow emerges. The third theme addresses the historic tension between Moscow as an urban community and Moscow as the locus of state power, with its Kremlin above and apart from the urban space in which it resides. A fourth theme follows the unique quality of Moscow's parthenogenesis, replicating urban patterns of itself across the landscape of its dominions, both imperial and Soviet, each a model of the world-view of its rulers. St. Petersburg, Moscow's near-nemesis, became the architectural expression of the rift that developed in the Russian identity that has continued to this day.

The triad of defence, domination and survival runs through each chapter as leitmotifs. The evolution of the physical means that Moscow devised to assure its continued existence has left a deep imprint on the city's psyche. Palpable evidence is still visible, and accounts for the city's concentric development, the strategic placement of monasteries on its approaches and even the siting of the Stalinist 'high buildings' within the city itself. Anti-ballistic missile systems ringing Moscow are the direct inheritors of ancient patterns of defence.

In later years, at the Canadian Embassy I observed first-hand the end-game of *perestroika*, the Moscow coup attempt of August 1991 and the emergence of Yeltsinite Russia. With the break-up of the Soviet Union I was subsequently appointed to Canadian Embassies in the former Republics of its collapsed empire, first in the Baltic States and then in Central Asia. Like a turned kaleidoscope, the images these countries had of Moscow and what it represented were sometimes widely divergent.

Personal circumstances and the hand that fate dealt me, seeing Moscow first as a graduate student, then as a bureaucrat and diplomat, and finally as a member of St. Antony's College at the University of Oxford, contributed to the differing images I had of the city before, during and after communism. This book seeks to reconcile them.

* Among the exceptions in English are Arthur Voyce, *Moscow and the Roots of Russian Culture*, Kathleen Berton, *Moscow: An Architectural History*, and Laurence Kelly, *A Traveller's Companion to Moscow*. In German, there is historian Karl Schloegel's *Moskau*. Amongst the many books on Moscow in Russian, there are surprisingly few that would satisfy the general reader. An encyclopedic, multiple-volume work on Moscow history produced by the Russian Academy of Sciences, *Istoriya Moskvy*, is aimed at specialists. A less exhaustive work, the Gorbachev-period two-volume *Moskva: Illyustrurirovannaya Istoriya,* (Y.A. Polyakov, chief ed.) is available in English. One of the most succinct accounts of the city is Yevgeny Ocetrov's *Moe Otkrytie Moskvy*, which takes a selective approach to the city's past in a series of short historical sketches. Translated from the German, Walter Benjamin's *Moscow Diary* offers a detailed description of the city in the 1930s. Jacques Derrida's Jacques *Derrida v Moskve: dekonstruktsiia puteshestvia* (1993), subsequently published in French as *Moscou aller-retour*, captures the spirit of post-communist Moscow.

The Palace of Soviets, approved final version, 1934. After many delays, plans for its construction were cancelled by Khrushchev. The Cathedral of Christ the Saviour has been rebuilt on its original site.

Chapter One
Moscow: Portrait of a City

> *No city on the continent of Europe has undergone such momentous change in the past one and a half decades as Moscow. Moscow has been the setting for the end of an empire and the rebirth of Russia; the scene of transformation of the world's grayest capital into a Babylon iridescent with colour, a place where time stands still and yet one of frenetic acceleration... Moscow is not identical with Russia. Moscow is almost a state in its own right, a city on a different planet.*
>
> Karl Schlögel, German historian, 1984

The world's great cities possess a quality of historical continuity. Continuity defines their identities from their beginnings to their maturity. Geography, climate and resources, the culture of the people who live in them, their social organization and their technology, all contribute to a city's personality. So does history. History means change. Moscow's various transformations over the centuries have been extreme, and have often obscured Moscow's identity as a place and of Muscovites as a people. The effect can be disorienting as one must juggle in one's head many Moscows at once.

There are many Moscows, each standing on the ruins of the other. Layer by layer, each of the earlier Moscows has contributed to the narrative of its successor, together informing the identity of the present-day city. Even within its layered past, Moscow's continuities are astonishing. The Englishman William Coxe, visiting Moscow in 1770, described a city of wretched hovels, blended with large palaces, cottages of one storey standing next to the most stately mansion: 'some parts of this vast city', he wrote, 'have the appearance of a sequestered desert, other quarters of a populous town; some of a contemptible village, others of a great capital.' Over one hundred and fifty years later, a fellow countryman, the Mayor of Manchester Sir E. D. Simon, headed a Commission of Enquiry that visited Soviet Moscow in 1936. He reported that the city, 'which for many centuries had developed in chaotic fashion, reflected, even in the best years of its development, the barbaric character of Russian capitalism. The narrow and crooked streets, the districts intersected by a multitude of lanes and blind alleys ... the low, decrepit houses huddled together.'

The Commission reported that Soviet communism would change all that, and indeed it did. The details were spelled out in the Ten-Year Plan for the Reconstruction of Moscow of 1935. A Stalinist storm of destruction which followed had no rival until the renovation of Beijing in the 1990s.

In his *Message of Greeting on the Eight-Hundredth Anniversary of the Founding of Moscow*, Stalin announced in 1947 that Moscow was 'the initiator of a new way of life of the working people ... a life free from wretchedness and want ... a model for all capitals of the world... Moscow has abolished slums and moved working people out of cellars and hovels into apartments.' According to Soviet publications, by the 1970s the USSR had reached the stage of a fully-developed socialist state. There was even a term for it coined in the Brezhnev years: 'actually existing socialism'. Moscow was then described as a capital of social equality, without slums or gangsters, without people deprived of work and homes.

The years of Stalin's ascendancy from the mid-1930s until his death in 1953 took a heavy toll on the city. Before the Second World War abortive development plans, large-scale destruction of neighbourhoods, overcrowding and the associated social costs of giving priority to prestige projects resulted in the grey desolation of post-war Moscow. With the fall of communism in 1991, and after a near-death experience in 1998, when the Russian economy came near to collapse, Moscow is reviving. Although challenged by the worldwide economic downturn beginning in 2008 and the consequent drop in energy prices, Moscow still has all the twenty-first-century glitter and urban glitz that comes from moving rapidly from the Third and Second Worlds to the First.

The Moscow Mystique

One word which does not describe Moscow is charm. My first reaction to the city was a mixture of fascination and repulsion. The very size and the impersonality of its faceless Soviet-era concrete blocks overwhelm one. It is a city that has inherited a tradition of giganticism. The Kremlin dominates. The hulking Stalinist silhouette of Moscow State University presides on the horizon. The city's architectural dissonances contribute to a vague feeling of disorientation. A small medieval church sits incongruously in the midst of a vast Khrushchev-era housing estate. Heavy rush-hour traffic stampedes outside the Kremlin walls along the Moskva River.

The Moscow mystique lies beyond the visual cacophony of its architecture, and is half-hidden in its layers of history. It emerges in unexpected ways. One of the long-term effects of a fixation on Byzantium has been the survival of the double-headed eagle, directly inherited from Byzantium, and reappearing phoenix-like after the collapse of the Soviet Union as a symbol of all Russia and of the Russian national identity. Its presence in Russia's new nationalism is ubiquitous. The equestrian image of St. George, Moscow's patron saint, is the logo of Russia's primary city.

Many view that mystique as a product of the tension between the deeply-rooted culture of the Russian countryside and the industrialized demands of urbanism. Yet the social gulf between city and countryside may not be as great as many suppose. This is best illustrated by the change in the social composition of Moscow following the liberation of the serfs in 1861, when many people, driven by rapid industrialization and radical changes in the social order on the land, came to the city to find work. This had the effect of 'countrifying' it. Despite various guises, the mystique of Moscow and its link to the Russian identity have been remarkably constant from the Napoleonic invasion into the revolutionary period, through Stalinism, the Second World War and beyond.

In one important sense, however, that gulf remains. In making the case for the presence of contradictions between the city and the countryside, some historians have argued that the former was parasitic upon the latter. The tsarist system of rule rested upon the landed aristocracy, even though the urban merchant classes bore the greater part of the financial burden in maintaining the state. Even now, if one drives beyond the perimeters of the city, the division between city and countryside is striking. The further one goes, the more one feels caught up in a time-warp.

The 'Moscow mystique' stands in sharp contrast with the civic personality of St. Petersburg, which since its founding has been Western-oriented as indeed Peter the Great intended, modelling his Window on the West after cosmopolitan Amsterdam, showcase of the Enlightenment. Even today, St. Petersburg residents tend to regard their cousins in Moscow as culturally inferior, and deride the Moscow accent. Aristocratic St. Petersburg looks west, to the sea. Merchant Moscow looks east, to the steppe.

The identification of Russians with their capital city remains an elusive quality. The thousand-day siege of Leningrad/St. Petersburg and the great battles of Stalingrad and Kursk during the Second World War point to a tenaciousness in defence of territory that is spectacularly missing in the case of Moscow. In 1812, Marshal Kutuzov ordered the Russian Army to abandon the city to Napoleon, and the Governor of Moscow, Count Fyodor Rostopchin, has been accused of arranging for it to be set alight. Again, in 1941, in the face of a relentless Wehrmacht advance, the Soviet administrative capital was temporarily moved to Kuybyshev. After a near-collapse, the defensive line established by Marshal Zhukov held against the Germans. In the midst of panic in the streets and general abandonment of the city, the NKVD had the Kremlin mined, and the main thoroughfares booby-trapped. It is possible to envisage what the ensuing Armageddon might have been like. In the midst of the Moscow campaign, Hitler diverted Wehrmacht Army Group South to Stalingrad in a misjudged strategy to gain the resources of southern Russia and the Black Sea. The epic battle which followed reversed the course of the war in Europe, but utterly destroyed the city. By a fluke, Moscow just missed Stalingrad's agony.

Moscow has an inexplicable capacity to exist outside the space it occupies. Received wisdom is that Russian military leaders learned by experience to trade distance for time, and that General Winter would eventually come to Russia's defence—as indeed turned out to be the case in 1812 and again in 1941. Tolstoy's basic thesis in *War and Peace* is that oceanic historical forces, nature and geography acting in concert beyond human will are the final arbiters of great events. In Tolstoy's version, Marshal Kutuzov understood this and used it to his advantage. Napoleon's occupation of Moscow was inconsequential. In Tolstoy's account, Moscow was greater than a place. It was Russia itself. Napoleon was at a loss to understand why his occupation of Moscow did not bring victory. Instead of suing for peace, the Russians destroyed their city.

What Tolstoy sought to convey was a sense that embedded in the Moscow mystique is a spiritual dimension intimately linked to Russian national identity. Tsar Alexander's Manifesto calling upon the population to resist Napoleonic aggression was cast in Old Testament terms, equating Russians with the Chosen People. (The Manifesto was originally drafted in French, but was wisely translated into Russian before it was promulgated.) A similar appeal from a starkly materialist regime was made in 1941 when the Soviet authorities issued broadsheets exhorting the people of Moscow to defend their city. One wartime poster depicts Mother Russia as a twentieth-century version of Delacroix's *Liberty Leading the People*. Another recasts Russia as a proletarian Mother of God.

Naming Moscow

Names are revealing. In Russian culture, last names frequently carry a mystical, quasi-religious connotation. Dostoevsky named his spiritually-tortured protagonist in *Crime and Punishment* 'Raskolnikov', literally 'schismatic', implying a deep division within his psyche. Names of cities or places exhibit a parallel phenomenon, sometimes named after prominent historical figures. St. Petersburg/Leningrad and Yekaterinburg, city of Catherine the Great and place of the murder of the last Tsar and his family, are examples. One legend has it that Moscow was named after a descendant of Noah, Musokh. Firmer historical evidence records a proposed name-change from Moscow to 'Stalinodar', meaning Gift of Stalin. In an unusual burst of modesty, its intended beneficiary turned down the suggestion. Of all Russian cities, Moscow has held its original name from the beginning.

The linguistic origins of Moscow/Muscovy are obscure. Most likely the name is a Baltic–Slavic hydronym of the first millennium, named after the rivers of the region, similar in sense to the word Mesopotamia. In that first thousand years,

Mosk/Mask/Mozg indicated a bog or swampy place. The twelfth-century stockade that became the Kremlin rose above a swamp on the opposite side of a river. The Old Russian Chronicle relates that in 1147, Yuri Dolgoruky ('Long-Arm', a name of Norse inspiration), the grand prince of Suzdal, 'laid down the town of Moskva' near the confluence of two rivers. On the north-western bluff overlooking a bend in the river, he built a pine-log stockade, converting his estate into a fortified place—the core of the present-day Kremlin. 'A fortified place' is still one of the key elements defining Moscow.

If its name has not changed, Moscow has been oversupplied with designations. This began with its early identification with Constantinople. By the fourteenth century, both were upon occasion referred to as 'Tsargrad', city of the emperor. By the sixteenth century, some Old Believers awaiting the Apocalypse regarded Moscow as the Second, or New Jerusalem of the Book of Revelation. Others were less impressed. A contemporary of Napoleon, Madame de Staël, famously called it the 'Rome of the Tatars'.

Moscow as the Third Rome

In 1310 Moscow became the see of the Orthodox Church. When Constantinople fell to the Turks in 1453, Moscow was increasingly recognized as the sole champion of Eastern Christianity.

Some believed that Moscow was founded on seven hills, like Rome. Unlike Rome, Moscow had kept the true faith of Orthodoxy, whereas Rome had fallen into apostasy and idolatry. There is much scholarly literature on the subject, the focal point being a letter dated 1511 from the monk Philotheus of Eleazer Monastery in Pskov to Vasily III:

> The church of ancient Rome fell ... to the second Rome—the Church of Constantinople... But this third, new Rome, the Universal Apostolic Church under thy mighty rule radiates forth the Orthodox Christian faith to the ends of the earth. In all the universe thou art the only Tsar of Christians. Hear me, pious Tsar, all Christian kingdoms have converged in thine alone. Two Romes have fallen, a third stands, a fourth there shall not be...

The secular dimension of Moscow's ecclesiastical succession to the seat of Orthodox Christendom had wide implications. The rulers of medieval Muscovy had a strong interest in reinforcing their claims to the legitimacy of their line and consequently their right of succession through the practice of royal intermarriage. This was frequently accompanied by the physical elimination of those who held differing views. In 1472, Ivan III, on advice of his counsellors, reluctantly married the hugely fat Zoe Palaeologus, niece and closest living relative to the last Byzantine emperor, thereby establishing his claim to the Byzantine throne. She is reputed to have broken their wedding bed with her weight.

There is a scholarly fascination with the notion of Moscow the Third Rome. Originally, the idea referred to ecclesiastical arrangements, and was not intended to buttress the worldly power of the grand princes, and later, the Romanov tsars. The tsar never became *pontifex maximus*, like a Roman emperor with temporal and spiritual authority combined in the same office. As a result, Moscow never became the equivalent of the Vatican City. This did not prevent it from developing a mystic aura which by tradition gave it a special calling, especially under communism when it became idealized as the headquarters of world revolution and the model city of the future.

As a political movement, communism represented a mixture of what its adherents held was objective analysis ('historical materialism', an economically-based set of Marxist principles) and faith, represented by the philosophically-obscure dialectic. In politics, the dialectic guaranteed the final triumph of socialism, and goes some way to explain why so many of communism's adherents were prepared to sacrifice themselves in the belief that they were building a better world. Marxist philosophy and Bolshevik ideology became simplified and codified in Nikolai Bukharin's *ABC of Communism,* the standard reference until Stalin had its author shot. It was replaced by *History of the Communist Party of the Soviet Union, Short Course,* which appeared under Stalin's own name. The story of Bukharin, a revolutionary true-believer, entered English political literature in Arthur Koestler's *Darkness at Noon,* whose main protagonist is based on him. In the novel, although innocent, he sacrifices his own life in the interests of the Party by admitting guilt.

'Revolutionary enthusiasm' and the prospect of world revolution with Moscow at its centre seemed a real possibility following the Bolshevik seizure of power in Russia, and amid the chaos of post-war Europe. At the end of the second decade of the twentieth century, Bela Kun in Hungary and Karl Liebknecht and Rosa Luxemburg in Berlin became prominent revolutionary figures, Kun heading a short-lived Soviet Republic. Many saw their movements as auguries of things to come. Under the inspired leadership and organizational skill of the Commissar of Military and Naval Affairs, Leon Trotsky, the Red Army consolidated its victory over the Whites throughout former imperial Russian territory, and obliged the withdrawal of a half-hearted Allied expeditionary force sent, in Churchill's phrase, 'to strangle infant Bolshevism in its cradle'. The victorious Red Army advanced deep into Poland, and was only stopped by the 'Miracle on the Vistula', the defence of Warsaw by General Weygand. Briefly independent, Ukraine became Bolshevik.

Moscow the Third Rome became Red Moscow, headquarters

of the Third International and capital of world revolution. At its founding conference in March 1919, Lenin expressed the revolutionary optimism of the time: 'All over the world, the association of communism is growing... In a number of countries, Soviet power has already triumphed. Soon we shall see the triumph of communism throughout the world; we shall see the foundation of the World Federative Republic of Soviets'[1]

The city's self-proclaimed role as the seat of world revolution became contradictory after Lenin's death in 1924 and as Stalin tightened his grip on power. Flamboyant and charismatic, Leon Trotsky emerged as Stalin's main political challenger. He was also the main advocate of proletarian internationalism. Flamboyance and charisma proved no match for the systematic plotting of Stalin, who wielded his grudges like an axe. With his associates, Trotsky was purged in the 1920s and was finally assassinated in Mexican exile in 1940. Stalin's policies of forced industrialization and collectivization, 'Socialism in One Country', took precedence over world revolution. The Third International continued as an organization until 1943 when it was disbanded in the interests of Allied solidarity against Hitler.

Throughout the Soviet period Moscow acted as a kind of holding pen for expatriate communists. Often defeated in their own countries, their Soviet hosts kept them as 'strategic reserves' against future use. The policy of harbouring refugee Communists could take bizarre forms. Following the defeat of the Republican side in the Spanish Civil War, a few districts of Moscow briefly took on a Hispanic air. Communists defeated in Greece in 1948 fared worse. Some were sent to populate distant valleys of Kazakhstan, presumably because their potential was judged nil.

But the policy paid off. In the wake of the Red Army advance into Eastern Europe, Moscow-based Communists were 'parachuted' into their home countries to set up pro-Soviet regimes. In distorted form, the image of Moscow, capital of world revolution, was kept alive: Moscow was 'The Centre'.

The KGB, in its various appellations and abbreviations, had as one of its assigned roles the protection and promotion of world socialism. That was the theory. These objectives, however, had to be compatible with the 'Party line' as laid down by the CPSU Central Committee. Somewhat confusingly, officers of the KGB's First Chief Directorate (Foreign Intelligence) continued to refer to *their* Moscow Headquarters as 'The Centre' as well. The poet of the early Soviet period, Vladimir Mayakovsky, summed up Moscow's global outlook best when he wrote that 'the Earth begins at the Kremlin'.

Even after the demise of the Third International, 'Proletarians of All Countries, Unite', the battle-cry of Marx's *Communist Manifesto*, continued to appear on the masthead of *Pravda*, the Party newspaper. For over seventy years it was also the lead slogan on banners carried by mass demonstrations on Red Square on 7 November. The end came in November 1991. Boris Yeltsin had just outlawed the Communist Party, and all its slogans vanished with it. A month later, on 8 December, the heads of state of Belarus, Ukraine and the Russian Federation announced that the Soviet Union ceased to exist. On 25 December Gorbachev resigned as President of the USSR. With that, Moscow's revolutionary calling, already dead, was buried.

Bureaucrats in the Russian state apparatus still call Moscow 'The Centre'. One should not look at the distinctions too closely.

Naming Moscow as Workbench, Museum and Proletarian Digs

In the late nineteenth century, with the capital of the country still St. Petersburg, Moscow was called the 'Calico City' because of its rapidly expanding textiles industry. The huge Prokhorov Tryekhgornaya Mill employed some 6,000 workers. In the 1920s, a time of remarkable intellectual creativity and great hopes for the future, the city was briefly called 'New Moscow'. Idealists and artists from all over Europe dreamed of refashioning it along presumptive Marxist lines, planning to turn the Kremlin into a museum and demolish the rest. The idea was stillborn when its main sponsor, Lev Kamenev, was the victim of an early Stalinist purge. Other idealistic projects were often wildly unrealistic. An earlier scheme, proposed in 1918, envisaged refashioning the Kremlin as an Acropolis of the Arts, described by one of its backers as 'a Pantheon of Past and Future'. The Civil War raging at the time saved it.

The terms 'Peasant Metropolis' and 'Big Village' gave the city another image. Rapid industrialization continued into the new century. The uncontrolled migration of peasants to Moscow added to already existing problems of rural depopulation and urban food shortages, conforming to a pattern already experienced in Western Europe. In the early nineteenth century Moscow's population was around 300,000; it had grown to about a million by 1905. Over two-thirds were peasants. That year the city was the scene of major disturbances following the Russo–Japanese War. Social dislocations caused by the chaos of uncoordinated industrialization, combined with the massive influx of liberated serfs, created conditions of extreme overcrowding. Its inevitable companions, filth, disease and despair, were brought to life on stage in Maksim Gorky's dark play *Na Dnye* (The Lower Depths). Figures quoted in official histories are damning:

> Unlicenced dumps and heaps of garbage and excrement littered the inner areas (of the city); cattle grazed, chickens pecked, and wild dogs wandered freely in the outer... Moscow was the unhealthiest big city in Europe. Between 1883 and 1917, it endured eight epidemics of smallpox, ten of typhus and four of cholera. In 1910, the death rate in Moscow was 26.9 per 1,000 ... infant mortality exceeded Western European levels by 50 to 75 per cent.[2]

Moscow's population dropped from 2 million to 1 million after 1917, but then resumed its growth at a dramatic rate. By the mid 1920s it had grown from 2.2 million to 3.7 million. Beginning in 1927, the First Five-Year Plan and its successors demanded what amounted to wartime mobilization of the peasantry. At great cost the peasantry was the source of the raw material for an urbanized, industrial labour force. The consequences were dramatic. In two years, 1931-2, the city grew by another million. In human terms that rate of growth was unsustainable, and brutal policies were devised to meet impossible targets. In the face of other priorities, urban infrastructure and public health projects were set aside. Expropriation of the larger flats and their division into communal living spaces could not absorb all the peasant newcomers, many of whose sanitary habits were rudimentary. A stopgap measure was the creation of barrack-like, one-storey wooden structures, built close to Moscow's rapidly multiplying industrial sites. They bore a chilling resemblance to the long wooden huts that were one of the features of Siberian Gulag camps.

In 1940 Moscow's population was 4.5 million. Growth (and by then efforts to control it) included a system of internal passports. Permission to reside in Moscow was determined by workforce requirements. Never particularly effective, the ill-conceived system eventually broke down under waves of corruption, double-dealing and abuse. Moscow had now reached its present level of about 11.5 million. If the Greater Moscow region is included, the figure rises to around 14 million. The exact number of unregistered residents is unknown.

Rural Moscow

The overwhelmingly peasant origins of Moscow's population continue to have subtle effects on the character of the city. The rough construction of post-war apartment blocks, themselves hastily put up in a strategy to relieve overcrowding, was specifically designed to be put into practice by unskilled workers. Like that other great immigrant city, New York, twentieth-century Moscow was divided into discrete neighbourhoods often composed of people from the same village.

In the twenty-first century, commercial forces—the sheer power of cash, the spread of *nouveau riche* high-rise apartments and the mass appearance of the automobile—are breaking up this pattern. At the same time Moscow is going suburban. Just as in Los Angeles, Kingston (Jamaica) or Cairo, 'gated communities' (as they are euphemistically called) are sprouting up beyond Moscow's outer ring, isolated from the rigours of urban living and violent crime.

As central Moscow goes up-market, some central apartment complexes still survive with central courtyards reminiscent of village greens, complete with small wooden dachas, swings and vigilant *babushkas* for the children. Like Tokyo–Yokohama, where land is at a premium, large industrial sites stay embedded in residential neighbourhoods. In the case of Moscow, however, this is the result of the relativities of power under the former Soviet system. Moscow's reconstruction plan of 1935 called for a forest belt of parks to contain uncontrolled urban sprawl, but the Soviet industrial commissars ignored the City Council planners and placed their enterprises where they wished. In the latter days of *perestroika*, it emerged that there was a high correlation between the incidence of certain cancers, particularly leukaemia in children, and the location of industrial sites working with radioactive materials. One unpublicized objective of contemporary planning is to remove such factories from the Moscow area.

Throughout the inter-war period there was a strong theoretical strain of thought, influenced by the Bauhaus movement in Germany and by left-wing city planners such as Le Corbusier, that the proletariat should not be alienated from their place of work, physically or otherwise. The idea died when its main sponsors were eliminated in the 1930s. The 1999 plan for the city called for industrialized zones in the heart of the city to be reduced by 25 per cent within a fixed period of time. When I discussed Moscow's future development with city officials and academics in 2007, the talk was all of infrastructure, waste management and zoning. Visions of the early-twentieth-century dreamers had disappeared.

Moscow's cityscape also has other references to its rural origins. Architectural historians make much of the eighteenth-century 'Moscow classical' style, and its main exponents, Vasily Bazhanov and Matvei Kazakov. They take less notice of the fact that many of the great private houses of the period were low-standing, urbanized replicas of those found on the estates of their aristocratic owners, complete with mews and outbuildings for staff. The urban bourgeoisie, which was responsible for the distinctly urban, high-density architecture of Western Europe, was largely missing or underdeveloped in nineteenth- and early-twentieth-century Moscow. This social fact had direct consequences not only for the cityscape, but also for the future course of Russian political history. No urban bourgeoisie, no development of civil society.

In addition, currents of Western liberal thought had little chance to flourish, much less prevail over more radical solutions to problems facing the country. Even as they absorbed the thinking of their Western European counterparts, the social and political thinkers of Moscow, St. Petersburg and other Russian cities were on their own.

Imperial Moscow

'Imperial' implies a function as well as being a description and a condition of state. Imperial cities take on a certain look, and Moscow is no exception. As in other great cities of empire, its cosmopolitanism is accented by ethnic diversity. The railway boom of the nineteenth century is in large part responsible. Imperial Russia's eastward expansion by rail matched the westward railway expansion in the United States, in fact more like the Canadian example as a state-sponsored enterprise driven by a combination of private capital and public policy. Security was provided by the state, in the Canadian case, the country was technically an imperial possession until well into the twentieth century. The Royal North West (later, Canadian) Mounted Police, had uniforms which copied the red tunics of the British Army. In the Russian case, imperial expansion was a military operation linked to commerce.

Many historians argue that Moscow's imperial vocation began with Ivan IV's victory over the Tatars in 1552. The impulse was strategy, mixed with *raison d'état* and religion. Contemporary records make this clear:

> With the aid of our Lord Jesus Christ and the prayers of the Mother of God ... our pious Tsar and Grand Prince Ivan Vasilievich, crowned by God, Autocrat of all Rus', fought against

> the infidels, defeated them and finally captured the Tsar of Kazan', Edigei-Mahmet. And the pious Tsar and Grand Prince ordered his regiment to sing an anthem under his banner, to give thanks for the victory; and at the same time ordered a life-giving cross to be placed and a church to be built, with the uncreated image of our Lord Jesus Christ, where the Tsar's colours had stood during the battle.[3]

Territorial aggrandizement had been supported by commercial interests well before the nineteenth century, but the technology of railways, which gave speed and economy of moving men and materials over vast distances, and the statism of the tsarist autocracy plus advances in banking and financing techniques, accelerated Russia's eastward expansion. Moscow, the commercial capital, not St. Petersburg, was at its centre. Already by the eighteenth century Moscow was the largest unified market zone within the empire, protected by tariffs and subsidies to its leading industries. In that romantic age, and in the eyes of many, Moscow was symbol of the Rus' of pre-imperial Russia. It was the *pervoprestol'nyi gorod*, the 'original capital city' where every emperor was still crowned.

Of all the architectural achievements of nineteenth-century Moscow, its nine railway stations are the most striking expression of Russia's imperial idea, rivalling the grand palaces of the tsars. Through the rapid growth of its railway system, Moscow became the centre of a vast communications network. Railways were the primary means by which Russia's wealth and energy were mobilized. Even now, at a length of over 9,000 kilometres and spanning seven time zones to reach the Pacific Ocean, the Trans-Siberian Railway stands as testimony to engineering achievement. Railways were also a strategic resource of the first order, as lessons about their military use in the American Civil War and the Franco–Prussian War demonstrated. Both wars saw the movement of unprecedented numbers of troops in astonishingly short periods of time. Railways were also the vehicle of revolution. On 11 March 1918 Lenin arrived at the northern-oriented station of Nikolayev (now St. Petersburg Station) to establish the Bolshevik government in Moscow.

In the absence of a modern national highway grid, the Russian rail system assumes additional strategic importance. Within this system it is often assumed that to get from A to B one must travel through Moscow. Each of Moscow's terminals had its own point of the compass and its distinct characteristics. The Belorussian station gives to the west, receiving travellers from Paris, Berlin, Prague, Warsaw, Minsk and Smolensk; the Kazan station from Kuybyshev and Omsk, and from the other side of the Ural mountains, from Samarkand and Dushanbe in Central Asia. Even with the growth of air travel, it is still the great numbers arriving at Kazan station from Central Asia that gives Moscow its slightly Asiatic air. Today a high-speed railway system is projected between Moscow and St. Petersburg.

In their dark corners these symbols of imperial power are also home to transient colonies of social cast-offs, victims of drink, drugs or simply bad luck. The *militsia* remove them, but they find their way back or others take their place. Perhaps more than those in the West, Moscow's railway stations disorient, and some arriving from distant provinces become lost in their cavernous interiors.

Locating Moscow in Time and Space

How a small twelfth-century stockade above a swampy bend in a river became a world capital is still an open question. The Russian historian Vasily Klyuchevsky (1841–1911) made a strong case for geography. He argued that its position within a network of rivers, the *mezhdurechiye*, starting with the Volga to the east and the Dnieper to the south-west, connected Moscow to both the Baltic and Black Seas. A short portage from the

Volga to the Don brought travellers and merchants to the Black Sea, and colonies of Genoese merchants - and thence to Constantinople.

Following the accession of Ivan III in 1462, Moscow gained control of the upper Volga, essential for its rival Novgorod's grain supply, thereby destroying its power. Building on Klyuchevsky's argument, the historian Sir Martin Gilbert writes that for four hundred years the river routes around Moscow 'were the focal point of all communications, whether for trade, settlement war or revolt'. This north–south pattern underwent a fundamental change to an east–west axis only with the advent of the railway system of the nineteenth century.

Geographical explanations underestimate the ferocious scheming, determination and sheer bloody-mindedness of the Moscow's thirteenth- and fourteenth-century rulers. More often than not they cooperated with the Tatar invaders. Novgorod, which originally had shielded Moscow from invasion from the north-east, was not the only city devastated by Moscow during this period. Ryazan suffered a similar fate. It sometimes protected Moscow from the south-east, but its leadership made the fatal mistake of choosing the wrong (Tatar) side. Amidst the gore of Kulikovo Field (1380) Moscow prevailed over the Tatars for the first time. To Russian schoolchildren, this date has the same familiarity and moment as the Battle of Hastings and the heroism of Agincourt combined.

The imprint of those violent days has given shape to the city. Moscow's layout is influenced by military considerations. The city plan bears a certain resemblance to walled, medieval Paris. The city's different quarters developed around the Kremlin in a horseshoe-shaped pattern, following the banks of the river on its northern, higher (and therefore more militarily defensible) bank. In the process, Moscow emerged as one of the strongest fortified cities in Europe. The Kremlin dwarfs the Tower of London and the Bastille.

As the city expanded, the military hand is seen most clearly in the concentric roadways which encircle it—the inner Boulevard Ring and the outer Garden Ring, both following the paths of defensive ramparts now filled in or destroyed. An earlier ring surrounding the commercial district of Kitai Gorod next to the Kremlin was torn apart by Soviet anti-historians in the 1930s. The 1999 Plan for the City had it restored as the innermost ring.

Framing the entire city of twenty-first-century Moscow is the equivalent of the Washington Beltway, the 109-kilometre diameter Moscow Ring Highway (Moskovskaya Kol'tsevaya Avtomobil'naya Doroga, MKAD) completed by 80,000 Komsomol volunteers in the early 1960s. It is known to traffic police as 'the road of death', having the highest fatality rate of any road in Russia. The MKAD also has a military purpose: to act as a military airstrip in the event of war, and has no centre-line or lighting. Some 25 kilometres further out lies another semi-secret circular highway of reinforced concrete, designed to carry the weight of anti-aircraft missile launchers.

Circular arrangements for Moscow's defence in depth have a long history. Six fortified monasteries, now all within the boundaries of greater Moscow, encircle and guard the city and the roads radiating out from its heart.[4] In response to threats at various times from virtually all points of the compass, they are strategically located more or less evenly about the points of the compass. They also occupied the best land in Russia.

Moscow in Stone and Steel

The spirit of Moscow is captured in a surprisingly small number of buildings and places. Among them are Red Square and St. Basil's, the great building and industrial projects of the Stalinist era (including the Metro and the 'High Buildings' of the

1950s) and the housing complexes initiated by Khrushchev and continued under Brezhnev.

These have now been supplemented by aggressive building and renovation projects undertaken in post-Soviet Moscow, the most prominent of which are the restoration of the Cathedral of Christ the Saviour, and the skyscraper district of the International Business Centre. In Soviet times physical revision of history was undertaken by means of dynamite, and large parts of historic Moscow were destroyed. Rampant urban self-destruction is an old Muscovite practice. Efforts to moderate it by organizations such as the Moscow Architectural Preservation Society (MAPS) have been only partially successful.

First of all of Moscow's monuments is the Cathedral of Vasili Blazhennyi, Basil the Blessed or St. Basil's. It was originally named Pokrovsky Sobor, or more formally Cathedral of the Intercession of the Most Pure Mother of God on the Moat. In plan, St. Basil's is an eight-pointed star built around a central core, each point a church representing a successive victory and its feast-day in the Kazan campaign. Its core is inspired by the wooden, tent-roofed churches of north-east Russia, their shape developed to protect against snow and wind. By dispensing with the rules of symmetry and proportion inherited from Kiev and Byzantium followed by the ecclesiastical architecture within the Kremlin, it announces the coming of age of an authentic Russian style.

Often overlooked in the guidebooks, St. Basil's also represents in one significant respect an advance over the sequestered Kremlin. It lies outside it. As a church commemorating the victorious campaign against the Kazan khanate, it also celebrates the victory of Orthodoxy over Islam, although this did not prevent Ivan the Terrible from adding the Islamic appellation 'Great Khan' to his list of titles. Thus, by tradition, the victory of Kazan is recalled on its onion domes by the triumphant cross rising above a supine crescent.

The early Soviet authorities were ambivalent towards the cathedral. In 1917 the first Soviet Minister of Enlightenment, Anatoly Lunacharsky, is said to have burst into tears on hearing that it had been destroyed by bombardment. In sorrow and protest, he resigned from the Bolshevik Party, but then executed an awkward reverse-step when the reports turned out to be false. A decade later, the Moscow Party first secretary Lazar Kaganovich wanted its demolition to make room for demonstrations on Red Square. The conservationist Pyotr Baranovsky threatened to chain himself to the front door of the cathedral (or, according to another version, to slit his throat) if any attempt were made on it. He was sent to the Gulag for his pains. Others were also ready to sacrifice themselves for the cathedral. One story has it that a city planner intentionally jogged Stalin's arm when he lifted a model of it from a Moscow maquette, to see what Red Square would look like without it.

An ambitious attempt to replicate St. Basil's is the Church of the Resurrection of Christ in St. Petersburg, built on the spot of Alexander II's assassination in 1881. Because of its association with the murder, it is commonly called the Saviour's Church of the Spilled Blood. In neoclassical, Westernized St. Petersburg, it never really fit into the landscape. St. Basil's belongs to Moscow.

St. Basil's sits at the far end of Red Square. An air of violence hangs over the square, originally the main market area of Moscow but also a place of entertainment, spectacle and execution. This is hinted at by the enigmatic circular structure in one corner, referred to as Lobnoye Mesto, sometimes translated as 'place of skulls', but probably more accurately as the place where the forehead touched the ground in an act of oriental obeisance. On 8 June1671, the Don Cossack Stepan Razin and his brother Frol were executed here for leading a peasant revolt numbering some 20,000. In the same century, Peter the Great directed and apparently watched the execution of some of the over a thousand *streltsy*—musketeers—who had revolted against him in 1698. After the risings in 1905, the square was cleared of its kiosks and shacks to allow an unobstructed field of fire from the Kremlin walls in the event of further disturbances. In *Dr. Zhivago*, Boris Pasternak has Pasha, the idealistic revolutionary and lover of Lara, receive a slash to the face from a tsarist cavalryman on the square. In 1941, Red Army troops went directly to the front before Moscow after Stalin reviewed them from atop Lenin's mausoleum. Two of the T-34 tanks broke ranks, and appeared to be heading directly towards members of the watching Politburo, Stalin included. The brief confusion ended when it turned out that one had broken down and, as was standard military practice, its partner tank had followed to tow it away. In 1945 the victory parade on Red Square was led by Marshal Zhukov, not Stalin, whose horse had thrown him during a practice session. Zhukov rode the same horse.

Like St. Basil's, Red Square has had a number of threats to its existence. In the nineteenth century there were plans to have it serve as a platform for an elevated railway. In early Soviet times, the Iverskie Cathedral at its entrance was torn down to clear the way for parades. Later a city planner, one Leonodov, proposed to use Red Square as the site to erect a fifty-storey office building in the shape of a factory chimney, symbol of the new proletarian age. Lack of funds and other priorities of the leadership stopped the project.

Red Square has also been the scene of dramatic events more recently. After an 800-kilometre flight from Helsinki over Soviet territory, on 28 May 1987, a single-engine Cessna 173P piloted by nineteen-year-old Mattias Rust landed on Vasilyevsky Street, on the immediate approaches to Red Square.[5] This precipitated a shake-up in the Soviet military which, besides removing the incompetents, could President Gorbachev calculated, be used to replace them with those more supportive of his policies. In the event, one of the leaders of the failed *coup* against Gorbachev of August 1991 was the very Defence Minister, Dmitry Yazov, whom he had personally chosen to replace the disgraced Marshal Sergei Sokolov. Again, a spectacle of history in the making occurred on New Year's Eve 1991, when a huge crowd gathered on the square before St. Basil's to celebrate what many hoped would be the birth of a new Russia to coincide with the birth of the new year. The Russian tricolour flew atop Senate Building from which the Soviet flag had flown. At midnight, the first six strokes of the New Year issued from the Kremlin's Spasskaya Tower, whose chimes were as familiar to Russians as were those of Big Ben to Londoners—but the last six came from St. Basil's, whose bells had been silenced for over seventy years.

Stalin's Moscow

In the post-revolutionary climate of the 1920s, the Civil War over and a period of economic relaxation at its height, an air of optimism and hope for the future generated an extraordinary flowering of the arts in Moscow. When Stalin finally achieved complete control by the early 1930s, all this changed. Stalinism, a term coined by Stalin's colleague Lazar Kaganovich, then Moscow Party first secretary, became the dominating *leitmotif* of all of Soviet society. In the arts and literature it was known as socialist realism. It rested on principles of simplicity and accessibility, optimism, and the social/political function of art and literature. These were laid down by the Party, regulated by elaborate organizational structures, unions of artists and their congresses, and enforced by the secret police. The threat of exclusion from the union (therefore no employment), exile or worse hung over those who chose a different path. The cultural and physical impact on Moscow was profound and long-lasting. Some have argued that its spirit continues in a post-Soviet form, particularly in government influence on the media.

In 1932 Kaganovich with his deputy, Nikita Khrushchev, directed the development of a new city plan from the Organizing Committee of the Union of Soviet Architects. In July 1935 the Plan was announced with great fanfare, 'proclaiming that the barbarous Russian city built by capitalism was to become a socialist city, the most beautiful in the world'.[6] The Plan's immediate effect was the widening and reinforcing of the city's roads, inevitably followed by the destruction of many historic places. Under Stalin, engineering trumped art, with one huge exception: monumentalism.

'Monumentalism' was the watchword of Stalin-era projects of the 1930s, a trend that continued after the Second World War. The pre-war Moscow–Volga Canal, 128 kilometres long, 70 of them up an incline, and the Volga–Don Canal were both dug by unskilled volunteers but also by thousands of ZEKs (a slang abbreviation, z/k in paperwork, for *zaklyuchyennyi*, meaning prisoner). These huge projects were portrayed as examples of how revolutionary ardour could defy the laws of physics. It was mind over matter: 'The water does not want to go into the Moskva River, so we must force it to go... there are no fortresses we Bolsheviks cannot storm.'

The American architect Frank Lloyd Wright hated the attitude that lay behind grandiose projects and told his Soviet hosts so. At the height of the Great Terror in 1937 and during the First Congress of the Union of Architects, the address by the chairman of the Council of Peoples' Commissars, Vyacheslav Molotov, stressed that the Party was the 'final arbiter' of rules governing architecture, and that monumental buildings, giving full expression to proletarian aspirations, would be the order of the day. In that atmosphere of fear and political compliance, the Congress unanimously denounced 'formalism', by which it meant modern architecture. Wright took exception, and in referring to skyscrapers as false architecture, declared to the Congress: 'I have seen a dismal reflection of that falsity in your own workplace... And elsewhere among you I see your old enemy, Grandomania—I see it even in your subways.'[7] Miraculously, Wright's speech was reprinted in a first edition of *Pravda*. It did not appear in the second edition.

Monumentalism in Moscow architecture was by no means new, and the verticality of Moscow's core has a tradition going back to the buildings of the Kremlin. Above ground, Stalinist monumentalism is most evident in the 'high buildings' (the Soviet authorities avoided the word 'skyscraper' because of its capitalist connotations) or the 'seven sisters' as Muscovites call them. These buildings, all designed under the direction of Stalin's chief architect, Dmitri Chechulin, were prestige projects, constructed at a time of post-war scarcity and hardship, and were later bitterly criticized by Khrushchev. The seven—two apartment buildings, two government offices, two hotels and one university—were meant to outdo capitalist skyscrapers in volume and height. Inspired by the buildings of New York's Rockefeller Center, which a Soviet architectural team had visited, they were specifically meant to put the Chrysler Building in the shade.

Like Hitler, Stalin had a keen interest in architecture, and insisted that these buildings be topped with spires that would act as references to the Kremlin towers. Of these the best known to visitors is the Hotel Ukraina, across from the White House, where Yeltsin gave his defiant speech during the failed putsch of 1991, and which he later had shelled to eradicate rebellious MPs. Best known to diplomats is the Ministry of Foreign Affairs (in Russian, the MID, *Ministerstvo Inostrannyikh Del*), and to students, the *Obshchezhyitye* of Moscow State University—*Moskovskii Gosudarstvennyi Universitet Imeni Lomonosova*—known by its initials MGU. Western architectural critics have not been kind to Stalin's tastes. One, for example, sourly observed that 'Stalin's generalized bridling of the country over several decades enabled the spirit of the petit-bourgeois vulgarity to spread, as it were, by official decree.'[8]

MGU stands above the city's skyline on Sparrow Hills and is self-contained. It is possible to be born in it (technically, this is illegal), live and die in it without ever leaving, although it has no graveyard on the premises. In keeping with its huge size, this single university building houses the bulk of its 40,000 students and provides lecture rooms for over 8,000 academic staff. In the event of an emergency, each of the four main residential wings can be closed down and sealed off. Built in its substructure is a secret nuclear laboratory, with equally secret communications and radar gear installed at the top of the building. The Russian security service maintains an office near the top of the building. German war prisoners were employed during its construction, and there are persistent rumours of their planning their escape by surreptitiously building gliders to launch off the eighteenth floor under cover of darkness.

Monumentalism above ground is matched by monumentalism below. The Moscow Metro, originally called the Kaganovich Underground Railway, preceded the Plan for the Reconstruction of Moscow. Work began in 1932, and then accelerated when the Nazis came to power in Germany a year later. The argument that the Molotov–Ribbentrop Non-Aggression Treaty psychologically disarmed the Soviet Union and that the country made no serious preparations for defence is contradicted by the way the Metro was constructed, built intentionally deep against air attack. Stalin personally approved the plans, despite the extra expense. As it turned out, the underground stations played a key role during the Second World War. Throughout the war, the Kirov station served as General Staff Headquarters. In 1941, as the Battle of Moscow raged, and because of security concerns, Stalin gave the October Revolution's anniversary address in deeply-underground Mayakovsky station. The next day, on 7 November, upon reassurances from his military, he stood atop Lenin's mausoleum on Red Square to take the salute in broad, snowy daylight. From the square the troops went to the front, only a few kilometres away, without stopping.

The Moscow Metro was born in controversy. Moscow was under-housed and overpopulated. As a result of early crash-industrialization programmes, especially those designated high-priority 'shock' projects like the Metro itself, workers and often their families were required to live in hastily constructed wooden barracks. Khrushchev, recently called to Moscow to coordinate plans, wrote in his memoirs that he objected, and instead of building 'underground palaces' for the workers, he believed decent housing should have been built. At the height of construction, some 70,000 workers were engaged and the work as a showpiece was declared a part of 'the great war for socialism'. Coal miners from the Donbass and peasant labourers ('rock carriers') were employed, as well as *subbotniki*, volunteers working in the underground shafts on their own time. For the more difficult or dangerous jobs convict labour was used, although the numbers involved are disputed, as is the number of casualties, which is known to be high. Progress in building the Metro improved and deaths decreased somewhat with the introduction of a technique for freezing the ground before drilling commenced. The soil was further stabilized by a technique developed by a German engineer working for Siemans Baer Union, a process still held under secret patent.

By 1980 the Metro was carrying around 6 million passengers daily (compared with New York, with 3 million, and London, with around 1.6 million) over 299 kilometres of track. Today these Metro figures are reduced as a result of Mayor Luzhkov's aggressive road-building programme, and of course the explosive growth in the numbers of automobiles.

As a monument to Stalinist giganticism the Metro has no

comparison. It has many dark sides. In some of the stations, many of the sculptures depicting socialist achievements are carved on the backs of gravestones taken from monasteries. Other gravestones are buried in the Metro's foundations to stabilize the soil. Many workers suffered the 'bends', an agonizing and potentially fatal condition caused by the presence of nitrogen bubbles in the joints, by working in pressurized mining cages operating at depth, and then surfacing too quickly. A good proportion of Muscovites believe that some Metro tunnels are the home of giant mutant rats which prey on the unsuspecting or unwary.

Also the subject of indirect references and rumours is Metro II, a still-secret line built under the main Metro. Composed of a network of branches and passageways radiating out from under the Kremlin, and about one-third the size of its sister line, it connected the main buildings of Soviet power—the Kremlin itself, the *Lubyanka* and Central Committee buildings. It was presumably designed to act as a bolt-hole for the leadership. One line is said to run to Sheremetyevo airport. The underground palaces of the Metro bear an uncanny resemblance to Nazi architecture, as do many of the above-ground buildings of the Stalinist period. The most prominent example of a public building that could have been designed by either Nazi or Soviet architects is the Palais des Nations of the United Nations in Geneva. In Moscow, however, Byzantium kept breaking through. Rich mosaics and tiles and iconographic figures adorn the Metro palaces of the 1930s, reflecting a long tradition of religious art. The decor of later Metro stations is less effusive.

Alongside Monumentalism

Four little-known buildings rarely seen by visitors, none particularly large by the standards of his later mammoth projects, together form a narrative of Moscow under Stalin.

The first, the House on the Embankment, is a large grey structure in the constructivist style slightly downstream from the Kremlin. Constructivism was a product of early post-revolutionary Moscow, drawing its inspiration from modernist paintings and sculptures of the 1920s. It was defined by one of its leading proponents, Aleksandr Rodchenko, as 'the contemporary demand for organization and the utilitarian application of materials'. In practice, constructivism meant that buildings should be simple in style and honest in their use of materials, with the structure of the building sufficient in itself to provide the aesthetics. Unfortunately for the architects, Stalin and his circle judged the results ugly. By the 1930s, experiments in *avant-garde* architecture came to an abrupt end. As Stalin's grip on all the arts tightened in the 1930s, constructivism did not survive its early promise.

Like many other buildings in Moscow, including the Kremlin itself, the House on the Embankment is better known by the time and events associated with it than its architectural inspiration. Completed in the late 1920s, it has three inner courtyards and holds more than five hundred apartments for the Party elite. Like the Kremlin, it is a sequestered, cloistered place, secure and secret at the same time. At the height of the Great Terror[9] of the 1930s (the *Yezhovshchina*, named after Yezhov, the head of the NKVD) it also became a Death Row. A novel written by a surviving son of one of the victims, Yuri Trofonov, describes how each morning the concierges would tell the residents who had been arrested the night before. It was customary to keep a packed suitcase by the door.

The second building is the Hotel Luks, now renamed Tsentralnaya. In a function it performed for over three decades, it housed expatriate members of refugee communist parties. Its original guests were Germans and Hungarians, survivors of their abortive revolutions, later joined by Poles and others.

The number of residents in the hotel grew after the Spanish Civil War. Mixing apples and oranges perhaps, the hotel also housed foreign members of the Comintern, but all were carefully monitored. As a place of semi-confinement, the hotel was ridden with informers. It was here that the Soviet secret services perfected sex as a method of entrapment, which in turn sent many to the Gulag or worse. There are persistent stories of twin female NKVD operatives who achieved spectacular intelligence successes. Residents who survived and still kept the faith were among those who returned to their home countries behind the advancing Red Army. Eventually they formed the nucleus of many pro-Soviet governments in Eastern Europe.

The third building is better known. It sits in central Moscow on a slight incline. Large but not architecturally significant, it originally housed the Yakor (Anchor) Insurance Company. A co-tenant was Lloyds of London. When the Soviet government moved from Petrograd to Moscow in 1918, Felix Dzerzhinsky, the first chairman of the Extraordinary Committee for State Security (better known by its Cyrillic initials Ch-K or Cheka) arrived in Moscow on the same train as Lenin. Elbowed aside from occupying more prestigious headquarters in the Kremlin, he took over the insurance building as his headquarters. Lubyanka, named after the square where it stands, has remained the property of the Cheka's successors ever since. Dzerzhinsky arranged for the building's basement to be fitted out with asphalt-lined torture and execution chambers. At the height of the Terror, most of the executions were in fact conducted in the sound-proofed chambers of a Red Army office building across the street. Moscow's main toy store, *Detsky Mir* (Children's World), is close by, leading to a weak joke that the adults' world is just up the square from Children's World. After the Second World War, the main headquarters of the KGB moved to larger premises outside town.

The fourth building, the Noblemen's Club, was renamed

the House of Unions after the Revolution. The bodies of both Lenin and Stalin lay in state here in 1924 and 1953 respectively. In this same place, the three great purge trials of the 1930s were held under the direction of the Public Prosecutor Andrei Vyshinski, who later won the Stalin Prize for his work *Theories of Judicial Evidence*, in which Vyshinsky wrote that confession was key. Sentencing was based on political considerations.

It is estimated that some 800,000 were killed during the Great Purge, directed and orchestrated by the bureaucrats and police of the Lubyanka in concert with the administrators and lawyers of the House of Unions. In a secret room of the latter, Stalin could watch the Public Prosecutor and his victims from behind a curtain. Possibly as an act of exorcism, the House of Unions was chosen as the venue for the United Nations Conference on Human Rights, held in the autumn of 1991. This was its last service to the Soviet state.

Khrushchev's Moscow

Nikita Khrushchev was responsible for the execution of the Moscow 1935 Plan. His priorities changed abruptly with the death of Stalin. Moving away from the monumental style of 'High Stalinism', his down-to-earth approach was to tackle Moscow's post-war housing crisis head-on, whatever the aesthetic cost. The result was known as Khrushchev's 'architectural revolution'. Huge apartment complexes mushroomed in the city's outskirts, utilitarian in form, simple to build and ugly to behold. They also represented a radical break from the studied monumentalism of the Stalin era, having the visual effect of 'flattening' the outskirts of the city, in contrast to the spires and Greco–Roman decoration of Stalin's tastes. They were also far more democratic than Stalin's inner-city housing projects, which were built exclusively for the *nomenklatura*, the Soviet bureaucracy whom Stalin alternately cosseted and murdered.

Under Khrushchev, the annual rate of housing construction in the Soviet Union increased dramatically as the focus turned away from housing for the elite. Between 1956 and 1965, about 198,000 apartments were built, with the greatest concentration in Moscow. Khrushchev encouraged rapid, assembly-line construction from standardized pre-stressed concrete slabs. The result was the appearance of apartment complexes with each building identical in modular design. In some cases even its layout had nothing to distinguish one complex from another. (In accordance with the Law of Unintended Consequences, the similarity of these vast housing estates caused a significant rise in the need for sobering-up tanks. Many of the inebriated would lose their way in the suburban maze, and needed emergency shelter.)

At least superficially, Khrushchev's building complexes resemble the large 1960s and 1970s housing estates of London or Rome, or the *banlieues* of Paris—but with a fundamental difference: those moving into them were going upmarket. Small as they were by Western standards, the flats were much in demand. Many years, red tape and sheer bribery were often needed to acquire one. Despite their aesthetic and other problems, they were a world away from the tuberculosis-ridden, crowded communal workers' barracks of the 1930s and 1940s.

Shoddy construction was still a universal problem, but each flat was heated (in principle, at least) and each had its own toilet and kitchen. Above all, each was *private*. Khrushchev dispensed with received dogma about communal living with shared cooking and eating facilities at the end of the hall. He also abolished theories about the seamlessness of workplace and living space for the proletariat. Even so, his apartment blocks soon became known as *khrushchoby*, a word combining Khrushchev's name with *trushchoba*, the Russian word for slum.

The shoddiness of Khrushchev-era domestic construction,

which extended into the Brezhnev and Gorbachev years, is often blamed for the structural failures of many buildings. There were other reasons as well. Builders did not always take account of the salinity of the subsoil, or the increasing frequency of 'acid rain' over Moscow, which ate away at the concrete, causing some buildings to develop a list from weakened foundations, or in extreme instances causing balconies to buckle or fall off. This problem was further exacerbated by the general Soviet philosophy of planning: the state planning agency, GOSPLAN, rewarded production from its managers, not maintenance. Consequently, maintenance facilities occupied a low priority in city and municipal budgets, which focused on rapid and cheap construction. It was a question of trade-offs.

Sanitation, not only in the nineteenth-century sense of building large public sewerage systems in the interests of public health (Moscow lagged behind Western European cities in this respect) but also in more modest conveniences, was a fixation Khrushchev shared with Stalin. After prowling around Moscow at night, Stalin ordered the construction of more public facilities. In a still peasant-based society, the stairwells of the new apartment complexes quickly became impromptu loos, and the residential Housing Committees faced the challenge of how to discourage this. One answer of the architects was Leonardo da Vinci's solution to the same problem: circular staircases. The idea was dropped because of the skill needed for their construction, and the fact that in the event of an emergency, they could not safely accommodate rushing masses of people.

By 1958 regulations decreed that every new apartment block in Moscow would be five storeys high. This was because the same regulations required a lift if they were any higher. The Soviet General Staff also determined that a five-storey building could be quickly evacuated in the event of an impending nuclear attack and, like the wooden buildings of medieval

Moscow, easily replaced. The buildings' standardized aspect repeated across the city, the military planners believed, would also thwart any incoming hostile aircraft from identifying navigational aids. In subsequent years these regulations were rescinded, but their impact on the look of the outskirts of the city endures with the massive housing complexes encircling Moscow. In their own way, they are Stalinist giganticism reborn: Novyi Cheremushki in the south-west, Novyye Kuzminki in the south-east, Khoroshevo-Mnevniki in the north-west, and Izmailovo in the north-east.

City of Dreams and Non-buildings

Moscow's ravaged face has at least been spared the effects of projects fortunately unrealized. Among the city's many names is yet another: Moscow, City of Dreams. Like other cities, however, Moscow's shape reflects the circumstances imposed upon it. From Moscow's founding, defence has been a dominant theme. The permission of the Tatar khans was necessary for the Kremlin's pine walls to be replaced with oaken ones. Only then could the Kremlin become a fortress, and the rest of the city grew around it, in the process becoming the epicentre of the 'gathering in of the Russian lands' first undertaken by Ivan the Great. By the fourteenth century this growing seat of power was sanctified by the construction of ecclesiastical buildings within the Kremlin. Their inspiration was Renaissance, and the architects Italian. This applied to secular architecture as well. The swallow-tail battlements of the Kremlin walls replicate those of Renaissance Turin. The only exceptions were St. Basil's and the isolated churches and monasteries of the deep northern forests.

Although some historians argue otherwise, citing as examples the Moscow baroque and Moscow classicism of the eighteenth and nineteenth centuries, Moscow never developed a distinctive Western imperial style like nineteenth-century London, Vienna, Paris or Berlin. Nor did it develop an *oriental* imperial style, like Istanbul under the Ottoman Empire. Peter the Great built his new capital, westward-looking St. Petersburg, as an imperial city, sea-oriented, classical in inspiration, planned, balanced and symmetrical, all things that Moscow was not.

In the nineteenth century travellers marvelled at Moscow, a 'city of forty times forty' churches. Reality imposed. As one traveller remarked, what looked like Jerusalem in the distance looked more like Bethlehem up close, complete with cows, chickens and ordure. The opportunity to refashion the city from its late-medieval appearance came with its destruction by fire in 1812. No Russian equivalent of Baron Haussmann, Louis Napoleon's visionary architect for Paris, came forth. Instead, William Hastie, a Scottish engineer-architect involved in the construction of St. Petersburg, was chosen by Alexander I to draw up a plan for the reconstruction of Moscow. Ignoring Moscow's legacy, his plan called for the complete destruction of what was left of Moscow's centre and its replacement with straight boulevards lined with classical-style buildings. This would have turned Moscow into a pale imitation of St. Petersburg. His plans, although approved by the Reconstruction Commission, foundered because of lack of funds.

The complete destruction of Moscow's centre is a recurring theme in the history of the city, from the Mongols in the thirteenth century up to Le Corbusier's similar idea of the 1920s. Foreigners, including the German General Staff and later the American Strategic Air Command, seemed particularly attracted to the idea.

Plans for the City of Dreams included great buildings to be erected within it. Inspired by the November Revolution, the Monument to the Third International, or the Tatlin

Tower, named after its designer, was to 'embody all previous architectural experience'. Conceived in 1919 amidst the chaos of post-revolutionary Russia and an ongoing civil war, it was never built. Not even its location was ever decided. But it is still regarded as an outstanding example of the constructivist architectural movement.

The Revolution meant absolute change, constructivist architects argued, and architecture should reflect its ideals. As a kind of proletarian Eiffel Tower (324 metres) and one-third as tall again, Tatlin's conception was of a gigantic steel tower 400 metres high, the tallest building in the world. It was conceived as two conical structures soaring upward around a tilted girder-like spine painted red. Suspended within this skeleton would be three enormous geometric structures of glass—a pyramid, a cube and a cylinder—to house the administrative and legislative bodies of the Comintern, the nucleus of a new world government. To some, including the distinguished British historian Eric Hobsbawm, it resembled nothing so much as an overgrown Ferris wheel or possibly a fairground Big Dipper. Others noted its close resemblance to the monstrous war-fighting machines of the aliens in H. G. Wells' *War of the Worlds*. To visionaries, it would symbolize the Third Rome reborn as the Third International's headquarters.

The project was wildly unrealistic, but it remained on the books until the late 1920s and the political eclipse of the revolutionary internationalism of Trotsky and his followers. Its direct successor in inspiration, but also its antithesis, was the projected Palace of Soviets, counterposing revolutionary idealism with the massive ambitiousness of the Five Year Plans.

At the end of the 1920s the gaze of many idealistic Western architects fell on the construction projects in Moscow and elsewhere that accompanied the first Five Year Plan. Hannes Meyer, Director of the Bauhaus School, settled in Moscow. A historian of the Palace of Soviets observes:

> These Western architects saw Bolshevism as the political analogue of artistic modernism, and like their Russian colleagues of the Russian avant-garde, they mistakenly interpreted the beginnings of industrialization and the start of the Stalinist cultural revolution as a return to the radicalism of the early revolutionary years... They believed that France still lived in the nineteenth century and Germany in the twentieth, but the Soviet Union had leapt ahead to the twenty-first.[10]

The centrepiece would be the Palace of Soviets, the new heart of the first socialist state. It would be the spiritual successor to the Kremlin as symbol of the new Moscow. Designed by the classically trained architect Boris Iofan, who won an international competition for its design against such participants as Walter Gropius, Le Corbusier (of whom more later) and Erich Mendelsohn, the 150-floor palace was to be 420 metres high, with a seating capacity of 21,000, crowned at Stalin's suggestion with a statue of Lenin 70 metres tall. Its 7 million-cubic-metre capacity would have equalled the combined volumes of New York's tallest skyscrapers, which of course was the whole idea. The Statue of Liberty would be outclassed.

The Palace of Soviets is a story of hubris punished by the gods, and its construction was ill-starred from the beginning. It became the Old Testament Tower of Babel. The site chosen was occupied by the massive Cathedral of Christ the Saviour, a monument to the Russian victory over Napoleon in 1812. It had taken the reigns of three tsars to complete. In its turn, the cathedral took the space occupied by the Alexeevsky Convent, and the territory was known as *chertolie*, hole of the devil. The cathedral's demolition in 1931 to make way for the Palace of Soviets also performed the anti-religious function of eliminating the Orthodox Patriarch's seat, and therefore the only remaining centre of organized resistance to Soviet rule.

Many believed that the site was cursed. Other priorities disrupted its construction schedule. Technical problems already faced by the builders of the Metro, including unstable ground and water seepage into the site, exacerbated by the huge projected weight of the building, plagued the project. Finally the Second World War intervened, and men and materials ordered for the building's construction were diverted elsewhere. During the Khrushchev era the massive pit was converted into a swimming pool, the largest in Europe. Rumours spread that the pool, with the memory of the Cathedral of Christ the Saviour hovering over it, was in fact a gigantic baptistry, converting atheists without their knowledge into the true faith. Others believed that a mysterious illness was affecting swimmers, who were being punished for the blasphemy of swimming in a sacred place.

In the end, the Cathedral of Christ the Saviour was rebuilt under President Yeltsin. Mayor Luzhkov played a leading role by squeezing the financing out of the newly arrived oligarchs and others. The symbolism was obvious. The cathedral represented the new Russia rising out of the moribund Soviet Union. Many critics called its construction a travesty—concrete and plastic instead of marble and bronze—but the new cathedral corresponded to the semiotics of late-*perestroika* Russia, with its jumble of red stars, hammers and sickles and double-headed eagles. According to Konstantin Akinsha, a historian of the cathedral, it was regarded by Moscow intellectuals as a Las Vegas copy of the real thing. They were ignored. President Yeltsin's funeral was conducted there on 25 April 2007.

Typically, Western cities developed the way they did because of the step-by-step growth of the legal and commercial power of the city-dwellers, and the need of the rulers for their money. The emergence of a relatively autonomous city-based commercial class, the bourgeoisie, was a major factor in the increasing ability of cities to moderate the arbitrary rule of the monarch, even to the point of negotiating with him to place legal limits on his power by means of city charters. Across Western Europe, beginning with the early Renaissance, commerce and manufacture developed behind the protective walls of cities; in Russia this development was inverted, with trade and industry developing outside cities in the countryside, and much later. Historically, the economic life of Russian cities tended to follow a quasi-Asiatic pattern. Cities functioned as *emporia*, places of trade and barter, with merchants and traders representing the main economic classes, not entrepreneurs or financiers. Industrialists came late to Russia.

In the case of Moscow, foreign traders were consigned to separate and restricted districts. Beginning well before Peter the Great, large sectors of economic life were the exclusive domain of the *gosudar*, the grand prince. He exercised his rights on the basis of monopoly. In the view of some economists, the monopolistic trading practices of the tsarist system were a major brake on Russia's economic development well into the early twentieth century. As a result of this system, financing for major infrastructural projects such as railways depended heavily on sources from abroad. Even by the time of the political upheavals of 1905, the bourgeois populations of Russia's cities remained relatively small. Being literate and educated, they belonged to what in Britain are known as 'the chattering classes', and the enormous intellectual ferment they generated provided many employment opportunities for members of the Okhrana, the tsarist secret police. Lacking an effective parliament (the tsarist-sponsored Dumas did not qualify) and with no control over state finances, their actual impact on the functioning of the tsarist system was insignificant. Reform, if it was to come at all, would be exclusively at the initiative of the authorities themselves, as demonstrated by the tortured process by which the serfs were liberated by tsarist fiat in 1861. Tsarist obtuseness and the deep conservatism of the bureaucracy smothered any hope that reform could be a real possibility. For a brief moment after the Revolution, and as a result of Lenin's economic liberalization policies of the 1920s, the urban bourgeoisie began to revive from its modest beginnings. In an act of social vandalism a decade later, Stalin gave it an abrupt, bloody end.

Stalin was not the first to destroy any chance of a Westerly development for Russian cities. Between the twelfth and fifteenth centuries, Western-oriented cities emerged in north-western Russia, Novgorod and Pskov in particular. They took their lead from the administrations of contemporary German cities and the Hanseatic cities of the Baltic, which in their turn copied in their laws the urban autonomy of the town of Magdeburg.

The historian Richard Pipes comments:

> Moscow could not tolerate privileged sanctuaries from which a genuine urban civilization might have developed because they violated the kingdom's patrimonial constitution. Moscow deprived Novgorod and Pskov of their liberties as soon as it conquered them... Long before the devastations of the Second World War, such once proud metropolitan centres as Novgorod, Pskov and Smolensk degenerated into seedy large villages; and the city of Moscow owes whatever grandeur it can claim not to its commercial, but to its autocratic and aristocratic heritage.[11]

This leaves Moscow the citadel as a sacred place. The Kremlin was built to keep the city's inhabitants and others out, not in. Life was cramped and circumscribed, openness of debate discouraged and public gatherings restricted to time-consuming church ritual, tsarist pageant or, upon occasion, the spectacle of increasingly imaginative tortures and executions.

Communication, 'networking', if it existed at all, was considered a plot. Behind the walls of the Kremlin was the only place where the means of communication multiplied, 'all the more because it was segregated from the population as a whole'. Thus the eminent historian of cities, Louis Mumford, observed that the great secret of centralized power was secrecy itself.

Modern Moscow, the ultimate mover of the Second Russian Revolution of 1991, is enigmatic. The city's original profile of spires and cupolas amidst a sprawling wooden village of peasants and tradesmen has been superseded by the urban landscape of High Stalinism, both rising upward. These profiles were supplemented by the horizontal apartment complexes of the Khrushchev and Brezhnev eras. Gorbachev left barely a trace on Moscow's architecture, his energies spent elsewhere. Now, in the post-Soviet era, massive architectural projects rise within Moscow's inner ring as a third wave of verticality. Idealism may have been replaced by the economics of real estate and industrialized urbanism, but with more than a hint of grandeur still.

Moscow is now a true cosmopolitan city, but not in the way its Bolshevik leaders had intended, brought about by the economics of internationalism. With the great weight of the city's history, it would be an illusion to expect a graceful transition to a civil society, meeting all Western criteria: impartiality within the rule of law, security of person and property, transparency in governance and competitive liberalism within a market-based economy. Instead, conforming to a deep-set historical pattern, the oligarchs who emerged to replace the Soviet *nomenklatura* during the Yeltsin years are in their turn giving way to a new class of *silniki* and *derzhavniki*, men of business and industry and upholders of the pre-eminence of the state. Behind them all stand the ghosts of the past, their whispers rising above the urban traffic of First World–Third World Moscow.

'Moscow at the end of the eighteenth century' by the artist Apollinari Vasnetsov. Moscow was an overwhelmingly wooden city; only public buildings and city walls were of stone and relatively fireproof.

Chapter Two
The Long Beginning

It is clear that neither the practice of centralized authority nor the theory of autocratic rule came to Muscovy from the Qipchaq Khanate since neither that practice nor that theory existed in the Qipchaq Khanate. Instead, autocratic theories entered Moscovy from Byzantium through written culture of the Church. From the late fifteenth century on, the theoretical justification of the Muscovite ruler's authority over society derived from Byzantium.

Donald Ostrowski, historian of the Mongols

The first view of the capital of the Slavonians, rising brightly in the cold solitude of the Christian East, produces an impression that cannot easily be forgotten.

Marquis de Custine, traveller, 1839

The writer Simone Weil gave an elegant reply to Henry Ford's famous aphorism that 'all history is bunk'. 'The present is something that binds us', she wrote. 'We create the future in our imagination. Only the past is a pure reality.' If an argument can be made for the past, it can surely be found in Moscow.

Like all cities, Moscow bears the stamp of its forebears, as well as of its recent and not-so-recent contemporaries. The wide boulevards of nineteenth-century Paris find their twentieth-century Soviet interpretation in Moscow; and the Stalinist 'high buildings' are conscious emulations of the skyscrapers of New York. There is a word in Russian for 'skyscraper'—*neboskreb*—but in Soviet times it was generally avoided because of its close association with the capitalist temples of Mammon.

Neither the tragically defunct World Trade Center buildings in downtown Manhattan nor the 50-storey-plus buildings of Moscow's International Centre are referred to as 'skyscrapers'. The term is obsolete.

Borrowed in the early twentieth century from Paris, Vienna and Berlin, Jugendstil/Art Nouveau architecture flourished in Central Europe and the Baltic, particularly in Prague and in Riga, but also as far east as Moscow, where after a kind of apotheosis its influence stopped. It coexists alongside romantic interpretations of the traditional building styles of medieval Pskov and Novgorod, architectural survivors of Moscow's 'silver age' architecture of the early 1900s. Both styles can be still seen in Moscow's Metropole Hotel (for Jugendstil); and in the Kazan railway station and the building now housing the French Ambassador's Residence (for ethnic architecture).

Today, the International Centre of Moscow represents urban internationalism as much as downtown Singapore or London's financial district of Canary Wharf. The centre's towers inadvertently act as reference to Stalin's vertical, heroic Moscow, but the shape of globalized, modern Moscow is being moulded by forces profoundly different from the Soviet capital of international solidarity of the working class and revolutionary socialism. Then, the medium of exchange was power, supported and justified by an ideology and enforced by a state apparatus at the disposal of the *nomenklatura*, so named because of their classification that defined their privileges within the socialist hierarchy. Now, international finance and the domestic economy drive economic life, and the terms of exchange range from the cost of land in central Moscow to global competition in the labour and resources market—most particularly in the fluctuating prices of gas and oil in Russia's lopsided economy.

To its citizens, Moscow is built on a layered, Trojan hill of the imagination. Buried beneath it are its many pasts. Deep in the first layer is Constantinople, capital of the Byzantine Empire. As an Eastern Rome, the heart of Eastern Christianity, it commanded a heritage that ultimately passed to Vladimir-Moscow. The next layer holds the collective memory of Kiev, the first capital of ancient Rus', destroyed by the Mongols in the thirteenth century. Kiev's traditions were passed to Moscow even as Kiev rose out of its own ashes to become, in alliance with Lithuania, the greatest European empire of the high Middle Ages. The third layer is Sarai, located near present-day Stalingrad/Volgograd. From the thirteenth to the fifteenth centuries Sarai (the name has a Turkic origin, meaning 'encampment') was the administrative centre of the Qipchaq Khanate, and the goal of the Muscovite grand princes was to have their authority confirmed by their Mongol overlords.

Atop this hill, the Moscow Kremlin still looms. It remains a functioning citadel of state power, unrivalled in age and continuity of purpose by any other comparable structure on earth. With its mystery and contradictions, the Kremlin dominates the city of Moscow as it does all Russia.

Byzantium

Byzantine influence on the formation of the culture of Muscovy/Moscow is the perennial subject of many a struggling graduate student's essay. The 'Byzantine connection' is often seized upon by journalists as a ready-made explanation for Russian political behaviour: dark plots, intrigue, factionalism and violence. In a dispute over the disposition of a Soviet-era war memorial in late 2007, the Estonian president, Henryk

Ilves, called the electronic jamming of his country from Russian sources 'Byzantine'.[1]

Seen from the Russian side, Byzantium remains an emotive subject, not only as a wellspring of Orthodoxy, but also because of what at least some believe are the lessons it holds through its negative experience in dealing with the West. As relations with Western countries continued to sour in the spring of 2008, Russian state television aired a programme entitled 'The Destruction of Empire: the Byzantine Lesson'. Acting as host and narrator, Father Tikhon Shevkunov asserted that Western hostility to the Byzantine spiritual inheritance of Moscow was 'genetic'.

Despite a tendency to see history through the prism of the present, the actual influence of Byzantium on the political culture of Moscow is remote, indirect and subject to interpretation. It also must be balanced against the later Mongol influence, a subject of equally emotive debate. Nevertheless, enough evidence suggests that the political culture of Moscow is conditioned at least to some extent by the Byzantine inheritance. Among the echoes of Byzantium is an outlook perhaps rooted in a kind of unconscious collective memory. In the sixteenth century Muscovy stood alone as the champion of Eastern Christianity. It was assaulted from the west by Catholicism, and from the south by Islam. Muscovy turned inward, isolated and self-referential. But it prevailed.

The historical record is surprisingly precise on the first date of contacts between the Byzantines and the Russians (or more accurately, proto-Russians): AD 8 June 860. That date records the appearance of some two hundred ships containing an invading army at the head of the Bosporus, heading towards Constantinople. According to Patriarch Photius' contemporary account, they were unsuccessful in breaching the city's massive walls, and the invaders withdrew. Deliverance was ascribed to the miraculous intercession of the Virgin, whose icon was carried shoulder-high around the parapets, a phenomenon next seen in 1169, when an icon of the Virgin was displayed by the besieged city of Novgorod to deflect the arrows of the forces of Suzdal. By the fourteenth century the use of an icon as a tactical defensive weapon became standard military practice, and the relationship between the icon and the ruler had been set. The Russian historian G. I. Fedotov has observed that the Orthodox conception of tsardom as a 'social extension of the dogma of icon-veneration' fits in already well-established Byzantine iconography to depict emperors as identified with Old Testament kings. Upon occasion, the identification is with Christ Himself.

The Byzantine conception of the ruler-as-icon was made explicit as the grand princes of Muscovy adopted the dress of their spiritual predecessors. The weighty sixty-pound ceremonial vestments for the tsar's coronation were modelled after those of the Byzantine emperors—and indeed the title 'tsar' is an adaptation of the Byzantine title, first accorded to Ivan the Terrible in 1547. Ivan was also the first grand prince to have himself explicitly painted, in saintly pose, as an icon.

The power of religious symbolism, intertwined with the mystical name of Moscow, persisted well into the nineteenth, and even into the twentieth century. The alien and godless 'army of twenty tongues', as Napoleon's invading Grande Armée of 1812 was sometimes referred to, evoked the heathen inhabitants of Babylon. The phrase suggested remorseless divine retribution. Unlike the proposition of the Russian Holy Synod to take up arms against Napoleon who had offended God, no appeal to the divinity was forthcoming in June 1941, either from Foreign Minister Molotov, who was given the unenviable task of announcing the Nazi invasion on Soviet radio, or from Stalin, who invited or rather told him to do it.

The Byzantine heritage of religious symbolism, however, continued just below the surface, even during Moscow's period of High Communism. The ritual ranking in order of precedence of Soviet leaders atop Lenin's mausoleum on state occasions replicates in detail the order of figures on the iconostasis in the Cathedral of the Assumption, including the intermingling of the worldly and the divine. But even here, caution is advised. In the tangled web of influences on present-day Muscovite and Russian history, it has been pointed out that seating arrangements at the Mongol Khan's banquet were critical because they determined the distribution of war booty; and under the Romanov tsars litigation on the part of the offended was sometimes provoked by what the plaintiff regarded as incorrect seating.

Without religion, questions of *placement* have bedevilled more than court officials and chiefs of protocol, and not only in Russia. From personal observation I can attest that diplomats share a universal concern in assuring the correct seating order at the table. A mis-step can result in social awkwardness and ensuing silence at best; and at worst, a lost promotion or damaged career. On the latter, the only greater failure for an aspiring young diplomat is not knowing where the nearest loo is when asked by a VIP. As a commentary on human nature, VIPs and others who feel that they are mis-seated rarely have a sense of humour. Without a loo, their sense of humour is even less.

In the frigid atmosphere of the Cold War, information was at a premium. This created an entirely new profession: Kremlinology. Its practitioners, many of whom were highly paid, devoted their attention to the arcana of precedence of senior Soviet officials: whether they were seating or standing, or walking in funeral processions (who behind whom), in an attempt to determine whatever shifts in Soviet policy the order of protocol might suggest. As a group, Kremlinologists were singularly unsuccessful in anticipating the collapse of the Soviet Union in 1991. A good number have since been consigned to well-deserved oblivion. Among them are exponents of the 'diaperology' school of Kremlinology, who maintained that the roots of Russian political behaviour could be found in the peasant practice of swaddling infants tightly, and the fits of rage that this provoked. Swaddling, the theory went, led in later life to unfettered violence. Unfortunately for the diaperologists' theories, a disproportionate number of the Soviet leadership were not Russian, and those who were did not have peasant backgrounds. Ethnically, they were Polish (Dzerzhinsky), Jewish (Trotsky, Kamenev, Zinoviev, Kaganovich), even Georgian (Ordzhonikidze, Dzhugashvili/Stalin). Boris Pugo, the last Soviet Minister of the Interior, was Latvian. None of the cultures they represented included swaddling. More certain are the vestiges of Moscow's Byzantine heritage surviving into the twenty-first century. In the subterranean vault of his mausoleum on Red Square, Lenin's body is arranged in a pose identical to that assumed by the early saints buried in the Monastery of the Caves in Kiev, with only hands and face uncovered.

The physical appearance of Lenin's mausoleum owes little else to Byzantium. After Lenin's death in 1924, the original wooden structure took two and a half days to build. It was subsequently rebuilt in red granite by the architect Aleksei Shchusev. It is said that the monument was inspired by the tomb of Tamerlane in Samarkand, this despite its columned appearance as a vaguely Greek temple. The elevation of Lenin's body to saintly relic, in line with Byzantine tradition, was opposed by Nadezhda Krupskaya, Lenin's atheistic wife, as well as some Politburo members, but not Stalin.

The ex-seminarian Stalin managed to have himself nominated as the head of the Party Funeral Committee and Lenin was duly entombed on Red Square. In 1953 Stalin's body was placed beside that of the man he always called his mentor. In a flood of emotion at Stalin's death, the Party Presidium resolved to build a pantheon housing the bodies and commemorating the deeds of all of the revolutionary leaders. Stalin's corpse was to be the *pièce de résistance*. The envisaged rotunda bore a startling resemblance to the St. Sophia Cathedral in Constantinople and was to be located on Red Square, replacing the GUM department store. This architectural homage to Stalin never materialized. On 31 October 1961, by resolution of the Twenty-Second Party Congress, Stalin's body was removed and buried in the ground behind the mausoleum. Liquid concrete was poured down the hole to discourage prospective relic-gatherers, followers of an old Byzantine custom.

Aside from the palatial boardrooms of the soaring, post-Soviet edifice of Gazprom, and the quasi-Byzantine edifice of the Cathedral of Christ the Saviour, indirect evidence of the city's Byzantine heritage is found below ground, in the Kievskaya Circle Line Metro Station. It was one of the first to be completed in the 1930s. On its walls mosaics celebrate in rich detail the fraternal relationship between Soviet Russia and Soviet Ukraine, and the union of these two Slavic countries in the creation of the world's first socialist state. Were it not for the fact that some of the figures, all workers and peasants, are executed in profile, the figures' resemblance to the mosaics of their Byzantine predecessors (who were usually depicted head-on) is striking. The unintended message is that in the man-made caves of Moscow, as in the natural caves of Kiev, the spirit of Byzantium lives on.

Moscow's history is full of ironies. In August 1991 the Eighteenth World Congress of Byzantology was held in Moscow, just days before the failed coup attempt of 18 August against Gorbachev, who by coincidence was vacationing in the Crimean Black Sea resort of Foros. Foros had been occupied by the Byzantine Greeks for over eight hundred years.

Kiev

As Moscow's mother-city, Kiev's contribution to the development of Moscow begins with its founding in 1147 by the son of Kievan Prince Monomach, Yuri Dolgoruky of Suzdal. Kiev was the original centre of Orthodox Christianity in Russia. Moscow became the ecclesiastical focus of Orthodoxy when it assumed responsibilities as the metropolitan seat from Kiev. The sack of Kiev in 1169 by Dolgoruky's son Andrei Bogolyubski had little effect on the emotional attachment between the two cities, and Monomach's crown still resides in the Kremlin, which tour guides (Russian ones, at least) still insist stands as witness to the civilization transmitted from Kiev to Moscow.

Kiev is wonderfully situated. Its centre rests on the western bank of the Dniepr, overlooking vast plains beyond. In summer there is a Mediterranean whiff in the air. The magnificence of its monasteries endures, cupolas glinting in the sun. All visitors, including myself, seem to end up in the vaults beneath Pechersk Lavra, reverently inspecting the bones of the saints.

Kiev is also a living monument to the human will to survive. It was completely destroyed by the Mongols in 1240. During the Russian civil war and the Soviet–Polish War from 1918 to August 1920, Kiev changed hands sixteen times. Almost exactly seven hundred years after its first destruction, the German Army razed it yet again. Kiev is also the scene of Babi Yar, the ravine on its outskirts where in 1941 over 30,000 Jews were machine-gunned and their bodies bulldozed over.

The massacre is the subject of the famous poem by Yevgeni Yevtushenko, translated into music by Shostakovich's monumental Thirteenth Symphony. It is said that even today people living near Babi Yar will not eat cabbages because of the belief that they are nurtured by the ashes of the dead. Just north of Kiev, the Chernobyl nuclear power station experienced a reactor meltdown in 1986. Lingering radiation has the same deterrent effect.

Most historical descriptions of Kiev's relationship to Constantinople have two main themes: trade and war, both in endless succession. Kiev is also the ancient capital of Eastern Orthodoxy, regarded by many as the most important factor of all in the development of the Russian national identity. The Russian historian Klyuchevsky, drawing mainly on the accounts of the Byzantine emperor and scholar Constantine Porphyrogenitus, emphasized the importance of Kiev's north–south trading pattern, from the Varangians to the Greeks along the lower reaches of the Volga and Don river systems into the Black Sea. Following the Mongol invasions in the thirteenth century, that pattern was broken, and as Kiev revived more than a century later, its attentions gravitated westwards, to the medieval Polish–Lithuanian Empire, itself becoming a formidable rival and enemy of Muscovy.

In those difficult times, Moscow's inheritance from Kiev was indeed religious and cultural, and not primarily economic. The southern Volga–Don river routes to the south were effectively barred by the Mongols, and the consequences were far-reaching. Moscow was cut off from Mediterranean civilization, including the wellsprings of Greek–Byzantine Orthodox culture. From that point on, and despite military campaigns that have persisted in one form or other ever since (some would argue right into the twenty-first century), the gravitational pull of Moscow's 'line of advance' would be east–west as much as north–south. Unlike Kiev, Moscow's governing ethos concentrated on military and political power, not trade, as the ultimate determinant of its survival.

Tsar Alexis' reign saw the return of Kiev to Russia after the defeat of Poland in 1667. With it came a higher level of culture than existed in Moscow. But the cultural tradition of Kiev, and the people who carried it, naturally gravitated to Westward-oriented St. Petersburg after its founding in 1703. Even then, Moscow was seen by its detractors as a creature of the steppes, removed in culture and outlook from enlightenment, a dark place of oppression and autocracy, having survived the Mongol catastrophe only by complicity in the invaders' crimes. Significantly, the Slavophile tradition of Moscow's special place in Holy Russia, and its mission in the world, held little resonance in Kiev.

Even today, the Westward orientation of Kiev, exemplified by the Ukrainian 'Orange Revolution' of 2004 led by President Yushchenko as head of a Western-oriented reformist coalition, had to overcome direct pressure from Moscow, which favoured a pro-Russia candidate, in addition to dealing with the after-effects of an attempted assassination. The election of a Russian-oriented president in the spring of 2010 served as a reminder that Ukraine's relationship to Russia remains contradictory. For Kiev, so closely bound to Moscow by faith and history, leaving Moscow's orbit is not only a political challenge but a cultural statement of independence as well.

Novgorod

If Kiev was Moscow's mother-city, Novgorod was its father-city. Velikii Novgorod or Novgorod the Great, it represented an alternative model and potential rival to fourteenth-century Moscow. Historians emphasize the role of Novgorod, and to a lesser extent Pskov, as Western-oriented cities with strong links to Baltic trade routes. They were closely modelled after the Hanseatic town of Magdeburg. Novgorod became a self-governing city-state with a large hinterland, which in the north and east was transited by navigable waterways, and out of reach of the Mongols. It was ruled by an elected council. Its rules of civic conduct were patterned after those of the commercial centres of north-west Europe with the powers of the princes limited by law and contract, an arrangement unthinkable in Ivan the Terrible's Moscow. In fact, Novgorod represents a counter-factual study in what Moscow might have become.

For almost three hundred years, between the twelfth and fifteenth centuries, Novgorod faced invasion. One historian[2] reports that Novgorod fought the Swedes 26 times, the German knights (Livonian and Teutonic Orders) 11 times, the Lithuanians 14 times and the Norwegians 5 times. Under Alexander Nevsky, Novgorod instituted a policy of cooperation with the Mongols, possibly because he recognized that resistance was hopeless. In 1471 the city surrendered to Ivan III, and in 1478 it was incorporated into the Moscow state. His successor Ivan IV (the Terrible) devastated the city in 1570. Nineteenth-century historians in particular saw in the demise of Novgorod as an independent state the end of any possibility that Russia would take a Western road to the development of a civil society. However, as another historian[3] notes, 'whatever the ambitions of the Moscow princes, a unified state could not simply be a reality so long as Novgorod led a separate existence'.

The Western-oriented Novgorod citizens' mistrust of Moscow lingers. Traditionally, governors of the Novgorod *oblast* have a record of resistance to the attentions of Moscow bureaucrats. The post-Soviet solution to this problem of control has been to appoint its governors direct from the capital, as in tsarist times. Putin's 'managed democracy' effectively abolished *oblast* gubernatorial elections, extinguishing the remotest possibility of any regional independence. Novgorod's last freely elected governor, a dynamic and forward-looking young man, told me in 2002 that his aim was to 'integrate Novgorod with its Western partners'. His attitude towards Moscow (by which he meant the city as well as its policies) was a mixture of scorn and contempt. Moscow was 'un-Western'.

Sarai

Located at the lower reaches of the Volga, Sarai was the seat of the Qipchaq Khanate, the westernmost component of the Mongol Empire.[4] In collaboration with their Mongol overlords, the Muscovite princes, in particular Ivan 'Moneybags' Kalita, ruled successfully at a time of Moscow's struggles against other principalities, particularly Tver. Under the circumstances, the wisest policy was no doubt voluntary cooperation with the Mongols, who occasionally offered military support. When that cooperation broke down, the results were disastrous.

Some distinguished historians argue that the 'catastrophic' appearance of the Mongols in Europe in the thirteenth century has been exaggerated, and that in fact the Mongol presence was a net contribution to the development of Eastern European civilization in general, and to Muscovy in particular. Some point out that the Orthodox Church benefited from the protection offered by the Mongol khan Mongke-Temur in 1267, which exempted the Church from taxation and confiscation of property in return for prayers for himself and his family. Others disagree, estimating that the Mongol invasion and domination of Russia retarded the development of the country by some 150 to 200 years. It has also been argued that the Mongols' general protection of the Church, however imperfectly observed, fostered a tradition of medieval conservatism amongst the clergy, even though the Church eventually turned against the Mongols. Whatever the case, there appears little doubt that the Mongol impact was profound.

The Mongol way of war was as terrifying as it was indiscriminate. The military historian John Keegan offers a graphic description:

> The horse-riding peoples, like the charioteers before them, brought to war-making the electric concept of campaigning over long distances and, when campaigning resolved itself into battle, of maneuvering on the battlefield at speed—at least five times the speed of men on foot... In their management of animals they showed a matter-of-factness—in mustering, droving, culling, slaughter for food—that taught direct lessons about how masses of people on foot, even inferior cavalrymen, could be harried, outflanked, cornered and eventually killed without risk. To the horse peoples, equipped with the composite bow... killing at a distance—of emotional detachment as well as physical space—was second nature. It was the emotional detachment of the horse warriors, ultimately manifest in their deliberate practice of atrocity, which the settled peoples found so terrifying.[5]

Moscow was repeatedly destroyed. One record reports the attack of 1571, when Devlet Girei, the Crimean representative of a then weakened and divided khanate, also attacked Moscow. Even in the Tatars' weakened state, Moscow lacked the ability, the *political will*, to offer resistance. At this distance it is difficult to comprehend the Muscovite grand princes' persistent belief that travelling to Sarai would reduce the possibility of Mongol attack, and that they should continue to act as Mongol agents and tax-collectors.

Sir Jerom Horsey, envoy of Queen Elizabeth I, described the effects of Devlet Girei's attack:

> The rever and ditches about Mosco stopped and filled with the multituds of people, loaden with gold, silver, jewells, chains, earrings, brasletts and treasur, that went for succor eaven to save their heads above water. Notwithstanding, so many thowsands wear ther burnt and drowned, as the river could not be ridd nor

> cleansed of the dead carcasses, with all the means and industrye could be used in twelve monnthes after...[6]

Less emphasized by historians (possibly because not many are horsemen themselves) is the physical challenges the Mongols faced as they headed north in large numbers to reach Moscow. This gave the city a fundamental advantage over them, for distant Sarai was some 1,500 kilometres away. In addition, Moscow was located in dense forest at the junction of two protective rivers. This caused special problems of attack. A nomadic people of the plains, accustomed to fighting on horseback with the composite bow as the principal weapon, faced difficulties in woods where manoeuvre was limited and cover for the enemy was close. The solution was siege. Vast Mongol encampments were laid down on the opposite side of the river from the Kremlin's southern walls, where they soon became mired in their own filth in the disease-ridden, marshy ground of Zamoskvorechiye. 'Across the river', as the encampment area was known, became in the nineteenth and early twentieth centuries a jumble of workers' housing and textile and machinery factories. In 1905 it was the scene of bitter strikes and demonstrations,[7] and again in 1917. Zamoskvorechiye became a core of proletarian Moscow.

Like the Wehrmacht six centuries after them, the Mongols' military weak point was their means of transportation. Hardy Mongol horses, short of stature and expert at finding grasses under snow, were choked by the summer dust of the western steppes, and died in great numbers. As they headed towards the vast northern forests, the grass of the plains thinned under the shade of trees, further stunted by the soil's acidity from black pine needles and stands of dense birch. By the development of defensive lines of felled trees, the Russians learned to meet them on a more-or-less equal footing. Already divided internally,

Mongol numbers could not be sustained, and their northern attacks, however appalling, did not match the devastation earlier visited upon Kiev.

According to contemporary accounts, Novgorod successfully resisted Mongol attack because the marshy ground turned to deep mud under the tread of the masses of horses. The same conditions applied to the environs of Moscow. The circle of heavily fortified monasteries around Moscow added to the difficulties of launching a sustained attack on the city. One of them, the Monastery of the Holy Trinity-St. Sergius, never did fall.

Pushkin once observed that the Mongol influence could not be seen as a parallel to the Arab influence in the West because 'they were Arabs without Aristotle or algebra'. Others have noted that up to the time of Peter the Great the tsarist mounted cavalry could be taken for Mongols, with their quilted jackets and composite bows, an impression borne out by the displays of medieval equipment in the Kremlin's Armoury Palace. Not only in medieval Muscovy, the Mongol experience had a long-lasting impression on the European imagination. The wild ride depicted in Albrecht Dürer's etching of the Four Horsemen of the Apocalypse, trampling all underfoot, clearly depicts the third and fourth Horsemen as Mongols, with peaked hat, furs and composite bow.

Many believe that the origins of Russian traditions of political administration lie deep within Moscow's historical experience with the Mongols. The threat of Mongol attack, and the consequent necessity to develop a strong centralized authority to withstand it, was reinforced by the autonomous and rigidly hierarchical Orthodox Church. When it eventually turned against the Mongols, it naturally supported the strengthening of the Muscovite state. By extension this included the undivided power of the tsar.

Two scholars in particular, Karl Wittfogel[8] and Tibor

Szamuely,[9] have both placed particular emphasis on the Mongol experience as laying the foundations of a 'system of government and administration that had served them so well, and that was so admirably fitted to the needs of a large, expanding and powerful state'.[10] A possibly more measured assessment of Mongol influence is offered by the historian Donald Ostrowski:

> The adoption of Mongol political administration resulted from numerous trips in the fourteenth century of the Moscovite princes to Sarai as subordinates to the Qipchaq khan. When they became grand princes of Rus', they adopted the structure and functioning of the Khanate's institutions... because they worked well for the purpose of collecting taxes and maintaining order over a wide area.[11]

Whatever the impact of Mongolian administrative techniques—many Russian words associated with administration, including *dengi* (money) and *tamozh* (customs duties), have Mongol origins—on the subsequent development of Moscow's political culture, the physical appearance of the Qipchaq Khanate's capital at Sarai appears to have had little influence upon Moscow's architecture or design. As in the massive stone-built Topkapi Sarai in Istanbul, founded in 1459 by the Ottoman Turks, also a horse people, the stone foundations excavated at Sarai suggest that permanent buildings and nomadic cultures are not necessarily mutually exclusive. In the end, the lasting effect of the Mongols on the face of Moscow is its development in concentric rings, following in a horseshoe-shape the turn of the river, each ring a successive rampart, first in wood, then earth, then stone, all meant for defence.

If there is uncertainty about Mongol influence on Muscovite traditions of civil administration, there is less doubt over Mongol influence on the Russian way of war, most brilliantly seen in the Battle of Moscow in 1941. Soviet operational doctrine along Mongol lines was developed by

General Mikhail Nikolayevich Tukhachevsky, and Mikhael Valilyevich Frunze. They had behind them the experience of the Russian civil war, characterized by rapid movements of men and cavalry over large distances, so unlike the grinding, blood-soaked war of attrition on the First World War's Western Front. They emphasized preparation before attack, later to become the massive barrages of Katyusha multiple rocket-launchers. 'Combined arms' was the essential element in this doctrine, by which Tukhachevsky meant the coordinated actions of all elements of the attacking force manoeuvring at speed to deprive the enemy of the initiative, and to paralyze his ability to concentrate his own forces. The guiding principle was the 'seizure and maintenance of the offensive over a long period of time'. Tukhachevsky was executed in 1937, a victim of the Stalinist purges, but by that time and thanks to his teachings the Russians, however weakened by Stalin's virtual decapitation of the officer class, 'possessed an army that was Mongol in doctrine and tactical sense'.

The whirlwind nature of the Wehrmacht advance was such that the principles Tukhachevsky espoused could not be realized until the Germans had been brought to a frozen standstill before Moscow in the winter of 1941. Ironically, the Germans had also learned from the Mongols by a completely different route, via the inter-war writings of Western military strategists. These *Blitzkrieg* principles were adapted and put into practice by General Hans von Seeckt and his subordinate General Hans Guderian on the Eastern Front with devastating effect. Ultimately the Wehrmacht was outdone by the Red Army as it advanced inexorably, and at horrendous human cost, to Berlin.

Like the Mongols, the Red Army observed the principle of revenge. In 1945, as Soviet troops approached the German capital, the Communist Party's Central Committee issued a slogan for the 27th Anniversary of the Red Army, making revenge explicit: 'Let us punish the fascist monsters for plundering and destroying our towns and villages, for their violence against our women and children, and for murdering Soviet people and driving them into German slavery! Vengeance and death to the fascist villains!' Some (but not all) Red Army commanders made an unrestrained interpretation of this slogan.

Under the Mongols, Moscow was both accomplice and victim, chief enforcer and rent-collector for the Mongols, and beneficiary of the Mongol presence. The confidence the Mongols had in the grand princes of Moscow allowed them to begin the famous 'gathering in' of the lands of Rus', more often than not by fire and sword, the bitterness even deeper because many of the rival princes shared the same Kievian roots. Not only Novgorod, but also Pskov and Tver, bastions against invasion from the West, fell under Moscow's control in the prolonged civil wars of the late thirteenth and early fourteenth centuries. In the end, it might be argued, Sarai and the masses of Mongol and Turkic horse warriors who acted under its hand were the decisive factors in the shaping of Moscow/Muscovy and its development. As influential in belief and culture as Constantinople and Kiev were (and as Novgorod might have been), Sarai bears little comparison.

Moscow Eclipsed

For two hundred years Moscow fell under the shadow of St. Petersburg, and when Moscow finally did emerge, it was to a vastly different world. Moscow itself had greatly changed.

Built only several decades before the French Revolution of 1789, St. Petersburg performed the same double function as the Versailles of the later Bourbon kings: a *venue obligatoire*, that is, a place of ritual, distraction and amusement for the nobility; and a place of high administration. The imperial court in St. Petersburg was isolated in more than one sense. It had a penchant for French and German over Russian, which was generally reserved for servants, workers and dogs. Its physical distance from the rest of Russia was matched by its mental distance. Despite the efforts of reformers like Stolypin and others, these are certain but often unassessed factors in undermining the ability of the Romanov dynasty and its supporting structure to face the challenges of 1905, Lenin's 'dress rehearsal' of revolution, the Great War and the 1917 Revolution itself.

Among the Old Believers, Cossacks and peasants, rumours spread that the founder of St. Petersburg, Peter the Great, was German, and that the Western ways he brought to Russia were the work of the Antichrist, if Peter was not the Antichrist himself. The myth of St. Petersburg took shape that, with its mists and slanting half-lights, it was a supernatural realm of fantasies and ghosts, a kingdom of oppression and apocalypse, ultimately damned. This myth was the raw material from which Pushkin fashioned his epic poem, 'The Bronze Horseman', in which the statue of Peter comes down from its pedestal to gallop into the unknown.

Peter hated Moscow. It was where as a boy he watched his close relatives being thrown onto the pikes of the Kremlin guards and hacked to pieces; it was the scene of the failed revolt of the *streltsy*. The city was also the stronghold of the Old Believers,[12] whose entrenched, medieval beliefs were at odds with the ideas of the Enlightenment, which held so much attraction for Peter. Paradoxically the Old Believers, with their Old Testament principles of frugality and hard work, were the backbone of Moscow's rapidly developing merchant class. Beyond the brooding nightmare of the murders he witnessed with his mother at the top of the Kremlin's Red Steps, his boyhood memories of intrigue and dangers were balanced against other memories, especially the sunny banks of the sprawling Preobrazhensky Palace on the Yauza River, on the outskirts of eastern Moscow.

The palace was by coincidence opposite the Foreigners' Settlement, which Peter frequented as he became older, absorbing the fashionable, progressive ideas of the time. In his early manhood, he moved to the Settlement, to be close to his Swiss friend Lefort, the namesake of the Moscow district where the KGB prison was later located. (The district is now best known as the location of the Tunnel of Death, a badly designed underpass where there has been an unusually high number of traffic accidents.) His antipathy to the city was such that when his wayward son Alexis, who had been lured back to Russia from the Austrian court where he was hiding from his father, admitted under interrogation that had he become tsar he would have moved the capital back to Moscow, Peter had him accused of treason and then severely beaten. Peter joins Ivan the Terrible as the instigator of his son's death.

Peter's maritime obsession, acquired during his travels to Holland and England (and possibly with the toy boats he played with as a child on the palace grounds), adds to the explanation of why he turned his back on Moscow and the oceanic sea of grassy steppe to the east. Succeeding Russian rulers were also caught up in the geopolitical logic in fashion at their time, with its heavy emphasis on control of the seas as the path to imperial greatness, a commanding theme that was later put into words with the publication in 1890 of Captain Alfred Thayer Mahan's book, *The Influence of Sea Power upon History.* Its misapplication to Imperial Russia—and the unpreparedness of the Russian Imperial Pacific Fleet—led to the disastrous naval defeat at the hands of the Japanese navy when empires collided in the Straits of Tsushima on 27 May 1905.

The historian Orlando Figes notes that the 'literary

conception of St. Petersburg as an alien and artificial place' seized the nineteenth-century romantic imagination, which contrasted it with Moscow and that city's ancient Russian heritage. But from its founding in 1703 to 1917, St. Petersburg was in the ascendant, the imperial capital from 1712, the foremost city of all the Russias.

In many respects, Moscow and St. Petersburg still remain in stark contrast, representing unresolved questions about Russia's future. St. Petersburg was rationally planned (if one leaves out of account the decision in the first place to build on a swampy and flood-prone sub-arctic site) by Domenico Trezzini, a Swiss-born architect of Italian descent. Trezzini had already worked on the palace of the Danish King Fredrick IV and had been influenced by Scandinavian and Dutch design, which happened to meet Peter's tastes exactly: it was Trezzini's Chancery for Construction which oversaw the construction of the city complete with grid plan and the ordered uniformity of the neoclassical design of its buildings. His rigorously enforced height restrictions (with one or two exceptions, including the steeple tower of the Peter–Paul Fortress) hint at Khrushchev's massive apartment developments encircling Moscow, of uniform height and of similar visual effect. The names of the architects who worked in St. Petersburg at the end of the eighteenth century together are indicative of the cosmopolitan outlook informing not only the design but also the spirit of the place: Trezzini (Italian); Schuelter (German); Michetti (Italian); and Leblond (French). Above all, Rastrelli, also Italian, who worked in Moscow as well.

The construction of St. Petersburg, a monumental project carried out at great cost,[13] established a pattern of giganticism in nation-building that has continued to this day—the Trans-Siberian Railway of the nineteenth century (which took the labour of 40,000 to construct), the Moscow Metro, the White Sea Canal and Volga–Don projects of the 1930s, and today the pipeline projects out of Siberia and the Caspian Sea into Western Europe. Beginning with the impassioned debates of the Slavophiles and Westernizers of the nineteenth century over the direction that Russia should take, and whether or not Russia was somehow different from other countries, the tension between Moscow and St. Petersburg provided the setting to one of the great debates in Russia's search for national identity. Partially obscured during the Soviet period, it has re-emerged as one of the dominant issues in contemporary Russia.

Beyond issues of identity and 'the poetry of place', access to the sea and its control for economic as well as military and political reasons remained an obsession of European strategists and statesmen for almost two hundred years. Until the mid nineteenth century, grain, along with wood for ship construction and hemp for sails and ropes, played the role of twenty-first-century energy as Russia's strategic export resource. St. Petersburg was meant to serve as the country's main entrepôt to Europe, but here the policy ran into difficulties, as Archangel and Riga (which is ice-free) were more naturally advantageous ports for export. Export restrictions were placed on them to favour St. Petersburg. By comparison with lands further to the south, northern grain production was limited by weather and soil conditions. Besides ice, the shallow waters on the approaches to St. Petersburg also count as a factor in the location of terminals of sea-routes out of the Baltic.

By the early nineteenth century, European grain prices had risen steeply, and Russia had acquired extensive Polish grain-growing areas through its role in the partition of that country. Russian military campaigns against Turkey gained access to the Black Sea, and the rise of the Russian cities of Sebastopol and Odessa further promoted the export of grain, driving the economic centre of gravity of the country southwards—in fact towards Moscow. Even in the mid eighteenth century Moscow was the 'largest unified market zone' of the empire, with a well-established industrial and commercial base where textiles and light industry provided the engine for economic growth. It was the only centre in the empire that produced consumer goods. The regulation of trade may have been out of imperial St. Petersburg, but its management was out of commercial Moscow, by the great Russian merchant and princely landowning families who even in Moscow's stagnant days of eclipse were to build mansions and estates that would transform it. Despite the vision of the northern city's founder, the realities of economics and geopolitics determined that Moscow would remain the heart of Russia, with St. Petersburg not only geographically but also economically on the periphery. It was the Moscow merchants' associations that saw clearly that the future of empire—and the profits that went with it—lay in its southern and eastern borderlands, across the 'oceanic sea of grassy steppe'.

And so it has come to pass. St. Petersburg does not figure in what some regard as the new Russian imperialism of oil, so called because of policies related to Russian state control of supply, routing and prices, and the vulnerability of third countries like Ukraine and the Baltic States. The new Russian port of Primorsk, which had a capacity of over one million barrels a day in 2005, was deliberately designed to trump Ventspils in independent Lithuania, once the largest port in the Baltic but completely dependent upon Russian-sourced oil. The same strategy has been applied in the Black Sea, where Novorossisk, Russia's largest crude facility, is at the centre of Russian strategies in the south Caucasus and Central Asia. It is already the terminus of the pipeline from the massive oil field at Tengiz, Kazakhstan. In the new Russia, St. Petersburg has been marginalized by Moscow.

During the two centuries that St. Petersburg flourished, Moscow withered. By 1725 its population, reckoned to be about 200,000 in 1700, sank by about a quarter, which gave Moscow an air of abandonment. Moscow suffered major fires in 1730 and 1748; and a 'plague riot' in 1771 was finally suppressed by the use of grapeshot fired into angry crowds. There was a ban on all stone or brick construction, and a travel 'tax in kind' was imposed on all visitors to the new capital. The traveller had to bring specified amounts of building material as the price of admission. Much was of such poor quality that it was unusable, and the scheme was finally dropped.

The job of providing construction materials was taken over by the Imperial Chancery for Construction, which arranged for state deliveries. In the 1930s and after, a similar function was performed by GOSSTROI, the Soviet state construction organization, which was the central agency for all major projects in the city of Moscow. In order to meet the construction needs of Moscow's defensive perimeter, bans on concrete or reinforced-steel construction were enforced throughout the Soviet Union during the Second World War. The only exception was the Moscow Metro.

St. Petersburg overtook Moscow in population in the 1780s and it was not until 1800 that Moscow regained the same level it had a century before. Moscow's nadir at the hands of St. Petersburg came in the 1770s when plans were drawn up to rebuild the city in a pale image of its northern sister. The architects Vasily Bazhenov and Matvei Kazakov convinced Catherine the Great to replace the greater part of the Kremlin with neoclassical structures. Some demolition did take place, but fortunately the project ran out of cash and was shelved. Moscow seemed particularly prone to grandiose projects abandoned through lack of resources—a pattern repeated into the nineteenth and twentieth centuries.

The return of the imperial court to Moscow for five years

did little to improve its second-class status within the empire. In 1732 Catherine the Great moved the capital back to St. Petersburg. In 1820 Pushkin likened Moscow to a dowager queen in the mourning dress of purple curtsying before the new ruler, St. Petersburg. Emblematic of St. Petersburg's pre-eminence over Moscow was its completion of permanent street lighting in 1724; Moscow did not even begin until six years later. St. Petersburg commenced a systematic paving of its streets in 1717; Moscow, although some stone paving had taken place there in the 1640s, would have to wait until the advent of asphalt in the 1870s before a similar project was undertaken on its streets, several decades after the first rail link between the imperial capital and Moscow was established, in 1851. It became the inevitable task of Moscow's governors to carry petitions on behalf of the city to the new capital, a role sardonically likened to the Moscow princes' abject carrying of petitions to Sarai.

St. Petersburg/Petrograd[14] also overshadows Moscow in the Soviet version of the Great October Socialist Revolution of 1917. There is an irony in that nineteenth-century St. Petersburg, bereft of the influence of a strong politically conscious middle class, refined in speech and manner, should in Soviet mythology be the cockpit of revolution, not Moscow. St. Petersburg's revolutionary credentials include the ill-led Decembrist revolt of 26 December 1825, staged by aristocratic and idealistic officers of the city's Preobrazhensky Guards regiment, and put down by the new Tsar Nicholas I with the loss of several dozen lives. It ended with the tragedy of exile and even death for the sons of many aristocratic families. Then there was Bloody Sunday of 1905, when some two hundred working-class demonstrators peacefully marching in supplication to the tsar in their churchgoing best were shot down by troops. The massacre and unrest of 1905 set the revolutionary stage for Lenin's arrival in November 1917 at Petrograd's Finland

Station in a sealed train, arranged by the German General Staff from Helsinki via Stockholm and points west.

Cheaply produced cardboard boots that fell apart in the autumn mud, and bad or non-existent food (which provoked riots as the war ground on), may have been as much a factor in prompting the Petrograd garrison to revolt and support the Petrograd Soviet as Lenin's rather squeaky rhetoric, the reactionary obtuseness and incompetence of the tsar (who in an astonishing error of judgment had put himself at the head of an already failed military campaign) and the dithering of Kerensky's provisional government. Were it not for Petrograd's relative accessibility by land and sea to Europe's borders, it was an anomalous place for proletarian revolution. Some historians question whether it was a revolution at all, or rather a *coup* organized by the Bolshevik Party operating out of the Smolny Institute, a finishing school for fashionable young ladies. The Bolsheviks managed to get control of the Petrograd Soviet, the springboard for wresting power from the provisional government.

Even as the cradle of revolution, the Bolsheviks' attitude toward the city was ambivalent. Amongst the Bolsheviks, first of all Lenin, the city did not inspire confidence. He ordered the mutiny in 1921 at the nearby naval base of Kronstadt in the Gulf of Finland to be mercilessly suppressed. In fact, the Kronstadt mutiny established a tradition of mistrust between the Party and the military, some of which rubbed off on the city itself. The mistrust came to a head during Stalin's culling of the Red Army of the late 1930s, but also recurring fears of 'Bonapartism', a charge levelled by Stalin in 1945 against the popular hero of the Red Army, Marshal Zhukov, whom Stalin suspected as a potential rival. In the 1920s Stalin held the same suspicion against Trotsky as Minister of War. The Soviet Minister of Defence, Yazov, was among the plotters who tried to overthrow Gorbachev in 1991.

Moscow Reinvented

Moscow's revolutionary credentials are as legitimate as St. Petersburg's, perhaps even more so. St. Petersburg had been the scene of Russia's first major strikes, beginning in the 1870s, which triggered the first hesitant labour legislation governing conditions of work, but by 1885 intolerable conditions in the massive Tryekhgornaya textile plant in Moscow prompted its workers to mount a strike that in the end had to be forcibly put down by the local authorities. A decade later, the Moscow League for the Struggle of the Working Class was established drawing together a number of disparate socialist groups, including that of Lenin, who had moved to Moscow from Simbirsk in 1890. The revolutionary newspaper he founded, *Iskra* (appropriately, The Spark), was clandestinely distributed from Moscow throughout the empire. The disturbances which gripped Moscow in 1905 and in 1917—much greater in terms of the number of casualties and extent than those in Petrograd—were particularly violent, mainly because of all Russian cities it had the largest underclass of urban peasantry existing in wretched conditions, as defined by Engels' Manchester slums, and therefore the nearest thing to Marx's proletariat. (Soviet writings omit Marx's disparaging remarks about their backwardness.)

In 1918 revolutionary Petrograd was faced with a triple threat. The German military was still a presence to the west; that year, British, American, Canadian, Italian and Serb troops landed in Murmansk and Archangel and other ports on the White Sea while Finnish troops under General Mannerheim fought the Red Finns not far from Petrograd. An army of 18,000 was massing in Narva under the former tsarist General Yudenich. The attack on the city was planned for 1919. In the event, Trotsky organized a successful defence against a less than determined enemy.

On 26 February 1918, with Petrograd still threatened, its Council of Peoples' Commissars resolved to relocate to Moscow 'for reasons of security'. A contributing factor may have been that Petrograd was judged not to be a reliable Bolshevik stronghold, given the chaotic situation in the city and the presence of many armed and disparate revolutionary groups. Originally it was intended as a 'temporary move', but this latter phrase quickly disappeared in later Soviet histories. Because of the aversion of some of the Bolsheviks to 'Asiatic and backward' Moscow, an alternative candidate for the new seat of government was proposed: Nizhni Novgorod, the same city where Prince Pozharski and Kuzma Minin organized resistance to the Polish occupation of Moscow in 1613. This idea was quickly put aside.

Posthumously, Lenin's concern about the military vulnerability of Petrograd proved correct. Beginning in 1941, Leningrad endured a siege at the hands of the Wehrmacht's Army Group North under appalling conditions, and before it was finally lifted 900 days later, isolated with no hope of relief. It is estimated that the siege killed 200,000 by bombing and shelling, with over 600,000 dead by starvation.

The move to Moscow was carried out in utmost secrecy.[15] On 11 March 1918 Lenin arrived in Moscow's Nikolayevsky railway station accompanied by a squadron of Latvian machine gunners, just in case. Moscow returned to centre-stage—and less than ten years later, under Stalin, it returned yet again, and this time with a vengeance. Centralization became the order of the day, if not the era.

As with almost everything and everyone else, Stalin's suspicion of St. Petersburg grew over the years. Bolsheviks native to the Baltic city were among the first to fall victim to his purges. In 1928 members of the Leningrad Party organization, headed by the 'Old Bolshevik' (i.e. having joined the Party before the Revolution) Gregory Zinoviev, unwisely criticized the Party's rapid bureaucratization and abandonment of revolutionary ideals. The Left Opposition, as it was called, was condemned by Stalin (who, they should have known, controlled Party and state appointments) and by his temporary ally Bukharin. Not too far off the mark, Zinoviev and his fellow Leningraders accused Stalin of fostering a 'Genghis Khan' plan of excessive coercion in the pursuit of industrialization. Stalin had them outmanoeuvred at the next Party Congress. With the elimination of the Left Opposition in Leningrad, the city's political threat to Moscow and therefore to Stalin's power base was also eliminated.

Stalin was implicated in the assassination on 1 December 1934 of Sergei Kirov, Leningrad's charismatic Party chief and potential rival. The official Soviet account blamed 'Trotskyite, Zinovievite and Bukharinite bandits' for the assassination. The same group was accused of plotting the death of Maxim Gorky, the revolutionary poet whom Stalin had lured back to Moscow from abroad, and who had begun to have doubts. Kirov's assassination served as the trigger for the Great Purge Trials of the 1930s.

Stalin's dislike of Leningrad continued after the war. In the early post-war atmosphere of trauma and still-open wounds, the 'Leningrad Affair' sent many soldiers returning to their home city to the Gulag instead. They were suspected of collaborating with the Germans. If Stalin suspected soldiers, he particularly suspected soldier-heroes, including General Kuznetsov, the hero of the Leningrad siege, and Marshal Zhukov, the hero of the Battles of Moscow and Berlin. Kuznetsov was involved in postwar power-struggles. His zealous enquiries into the Kirov assassination and his reputation as a potential successor to Stalin led to his demotion and ultimately execution in 1950. Too popular to eliminate, Zhukov was shunted aside.

Stalin was also suspicious of hero-cities. Leningrad represented an alternative totem of military patriotism to himself and Moscow. Priority was given to Moscow in post-war reconstruction even though the damage to Leningrad was much greater.

The wheel has now come full circle, for the present leadership in the Kremlin is dominated by representatives of the old imperial capital. Leningrad had received its post-revolutionary name shortly after Lenin's death in 1924, but had lost out to Moscow in the competition for the honour of housing Lenin's body. Both Prime Minister Putin and his successor President Medvedev are Leningraders and both worked with Anatoly Sobchak when the latter was mayor during the tumultuous days of the early 1990s. Vladimir Putin had been Anatoly Sobchak's pupil in Leningrad University's law faculty, and in the mayor's office KGB representative, although his functions were obscured under a less eye-catching title. As professorial mentor to Putin and to other law students, Sobchak was famous for his insistence on the primacy of the rule of law in the management of the state, however much he may have strayed from this principle himself. As president, Putin rephrased this as the '*dictatorship of law*', which at least in theory had a less ominous ring than the '*dictatorship of the proletariat*', the term coined by Marx to describe the inevitable outcome of class war.

Following the turmoil of the Yeltsin years, in a prolonged and convoluted adjustment of Kremlin power structures, President Vladimir Putin brought to Moscow a group of Leningraders, most of them associated with him during his earlier days in Leningrad. They became the inner core of *silniki*—the group of men (they are all men) who control the 'commanding heights' of the government apparatus. Among the most prominent are Foreign Minister Ivanov, formerly head of the Security Council,

Viktor Cherkassov and Nikolai Patrushev, both of the successor organization to the KGB, the FSB. Perhaps unsurprisingly, but to the delight of Kremlinologists who built careers by following the patterns of recruitment of senior Soviet officials, this 'old boy' networking has a history beginning with Khrushchev in the 1960s, with his power base in Kiev, and Brezhnev, who 'had no Moscow vassals to speak of'.[16] There was also a kind of 'old boyism' among Eastern European Communists who had spent the late 1930s and the war in exile at the Luks Hotel.

Even a generation later this pattern persisted in Eastern Europe, famously where with Edward Gierek's Katowice Mafia, Polish Communist Party members from that southern industrial city held virtually exclusive authority in running pre-*Solidarnosc* Poland. In Russia, only Lenin the internationalist and Stalin the Georgian were exceptions to the general rule of recruiting 'old boys', as was Gorbachev, each in his own way an outsider. Beginning with Putin and Medvedev, Russia is again run by insiders, with strong representation from Leningrad/St. Petersburg. In a departure from Soviet times, beginning with the old-style hand of former Mayor Luzhkov, Moscow is now run by Muscovites.

Beloved city of Pushkin, St. Petersburg received long-delayed international recognition as a World Heritage Site in 1990. As host to the G-8 Summit in July 2006, the city provided the setting for Russia's symbolic emergence as co-partner with the seven great industrial democracies. Because the country was still recovering from the economically troubled years of the 1990s—Russia came close to economic collapse in 1998—the summit had a slightly Potemkin village atmosphere with the main venues and streets expensively cleaned up for the occasion. With all-out preparations for the G8 Summit, St. Petersburg was finally released from Stalin-inspired neglect. But UNESCO has threatened to strip it of its World Heritage title. High steel and glass buildings have grown to deface the city's skyline.

In spite of the overwhelming personality of its founder's namesake, Petersburg (as it was then known) had little chance of overcoming the great weight of Russian history which Moscow represents. There was a prescience about this. Mikhail Shcherbatov, in his metaphorical *Journey to the Land of Ophir* (1784), contrasted Ophir's old and new capitals, with the new capital collapsing and the old capital returned to its former station because of its commitment, Rousseau-like, to a simpler, more virtuous way of life. Moscow had always remained the commercial and economic capital of Russia; and the place of the coronation of the Romanovs had never migrated out of the Kremlin. Like Rome for the historical Christian West, Moscow was also the spiritual capital of Russia and the Christian East.

Beyond the military situation imposed upon Petrograd by its geographic realities in 1917-18, authentic Russian Moscow still holds the historical and cultural balance of advantage against Westernized St. Petersburg. The G8 summit was after all a *Western* event attended by foreigners; Nicholas II called St. Petersburg home but did not have a drop of Russian blood in his veins. Moscow, not St. Petersburg, was the Soviet capital of world revolution. Strategically placed between East and West in spirit as well as geography, between the First and Third Worlds, globalized Moscow is now transformed, a city among other great cities. Moscow's past is with it yet, from Mongol to tsar and to commissar, to the world of today's *silniki* and *derzhavniki,* practitioners of state and power in the Kremlin.

'The Four Horsemen of the Apocalypse' by Albrecht Dürer, from the Revelation of St. John: 4. The two riders to the right wear Mongol headgear; the double-curved bow is of Central Asian origin. Dürer however was probably portraying Turks who were then threatening Europe.

Chapter Three
Pestilence, Fire and Sword

> Yt was God, that suffereth this wicked people, whoe live, flow and wallowe, in the verie hight of their lust and wickednes of the crienge Sodomiticall sines, to be thus justly punished and plaged with the tirrannie of so bloody a kynge: God, I say hath now appointed a tyme and prepared owt of his great justice a fearful reveng...
>
> Sir Jerom Horsey, on Devlet Girei's attack on Moscow, 1571

Moscow is not alone as a city that has endured and survived catastrophe. In the distant past, Rome, Baghdad and Constantinople come to mind. In more recent centuries, the Great Fire of London of 1666 caused the inner, pestilential core of the city to be cauterized, though miraculously only five died. The Blitz conducted by Goering's Luftwaffe between September 1940 and May 1941 cost Britain some 43,000 people killed, the greater number in London, and a million houses were destroyed. An Allied incendiary raid on Dresden three years later in a single terrible night created a funeral pyre in which 24-40,000 perished. Nanking, which was capital of China during the winter of 1937, suffered an estimated 300,000 deaths—half the city's population—in six weeks of atrocity and murder at the hands of the Japanese. Warsaw was destroyed three times by the Germans during the second World War, and its rubble further reduced by the Soviet Forty-Seventh Army. Only the fact that the underground infrastructure was relatively intact weighed against a post-war decision to move the entire city further north up the Vistula. In August 1945, the sacrifice of the Japanese cities of Hiroshima and Nagasaki, and the deaths of 140,000 and 80,000 respectively, established what passed for the ground rules of strategic nuclear stability as they developed over the next fifty years.

Moscow belongs to the same category as all these cities. It has been argued that the apocalyptic vision in Russian culture, from the fires of the End of Days to Nuclear Armageddon, stems from Moscow citizens' collective memory.

Moscow is no stranger to despoliation and even abandonment by its own people, either by its inhabitants or by its rulers. Moscow was deserted by Ivan the Terrible in 1564 when he transferred his seat to Aleksandrovskaya Sloboda and renounced the throne. He was persuaded to return, but again sought refuge out of the city in 1571 as it was burned down by the Crimean Tatars, who had sworn to send his ears to the Turkish sultan. Peter the Great forsook Moscow for St. Petersburg, leaving the city to its own devices. With the help of the French, the Russians destroyed it again in 1812.

Then in the first week of October 1941 they made preparations to repeat the act: before Moscow was an impossibly thin line of defence standing between it and Panzer Groups III and IV of Army Group Centre, approaching due east along the Mozhaisk Highway. It had already been breached; had the line of advance continued it would have taken the same route as Napoleon, entering the western approaches of the city and proceeding down the Arbat to the walls of the Kremlin. On 15 October, a top secret decree by the State Defence Committee issued instructions for evacuation to Kuybyshev: 'Comrade Stalin will be evacuated tomorrow, or a little later.'[1] An underground bunker was prepared for him there by the same workers who had constructed the Metro. As in Napoleon's time, plans were made for the destruction of Moscow. Word got out, and precipitated the notorious Moscow Panic. It lasted several days as rumours spread that officials were fleeing, leaving the rest to the devil. In sad repetition of other urban disasters, food riots and looting—sometimes abetted by store and warehouse managers themselves—spread throughout the city. Some of the most chaotic scenes took place before Kazan railway station as masses of people sought to escape to the east from what they thought was a doomed city.

In one of the defining moments of the city's history, Stalin made a decision to stay. A state of siege was declared, and the NKVD set to work bringing order to the city by summary execution. Within the space of a week Stalin had gone from potential refugee, ready to flee his own capital, to the heroic guardian of the gates of Moscow. Three weeks later, on 6 November 1941, Stalin gave his customary address on the occasion of the anniversary of the Revolution from the deep Mayakovskaya underground station, surrounded by flowers and a picked audience. A day later, on the advice and assurance of his generals, he stood atop Lenin's mausoleum to review troops marching directly to the front. Snowfall and an umbrella of fighter aircraft kept the Luftwaffe away. As in the past, Moscow had brushed extinction and survived.

It is tempting to speculate that Moscow was star-crossed from the beginning. The old Russian chronicles record that in 1147, the year he founded Moscow, Yuri Dolgoruky had executed Stefan Kuchka, the unlucky owner of a hunting lodge and surrounding territory that Yuri wanted for himself. The next mention of Moscow in the chronicles is in 1177, when Gleb, Prince of Riazan, came upon Moscow and burned the entire settlement, the stockade and surrounding villages.

This ancient act of vandalism set the pattern of destruction and regeneration as one of the distinctive features of the city's history. Threats to survival have taken many forms, from the consequences of invasion from all points of the compass, to the risks of living in a city which until the nineteenth century was built almost entirely of wood. Epidemics have convulsed the city over the centuries. Some disasters defy comprehension. On 9 June 1909 a massive tornado struck the eastern suburbs of Moscow destroying three villages and the Lefortovo district, killing several dozen. Many Muscovites at the time saw this as a divine omen, promising damnation on a distant, corrupt and incompetent tsarist regime which had brought humiliation upon Russia in the Russo–Japanese war, and had loosed a war of oppression against its own people.

Beginning in the 1930s, purges, executions and wholesale deportations of entire social groups had an inevitable effect on the city's population and make-up. In an attempt to disguise the extent of this human tragedy, the Soviet authorities suspended publication of the city's directory *Vsya Moskva*, as there would be too many blank pages and missing names. It did not reappear until the end of the 1980s. The habit of secretiveness dies hard, and even in Gorbachev's Moscow there were secrets. For fifty years, between 1937 and 1987, there was also no detailed city map publicly available.

As a student in the 1960s, I was warned by the *militsia*, but also by *babushkas* who practised their own surveillance, not to photograph bridges. These small acts of being watched, plus the seemingly endless hierarchy of permits and passes and restricted areas, though individually insignificant and only mildly irritating all contributed to a debilitating sense of helplessness in the face of a vast system of control. Secrecy extended to the rules as well, and arrests could be made with the charge presented after the fact. One of the more chilling features of the Purge Trials of the 1930s was that prisoners were often interrogated on what the charge should be, and if necessary they were required to invent one.

One of the greatest secrets of all, the disaster at the Chernobyl nuclear power station on 26 April 1986, was forced by overwhelming evidence to become a public issue and a test for Gorbachev's policies of *glasnost* or openness. By luck, unusual wind conditions made the radioactive cloud drift to the west, irradiating much of rural Belarus, brushing the edges of the Moscow region but just missing the city itself.

Gorbachev's strong aversion to nuclear weapons was attributed to the potential for even greater catastrophe that this experience forewarned.

In more recent years, Moscow has experienced its own version of the London Underground terrorist bombings, hostage-takings in theatres, and the tragedy of Beslan, where the deaths of so many children transformed the politics of Russia and served as a permanent warning against terrorism: intended or not, it had the side-effect of justifying authoritarianism in the interests of security. At the ultimate level, like many other cities of the twenty-first century, Moscow remains hostage to the strategic end-game of nuclear annihilation, or of falling victim to other weapons of mass destruction.

Even from the beginning, the city prevailed and grew, perhaps against the odds, as indeed most versions of the history of Moscow and the state that derived from it take as their principal theme.

Pestilence

More than once, plague threw its dark shadow across Moscow. The bubonic plague or Black Death first appeared in Pskov in 1352. According to the chronicles, in an act of self-denial Archbishop Vasily of Novgorod went to Pskov in order to bless the city in its time of distress. He died there of the disease. His infected body was returned to his home city. From Novgorod the plague quickly spread to other Russian cities, and reached epidemic proportions in Moscow by 1364;[2] it was to have profound long-term social and economic effects from its beginnings in the fourteenth century.

In Western Europe, shortages of labour supply as a result of the medieval epidemics tended to drive up the wages of the surviving artisans and other urban workers. The indirect result was the increasing independence of towns, or more precisely the guilds to which the artisans belonged. In contrast, the plague's devastation of the city's population placed Muscovy peasants under an urban corvée, in most cases to build and extend the city walls. Muscovite princes treated their city and, by extension, its inhabitants as private property. In collaboration with the great land-owning monasteries, the princes drafted the workers attached to them into city public works, and in legal terms there was no judicial distinction between townsman and peasant; all were in effect chattels. No tradition of independent self-government ever developed in Moscow or in other Russian cities. This was to have ruinous consequences, and was a major contributing factor to the urban upheavals of 1905 and 1917.

Bubonic plague and its sister pneumonic plague struck Moscow among the first of European cities, and after a respite of a couple of centuries Moscow was the last to see the epidemics leave. Only the advent of systematic urban sanitation, beginning in the nineteenth century, brought it under control. Moscow's misfortune was to be closest to the Gobi region of Central Asia where the disease is thought to originate, carried first by the Mongol invaders of the thirteenth century, and later in the cargo and the rats accompanying travellers along the Silk Route during the *Pax Mongolica*. For centuries, the Kremlin palaces were reported to have smelled of rats.

Rats and the plague also had an effect on political events in Russian history. In the fourteenth century the Mongol khan conferred the title of grand prince on Simon the Proud, in effect giving him implicit permission to expand the territories of Muscovy. He died of plague-like symptoms in 1353 at the age of 36, triggering an extended contest for power, and putting into abeyance any expansion of the Muscovite state for over a generation.

Moscow's urban structure was, in fact, particularly vulnerable to infection because of the close proximity of its wooden buildings, and the practice of keeping livestock inside together with the fodder, which attracted vermin. Outside, filth and slops collected in cesspools, and only the onset of winter would bring frozen relief from the stench that pervaded many public places. Spring and autumn brought mud. European visitors reported that their horses had to wade through passages of offal. The general condition of the city was exacerbated by other practices. Unsold fish were left to rot in the main trading rows (the *riadi*) next to Red Square. In the same district of Kitai Gorod, barbers worked in open booths littered with unswept piles of their clients' shorn hair infested with lice. Further down the *riadi*, desperate women sold both themselves and the risk of venereal disease.[3]

Some of the same conditions that made Moscow so noisome served as an impediment to invasion. Moscow's swampy Zamoskvorecie district opposite the Kremlin was a case in point. Contemporary descriptions of Devlet Girei's besiegers of Moscow record plague-like symptoms as well as diarrhoea among them. For an infected man, it would have been impossible to ride. The affliction was common to medieval armies. The French historian Froissart reports that the English archers, facing the French army drawn up before Agincourt in 1415, suffered from intestinal disorder, but they dealt with the problem before the battle by dispensing with their breeches. Girei's Tatars as well as the Mongols themselves, however, fought almost exclusively from horseback and many were immobilized.

The eruption of the Moscow plague of 1570 may have affected the ability of the Mongols to wage war, but not to the extent of preventing them from reducing Moscow to ashes. The wooden city was rapidly rebuilt, but in 1654, after several years of famine, the plague flared again, reaching its peak in 1661. By September of that year, as a result of seven years of plague, nearly half of the city's population had died. Others perished for reasons discovered only after advances in knowledge of public hygiene: in a city with a vestigial sewerage system, many were asphyxiated by hydrogen sulphide gas seeping out from cesspits below the floorboards.

Bodies were left in the streets as the gravediggers themselves had succumbed. Sometimes the corpses were hidden for fear that they would attract looters to the victims' vacant houses, and this contributed to the further spread of disease. Dogs were killed in the mistaken belief that they were the main carriers, this idea apparently imported from recent contacts with the Ottoman Empire. (In the Islamic world, belief in dogs' uncleanliness derives from their medieval association with the plague.) Moscow lost an estimated 80 per cent of its taxpayers, and the government was obliged to offer incentives to provincial inhabitants to come to Moscow to occupy empty houses and abandoned trading rows.

As the plague of 1661 reached its height the authorities undertook strict measures. Moscow and Smolensk, where the plague had also broken out, were isolated with checkpoints set up at their approaches. Those who tried to avoid them were summarily executed. All the gates to the Kremlin and all its windows were sealed from the outside with bricks, and the tsar sought refuge at the Troitsko-Sergieyev Monastery, some 130 kilometres from Moscow; the dispatches he received there were copies of the originals, which were burnt as a precaution. In an early form of quarantine, the tsarina and the tsarevich were given refuge separately in the Kalyazin Monastery, kept under close guard against visitors.

In September 1771 unusually warm weather brought a further outburst of the plague, which was responsible for 52,000 deaths (some reports put the toll at twice that number) out of a Moscow city population of 300,000. At its height it was killing 500 people a day, and survivors were fleeing the city. As a preventive measure the city ordered buildings near the

Kremlin to be destroyed, but did not offer compensation. This move triggered demonstrations in the Lefortovo district, which then spread to the centre. A clumsy attempt by Archbishop Ambrosius to disperse demonstrators who had gathered before the Icon of the Virgin Mary of Blagolyuovo in Kitai Gorod prompted the large crowd to riot, growing and spreading throughout the city and into the Kremlin itself. It was finally broken up by sabre and gunfire. By order of Catherine II, the tongue from the bell that sounded the alarm at Ambrosius' interdiction was cut down by an executioner. In 1803 the bell was removed from the Bell Tower to the Kremlin Arsenal where it hung silently for thirty years before being replaced.

In the nineteenth century, as Moscow underwent rapid industrialization and the housing conditions of factory workers reached appalling levels of overcrowding and lack of sanitation, there were several major outbreaks of typhus, a pestilential disease already endemic. It had a psychological as well as a physical effect. Anton Chekhov, the great Russian writer (who happened to be a doctor), complained that the outbreak of typhus in 1885 'sapped his creative energies because of his medical responsibilities'. Not so long afterwards, Moscow was badly hit, as were many other cities, by the global influenza outbreak of 1918-20.

The collapse of the Soviet system in the 1990s had the side-effect of a dramatic increase in cases of tuberculosis in Moscow and in other ex-Soviet cities. This was caused by the rapid decline in housing standards and related social dislocations as extensive Soviet public welfare programmes, including military and civilian pensions, medical care and public health infrastructure, disintegrated. The social disaster that this represented was exacerbated by the attempted imposition of a rapid transition to American-style free-market capitalism—'shock therapy', it was called, as prices were freed in 1991. This policy was advocated by Western-oriented economic reformers, led by acting prime minister Yegor Gaidar. The 'Chicago School', from which Gaidar drew inspiration, focused on distinctions between marketization and privatization, and their sequencing during the transition from a command-driven to a free-market economy, where prices, at least in theory, determined all. This meant little to the average Muscovite on a fixed income who was suddenly confronted with rent increases and the need to pay for bread with money of depleted value.

The city drifted towards a primitive economy of personal survival based on barter trade in goods and services. On the streets, family *babushkas* offered their grandchildren's shoes in exchange for food. It was here that tuberculosis struck. In a society with weakened public health defences, the sudden release from the Gulags and prisons of thousands of political prisoners (and in some cases, outright criminals) infected with the disease threatened to bring further tragedy upon the city. The unsung heroes of Moscow are those who worked under these difficult conditions to contain the impending pestilence. In large part, they succeeded where Archbishop Vasily had failed over four hundred years before.

The last reported case of the plague was registered in 1979, but a plague warning was issued for all of European Russia on 27 March 2004. It was apparently issued after the accidental release of research material housed at the experimental biological weapons facility on Vozrozhdeniye Island, in the Aral Sea, an incident (if it was one) that has always been denied by the authorities. There have been no reports of that infection ever having reached Moscow.

As more ordered systems of government returned to Russia under Presidents Putin and Medvedev, the threat of large-scale epidemics has diminished in Russian cities. The exceptions are alcoholism and the explosive growth of AIDS, or SPID in Russian. At a public health conference sponsored by the World Health Organization in 2009, the Russian Minister of Health recognized the existence of AIDS but was reluctant to adopt measures common in the West to combat it, e.g. offering sterile needles along with methadone to drug-users. Public health information programmes were rudimentary and are only now improving. One 1990s poster in a Moscow Metro station reads: 'AIDS? See a doctor.'

Fire

The history of fire destroying Moscow is a long and sorry one. The Mongols first burned Moscow to the ground in 1237, and again in 1293; during their period Moscow was repeatedly attacked by fire. The popular name of Red Square remained until the second half of the seventeenth century Pozharnaya Ploschad, the Square of Conflagration, because of the fires that burned to death the crowds on the square seeking refuge in the stone Kremlin from Devlet Girei and his Crimean Tatars; its doors had been locked and bolted. The same square with its densely packed trading rows was again set alight by the Polish occupiers of the Kremlin as they retreated from Moscow in 1612 (at that time, its official title was Troitskaya Ploschad).

Nature added to the history of destruction by fire. The first recorded mention of the Kremlin is contained in a report of a fire dated 1331; its cause, apparently, was non-hostile. To escape a fire in April 1547, Ivan the Terrible took refuge in the village of Vorobievo, located in the Sparrow Hills overlooking Moscow; two and a half centuries later, Napoleon would look down from the same village to see Moscow yet again in flames. From the sixteenth to the mid eighteenth century, wooden Moscow was burned to the ground at least more than a dozen times. Two of the dates, 1612 and 1712, have a familiar ring, occurring at exactly one-hundred-year intervals before the Great Fire of 1812 which forced Napoleon's withdrawal from the city. The regularity and destructiveness of fires, even in times of peace, are a steady drumbeat in the city's history, at least until stone replaced wood as the building material of choice. This took time: the first Kremlin church, Spas na Boru, was built of wood in the thirteenth century; it was later rebuilt in stone because of fires, having survived the depredations of the Mongols, but finally succumbed to the anti-religious campaigns of the 1930s. The first stone buildings of Moscow were the Cathedrals of the Assumption and the Archangel Michael, built in the Kremlin in the fourteenth century, about the time that the first stone houses appeared.[4] This became more common practice by the late eighteenth century; but even then the urban estates and palaces of the boyars and rich merchants were often of wood overlaid with plaster. Despite the risks of wood, the cost, abundance and the comparative ease of working the material all weighed in its favour. The embargo on stone construction in Moscow during the building of St. Petersburg reinforced the continuing preference.

Following Napoleon's retreat from Moscow, a plan view of the city was prepared by Russian Army cartographers to produce a (possibly exaggerated) inventory of the extent of destruction. The plan shows the stone and brick Kremlin standing alone in a devastated landscape, with the only surviving buildings on the opposite side of the river. Some decades later, in defiance of fate, but within living memory of the Great Fire, some 9,800 houses out of 14,900 were still made of wood.

A combination of circumstances contributed to Moscow's extreme vulnerability. Closely-packed buildings along narrow streets littered with all manner of combustible material were an open invitation to fire and plague. Choked lanes and winding alleys acted as a barrier to efficient fire-fighting. Prevailing winds from the west guaranteed the fires' rapid spread. Wood-burning stoves kept alight for nine months of the year added to the risk. A number of cases of arson have been recorded, such as a major fire in 1611, committed either by disaffected citizens or drunks, given the general rowdiness of the place. The Muscovite expression for arson is 'letting loose the red rooster'.

After the 'civilian' fire of 1547, Ivan the Terrible took a number of steps to rectify the situation, including razing buildings to create firebreaks, particularly around the Kremlin. Before Ivan, the standard method of fire-fighting was to demolish buildings downwind from the fire, but of course only after it had started, often too late to prevent its further spread. Other measures were adopted, such as a ban on the use of wood-burning stoves in the summer months, and the use of watchdogs tethered to lines strung along city streets. These were supplemented by night guards stationed on the roofs, and the ringing of church bells in the district where the fire had broken out to summon the fire brigade and security squads, the latter to deal with thieves attracted by the confusion. *Droshki* drivers were put on permanent call to transport fire-fighters. By the seventeenth century, Moscow had a corps of fire inspectors and a fire brigade numbering 200 which grew to to a million-strong force that defended Moscow against Luftwaffe incendiary attack in 1941.

In other ways as well, fire left its mark. A 1748 rescript of fire protection marked off streets for straightening by means of red lines drawn on Moscow city plans. These *krasniyye linii* appeared on maps of city planners until well into the twentieth century. City-wide bans on fire, or *chistkas*, continued into the twentieth century when city water systems were closed down for cleaning and repair. The Great Fire of Moscow of 1812 was the culmination of the city's experience with fire. How it began is still the subject of some debate, but the balance of evidence suggests that it was started on the orders of the Governor of Moscow, Count Fydor Vassilievich Rostopchin, described as 'destroyer of Moscow, intelligent, cultivated, and possibly mad'. Once he was informed that General Kutuzov would not defend the city against the Grande Armée (he had just fought it to a draw at the Battle of Borodino) the count ordered the police superintendent Veronenko to torch anything useful to the French, and to evacuate all the fire-pumps of Moscow, along with their crews.

One of Napoleon's entourage, De Larrey, described the whole city on fire 'with thick streams of flame of various colours rising up on all sides, blotting out the horizon and sending in all directions a blinding light and a blinding heat'.[5] A number of romantic paintings of the time show Napoleon's profile depicted against the background of a warm, red glow of Moscow aflame, smoke curling artistically skyward. The reality was otherwise. Contemporary reports record that the heat was so intense that convection currents from the maelstrom blew the tin roofs off buildings and shot golden cupolas into the air. Above the roar of the inferno, they reported the screams of women being raped and the howls of tethered dogs being burnt alive.

Over time, however, Moscow had come to terms with its own vulnerabilities. Because of the embargo on stone and brick for construction in Moscow as the St. Petersburg project got underway, the majority of Moscow's private buildings continued to be constructed of wood. Large markets on the outskirts of Moscow, near the present Vysoko-Petrovsky Monastery on the Boulevard Ring, specialized in selling pre-cut timbers, early examples of modular construction. If the weather cooperated, an incinerated house could be rebuilt in a matter of weeks. The overall effect was that, well into the nineteenth century, the life and appearance of the city were marked by a cycle of destruction and regeneration, like a living thing marking in its own way the passage of the seasons—fire being most prevalent in the winter and spring months. Only the stone and brick Kremlin seemed immutable.

The impulse towards regeneration is reflected in nineteenth-century Russian art, and its experiments in visual metaphor. One of the most powerful and moving examples is Saurasov's famous painting *The Rooks have Returned* (1871), in which a village scene of a flock rebuilding nests against a bleak early spring day is elevated to poetry by its symbolism of rebirth.

In the twentieth century, fire brought to Moscow by its enemies repeated a pattern of grim familiarity. On the eve of Operation Barbarossa, the Wehrmacht military plan for the attack on the Soviet Union in 1941, an estimated 70 per cent of Moscow's residential buildings were still wooden, this despite the massive steel and concrete domestic housing programmes of the 1930s.[6] Many of the new structures had roofs of inflammable material and tarred paper. Combustible material left from construction sites littered the streets. Under Operation Barbarossa, Hitler's instructions were clear. Directive 33 ordered the Luftwaffe to obliterate Moscow by fire. In accordance with this directive, heavy incendiary and high-explosive bombing of Moscow by over 200 aircraft began on the night of 22 July 1941, a five-hour engagement that extended into a year-long campaign lasting as long as the London Blitz. Many of the German pilots involved in both were the same individuals.

The association of fire with destruction and rebirth extends beyond imagery in Muscovite history. Before the beginning, at a place where Moscow was to be built, the pagan god Perun, creator of fire and god of thunder, was accorded mystical significance. Moscow was the centre of Old Believers' resistance to the officially sponsored Nikonian reforms of the Orthodox liturgy in the seventeenth century. Patriarch Nikon had the Old Believers anathematized in 1667. The response of many was self-immolation in oil-soaked wooden churches in anticipation of the purgative fires of the imminent Last Judgment, chanting hymns of their childhood to the last. The leader of the Old Believers, Avvakum, was burnt at the stake, a method of execution unusual in Russia at the time, in imitation of the methods of the Spanish Inquisition. Before his death, he advocated self-destruction, separating body from soul: 'By burning your body, you commend your soul into the hands of God.'

Death and rebirth through fire had acquired a cosmic meaning, largely through Moscow's experience with it. Modest Mussorgsky's opera *Khovanshchina* (first performed 1886), which takes as its theme old Russia being replaced by the new, ends with the self-immolation of Old Believers, while offstage is heard the music of the Preobrazhensky Regiment—based, as it happens, in Petersburg—representing the death of Old Russia and the impending birth of the new.

Memory of the conflagration emerged, recreated in the myth of a Moscow purified and reaching a sacred state that would be impossible for worldly Petersburg ever to attain. It has been suggested that beliefs in Moscow's special calling and destiny spring not only from the Third Rome myth, but also from Moscow's ancient experience with fire. On a more prosaic level, fire acquired a political meaning as well. The title of the official organ of Russian Social Democratic Labour Party, co-edited by Lenin until 1903, was *Iskra*, The Spark. Its masthead carried the slogan, *Iz Iskry Vozgoritsya Plamya*: Fire Bursts Forth from a Spark.

Sword

Pestilence and fire have interacted with human agency throughout Moscow's history, but since the Second World Was they have largely retreated to the middle distance.

Moscow survived the bombing with surprisingly few casualties and relatively little damage as compared to the wholesale destruction of parts of London or Rotterdam,[7] mainly because of the systematic preparations the city had made before the war. Besides the deep underground Metro stations planned to double as shelters (the London authorities initially resisted the use of tube stations), a network of smaller shelters covered the city, with a total holding capacity of 400,000 people, about one-tenth of the city's entire population. At the onset of the war, many more citizens were evacuated and dispersed. In addition, the Kirov Metro station in north-east Moscow served as the command post of the *Stavka*, the headquarters of the Soviet General Staff.

The commander of air defence, General Gromadin, had 600 fighters for Moscow airspace alone, while at the height of the Battle of Britain, the British had only 800 fighters to cover the whole country. Succeeding concentric lines of air defence around Moscow, beginning some 180 kilometres out, reaffirmed traditional military logic, a pattern repeated in the present era of ballistic missiles. About one million—one quarter of the city's civilian population—had been trained in air defence and fire suppression. Iron tongs were issued to pick up incendiary bombs that could then be thrown into barrels of water distributed through the city. Advice from a visiting British experts' delegation that fire observers should seek shelter until the 'all clear' alert was sounded was ignored, saving many lives but at the cost of some of the observers' own. Other factors as well contributed to Moscow's relatively light escape from the massive German bombing campaigns. German aircraft were flown from forward positions as the Germans approached Moscow, and there were few usable ground facilities. Many had been sabotaged. As the ground advance continued, the onset of winter meant that the aircraft had to be dug out of snowdrifts in sub-zero temperatures and their flight strips cleared. Soviet planes were housed in prefabricated shelters. Distance, weather and problems of logistics were constant enemies of the Luftwaffe.

Operation Typhoon, the German plan for the ground attack

on the city, encountered the same challenges. The invasion began in early October 1941. Confident in an uninterrupted *Blitzkrieg*, Hitler promised his soldiers that they would march on Red Square before the turn of the year. From the west there is a single route to Moscow which despite centuries of human presence remains governed by geographical fact, impervious to change. This route was transited by the Poles in 1612, the French in 1812, and then the Wehrmacht in 1941.

Moscow stands behind a formidable barrier, measured not only by distance—between Warsaw and Moscow it is 1,149 kilometres, between Berlin and Moscow 1,608 kilometres and between Paris and Moscow 2,485 kilometres. These distances are crossed by a complex European river system, beginning with the Rhine, further east the Oder and the Vistula, and ending with the Dvina/Daugava flowing north to the Baltic, and the Dnepr flowing south to the Black Sea. To reach Moscow from the west they cannot be avoided.

Nowhere else in European history has the quotient of time multiplied by distance had such effect as in approaching Moscow, where autumns bring mud and spring the famous *rasputitsa*, the thaw that turns roads into melting, icy bogs (the origin of the Russian word meaning 'thaw' is closely related to words for 'disbandment' or, in another context, 'disarray' and 'dissolution'). In winter, temperatures on the roads to Moscow can reach 40 degrees below. Summer brings no relief, because of the dust, stirred up by armies as they pass, clogging lungs and engines. None of these remorseless facts was visible on the maps spread before Hitler.

Across the direct route to Moscow from the west, spaced along the highway, lie another three barriers: the fortress city of Smolensk, and the towns of Vyazma and Mozhaisk/Borodino. It was along this route and on either side that the Battle for Moscow was fought, beginning in early October 1941, when early snows were turning into mud, and winter was approaching.

Despite a chain of brilliant encircling movements along this line of advance, the late timing of Operation Typhoon condemned the Panzers of Army Group Centre to certain defeat.

Hitler called the Battle for Moscow 'the Final Decisive Battle'. Estimates of casualties differ, partly because of different counting rules by the participants, partly because of political considerations. The total number engaged, officers and men, was 7 million, fighting in an area the size of France. There is general agreement amongst Western military historians, however, that the Soviet Union lost more people in this one battle—almost 1 million soldiers—than the British lost in the whole of the First World War.[8]

Had Moscow been taken, the consequences would have been dire. Hitler had already noted with satisfaction that Red Army soldiers were being 'reduced to chopped meat' and he anticipated bringing about 'ethnic catastrophe' in Russia. Plans had already been drawn up to isolate ethnic Russians in a kind of Bantustan, a territory that would extend from Moscow to Vorkuta and the White Sea.[9] In one of his more effusive moments, Hitler announced that his plan for Moscow was to create a giant water reservoir, 'extinguishing all memory of the city and what it had been'. [10]

In mid October 1941 the Germans were some 150 kilometres from Moscow, and had opened a large gap in the outer Russian defensive line encircling the city at Mozhaisk. Even as the Germans drove (possibly the correct term is *pushed*, given the state of the roads) through this gap, and as the Soviet Fifth Army retreated, it had bought enough time for Marshal Zhukov to organize a stiffened defence sufficient to stop the Germans. The start of this battle was 13 October. Amidst a deafening Soviet artillery bombardment on 31 October, the breach was finally closed at the cost of appalling casualties on both sides. Ruthless and skilled leadership by the survivors of Stalin's purges also played a part in the successful defence of

Moscow. General Konstantin Rokossovsky, a Russified Pole, was one such leader. On Stalin's orders, he later halted the Red Army before Warsaw as it rose against the Nazis, even though this put at risk his own sister who was sheltering there. He was later assigned the job of Polish Minister of Defence, partly to get him out of Moscow where his popularity was second only to that of Zhukov. Victor of the Battle of Moscow, Zhukov was given the honour by the Western Allies of taking Berlin in May 1945. The military 'stop-line' to the west which that arrangement required defined the early post-war zones of occupation. Most contemporary photographs show comradely smiles and handshakes between the wartime allies. Only later, and with some modifications, did that 'gesture of honour' become frozen in political geography as the Cold War deepened.

On the highway running due west of Moscow to Smolensk, an orchard stands near Mozhaisk/Borodino planted by surviving soldiers, one tree each, as they returned to Moscow at the end of the Second World War. This is the site of two great battles, over a hundred years apart. In 1812 Napoleon waited on the low hill of Poklonnaya Gora for a delegation to offer him the surrender of the city. It never came. In October 1941 an Austrian reconnaissance unit somehow penetrated the front lines and succeeded in entering the outskirts of the Krasnaya Presnya district of Moscow before it was forced to turn back, leaving a rough sign staked in at their point of furthest advance, *Hier unser Glück hat uns verlassen*: 'Here our luck abandoned us.'

Where the orchard now stands, in 1941 the Mozhaisk/Borodino road led to Moscow through a massive belt of anti-tank ditches and redoubts. Closer to the city there was a forest of 24,000 hedgehog defences and over 12,000 reinforced-concrete gun emplacements. On the nearest approaches to the city, barricades had been set up composed of logs, concrete slabs and heavy vehicles, making rapid movement impossible.[11] During the putsch attempt of August 1991, similar barricades reappeared around the White House, erected by the sons and daughters (and sometimes grandchildren) of the veterans who planted that orchard and of others who had dug the defensive trenches in the desperate days of 1941.

The barriers of Mozhaisk/Borodino have now been replaced by equally formidable defences, their twenty-first-century equivalent, holding the city in a protective embrace. The Moscow ABM system consists of two phased-array radar systems which control four long-range (Gorgon) and four short-range (Gazelle) launch complexes. The entire system, encircling Moscow at about 80 kilometres, is supported by a dense ring of SA-1 missiles at some 40 kilometres from the city centre. In 1968, as the system was being deployed (which was allowed under the 1972 ABM Treaty, until it was abrogated by the second Bush Administration), it was calculated that to overwhelm it would require the combined strike force of 65-68 megatons, the equivalent of 3,800 Hiroshima bombs.[12]

Over time, the greater accuracy of incoming missiles has reduced to some extent the need for such gigantic 'throw-weights'—for their explosive charge or yield. Changes in nuclear doctrine have also altered the strategic landscape. Nuclear planning envisages a 'counterforce strategy' to neutralize offensive weapons and their defences, leaving cities untouched. However, as the *Bulletin of the Atomic Scientists* pointed out, 'Central Moscow would be initially undamaged but surrounded by a semicircle of fire soon after the attack.'[13] That is, Moscow would be incinerated.[14]

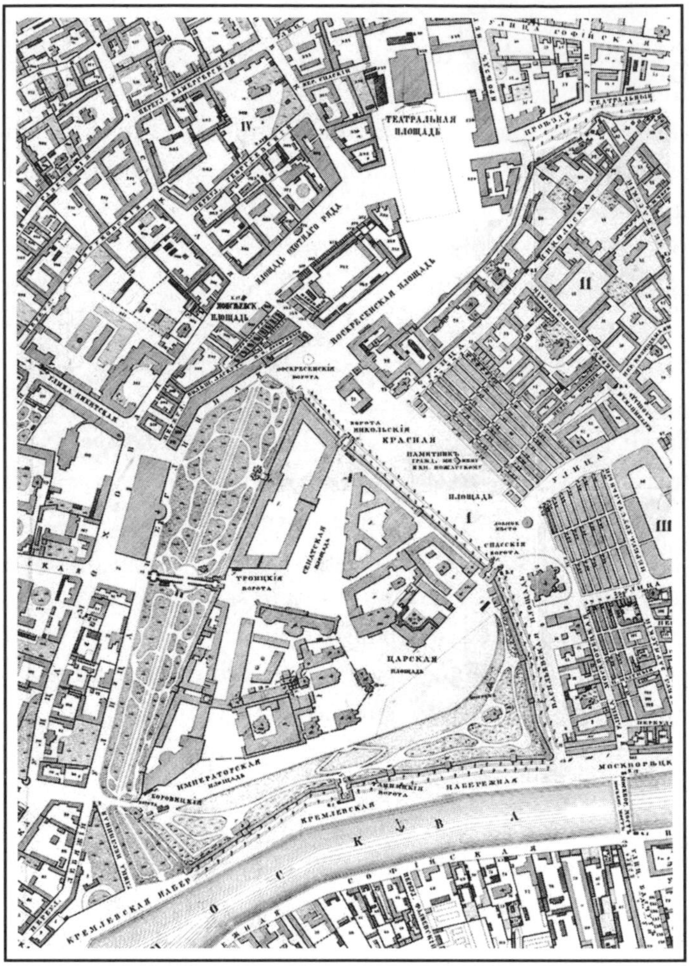

'Kremlin, Kitai Gorod and Trading Rows' from Khotev's Atlas of 1852-3. The Kremlin is centre left; Red Square and St. Basil's are along the eastern wall; and Kitaigorod and the Trading Rows are on the opposite side of Red Square.

Chapter Four
City of Darkness, City of Light

'In Moscow,' Chaadayev used to say, 'every foreigner is taken to look at the great cannon and the great bell—the cannon which cannot be fired and the bell which fell down before it was rung. It is an amazing town in which the objects of interest are distinguished by their absurdity...'
Alexander Herzen, *My Life and Thoughts*, 1868

Moscow is haunted by its past. Away from the noise and neon lights of twenty-first-century Moscow, ghosts of history and recent memory stand in dark places, seen or felt by all who live in this city. These lost shadows of the spirit and the intellect are the debris of a twentieth-century war conducted by the Soviet government against its own citizens. In his novel *The First Circle*, Solzhenitsyn has his Stalin at 'his most creative in the hours of darkness'.

The shadows have marked the city in ways more profound than the physical consequences of forced industrialization and social engineering to create an urban industrial class. The old quarters of Moscow have been destroyed, replaced by the Soviet structures still dominating the city's skyline. New buildings have sprung up, described by architects as 'international commercial modern'. The natural rhythm of the city is broken by highways and urban clearances, now the domain of stampedes of traffic.

Repelled by the carnage of the First World War and by what they believed about the economic and social systems that lay at its roots, many in the West looked to Moscow as the city of the future. The elegance of Marxist theory was soon belied by the reality, although *that* reality was not believed by many in the West, or else was wilfully ignored. The hopes that many intellectuals held for Moscow in the early 1920s were based on the illusion that the Revolution equalled liberation and social justice on a global scale. They looked to Moscow, the Red Army's victorious command-post in the civil war, with great hopes for the future. These hopes were expressed in a starburst of architectural innovation and artistic creativity. Between 1921 and 1929, when the rest of the world went from boom to bust, Lenin offered a respite in the Bolshevik drive towards comprehensive state ownership: his New Economic Policy (NEP). After nearly eight years of continuous conflict, Moscow began its post-war recovery. The respite was exactly that, a respite. It did not signify the end of Moscow's long agony.

Just over four years after Lenin's death in 1924, in 1928 the NEP was abolished. In January 1929, the First Five-Year Plan, a crash programme of industrialization and collectivization, was promulgated. By the early 1930s Moscow was becoming a place of grey buildings and long dark queues. Only the crimson of communist banners and the darker red of the plaques on official buildings relieved the drabness of the urban landscape. Moscow became its own building-site surrounded by a vast complex of tenements and *kommunalki.* More often than not, these were older houses expropriated and converted into cramped, multi-family living-spaces (they could not be called apartments) with shared bathrooms and kitchens, the use of which was governed by strict timetables set down and enforced by the Building Committee in the new order of communal living. They became a permanent feature of Moscow's socialist landscape.

Destruction was as much in evidence as construction in the Moscow of the 1930s. Waves of anti-religious campaigns wrought lasting damage to the city's heritage as churches and monasteries were looted and desecrated.

At the same time, plans were developed to reflect in city design and architecture Moscow's new status as the capital of the first socialist state, a beacon for the world of the future. In this vision, the past had no meaning, except as it related tsarist oppression and an inward-looking Orthodox Church, 'bastion of medieval obscurantism'.[1] While there were some efforts in the upper levels of the Party to respect Russia's cultural heritage and to maintain pre-revolutionary museums, there was also an opposed attitude among many rank-and-file Party activists engaged in *agitprop*—agitation and propaganda—whose function was to 'mobilize the masses' in support of Party programmes. The works of the New Soviet Man, who transcended class and nationality, would replace the now-defunct historic buildings, mere representations of the previously dominant classes—the feudal landlords, officials and dependents of the tsarist system and of the Church as well as the bourgeoisie; all and everything would be thrown on 'the ash-heap of history'.

This attitude on the part of the Bolsheviks did not prevent them from expropriating some of the most magnificent of Moscow's mansions. Not all of them were turned into *kommunalki,* but as state property, some became residences reserved for the new elite.

Under Moscow's socialist transformation, church buildings in particular were re-cast to serve as museums, warehouses, and in some instances stables or public toilets. The beautiful Novodyevichi Convent was converted into the Museum of Female Emancipation. The ultimate profanation for many of these buildings—if they were not destroyed—was to receive the designation *pamyatnik arkhiteckury,* architectural monument, which turned a living showcase into a dead shell. This was the fate of St. Basil's and of all the Kremlin churches.

Following the Second World War, the city moved into a half-light, beset by its consequences, crippled by its effects and burdened (although it was not seen that way at the time) by its new empire in Eastern Europe. Stalinism lingered. With the collapse of the Soviet Union in 1991, Moscow became the capital of Russia alone, for the first time since Ivan the Terrible, casting the city and the country into a post-imperial crisis of identity.

Moscow's past was a subject of deliberate forgetfulness in the 1990s as the city and the country descended into a kind of economic free-for-all, from which emerged the oligarchs, men of influence and power, the Russian equivalent of the nineteenth-century American robber-barons minus their contribution to the development of the country.[2]

Once again Moscow was neglected, this time not because of the competing demands of imperial St. Petersburg, but because of the general economic situation following the Soviet collapse. The post-Soviet elites, moreover, had priorities other than exercising civic-mindedness. In the Moscow of the 1990s there was no Rockefeller or Carnegie, no latter-day Tretyakov, the philanthropic founder of the Moscow gallery to Russian culture that bears his name. As in the St. Petersburg period of the eighteenth century, by the mid-1990s disrepair, beggars and refuse were commonplace on Moscow city streets. In a cruel parody of Potemkin's famous villages, Moscow's core suffered yet again many cases of abandonment and misuse as once-proud buildings were converted into glitzy casinos and night-clubs for the *nouveaux riches* and their hangers-on. From the street, Moscow took on the pretensions of Las Vegas; behind the glitz lay a sadder world of despair, worthless pensions, unaffordable rents and the omnipresent ghosts of the Stalinist past.

In a misreading of the principles of Western capitalism, often abetted by Western economic advisers themselves, economic instability combined with a fundamentally lawless marketplace brought the establishment of banks short of reserve capital and with little outside financial regulation. Their failures were at the expense of the depositors and to the profit of the erstwhile boards of directors whose members sometimes fled abroad with the cash. The fluidity of property laws and the retreat of the municipal authorities from their civic responsibilities, combined with their susceptibility to graft and corruption, were factors contributing to the city's declining birth rate and rising incidence of alcoholism and mortality. By 1998 Russia had come close to economic collapse. By supreme irony against the vision held for it in 1918, Moscow became a city without a future.

As the city continued its steep decline, the new rich sought refuge from its immediate effects. Like their eighteenth-century aristocratic predecessors seeking refuge from the stifling atmosphere of imperial St. Petersburg, the new economic and power elite built their new villas or refurbished old ones in a ring around Moscow on land previously occupied by garden-plots, but whose tenants had been evicted or otherwise removed by speculators. Often copied from the most vulgar of oversize house-plans then popular in the United States (and ignored by most guide-books as they 'do not fit the image'), these super-dachas remain a permanent blemish on the Moscow regional landscape. The prevailing winds over Moscow have determined that most are built on the western side of the city, up-wind from the pollution that generally drifts to the east.

Even with these difficult post-Soviet beginnings, for the first time in its history Moscow was 'suburbanizing', as not only a car but also a free-standing house (complete with mortgage arrangements) came within reach of middle-class Muscovites. Today, a new Moscow is emerging from a kind of time-warp, resplendent with steel and glass examples of petro-dollar wealth and new self-confidence and creativity, based on the Russian version of a market economy. Moscow is now experiencing another revolution projecting it in a fast-forward to a global city of the twenty-first century looking even further ahead.

With this comes heavy state involvement in determining the shape and texture of the city. This involvement has had costs, and the close relationship between the state and 'the commanding heights of industry' bears an uncomfortably close similarity to some of the practices of the past. Economically, the city runs perilously close to contracting the 'Dutch disease', a condition in which new wealth based on unearned commodities like petroleum and other natural resources destroys the existing manufacturing base and creates uncontrollable inflation as imports soar. The 'dictatorship of law', as Putin has called it, has also had costs, particularly in the fields of due process, property rights and freedom of opinion and information. Successor organizations to the KGB have been implicated in a number of apartment bombings and murders, most notably that of Anna Politovskaya, a bitter anti-Chechen War reporter whose body was found dumped in a Moscow lift on 7 October 2006.

As in other cities, the physical development of Moscow, how the city looks and why, is a reflection of its own 'life experiences'. The city's outward growth in widening circles from the Kremlin is still perceptible, like the rings of a tree, although they have been broken in many places because of succeeding catastrophes that have ravaged the city. In the nineteenth and twentieth centuries, these included visionary master plans aimed at the city's transformation, as if to lift it from its own past.

Besides the General Plan of Moscow of 1935, designed to turn the city from a peasant metropolis into a living example of the proletarian future, and the most recent 1999 and 2004 Plans, there have been two other major plans. That of 1971 aimed at moving heavy industry out of the inner core, thereby erasing the early Bolsheviks' belief that 'life should not be separated from work'; and in 1992 a further revision of the overall plan focused on ground transport and communications, both integral to a strategy of improving urban living conditions by moving residential areas farther from the centre, to 'micro-rayons'. This latter plan also envisaged the replacement of the dense, concrete tenements of the 1960s and 1970s, a process still continuing against a background of chronic housing shortages.

The 1999 and 2004 Plans, 'The Reconstruction and Regeneration of Moscow' and 'General Plan for the Development of Moscow' respectively, continue to shape the look of modern Moscow. Early in the implementation of the plans, they called for improving communist-era public amenities and building an inner ring road as well as the rebuilding of monuments. Besides the Cathedral of Christ the Saviour, the best-known are the Kazan Cathedral on Red Square and, at the square's entrance, the Iversky Gates, where even Communists used to cross themselves before entering the square's sacred precincts. In unconscious emulation of Soviet behaviour, Mayor Luzhkov had also been merciless in his acts of destruction, his most notable achievements being the razing and subsequent rebuilding of the Moskva Hotel (the same one whose competing designs were ambiguously approved by Stalin when he wrote his concurrence on the top of the folder containing them) and the demolition of Khrushchev's Hotel Rossiya, at 3,000 rooms the largest hotel in the world when it opened in 1967. The historic Zaryadye district, where it was located, had been largely bulldozed in the 1940s. The hotel's destruction, also by ball and bulldozer, represents a kind of rough justice—particularly to those who objected to its grotesque size, and to others who took exception to the hotel's culture of prostitutes and pimps with their links to the intelligence services who inhabited this vast colony of foreign travellers.

However glittering the surface of contemporary Moscow appears to the visitor, in its reality it is still far removed from the utopian fantasies of some of its well-wishers of the past. Even as

Stalinism was taking hold in the late 1920s, there was still room for dreams. An architect in the grand manner, Le Corbusier presented a plan to transform Moscow into a '*ville radieuse*' in the course of the competition for the design of the Palace of Soviets in 1928. His plan would have wiped out the centre of Moscow, including the Kremlin, to be replaced by massive rectilinear structures surrounded by 'green spaces'.[3] His plans were rejected, and Le Corbusier had to content himself with the construction of the Tsentrosoyuz (Headquarters for Workers' Councils) building. It took several years to build because of material shortages—and, one suspects, because of its low place on the Soviet list of priorities.

Moscow is now making up for lost time. This was a problem also faced earlier by the Soviet planners, with or without Le Corbusier, and only partially realized before the intervention of other priorities, beginning with winning the civil war, and then collectivization of the countryside and the demands of the First Five-Year Plan (1928) with its emphasis on electrification and industrialization. Other distractions included the Terror, successive famines and the Second World War. Even into the 1950s, beyond its inner core Moscow still kept a nineteenth-century urban industrial flavour, with electricity and sprawling factories its main concessions to modernity. If some parts of the city were visibly modern, or at least of the industrial age, other districts were still medieval in appearance, technology and sanitary conditions.

Moscow's Time-Lag

The problem of Moscow's time-lag, as a city on the easternmost periphery of Europe, is an old one. The cause of urban retardation has been the subject of scholarly dispute, but the evidence is that Moscow had no geodesic plan until 1739, and the first attempt at town planning did not come until Catherine II's Great Commission of 1775 when town planning had been commonplace in the rest of Europe for decades: the name and reputation of Moscow as a 'big village' rested on fact.

Symptomatic of Moscow's arrested development is a timeline of events that had occurred in Europe decades, and in some instances centuries, earlier. In fire-prone Moscow the first brick-plant was not established until 1475, and the great majority of its products were then used in the building and reinforcement of defensive walls, not houses. The first locally printed book appeared in Moscow in 1564, almost a hundred years after William Caxton printed *Recuyell of the Historyes of Troye (*1473), the first such book in English. The Moscow printer Ivan Fyodorovich Fydorov was accused of heresy for his work, and his printing-yard was attacked by arsonists two years later. Private printing-houses were banned in Moscow in 1769, and again between 1796 and 1804. This pattern was to repeat itself in Soviet times with such underground *samizdat* productions as *Chronicle of Current Events* defying the Soviet system.

Education also conformed to this general pattern of historical time-lag. Ivan the Terrible attempted to establish a university, but his efforts were defeated by the clergy, who held a monopoly on higher education. Consequently, the first educational institution was not established until 1686, at the Zaikonnospassky Monastery, the 'Slav, Greek and Latin Academy', whose curriculum avoided any subject that held the potential for controversy or which could invite dissension. This included law and history. Basic public education, established by Peter the Great in the eighteenth century, was confined to the children of the aristocracy and senior officials. The world-famous Moscow State University had its beginnings when its founder Mikhail Lomonosov established its premises above a chemist's shop on Red Square in 1755.

Before the Revolution, Moscow University (its full title is Moscow State University in the Name of Lomonosov) was a citadel of learning, a nest of anti-tsarist activity and revolutionary thought—and after the Revolution, an institutional gathering-place for the politically naive but ideologically committed. Many subsequently became victims of the Terror. Along with the Soviet Academy of Sciences, it also became associated with politically motivated abuse of the social (and sometimes natural) sciences, which were obliged to conform to Marxist philosophical principles.

Beginning with Stalin (some would argue, even earlier) the objective study of sociology, linguistics and psychology, not to mention history, effectively vanished or survived only in a truncated, distorted form. Soviet psychology did not progress beyond Pavlov and his research into the dynamics of stimulus and response. At an international psychological conference held in Moscow in the 1960s, interpreters failed in their attempts to translate mutually incomprehensible ideas across the East–West divide. English-speaking graduate students were co-opted as translators, including myself. We discovered that Freudian clinical terms, for example, did not exist in Soviet medical literature, not even in specialized dictionaries. Karl Jung was unknown.

In linguistics, the theories of N. Y. Marr (Marr, a Georgian, had a Scottish father, like the classical writer Lermontov) held that language had a class basis and the structure of the victorious proletarian language of Russia would be different from the defeated bourgeois language. Although refuted by Stalin in 1950, Marr's ideas still attracted some Marxists. The East German authorities in particular went to great lengths to demonstrate that the socialist system in the GDR was creating a new, advanced culture that set it apart from West Germany not only in social structure but in language as well.

Biology and especially genetics suffered as well. Because of their connection to national security, only the 'hard' sciences seemed immune, although nuclear research was hampered by political concerns about some of the findings in sub-atomic physics that contradicted Marxist philosophy, specifically the Hegelian dialectic, and hence held the potential of calling into question the principles on which the Soviet regime was founded. The Heisenberg principle of uncertainty (by which the actual position of a sub-atomic particle is expressed in terms of probability only) caused particular difficulties. Beginning in the 1950s one solution was to move many nuclear physicists out of Moscow to purpose-built, semi-secret and privileged communities such as Akademgorodok in Siberia, which at its height held over 65,000 academics and their families. This was done primarily for reasons of national security, but also to ensure that discussion on these topics would be safely isolated.

The most striking evidence of Moscow's arrested development has always been its cityscape, which seen from the distance has enthralled visitors from Napoleon and Custine to this day. Closer up, the practicalities of living and moving around in densely populated space held their own reality. There were no cobbled or stone streets in Moscow before 1643, when the first paving-stone—later to become in communist mythology the preferred weapon of the proletariat—was laid down. Street lighting was not installed until the middle of that century. Before then, logs were placed across city streets at night as a security measure, and if one was obliged to go out after dark, it was best with an armed escort.

Regulations for public sanitation were not promulgated or enforced until the seventeenth century, and construction of a communal sewerage system did not begin until 1898, a generation after work began in St. Petersburg. As Moscow moves through the first decade of the twenty-first century, a down-to-earth priority of city planners is the renovation and rehabilitation of the vast network of antiquated sewerage systems, drains and medieval cesspits lying beneath the city's streets. It is rumoured that in them are the secret torture chambers of Lavrenti Beria, and obscure burial passages holding the remains of 'non-persons', as well as blind alleys stashed with treasures hidden by the tsars. It is also believed that many points in the system register unusually high levels of radiation because of lax nuclear waste disposal methods in Soviet times. Urban myth has it that the radiation has been responsible for the appearance of deformed reptiles in the sewers' dark recesses, including a savage eyeless alligator. Illegal clubs of the adventurous have recently sprung up in Moscow to explore the system.

The Twilight Struggle towards Modernity

Moscow's struggle towards modernity has been attributed to many factors. According to some contemporary historians, the main culprits were the Mongols,[4] but also a debilitating climate and poor agricultural conditions. At the same time, the greatest responsibility for Moscow's failure to keep pace with the way Western cities developed may well lie with political and social systems that evolved under the Romanovs and their successors. The Soviet contribution to Moscow's viability lay more in the direction of destruction and vandalism, a judgment that the huge building projects of the 1930s and later do little to counterbalance. Much admired by architectural historians, Moscow's innovations of the 1920s—particularly the constructivist movement—were no more than brief explorations into modernity. As the state was the sole client for architects in Soviet Moscow, the movement did not survive. Only after 1991 did Moscow's cityscape begin to exhibit any contemporary architectural variety.

Textbooks continue to emphasize the peasant, agrarian

nature of Russian society from the early days of the Muscovite state, and then trace its evolution into an all-encompassing tsarist autocracy supported by the Orthodox Church and resting on an economy in which the peasants lost any landowning status they possessed, became indentured and in time became serfs, effectively without any meaningful legal rights. Their emancipation in 1861 represented no 'revolution from above' by the gracious hand and Manifesto of Alexander II, for they had to buy their freedom, and more frequently than not were weighed down with debt or other legal obligations. Others became landless and therefore rootless.

One of the side-effects of a system that effectively tied labour to the land was the arrested development of Russian cities, above all Moscow. The rigidities of the agrarian-based economy worked against the emergence of an independence-minded, city-based entrepreneurial class, owing their status to finance and manufacture, not land. Many of the wealthy in Moscow during this period were merchants, not financiers or entrepreneurs, dependent upon governmental patent for their activities, and beholden to tsardom. Specialized light industry, however, did grow rapidly at the turn of the century (hence 'Calico Moscow'), often with a single village or region supplying the manpower for a single factory or industry. In Western urban development 'civil society' was based on contract law to protect property, and the rule of law to defend the rights of the citizen against the power of the state. Rights of citizenship as they developed in the West had no place in tsarist Russia. The concept of a city charter, establishing respective rights and duties between the sovereign and the city, was unknown.

For all practical purposes, the under-represented bourgeoisie of pre-revolutionary Russia had neither the numbers nor the influence to construct a civic culture. In addition, before 1917 there was no legal classification for the term 'worker', and hence no legal framework for the protection of workers' rights, pay or conditions of work. The contractual wage relationship simply did not exist.

As Moscow's rapid industrialization progressed in the latter half of the nineteenth century, the city was swamped with waves of recently liberated or landless peasants, their very numbers generating appalling conditions, disease and filth. Close on half of Moscow's industrial workforce retained ties to the land, either legal or familial: they were in effect the nineteenth-century equivalent of the German *Gastarbeiter,* and at least economically bore a passing resemblance to the North African inhabitants of the Paris *banlieues,* the setting for such widespread violence in 2005. Called 'temporary migrants' (*otkhodniki*), the urban peasants of Moscow were expected to return home after their stay in the city. In many areas the primitive infrastructure of public services was overwhelmed, reducing entire districts to the level of a barnyard.[5] That, and the barbaric conditions of work in turn-of-the-century factories of Moscow, made the insurrection of 1905 inevitable.

Prior to the revolt, the niggardly funds that the imperial court of St. Petersburg advanced for the Moscow budget reflected the court's indifference to Moscow's social conditions, an attitude matched only by its brutality in the revolt's suppression. The working-class industrial district of Presnya where 150,000 workers had revolted was sealed off, and on the orders of the recently appointed military governor Vice-Admiral Dubasov[6] was subdued by artillery fire at point-blank range. Nor did the situation change after the rebellion was put down. The Moscow City Duma, established after 1905 as a weak effort at reform, lacked any powers to redress the desperate social conditions as they would have reduced the powers of the governor, whose mandate extended to order, not reform. More than Lenin's often impenetrable Marxist theorizing (to make himself clear, he sometimes underlined his sentences four times) and the intellectual hubbub of Moscow's grand salons, the tsarist atrocity at Presnya, henceforth called Red Presnya, turned Moscow into Red Moscow.

Marx's *Communist Manifesto*, published in the midst of the urban disturbances that swept across Europe in 1848, was a call to class revolt. The legend of Red Presnya tied it to the Paris Commune uprising of 1871. That rebellion was one also conducted by the urban underclass against authority, also ending in defeat. The association of the insurrection of Paris 1871 with Presnya 1905 became a founding myth of the Bolshevik Party, and a key argument in its legitimization to power. In Russia's cities the lasting effect of Presnya was its contribution to the transformation of workers' councils, originally established to coordinate strike activity, into nascent instruments of political power: the Soviets.

By yet another of the many ironies in Moscow's history, the Presnya district is now Moscow's greatest building site—the Moscow International Business Centre. It is a modern, still-unfinished complex which stands as a monument to New Russia and its own version of capitalist power. The dilapidated factories and their surrounding tenements have been bulldozed, along with their memory.

Moscow's thinkers of the nineteenth century saw the twentieth-century crisis coming long before it broke. In 1836, less than a generation after Napoleon's defeat and the tragic-comic Decembrist revolt[7] of Petrograd's aristocratic officers, Peter Chaadayev, a leading advocate of Westernism in Russian intellectual circles,[8] seized upon Moscow's riverine circumstances to trace a pessimistic analogy of Moscow's and Russia's backwardness: 'We live in the present in its narrowest confines, amid a dead calm. Russia was a kind of historic swampland, a backwater where things stirred now and then but never flowed anywhere.'[9]

That pessimism derived from what he saw as the provincialism of the Russian aristocracy, a theme brilliantly taken up by Russian writers and playwrights from Chekhov to Gogol. The tsarist anachronism in distant St. Petersburg and the reactionary Orthodox Church (which Chaadayev maintained had 'drunk from the poisoned waters of Byzantium') deepened his pessimism even further. He was convinced that Russia's culture of passivity and obedience to the tsarist state was responsible for the country losing its way.

Many Westerners shared Chaadayev's bleak view. Henri Troyat, the French biographer of Ivan the Terrible, said of the Church's role in the time of Ivan the Terrible:

> A horror of profane pleasures taught by the Orthodox Church stifled any impulse toward original creation in Russia. Only architecture was free from this iron restraint. Painting, sculpture, music and literature were interdicted by the clergy. The painter's imagination was liberated—within strict rules—only in icons... So far as the life of the mind was concerned, the great Russian land lay shrouded in darkness.[10]

More succinctly, perhaps, the Marquis de Custine, the French aristocrat and refugee from France's own Terror of 1790, also placed Moscow's backwardness at the door of the Orthodox Church: in his *Letters from Russia* (1839) he described it as 'an object of pity'. Its anti-intellectualism and unwavering support of reaction eliminated the Church from having any role in reform. (Sometimes the Church's mind-set takes on bizarre forms. In the early 1900s the deeply Orthodox rector of the University of Kazan, Michael Magnitsky, instructed his professors, 'notwithstanding the calculations of the pagan Pythagoras', to point out 'for reasons of piety' that the hypotenuse of a right-angled triangle represented the 'mercy of God descending to man through Christ'.)

Isaiah Berlin perceived the connection of the Orthodox Church to the advent of communism, seeing 'a strong craving for teleological and indeed eschatological systems in all societies influenced by Byzantium or the Orthodox Church'.[11] He might as well have said that this observation applied to Judaism or Christianity as well, for his judgment should be weighed against the mutually dependent relationship between Church and state in tsarist Russia, and the condemnation by Marxists of all religions and their doctrines, 'the opium of the people'. By the end of the nineteenth century, many of the young men of the Russian intelligentsia had discovered German philosophy and Hegel, 'who had substituted History for God' or at least History, teleology and all, as the expression of Divine Will. Marx's *Communist Manifesto* found a special resonance among the Moscow intelligentsia, particularly after the social upheaval of 1905. This put them on a collision course with Orthodoxy, which by definition remained staunchly opposed to the demotion of God, and hence anti-revolutionary. With others, the priesthood suffered for it.

Many of today's Eastern Christians see their faith as having transcended this history, now purified through the long martyrdom of the communist era, and its perversion under the tsars. Its spiritual survival has even been depicted as an opportunity for Western Christians to rediscover their true roots. This in turn has led to a revival of the idea of Moscow's unique spiritual significance. Among the Orthodox, the flood of proselytizing, born-again Westerners who came to the city in the early 1990s in search of converts are regarded with particular distaste, as spiritual primitives in their midst. A recent Orthodox publication declares that 'after many centuries of isolation, Western Christians are slowly finding their way back to the wellsprings of Christianity in the East'.[12]

Indeed, in their focus on hierarchy, Church structure and doctrine, and their relationship to the state, many non-

Orthodox historians may underestimate the deep spiritual satisfaction that Orthodoxy confers upon the faithful, its guiding mysticism extending far beyond the rationalism practised by the Roman Catholic Church. The reverence the faithful hold for *sobornost*, the holiness of the community of believers gathered together for prayer, is only approximated in Western Christianity at the Eucharist. Orthodoxy's effect on pre-revolutionary Moscow was that it lent to the city a cohesion uniting all believers, reaching across a deepening social divide. This in turn gave the city a stability that only the most extreme conditions could shake.[13]

In the 1880s the relationship of the Orthodox Church to the state, and the hierarchy's integration into its structure, formed the basis of Imperial Russia's official state policy. As pronounced in 1883 by Count Uvarov, the Minister of Education under Nicholas I, that policy was 'Orthodoxy, Autocracy, Nationality'. Ever since Peter the Great, official portraits of the tsars depicted them in Western-style military uniforms. The last tsar, Nicholas II, wore the uniform of the Imperial Hussars, and enjoyed watching his cavalry on parade. In a touching attempt to strengthen the legitimacy of Romanov rule in accordance with Uvarov's state policy, he also appeared in the vestments of Byzantine emperors, symbolically tying himself and his dynasty to the religion. Even then, the time had passed. In May 1896, at his coronation in the Kremlin's Cathedral of the Assumption, the atmosphere and the rite were Byzantine, but as he ascended the steps to celebrate mass as a priest for the only time in his life, the Order of St. Andrew he was wearing fell to the floor. Other disasters followed.

Midnight

By the 1930s Moscow and the entire country had entered into a period of darkness where the absurd mixed with terror. Moscow was at the very centre of this darkness. The great show trials of the mid and late 1930s were held in the Hall of Columns of the former Nobles' Club in downtown Moscow. Several blocks away in the Kremlin, plans were conceived that amounted to a war conducted by the regime against its own people. The trauma of this period lives on, but in the face of growing Stalinist nostalgia, President Medvedev was constrained to warn against 'historical revisionism'. Stalin's achievements as a wartime leader and in transforming Russia from a backward country to a superpower, he said, will always be overshadowed by his crimes.[14]

Robert Conquest's pioneering study *The Great Terror* (1968) recounting the three Purge Trials of the 1930s, and subsequently his *Harvest of Sorrow* (1986), estimated that some 18-20 million perished as a direct result of Stalin's policies through artificially created famines, class wars eliminating entire social categories of people or ethnic groups, and political trials leading to immediate execution. A sentence to the Gulag[15] was a sentence tantamount to death. In a later edition, he revised his estimates downward, to some 13-15 million.[16]

Roy Medvedev, the Russian historian, agrees with the latter figure, but on the technical grounds that a good proportion of the victims were in fact perpetrators of Stalinist crimes themselves, such as the police who had fallen under suspicion and then accusation and who did not count as actual victims.[17] For the unscrupulously ambitious, the purges were a ladder to get ahead. Dmitri Volkogonov, the Soviet *glasnost*-era historian, estimates that there were about 5 million people shot (as opposed to other causes of human-instigated death) during this period. Although his figure is generally considered an exaggeration, it should also be reported that Solzhenitsyn, writing in *The Gulag Archipelago,* claims that a total of 60 million deaths can be directly or indirectly attributed to Stalinist policies.

Among the many appalling spectacles of Stalinist justice were the courtroom scenes held under the tutelage of Andrei Vyshinsky, Procurator-General, a title he assumed in 1935. Like Felix Dzerzhinsky, the founder of the Cheka and succeeding organizations, the NKVD and the KGB, Vyshinsky was of Polish descent. He was also a former rector of Moscow State University. In a statement similar to those last heard during the Paris Terror, Vyshinsky, a legal scholar, declared that 'there are periods... when laws turn out to be obsolete and we have to put them aside'.

Like the Old Believers who practised self-immolation for their faith, some of the Old Bolsheviks on trial were induced to confess to crimes they did not commit in the interests of the Party—or if their convictions were not deep enough, in the interests of their families. Set in the interrogation room of the Lubyanka, this was the tragic theme of Arthur Koestler's *Darkness at Noon.* Rubashov, modelled after the Bolshevik intellectual Bukharin, commits 'an act of sacrifice' for the sake of the Party.

At the first of the three great show-trials, Zinoviev, former chairman of the Comintern, was accused of the trumped-up charge of 'organizing the joint Trotskyite–Zinovievist Terror Centre' for the assassination of Party and government leaders, specifically the death of Kirov, the Leningrad Party leader. A slogan was pinned behind his witness chair: 'For Mad Dogs—a Dog's Death'. For the Old Bolshevik elite and stars of the show-trials, executions were often carried out in the basement of the Lubyanka. There, wearing an ankle-length black leather coat, a black fedora and leather gauntlets up to his elbows, the state executioner dispatched the accused by a bullet in the back of the head. Several Makarov .38 pistols were arranged on a shelf in the event that the one he was using overheated.

The Moscow purges lasted for several years, and in their final phase beginning in 1938 decimated the Red Army officer corps, a major factor contributing to the Soviet Union's vulnerability to invasion. In 1937 the results of a major Soviet census showed a dramatic fall in population, particularly in Ukraine and in the Asian republics. Great areas of Russia were affected as well. The contents of the census were classed as a state secret and so, to ensure confidentiality, its authors were shot. Recently opened Soviet documents indicate that quotas for victims of the Terror were established for every region and workplace in the USSR.

In a passage in Anatoly Rybakov's *Children of the Arbat*, one catches a glimpse into the mind of Stalin. Poskrybyshev was Stalin's real-life secretary:

> Poskrybyshev followed Stalin and closed the door behind him carefully (Stalin did not like doors being left open, nor did he like them to be slammed) and stopped a few paces from the desk in order not to stand right next to Stalin (Stalin didn't like that either) but close enough to hear Stalin's quiet voice and not to ask him to repeat anything (Stalin didn't like having to repeat things). 'Take this letter' said Stalin.[18]

Even as the purges and the Terror were unfolding, Moscow had become a vast construction site. The guiding document was the General Plan for the Reconstruction of Moscow of 1935. Construction of the Metro tore up many of Moscow's streets to make way for the stations. Trenches and excavations crisscrossed the city. Large sections of Moscow's historic past were also destroyed, including the white stone and brick walls that defended Kitai Gorod and the eastern part of the inner city from Mongol attack.

In addition, entire neighbourhoods were removed to make way for dwelling-complexes for the elite. These bordered the main thoroughfares of Moscow, themselves widened without regard to the original pattern of the city's growth. In many parts of the city, roads were widened to broad avenues, in some instances eight lanes wide, with a lane down the middle reserved for the high-speed travel of the elite.

Workers were exhorted to surpass their targets under the plan, and to emulate the achievements of the (not terribly bright but apparently very energetic) miner Stakhanov, who was lionized for over-fulfilling his norm several-fold. Here too, Rybakov paints a subtle portrait of Stalin's motivations on the rebuilding of Moscow:

> The monument to Stalin's epoch would be Moscow itself, the city he was going to create anew, for only cities were perpetual. The modest architecture of the twenties had been a mistake. Contrasting revolutionary asceticism with the ostentatious opulence on the New Economic Policy had allowed modernist architects to ignore the classical heritage above all that had to be incorporated. Moscow would appear to future generations as a city that reached upward. Stalin was going to build the Palace of Soviets, which would be the focus of new Moscow; he would lay new highways, install the Metro put up new, modern apartment houses and administrative buildings, erect new bridges and embankments, hotels, schools, libraries, theatres, clubs, gardens, parks. It would all become a majestic monument to his epoch.[19]

The effects of this period of Soviet history are still visible. These are seen not only in the Metro or the apartment buildings of the *nomenklatura,* or the great circular roadways running through and around Moscow, or even the Soviet-era parks. Four great prisons 'for politicals' are integral parts of Moscow's urban landscape. The largest is Butyrka prison, extended in the eighteenth century to hold the leadership of the Pugachev rebellion by the architect Matvei Kazakov, better known for his elegant, neoclassical structures in downtown Moscow. At the height of the Terror and the purges, it held some 20,000 prisoners. Some were finally deported to the Gulag. Others were buried in the grave-pits of Donskoy Monastery. It was nevertheless the 'prison of choice' as its conditions were considered better than elsewhere.

Lefortovo prison, a KGB institution, now operated by its successor, the FSB, was host to Solzhenitsyn, Mattias Rust and participants in the abortive August 1991 coup. Raoul Wallenberg, the Swedish diplomat credited with saving thousands of Hungarian Jews in Nazi-occupied Hungary, is reputed to have been incarcerated here before he was apparently shot in the Lubyanka. The latter, headquarters of the KGB/FSB and its affiliated prison, stands on Dzherzhinsky Square in central Moscow, close to Detsky Mir, the Children's World department store. Following the Second World War, the Lubyanka building was modified and reworked by Aleksei Shushev, the architect of the Lenin mausoleum.

In *The Gulag Archipelago,*[20] Alexander Solzhenitsyn has long passages on the interrogation techniques practised at Sukhanovka, a prison intended for 'particularly dangerous' enemies of the people. Known as 'The Dacha', it was established by the NKVD in 1938 on monastery grounds near Lenin's estate. Solzhenitsyn knew of only one survivor who emerged coherent. It was routine to cover the carpets with plastic sheets to protect them from the blood of interrogation sessions.

Finally, Taganka prison holds both political and criminal prisoners. A number of prison songs have emerged from it. Unlike the elegant ballads of Johnny Cash's *Folsom Prison,* or Leadbelly's famous song *Midnight Special,* where the light of a freight train on a prison cell wall brought hope of freedom, a shining light brought no hope of release from Taganka. In Taganka, 'shine a little light on me' had an entirely different meaning:

Taganka, vsye nochi, polnye ogna
Taganka, zachem sgubila ty menya?
Taganka, Ya tvoi bessmennyi arestant
Pogubili yunost' i talant v tvoikh stenakh...

Taganka, bright light all night
Taganka, why have you done me in?
Taganka, I am your unreformed con
Behind your walls youth and hope are gone...

Moscow's best-known grave-pit is the Butovsky Poligon, at Butovo on the outskirts of the city. Between 1937 and 1938 it was the site of the deaths of an estimated 20,000 people, shot by the NKVD. Muscovites call this place 'our Russian Golgotha'.[21] The ground has since been sanctified by the Russian Orthodox Church. President Putin attended a memorial service there on 31 October 2007. In the new Moscow, Butovo is threatened by real estate development.

The False Dawn

Like other European cities, Moscow was faced with the massive task of post-war reconstruction. Stalin's 1935 Plan for the Reconstruction of Moscow had been put into abeyance because of the war, although some projects continued all the way through it, including the Metro. Never formally cancelled, resumption of work on the Palace of Soviets was subject to continuing delays. Some were caused by other early post-war priorities, including repair of the Bolshoi Theatre, which had suffered bomb damage. Further delays were caused by other intervening priorities, including the construction of the seven new 'high buildings'. Work on them began in 1947. Despite Stalin's dislike of the city, the reconstruction of Leningrad also received early attention. After that, there were Stalingrad and Kiev as well as a host of towns and villages in European Russia devastated by the war. In truth, the most likely cause of the demise of the Palace of Soviets project was not technical or financial, but that Stalin had lost interest.

By 1952, the Nineteenth Party Congress issued its directives for the current Five-Year Plan envisaging an ambitious reconstruction programme, with emphasis on housing, for the western part of the Soviet Union. In the early post-war years Soviet planners paid special attention to London's plans for reconstruction and made several trips to the city for ideas. In the end, they concluded that Western planning, led by such figures as Sir Patrick Abercrombie in the UK and Lewis Mumford in the United States, 'were a deceit to the working classes' because of the strategies they espoused of satellite and over-spill towns; that is, to remove the working population from the city centres, where the potential for landlords' profits was higher without them. Somewhat contradictorily, they also criticized the construction of cheap, high-density, multi-storey housing estates in bombed-out areas. The absence of anything but the most basic amenities and their lack of open spaces and sense of community, the Soviet planners believed, were a form of exploitation of the workers.[22] The tentative dialogue with Western architects and planners dimmed and was finally extinguished as the climate of the Cold War descended in the 1950s, and Soviet architects went their own way.

Work on the Moscow Plan was then renamed Socialist Reconstruction, when the Moscow Design Institute, Mosprojekt, was established in 1951; by the 1970s it had grown into a huge bureaucracy. One of its peripheral organizations alone, the Institute of Economic Problems of Moscow, had a staff of 250. The total number of people involved in city planning during those years may have been around 3,000, well above anything in the West, or for that matter elsewhere in the East. The rebuilding of Warsaw, little more than a pile of rubble at the war's end, was overseen by a handful of city architects. The centre of Berlin, completely destroyed and subsequently rebuilt in its two halves by two opposed political systems, did not command the numbers committed to the Moscow city project, even if its two halves had been added together.

Beginning with the Khrushchev period, Soviet architectural philosophy underwent a major change, away from Stalinist baroque. In part, it was due to the gathering de-Stalinization campaign which began shortly after his death in 1953, when Stalin's nascent anti-Semitic campaign was halted. Shortly thereafter, Lavrenti Beria, the head of the NKVD, was arrested and shot. Party colleagues, led by Khrushchev, suspected that he was planning a 'power-grab' and led him into a trap at a meeting of the Party Presidium. Eyewitness reports describe the scene of his arrest as having a dramatic, almost theatre-like quality. This is the putative explanation of why Shakespeare's *Julius Caesar,* also the victim of a conspiracy, was banned from the Moscow theatre for years afterwards.

The shift away from Stalinist-inspired city planning and architectural philosophy may have happened even without anti-Stalin campaigns. Khrushchev (a rather down-to-earth figure) and his colleagues maintained that there was excessive attention to detail and decoration as well as too much *gadost* (bad taste) in architectural interpretations of socialist realism. The change came early. At the end of 1954, even before Khrushchev had consolidated his power, a week-long 'Builders' Conference' was held in the Kremlin Great Palace, sponsored jointly by Party and government. Khrushchev was the keynote speaker. In his closing speech he denounced the Academy of Architecture, and attacked the leading exponents of Stalinist architecture by name. He demanded attention to economy and quantity. Khrushchev's directive—for that is what it was—had an immediate effect. Almost overnight, as the Metro continued its expansion, the design of new stations became more functional. Even today the sudden appearance of functionality and restraint in Metro decoration is striking as one travels outwards from the centre.

What began with the re-styling of the Metro and the cancellation of other Stalinist-inspired building projects culminated in what became known as 'the Ninth Quarter' of the city. There, at Novye Cheremushki, is a large dwelling complex containing high-density, single-family apartments, each with independent facilities. The Ninth Quarter was the beginning of all the other schemes that encircle Moscow, through the Brezhnev and Gorbachev eras into the twenty-first century. In their repetitious design they are tedious to look at and soul-destroying to live in. In their execution, building standards are lax, often further undermined by corrupt practices. They disintegrate rapidly. Their vindication is that in Khrushchev's Moscow the Marxist notion of communal living for the workers in shared facilities was finally buried.

Lenin once defined communism as Soviet power plus electrification. Nowhere did the Bolsheviks succeed more brilliantly than in the electrification of Moscow. Starting with a private electrical company established in 1887 and then nationalized after the Revolution, by the 1930s Moscow was the major part of a Soviet electrical system that ranked second in Europe, and third globally.

Even greater success in making up for lost time was in the field of education, which puts it among the first rank of Soviet achievements, but also one of the most enigmatic. At the beginning of the nineteenth century, there were some 16,000 Russian officials (for whom literacy was presumably a prerequisite) whereas in Prussia, with a population of 1 per cent of its neighbour, there was almost the same number.[23] Moscow University was the only one in the country. At the outbreak of the First World War Russian literacy stood at only 28 per cent. According to Soviet sources, the number of students in primary school rose from 8 million in 1914 to over 33 million in the 1930s. Possibly with more pride than accuracy, a Soviet publication in 1968 asserted that Moscow had '74 universities and colleges, with a total enrolment of over 600,000'. The dramatic increase in literacy throughout the country in an astonishingly short period was nevertheless real and a major accomplishment.

At the higher level, however, there were also costs. In the 1920s, experiments in creating the 'New Soviet Man' demanded a revolution in education which would be proletarian-oriented, combining academic study with practical work. A widely distributed reproduction of the period shows the greatest teacher of all, Lenin, carrying a log, working on a *subbotnik*, a day of freely donated labour (technically, Subbota/Saturday was a day off) for the improvement of the Kremlin grounds.

At the high tide of Marxist enthusiasm in the 1920s, innovators at the Peoples' Commissariat of Enlightenment (Narkompromos) devised an elaborate educational programme entitled 'the complex method' to integrate study with labour. It led to a nosedive in educational standards, and was eventually abandoned. What remained was a production-line approach to learning, the attitude behind it clearly evident in an official history of the USSR: 'The Soviet intelligentsia, which during the Second Five-Year Plan grew to 9,600 persons, will grow still more as the main task is filled in the sphere of cultural development; namely to raise the cultural and technical level of the entire working class to that of engineer and technician.'[24]

Marxism remained a compulsory subject at all Soviet educational institutions. At Moscow State University, *diamat*, as the course on dialectical materialism was called, was obligatory. Fail that, and you failed the year. The course became an object of amusement and even contempt for many of the students. A possibly underestimated factor in the collapse of the Soviet Union was the failure of the system to convince the educated, post-war young of its own legitimacy. When measured against the everyday reality of the Soviet state, Marxist theory was clearly insufficient to inspire either enthusiasm or faith.

This problem was, in fact, anticipated. Sensitive to the educational (and possibly, doctrinal) challenge, the Institute of Red Professors was established shortly after the Revolution. In a weird if unintentional back-reference to the Orthodox rector of the University of Kazan and his religious interpretation of Pythagoras' theorem, its objective was to ensure that Marxist philosophy was embedded into the social and even the physical sciences. Only with post-war developments in nuclear physics and related military potential were there any exceptions: there is no place for Marxism in Relativity Theory. The consequences were the deceits of academicians. Even into the 1960s, to supplement their studies of *diamat* Soviet law students were expected to master 'class-based' principles of jurisprudence, as opposed to Western principles of impartiality. My fellow graduate students swallowed hard and did the minimum to satisfy this requirement. In the end, it turned into a kind of charade, professors and students alike knowing that 'the requirement wasn't serious'. With Gorbachev, himself a graduate of Moscow State University's law faculty, it was finally dropped.

Students of Moscow State University as a group were not prominent on the barricades set up before the White House housing the Russian parliament and its presidency during the failed August coup of 1991, although they belonged to the same tradition of protest shared by students in the West. One Western scholar summarized the role of students in early-twentieth-century Russia as providing the revolutionary fervour, turning the universities into a political battlefield, where they fought the authorities to a standstill. Arkady Timiriazev, the son of the Russian botanist and geneticist Klement Timiriazev, records the battle between some 4,000 students and the tsarist police supported by the vigilante organization, the Black Hundreds, in October 1905.[25] In 1917 many were already members of the Bolshevik or other revolutionary parties, and played a role in establishing Soviet power in the capital. Their numbers had been diminished, however, by forcible drafting the obstreperous ones into the imperial army if their activities came to the attention of the tsarist police.

Soviet power anaesthetized student rebelliousness in Moscow. Although there were a few scattered protests, neither the suppressed Hungarian Revolution of 1956 nor the failed Prague Spring in 1968 brought much visible reaction from the students of Moscow University, although a number of underground pieces were circulated protesting at the latter's armed suppression in Czechoslovakia. Their authors were quickly rounded up, but among the student body a free-floating malaise remained.

As a contribution to their *subbotniks* Moscow University students were held on a roster, according to faculty, to await their turn at participating in demonstrations in downtown Moscow against the Suez intervention, and later against the Vietnam War. At the high-water mark of the Sino–Soviet dispute in the mid 1960s, Moscow University students were issued bottles of ink by the Komsomol to throw against the walls of the Chinese Embassy. It was conveniently within walking distance of the University building on Sparrow (then Lenin) Hills.

There was no echo in Moscow of the student protest movements of the 1960s; the Paris student uprising of 1968, the famous *jours de mai,* the same year and time as the Prague Spring, passed in silence. Before 1991, any non-official 'politics of the crowd' was absent from Moscow city streets. The only major exception was on Manezh Square, already in times of *glasnost* against the Soviet invasion of Afghanistan, and for immediate Soviet withdrawal. Its leaders and participants were the distraught mothers and wives of Red Army soldiers, not students.[26] Student passivity right into the 1990s accounts for their reputation of belonging to a 'lost generation'. Whether the student activism associated with the government-sponsored youth organization Nashi is a genuine movement or a pale reflection of its Komsomol predecessor is still an open question.

Even with Moscow's turbulent history, there are few places that can be readily identified where citizens rose up to drive history forward. There is no Bastille of 1789 or Alexanderplatz of 1953 where stone-throwing East Berlin crowds faced Soviet tanks; no Wenceslas Square where the people of Prague celebrated the end of communism. There is no Brandenburg Gate where the Berlin Wall was first breached on 9 November 1989, nor is there any equivalent of Tiananmen Square, where in the same year over 1,000 pro-democracy student protesters were killed by security forces.

Red Square comes closest, but ever since the days of Ivan the Terrible it has been a place for the open demonstration of state power, executions and parades. The few scattered, unauthorized demonstrations were always quickly swept away. In 2008, after a hiatus of eight years, Red Square again became a theatre for the Red Army, its military parade symbolizing the emergence of a newly assertive Russia. The White House, the Russian government building, may be considered by some as a symbol of liberation, but its image of democratic defiance to the putschists in 1991 is compromised—by a rambunctious showdown with uncooperative MPs, by its tragic-comic shelling on President Yeltsin's orders in 1993.

Opposition and dissent have an honourable and often brilliant place in Russian history. In post-Stalinist Russia, they were more often than not found in Moscow's quiet places. The most revolutionary place in the Moscow of the 1970s was probably the kitchen table, a place of private, trusted conversation. For the more daring, there were writers' desks or Xerox machines, used surreptitiously until the authorities started keeping track of who was making the copies. Private ownership of print or reproduction machines was illegal. The majority of the dissident groups, such as Helsinki Watch, which monitored Soviet adherence to human rights agreements of the 1970s, were based in Moscow. Other places were not in Moscow, but near it. Pasternak's village of Peredelkino was one such place, where he and others conducted a complex relationship with the Soviet Writers' Union, guardian of official cultural policy of socialist realism. The latter demanded simple, uplifting and unambiguous stories with proletarian heroes. Titles such as *How the Steel was Tempered* were common.[27] Some dissidents lived with their influence intact amongst the intelligentsia but in enforced internal exile, like the physicist Andrei Sakharov in distant Gorky, or in the farthest reaches of the Gulag, like Solzhenitsyn. They were Nobel Prize winners.

In the Soviet Union's later years, a few quiet but most unlikely places for revolutionary change came into being. Of these, two stand out: the eighteenth-century Administration Building of the Kremlin, and the Party Central Committee headquarters on Staraya Ploshchad in downtown Moscow. In those two buildings Gorbachev and a small circle of advisers elaborated the policies of *glasnost* and *perestroika,* improvising as they went along, conscious of the need for far-reaching reform.[28] 'Revolutionary change' was a term they avoided, but was the outcome of what they devised.

The crisis broke in August 1991. Its setting was almost entirely within the confines of Moscow. Other Soviet cities played no major role. In reaction to an incompetently organized coup, Boris Yeltsin, the democratically elected Russian president, faced down a loosely knit cabal of hard-line conservatives intent on restoring Soviet power. 'Democratically elected' was a qualification that Gorbachev, the presumed target of the coup, could not match. Yeltsin's victory was directed not from the Kremlin but from the White House, and supported by the people of Moscow. It was led by the leaders of Russia against the Soviet Union and its representatives, including ultimately Gorbachev, the Soviet president.

A common belief is that crows are the protectors of Moscow. It is said that between 19 and 21 August 1991 their flocks around the White House were unusually dense. The White House still stands on the embankment near the Kutuzovsky Bridge. Opposite is the Ukraina Hotel, one of Stalin's seven signature buildings, casting its dark shadow across the Moskva River.

The coat of arms of the Russian Empire, 'The Double-Headed Eagle' by the artist Kirill Kovalenko. The double-headed imperial eagle was adopted by Ivan III from the Byzantine crest, looking both east and west; the coat of arms of Muscovy/Moscow, depicting St. George and the Dragon (originally, the Bringer of Victory), appears at the centre. As of 1993, the imperial crest represents the Russian Federation.

Chapter Five
Empire and the Trial of History

The state and cities developed their own institutional features in close consort with each other. There can be no finer case in point than Moscow. This once-obscure appanage town loyally supported its ruling princes in their successful quest for national leadership and became in time the capital of a vast state and the claimant to the mantle of Rome and Constantinople. Political and ecclesiastical power—not the volume of its trade nor the products of its artisans—made Moscow the city it was.

Michael J. Hittle[1]

Moscow is a twelfth-century city-state perched on a hill. It grew from the humblest and most subservient beginnings into three empires: Muscovy and the possessions of the House of Rurik, with the reign of Ivan the Terrible as its culmination; after the time of Troubles of the late fifteenth century, the vast territories accumulated over the two hundred years of the Romanov dynasty; and the climax of Russian empires, the Soviet, when Moscow was the capital of a state encompassing one-sixth of the earth's land surface, with a chain of vassal states in Eastern Europe and Asia. Besides the usual strategic and economic determinants, in each of Moscow's empires it was ideology and belief, and the role they played in legitimizing its rulers, that occupied a pivotal role in the creation of the city's ethos—and even the city's shape and architecture.

Moscow Imperium

Only the state of the Romanov tsars, beginning with Peter the Great, bore the designation 'empire'. Copied from Western practice of the eighteenth and nineteenth centuries, this designation was intended to carry within its meaning not only an evocation of the traditions of Rome and Byzantium, but also the idea of dominion over distant lands and peoples. The supreme irony was that imperial Russia's capital, and imperial by name, was not Moscow, but the new Baltic city founded by the man who hated Moscow.

The history of Moscow's expansion to empire reveals the imprint of two hundred years of Tatar domination, when Moscow itself was the object of imperial subjugation: successor to Genghis Khan, the great khan at Sarai, the Crimean Tatar capital, favoured the Moscow princes with authority to rule, and in particular to collect tribute in the name of the Golden Horde. Beginning with Ivan Kalita in the thirteenth century, this authority, or *yarlik,* was vigorously—even cravenly—exercised by the grand dukes of Moscow, who with fire and sword also adopted Mongol methods of dealing with other Russian principalities, in particular Tver, which with Mongol assistance was destroyed in 1327. In the process the grand dukes expanded Muscovy and enhanced their own power to dominate other cities of Russia proper and to absorb them into the Muscovite state. Besides Tver, Novgorod, Pskov and Riazan were overcome even as Muscovy conducted wars with Lithuanians to the west and Swedes to the north.

From the Kremlin to the constellation of fortified places that spread out from Moscow, traces in stone remain of Muscovy's first empire, deeply embedded in myth but still an integral part of the Muscovite identity. By the mid sixteenth century, the Khanates of Kazan and Astrakhan had been annexed, and a chain of stockades built along Muscovy's southern border.

Orthodoxy and Empire

At the centre of Muscovite expansion stands Uspensky Sobor, or the Cathedral of the Assumption. The tsars are buried here, as their Bolshevik successors are buried in the Kremlin wall, less than a kilometre distant.[2] Drawing inspiration from architectural styles inherited from Vladimir-Suzdal and Pskov, and instruction from Renaissance practice, Italian architects under the leadership of Aristotele Rudolfo Fioravanti took over from local builders, whose attempts to build the massive cathedral for Ivan III the Great had ended in failure. Fioravanti built it in four years, between 1475 and 1479. To do so, he first dismantled the remaining walls of the first attempt, a task he accomplished within a week, to the astonishment of local builders. They had needed three years to construct them. (In 1934 a similar feat was repeated but with less honourable intention when the Cathedral of Christ the Saviour was dynamited into rubble. This took less than a week, but longer than planned.)

The stones of Uspensky Sobor stand as mute witnesses to the facts of life of fifteenth-century Moscow, for the Orthodox Church was a major purchaser of slaves, and bought slave artisans for the cathedral's construction. Free artisan labour had been drastically reduced by the Black Death. The same pestilence undermined Moscow's tax base, and the cathedral was financed by levying a duty in silver on tax-exempt monasteries, a step not even the Mongols had undertaken.

Fioravanti's cathedral represents in one monumental act in stone 'the felicitous meeting of two cultures':[3] the Russian, with its Byzantine heritage; and the Western, as expressed in the Italian Renaissance ideas of proportion, symmetry and space. The 'meeting' may have been felicitous, but the tension it implanted in Russian national identity between the Byzantine and the Western bedevilled the Russian state and then empire from the beginning. The supreme symbol of this schizophrenia is St. Basil's Cathedral on Red Square, which was the Slavic answer to Byzantium and the West, as represented by Uspensky Sobor. St. Basil's Cathedral's inspiration is derived from the authentic wooden churches of the Russian north, their style set in stone some ninety years after the completion of Uspensky Sobor.

Uspensky Sobor's significance lies beyond architecture, for besides being the first stone church built in Moscow, it stands as a monument to the nascent imperial state of Muscovy. It was there that Ivan III tore up a Tatar document demanding tribute, thereby launching Moscow's long journey from submission to empire. Until the Revolution of 1917, Uspensky Sobor was the main theatre for the great occasions of state and empire, the venue for weddings, funerals, coronations and declarations of war.

It is also the place for investiture of metropolitans and patriarchs of the Russian Orthodox Church. In the early fourteenth century Moscow became the capital of Russian Orthodoxy when the metropolitan took up residence in the city. In 1589, at Ivan the Terrible's instigation, the Eastern patriarchs consented to raise the title of the Metropolitan of Moscow to that of patriarch, thereby confirming his pre-eminence within the Russian Orthodox community—and with it, the city of Moscow now became a spiritual beacon to Orthodox Slavdom as well as a place of earthly power. In a turbulent time, the chief prelate frequently intervened to mediate in princely quarrels and struggles for power or aristocratic rights. Besides bestowing advice and admonition, he also wielded the fearsome threat of excommunication, which meant for the recipient, bereft of the Church's sacraments, eternal damnation. Moscow remained under constant threat from the north and west, but this did not prevent Muscovy's relentless eastward expansion, carrying the undertones of a religious campaign, a struggle for the triumph of Orthodox civilization rooted deep in the Russian historical experience.

Spiritual beacon to Orthodox Slavdom Moscow might have been, but even the installation of the patriarch in the city did not necessarily guarantee unity amongst the community of believers to create common agreement that Moscow was indeed 'the Third Rome'. That doctrine lay more with the rulers and clergy of the Muscovite state. This was a calling that Moscow took on for itself, acquiring in the process a self-declared responsibility for all believers within the Orthodox rite. The idea of Moscow's special responsibilities for those beyond its pale bears a certain resonance to the concept of the 'near abroad', i.e. responsibility for ethnic Russians beyond Russia's frontiers. The practical effect of the original doctrine was that it conferred upon the city of Moscow, the spiritual capital of Russia, the responsibility for all Orthodox Christians, including those living in Catholic (Lithuanian–Polish) and Muslim (Ottoman) lands, thereby often giving the wars on Russia's periphery a crusade-like quality, the echoes of which are still evident, most recently in the two Chechen wars of post-Soviet Russia and the Russian interventions in Georgia.

With no equivalent of the Bishop of Rome, Orthodoxy lacks the organizational unity of the Latin Church. Every patriarch was 'autocephalous', independent in his own land. With no independent authority, the effect of this relationship between spiritual and temporal power was to tie the patriarchate tightly to the state, a matter put specifically to the Grand Prince of Moscow at the end of the fourteenth century. In a letter reflecting Byzantine tradition, the patriarch of Constantinople advised Prince Basil that it was not possible for Christians to have a Church without an emperor, for 'imperial authority and church exist in close union and communication with one another and the one cannot be separated from the other'.[4] To testify to the legitimacy of the Muscovite princes' claim to rule, the Church devised a genealogy supporting the idea that the princes of Moscow were the direct inheritors of an imperial line back to the Roman Emperor Augustus. This exercise in state propaganda was the work of Metropolitan Makarius in the *Stepennaya kniga tsarskogo rodosloviia* (Book of Degrees) of the mid sixteenth century.

The identification of Church and state with tsar and city outlasted the change of dynasty from the House of Rurik to the Romanovs. At the height of the empire under the Romanovs, it was elevated to the level of official doctrine. Even when St. Petersburg was the Russian capital, the Church continued to refer to the Romanov dynasty as 'the princes of Moscow', and conferred upon them imperial legitimacy.

The close connection between Orthodoxy and the growth of empire is clearly seen in the battle standard of Yermak, the Cossack adventurer who conquered much of Siberia in the latter part of the sixteenth century. It shows him kneeling before the Archangel Michael, the guardian of tsars, who according to legend had led Ivan the Terrible's troops to victory at Kazan, the capital of the rival Muslim Tatar khanate in 1552. In the nineteenth century this idea was further elaborated in monumental form. As the empire expanded, a monument to Ivan's victory was constructed in Kazan in 1823. In the shape of a pyramid surmounted by a large golden cross, and containing the remains of Muscovite soldiers like the *bogatyri*, legendary Russian warrior-heroes who were killed in that battle, it became a place of pilgrimage for nineteenth-century Russians, as much a symbol of the triumph of Orthodoxy over Islam as a monument to Ivan's victory itself. Miraculously, the Pyramid of Kazan (its official name is *Panyatnik pavshim Voinam,* Monument to the Fallen Warriors) survived the anti-religious campaigns of the 1930s, whereas many in Moscow did not. Like St. Basil's it rises beyond Orthodoxy, becoming a national monument.

The very word in Russian for state, *gosudarstvo,* carries within its origins the combined idea of possession, authority and domination.[5] The system grew to grotesque proportions under Ivan the Terrible, styled tsar and, after his victory against the Tatars at Kazan, great khan. He appropriated vast tracts of land from erstwhile owners to create a state within a state, directly ruled by him, with the black-cloaked forerunners of Stalin's NKVD, the *oprichniki,* acting as his private army in a war against his own people. Only the monasteries, vastly wealthy islands in a sea of Mephistophelean nightmare, remained exempt.

Interregnum

The aftermath of Ivan's reign was tragic beyond invention. In a scene captured by Ilya Repin's famous painting, *16 November 1581*, Ivan clubbed to death his first son in a fit of rage over a breach of dress etiquette by the latter's wife. Ivan's Christ-like first son is depicted gathered up in the arms of his bloodied, guilty and terrified father. The painting brings an image of *pietà* unmatched by any other painting of regicide. Three years later, Ivan was dead. After a brief spell of able rule by Boris Godunov, the darkness over Moscow deepened further.

Godunov stood as regent. His charge and brother-in-law Fedor succeeded his father as second son in 1584. In poor health and feeble-minded, his chief occupations were prayer and ringing church-bells, to the extent that he failed to produce an heir, thereby demonstrating the remorseless principle that in matters of princely succession, theology is no match for biology. Feodor died in 1598. Ivan's third son, Dmitri, was found with his throat slit. Having run out of sons, the Zemski Sobor, an 'Assembly of the Land' representing 'all ranks of the Muscovite

State', elected Boris Godunov tsar in 1598. Suspicion of his involvement in Dmitri's murder dogged Godunov's brief reign and has clouded his reputation ever since. This provided the inspiration for Modest Mussorgsky's great opera of complicity and guilt which drew from Pushkin's drama, *Boris Godunov*, as well as from the account of nineteenth-century Russian historian Nikolai Karamazin, a strong advocate of state power. If the immediate cause of the Time of Troubles (1604-13) was the question of succession to the throne, for which Ivan had left no provision, the underlying cause stemmed from the policies of Ivan, whose creation of the *oprichnina* state (a period of terror, literally meaning 'apart from') and its aftermath had rendered the traumatized country essentially ungovernable, weak and vulnerable.

Within less than two years, there were four tsars: Feodor; after his death, Boris Godunov; then the False Dmitri (who claimed to be the third son of Ivan, supposed murdered, but actually a Polish prince who was apparently convinced he was who he said); and finally Basil Shuisky, scion of a noble family. Government disintegrated under intolerable pressure from relentless intrigue, rebellion and invasion.

Under such conditions, the Horsemen of the Apocalypse, as foreseen in the Book of Revelation as the Time of Troubles in the Orthodox Bible, took their wild ride across Muscovy. In 1601 and 1602 drought brought crop failure, famine and plague. In scenes likened to the Thirty Years' War that ruined Central Europe, Russia in the Time of Troubles was beset by bands of desperate men ravaging the countryside, destroying villages, crops and livestock. Petty warlords—but also a major insurrection led by a Cossack and ex-Turkish galley-slave, Ivan Bolotnikov—challenged the power of Moscow, giving battle to regular troops. In company with dissident *boyars*, he besieged Moscow in 1606, was defeated, blinded and drowned. Despite the violence issued to its enemies for over a decade, the House of Rurik came close to collapse, and as Thomas Hobbes postulated, life without a strong central authority was 'nasty, brutish and short'. But as one dissident Russian academic quietly reminded me, life under one of the strongest central authorities in history, that of Stalin, could have exactly the same result.

The Time of Troubles devastated Moscow. Its population fell to about 80,000 during its two-year occupation by Polish–Lithuanian invaders. Their expulsion in September 1612 in a 'national rising' led by Prince Dmitry Pozharsky and Kuzima Minin, citizens of Nizhny Novgorod, is commemorated in the famous nineteenth-century statue originally standing in the centre of Red Square, now moved to the side to allow for parades and public demonstrations (Nizhny Novgorod has a copy). As they withdrew, the Poles burnt the Kremlin, and much of the city besides. With the great national victory against the Poles, Moscow was elevated to the level of national myth as a rallying-point for the defence of Russia.

The Minin–Pozharsky legend was to become a permanent fixture in Moscow's history, the story of how the people—the *narod* of all classes united against the invader. The sub-text to this legend, avoided during Soviet times, was that Orthodox Moscow triumphed over its Catholic usurpers by its piety, purity and fidelity to the true faith. It is said that the cowl worn by the metropolitan reflects these qualities, in emulation of the headdress of St. Peter, and the faithfulness of Orthodoxy to the founder's principles.

Piety, purity and fidelity to the true faith are taken up as themes in Mikhail Glinka's opera, *A Life for the Tsar* (1836), in which the simple villager Ivan Susanin deceives an invading Polish army intent on deposing Alexander Mikhailovich by guiding it into a dense, uncharted forest from which there is no escape. He pays for this deception with his life, but his name lives on in the colloquial Russian expression, 'to lead astray, like

Susanin', a term often used by our frustrated embassy driver when he misread a map or lost his direction.

The Susanin legend was a source of embarrassment to the Soviet state, which preferred the Minin–Pozharsky alternative. It focused on the rescue of Moscow, as opposed to the rescue of the tsar—and the anniversary of the liberation of Moscow from the Poles was abolished as a public holiday by the Bolsheviks. Following the collapse of the Soviet Union in 1991, the original version was restored.

Unity Day, commemorating the liberation of Moscow in 1612, is now celebrated on 4 November, replacing 7 November, the anniversary of the Great October Socialist Revolution, the highlight of Soviet Moscow's annual open-air military spectacle on Red Square. In post-Soviet Moscow not only opera librettos, buildings and street names have been restored, but public holidays as well. In television broadcasts, school lectures and newspapers, the government of then-President Putin went to extraordinary lengths to publicize Unity Day, effectively re-educating the country away from the 7 November celebrations with their demonstrations of military hardware. The military parade on Red Square now takes place on Victory Day, 9 May, the day of German surrender in 1945.

Moscow Betrayed: the Romanovs

The Time of Troubles was brought to an end by the election in 1613 of 16-year-old Alexander Mikhailovich, the first Romanov, by the Zemski Sobor. He would be the last elected Russian leader until Boris Yeltsin 350 years later.

In the process of its recovery from the Time of Troubles, Moscow underwent a subtle transformation which over time was to have profound effects on its future development. The Zemski Sobor, which elected Alexander Mikhailovich in Uspensky Sobor, bore some relationship to the États Généraux (States-General) of seventeenth-century France. Attendance at the assembly was a duty, not a right. After this modest but promising beginning, the Zemski Sobor faded, its meetings held less and less often, and its power exercised with diminishing frequency. The fact that Moscow did not develop a 'civic culture' to promote the interests of the city and the independence of its citizens set Moscow's political development apart from Western cities. Like Hanseatic Novgorod, an earlier model which Moscow's rulers could have emulated but instead destroyed, the Zemski Sobor represented a second chance to develop a civic culture. That chance was missed as well.

More broadly, under the Romanovs Moscow never evolved from a fortress and surrounding settlements into an integrated city. The reasons were deeply embedded in the political culture of late-medieval Russia and the necessity of reinforcing the strength and authority of the state at all costs: it was a matter of survival. In the process, the state became separated from the city. The city and the townsmen's activities of fairs and commerce could no longer shelter behind or even in front of the walls of the Kremlin. From its heights overlooking the city the Kremlin became a remote, sacred place of religion and power. As the seat of rule, the fortress became the supreme embodiment of the state, a forbidden city, above and aloof from the urban conglomeration surrounding it.

The power of the tsar was boundless, the nobility increasingly his servitors, dependent upon his word for their lives and property. Inherited traditions dictated that Muscovy (soon to be called Russia) was a tsarist patrimony, meaning that there was no distinction between the properties of the ruler and those of the state. There was no Magna Carta to moderate his authority, no independent class of nobility. Western concepts of sovereignty limited by property rights and the rights of citizens—during the Enlightenment called Natural Rights—

were imperfectly transplanted, never took root or were lost on the way.

In Moscow, rudimentary merchant and artisan guilds lacked the organization, authority or tradition of Roman law to promote a civic culture, the founding principle emphasized above all the independent rights of citizens and the security of their property. Without the development of an urban bourgeoisie, such as had occurred in Western Europe, the implications for the economic life of the city were far-reaching. Moscow was the property of the tsar, and the notion of state ownership of land survived well into the Soviet era. Moscow's ruler became in effect its chief merchant and dispenser of monopolistic prerogatives.

Occupying the same space, the state, as represented by the Kremlin with its national preoccupations, and the city, with its more immediate, practical concerns, remained distinct and separate entities, the former parasitic upon the latter, imposing ever-increasing burdens of taxation. The main sources of taxation were the *posady,* commercial and other related districts of Moscow. Only a minor portion of the taxes collected was allocated to the city itself. Muscovite taxpayers were referred to as *posadskiye lyudi*, the rough equivalents of commercial and professional classes of Western Europe, except that they shared a proportionately greater burden of supporting the state as Moscow maintained a long list of tax-exempt classes—military personnel, service nobility, ecclesiastical organizations and their property as well as foreigners who had been granted concessionary rights as traders. In the sixteenth and into the seventeenth century, these taxes, the so-called *tiaglo*, required of the taxpayer not only contributions in cash but also in service, reminiscent of the *corvées* of Bourbon France. Each *posad*, for example, was required to supply its own customs and tax officials from its own inhabitants, and to administer and account for certain state monopolies, like the sale of alcohol.

The state also held a virtual monopoly on tax revenues, and Moscow received (or did not receive) funds according to the behest of the state, a situation that became more acute when the centre of fiscal decision was moved in the eighteenth century to the distant capital of St. Petersburg. The problem was further exacerbated by the fact that the taxpayers of Moscow, already bearing heavy tax burdens, had little control over the city and its further development.

The state *qua* state had one over riding interest in Moscow and other Russian cities: as a source of tax. The state also held profitable export monopolies, reducing opportunities for the local merchants. Some successful merchants were co-opted into acting as agents for state monopolies, the 'Cloth Hundreds' for example, further contributing to the dissatisfaction of urban taxpayers, many of whom were in competition with those favoured with concessions and tax-exempt. Various stratagems were devised to co-opt wealthy merchants, the so-called *gosti*, to act as tax-collectors to lesser members of their own class in return for certain concessions and privileges. Preferential concessions offered to foreigners, mainly English and Dutch traders, complicated the situation. Over time, the tax burden of the townsmen increased as tax concessions granted by the tsar continued to grow, and the tax base effectively narrowed, leaving the city's tax burden unequally shared amongst Moscow's citizenry. Many departed Moscow.

The heavy taxes were necessary to support Peter the Great's huge public works projects, including the building of St. Petersburg, the establishment of a modern navy and the creation of the largest army in Europe. Along with the peasants and serfs, the *posady* in cities across Imperial Russia, including those in Moscow, were also required to produce a fixed number of recruits to the armed forces, and, as in the taxes themselves, quotas were set not according to the ability of the individual *posad* to contribute, but on the needs of the state.

Well before Peter the Great became tsar in 1689, one of the first of many civic outbursts of Muscovites against the fiscal excesses of the state (tsardom was not yet identified with the state and was still off-limits for criticism) erupted in June 1648. Violence broke out in protest against a sharp reduction of *streltsy (*musketeers') salaries, and then rapidly escalated and spread to embrace a catalogue of issues feeding already simmering popular discontent. At its height, it had developed into a full-scale urban riot which left half the city's houses burnt to the ground.

The response of the state authorities was the promulgation by the Zemski Sobor of the hastily drafted *Sobornoe Ulozhenie* or Law Code of 1649, which provided a basic legal framework for all of Russia until the nineteenth century. Among other reforms, it gave the citizens of Moscow greater control of their city, and to a certain extent regularized the tax system. The state remained the final arbiter: serfs seeking freedom in Moscow were expelled and sent back to their estates. The Law Code also increased the number of tax-paying townsmen by reducing the number of exempted classes, reduced privileges and confiscated property from magnates and ecclesiastical institutions. Privileges to the taxpayer were correspondingly extended; for example, they were given exclusive right to trade within the city limits. The Law Code kept the *posad* system, and provided for each to be administered by a separate bureau. As a result, the *posady* never coalesced into a single legal entity representing the city as a whole.

For all its positive features the Law Code thus had the effect of freezing Moscow's social mobility, and even discouraged movement within the city, a practice which would reappear under the Bolsheviks. The Law Code rigidly divided Moscow horizontally by district, and vertically by class. Differentiation in taxation was reflected in social differentiation, and even generational mobility became more an exception than a rule. Taxation reached grotesque proportions. Ice and even watermelons were taxed. In order to simplify increasingly complex taxation schemes, a 'soul tax' (the same in inspiration as British Prime Minister Margaret Thatcher's 'poll tax' that led to her removal from power in 1989) was imposed on every adult male in 1784, the assessment being defined by social category of the taxpayer. It tripled revenues by one estimate, and continued unrevised until 1887. The Law Code was also inconsistent and lacking in clarity, possibly reflecting the haste with which it was drawn up. In a number of instances the old tax systems continued in effect even though in principle they had been overtaken by the Law Code. Although there was nothing specific in the Law Code about this, tax paid as labour was still expected and enforced. Under the Romanovs, Russia had developed a system of ranks (*chin*) which defined one's position in the state and in relation to the tsar. This arrangement became formalized and detailed with Peter the Great's elaborate 'Table of Ranks' of the eighteenth century, the precursor of the Soviet Union's *nomenklatura* system, which defined the country's elite according to the privileges they were to receive according to their place in the Soviet hierarchy. Even today the Russian word *chinovnik*, meaning 'bureaucrat' or 'official', carries a slightly derogatory back-sense, possibly rendered as 'pencil-pusher' or even 'eye-shade wearer'.

The principle of shared executive power never developed in Russia, and the last Zemski Sobor met quietly and without issue until 1653, when it then dispersed. In circumstances where mere residence did not mean urban citizenship or participation in the overall life of the city and influence over the decisions affecting it, the Muscovite's legal status was exposed, directly and uncompromisingly, to the state and to the tsar.

At this point fate intervened. Two years of crop failure, famine and then plague followed the urban reforms of 1649, and the state was obliged to offer incentives to townsmen from the provinces to move into vacant houses in Moscow, and of course to assume their previous owners' tax burden.

Only four Romanov monarchs paid any attention to their cities. Peter the Great was one, obsessed with his grand project and namesake on the Neva; Moscow was out of his range of vision. Another was the Tsarina Anna, who re-established Moscow as the capital following her coronation in 1730. Two years later she changed her mind and returned to St. Petersburg, at which point her interest in cities faded. Following the plague riots of 1771, Catherine the Great inspired by eighteenth-century rationalism, sought to transform Moscow into 'an enlightened metropolis' through the creation of 'a new race of men' that would become the Third Estate, effectively the middle class. Her efforts were only partially successful, and faltered after her death. Finally there was Alexander I, who in 1813 set in motion elaborate but unrealized plans for the rebuilding of Moscow in neoclassical style.

Despite the monarchy's general indifference to their cities,[6] outward appearances and being a source of revenue excepted, the final authority for their governance and welfare rested ultimately with the tsar. This was laid down in the *Complete Collection of Laws,* in particular its *Building Statute,* the first entry of which is dated 27 January 1649:

> No city plan could be altered to the slightest extent without the approval of the tsar and no building could be erected that did not conform in its outward appearance to prescribed features in design and scale... in the eighteenth and early nineteenth centuries the main goal of the state was to reconstruct the existing cities of Russia and to build new ones (primarily those recently absorbed into the Empire) with the rationalistic town planning concepts associated with the Age of Enlightenment.[7]

Even under these conditions and before, the face of Moscow continued to change. In the north-west outskirts and gradually closer in, traditional *izbas,* the small houses of the countryside, were giving way to larger villas, also made of wood. Some of the villas belonged to Ivan's *oprichniki,* but these had lain vacant after Ivan disbanded the organization and executed its leaders for failing to defend Moscow against the Crimean Tatar attack. Stone buildings began to appear: first churches, and less frequently private houses of the *boyars* or wealthy merchants, heavily fortified with windows high up, Italian Renaissance-style. Expensive to build, doubly so because of the shortage of labour, they had the great advantage of being fire-proof. The nobility kept to their country estates, and did not establish residences in Moscow in any numbers until the latter half of the eighteenth century. When they did, they brought the inspiration of their estates with them. This is what gave Moscow its countrified look.

By the time Alexander Romanov ascended the throne in 1613, Moscow had reached the shape it was to keep with few changes into the Napoleonic era. It now extended in a great horseshoe-shaped arc on the north side of the Moskva River with the roughly triangular Kremlin at its core. A moat ran down the Kremlin's eastern side. The Kremlin's walls, clad in white, enclosed the seat of temporal and ecclesiastical power.

All commercial activity had been removed. A second ring of walls on the east side of the Kremlin now sheltered the market and trading district of Kitai Gorod, or 'the Grand Posad'. At the time it was built in the 1530s, Kitai Gorod was known as the 'middle fortress'. ('Kitai Gorod' does not mean 'Chinatown' as many believe, but probably derives from *kita,* a Mongol word meaning 'fort'.) The trading rows (the *riady)* had also been removed from Red Square and relocated on its eastern perimeter. There were some 48 of these rows, leading down to the water's edge, where pre-cut logs waited for sale to rebuild houses after the next fire. The 'upper trading rows', beginning further up the gentle incline from St. Basil's, specialized in elegant manufactured goods and luxury items.[8]

The third ring of defences, the high earth ramparts built further out in the fourteenth century (as protection against attacks from Tver and the Lithuanians), were topped with whitewashed brick walls in the sixteenth century to enclose the outer reaches of Moscow and the district of Belgorod, forested to the east, with villas to the west, so named because its residents were classified as 'white', a classification that exempted them from taxes. This walled outer ring was built in the latter half of the sixteenth century by Fyodor Kon, the military architect of the fortress of Smolensk, the guardian of the western approaches to Moscow, and later a military obstacle to Napoleon and Hitler. Formally known after its earthen ramparts as Zemlyanyi Gorod, but more usually as Skorodom, a reference to the fact that it was built at great speed, the outer ring of imperial Moscow, some 10 kilometres in circumference and 4-5 metres thick, enclosed a population of 100,000, making it at the turn of the century one of the largest cities in Europe.

In a parallel development, as the institution of serfdom grew, and as various laws were passed to keep serfs on the land of the estates to which they were bound, Moscow fought a continuous rearguard action to control their migration to the city. The floodgates burst after 1861, the year that serfdom was formally abolished. The liberation of the serfs (by no means as straightforward as it sounds, as many serfs immediately found themselves in debt or indentured) coincided with the early stages of the industrialization of Moscow. The serfs supplied the labour-force, typically the men as industrial workers, the women as domestics. Dense shanty-towns and, in more fortunate cases, barracks provided by their employers became permanent features in outlying areas of the city well into the twentieth century.

Until the beginning of the Soviet period, the hierarchy

of city development was from the centre outwards, with population density following suit. Beyond the Outer Ring there was an administrative vacuum. Technically not included in any of Moscow's districts, these areas became heavily populated. Succeeding city administrations took no responsibility for them, and like South American *barrios,* these disease-ridden places lacked basic civic amenities, including clean water and sewerage. From these outer areas and from the city district of Zamoskvorechye, to the south side of the river, came the human material that fuelled the Russian industrial revolution of the late nineteenth century. The very centre of Moscow, the Kremlin, remained a cypher, not a part of the city, but in it. From the time of Peter the Great, it had forfeited its role as the centre of imperial administration to St. Petersburg.

By the mid nineteenth century Moscow had reached a total population of well over 300,000, and had enjoyed several decades of more-or-less peaceful development. Local wars were a chronic fact of life on imperial Russia's outer reaches, in Poland to the west, and to the south against the Ottoman Empire (and Crimea in the 1850s). To the east there was the empire's continued expansion across Siberia to the Pacific. All these wars, mini-wars and consequences of imperial ambition had a direct impact on Moscow and its finances. It was a question of taxes.

The long-term implications were that as imperial demands for revenue to finance its wars increased, Moscow's ability to develop an infrastructure with supporting political institutions was frozen. Under the empire, Moscow included, city governors were little more than keepers of the peace and tax-farmers in gold braid, appointed by and answerable to the tsar. At the same time the ethnic character of some of Moscow's outlying districts and open-air markets—those small shops and stalls at the bottom of Moscow's commercial hierarchy—noticeably changed as in-migrants from the empire's periphery gravitated to the city. This development accelerated following the great railway boom of the 1850s. The lasting result is the ethnic diversity of Moscow, which continues to distinguish it from St. Petersburg. Moscow is sometimes held in disdain for its 'countrified' accent and the provincial flavour of its open-air markets.

The indifference of the Romanov tsars to their cities also extended to such urban issues as public health, civic infrastructure and city planning. The outward appearance of their cities might provoke in them a brief, but languid interest. The cities' potential as a tax source might generate perhaps a few moments of genuine alertness. Suggestions for even a modicum of self-rule met the rigid opposition of the autocracy, and the incompetence and venality by which the governors, the Romanovs, chose to run their cities would in the end cost them dearly.

Where the rural *jacqueries* of Bolitnikov (1606-7), Razin (1670-71) and Pugachev (1773-4) would fail, the urban revolutions of 1905 and ultimately of 1917 would succeed. Significantly, these uprisings aimed at the heart of Russia, Moscow, not the city on the periphery, Petersburg. Empire was no match for revolution in the streets. Growing signs of the power of the streets had appeared in the mid seventeenth century, when general discontent materialized into the violent riots of June 1648 which prompted the government's response by promulgating the reformist *Sobornoe Ulozhenie.*

The long-term effect of the disturbances of the mid seventeenth century was to establish Moscow as a city of revolution. Some Marxist historians later argued that by the 'logic of history' it was inevitable that Moscow would turn Red.

St. Petersburg Eclipse

During Russia's three empires, St. Petersburg was the only city formally designated as imperial capital. As imperial capital it reflected the outlook of the Peter who had already let it be known that he should be styled 'the Great', and was the first of the Romanovs to accord himself the designation of 'emperor'. Both titles stuck.

The notion of 'empire' outlasted the Romanovs into the Soviet era, as revolution shifted the imperial capital from St. Petersburg to Moscow. 'Empire', with its capitalistic connotations (one of Lenin's original contributions to Marxism was *Imperialism, the Highest Stage of Capitalism*), was an anathema. Officially, the Soviet Union was an association of states united by class identity and whose national character was of secondary importance. The justification for the 'leading role' of Russia, a backward and primarily agrarian country, posed awkward questions of doctrine. Moscow's status as the 'beacon of revolution and hope of all progressive mankind' supplied part of the answer; the rest was supplied by crash programmes of industrialization and collectivization. The objective was the radical social remodelling of Russia and the rest of the Soviet Union into a unified workers' and peasants' state. The forced incorporation of the economically sophisticated and politically advanced Baltic States into the Union made a nonsense of this line of thought, as did the Soviet takeover of industrialized Czechoslovakia in 1948.

This led to some ideological contortions. At the height of the Sino–Soviet dispute of the 1960s, Mikhail Suslov, the chief ideologist in the Soviet Politburo, developed a rationale to explain why the USSR, as the world's most 'economically and historically advanced' state, should play a leading role in the world socialist movement, and why its dominion over the states of Eastern Europe was justified. His main target, however, was Mao's assertion that the peasantry of the Third World were the standard-bearers of revolution, and that 'the countryside would encircle the cities'. This was a direct challenge to Soviet leadership of the world communist movement.

The last book by Dmitry Volkogonov, a decorated Soviet general appointed by President Yeltsin to examine the Communist Party's secret archives, was entitled *The Rise and Fall of the Soviet Empire*. Even as he published his research into the crimes of the Soviet leaders, including the revered Lenin, he told me that his most difficult moment was deciding the book's title. By choosing the word 'empire', he was equating the Russian-led *sotrudnichestvo* or 'commonwealth' with other empires. By this choice, his was the final rejection of a belief system that he had devoted his whole professional life to uphold.[9]

There is little in Moscow's outward design that marks it as a self-consciously imperial city, unlike Haussmann's Paris with its Arc de Triomphe, or *fin-de-siècle* Vienna or Berlin with their Ringstrasse and Brandenburg Gate respectively. In Moscow, triumphal arches were few. Baroque triumphal arches were erected in wood to honour the taking of Azov in 1696, and victories over the Swedes in 1709 and 1721, but these did not last. The best-known, the Krasnye Vorota ('The Red Gates'), was constructed in the 1750s, this time in stone, by Prince Ukhtomsky to celebrate the accession of Empress Elizabeth.[10] In 1928 it succumbed to the demolition hammer in company with many other buildings, to make way for heavy road traffic. At the time, there was none.

The formal expression of empire in architecture was reserved for St. Petersburg, not Moscow. At the centre of Palace Square stands the Alexander Column as a monument to the Russian victory over Napoleon. Standing on its own weight, and surrounded on three sides by the Winter Palace and the huge neoclassical curve of the Staff Headquarters of the Imperial Russian Army, it took 2,000 soldiers and 400 workers to winch the 704-ton monolith upright in 1834. As envisioned by Peter the Great, St. Petersburg *was* the state, and the state was the sole reason for its existence: the capital of a great European power, embodying 'the architectural–bureaucratic utopia of the eighteenth century'.[11]

Besides Peter the Great's need for cash to conduct his not always successful wars in the north and his obsession with building a fleet, it is generally accepted that Moscow's decline in the early decades of the eighteenth century was directly attributable to the St. Petersburg project and its consequences. As a city whose sole purpose was the glorification of the eighteenth-century imperial state, replete with palaces and public buildings of neoclassical grandeur, St. Petersburg lacked a 'critical mass' of taxpaying townsmen—*posadkiye lyudi*—to make the city self-sustaining, and efforts to attract them by fostering trade out of St. Petersburg bore lukewarm results at best. According to Muscovites, their city paid for St. Petersburg with their taxes and with their talent. Moscow artisans were co-opted to move to St. Petersburg, leaving Moscow bare. An equally compelling case, however, can be made that the system of government of the Romanovs, and indeed the methods of rule they exercised on all cities of their empire, made Moscow's decline inevitable.

The immediate and the most visible result of the construction of St. Petersburg on Moscow was urban stagnation. Decay set in as great public buildings were left to moulder, including the Kremlin. Spreading out from Red Square and Kitai Gorod, shack-like, impromptu structures of wood and cloth sprang up like mushrooms after the rain, housing street-hawkers, the homeless and the destitute. Starved of revenue, demoralized and neglected, city administration was moribund. Only the churches and the stone buildings of the wealthy seemed immune to advancing decay. The few large buildings that were constructed, such as Countess Razumovsky's palace and the Annenhof, were built under the direction of Moscow artisans according to plans sent out from St. Petersburg by Rastrelli and his assistants.

Another case in point is the Kremlin's Oruzheynaya Palata, or Armoury. In the sixteenth and seventeenth centuries it housed the Muscovite school of decorative arts, its productions representing the supreme expression of the city's culture in iconography and design, as well as clothing and household goods for the aristocracy, the tsar and his household. Before the Time of Troubles, the Armoury was the source of the best that was manufactured in Russia.

Originally established under Ivan III in the early sixteenth century as a factory for the manufacture of the tsar's weapons, its functions were successively broadened to include an office for the maintenance of the tsar's treasure, and an icon painting chamber, as well as *ateliers* for working gold and silver. The most recent innovations from Western Europe were frequently reflected in the various designs, which were incorporated into a distinctive 'Moscow style'.

As the Time of Troubles deepened, the Armoury ceased to function, and many of the craftsmen fled. Moscow suffered a cultural near-death. Following the accession of the Romanovs, it was revived by Tsar Mikhail Feodorovich, and continued as the creative leader of Moscow until Peter the Great transferred its personnel to the new armoury in St. Petersburg in 1711. According to some historians, by this single act the original Muscovite genius in art was rendered extinct. A somewhat overwrought Russian art historian wrote that this 'most remarkable institution, the only one of its kind, in the truest sense of the word, an institution, the like of which never existed anywhere at any time, was destroyed by the single stroke of a pen, with the scribble of five letters (Peter)... with it died the heart of national Russian art. It never beat again.'[12]

In 1757 the Empress Elizabeth founded the Imperial Academy of Arts in St. Petersburg. It was given its first statutes by Catherine the Great in 1764. The entire orientation of the academy was Western. Like St. Petersburg itself, its products were an accurate (some would say slavish) reflection of the Enlightenment, indistinguishable from the aesthetics and conventions of the baroque period. But conspicuously missing were the spirit of rationality and the logic of Natural Law. In the view of some, without that spirit the academy was stillborn.

The building that Catherine commissioned to house the academy still stands, next to the Neva River, where it presided over the development of high Russian (read: European) culture, unchallenged for over a hundred years. Even the founding of the Moscow School of Painting and Sculpture in 1843 did little to challenge the dominance of classical motifs and academic models emanating from the St. Petersburg academy, which in turn took its lead from the French Académie de Peinture et de Sculpture. This meant that until the last quarter of the nineteenth century, artists were rigidly trained to paint according to the Greek historical ideal, as interpreted through the lens of neoclassicism, with their own national historical experience ignored. The artistic revolt came later, and coincided with the momentous changes in Russian society at the turn of the century.[13]

The Re-emergence of Moscow

St. Petersburg towered over Russia, leaving all dwarfed before it:

> The dazzling radiance of St. Petersburg reached its apogee during the reign of Catherine the Great the opulence of whose court rivaled, and in most areas surpassed, that of all other courts if Europe. Through the imposing magnificence of the Winter Palace and its armies of liveried servants and well-built guardsmen in their resplendent uniforms and through the technicolour brilliance of the great aristocrats, draped in lace and satin and adorned with ribbons and jewels, the Russian court proclaimed its power, wealth and taste to the entire world.[14]

How in the late nineteenth century Moscow survived and revived in the face of such brilliance from the north may well be more related to the city's place at the core of Russian national identity than to the great social changes taking place and their accompanying political and philosophical debates, in polite salons over tea and in vodka-drenched student digs alike. Moscow was *Russian,* and it is difficult to imagine that any court residing in the Kremlin could cast off one language for another, as if changing clothes, with the insouciance of Elizabeth, the daughter of Peter the Great. In 1742 she decreed that henceforth the court language of the Winter Palace would be French, not German. Pushkin, the master of Russian vernacular, was not born until 1799. His birthplace was Moscow.

Eighteenth-century St. Petersburg was indeed 'all ribbons and jewels'; like its court languages, it was also foreign. Moscow was homespun, with felt boots, mud and furs in winter, and the smell of hay and manure in summer. The nobility of the St. Petersburg court, pomaded and shaven, belonged to a world apart from that of the *muzhik,* with his calloused hands and beard. They were two different species of being, increasingly distant from each other, often incapable of anything but the simplest form of communication between them, if not in language then in outlook; two cultures, tenuously bound together by Orthodoxy and loyalty to the tsar. A similar gulf existed in patriarchal Moscow, but its inhabitants shared a common awareness of the city's close connection with the countryside and were the inheritors of a long urban tradition, completely absent in the imperial capital.

Palace Interval

Early ground for Moscow's revival was prepared in the 1730s. Empress Anna, crowned in 1730, whose reign was marked by baroque frivolity, Germanness and the secret police, resolved to move the capital back to Moscow, and directed a new imperial court centre to be built. The small wooden palaces, the Winter Annenhof and the Summer Annenhof, were constructed by Rastrelli within the Kremlin walls, but the fortress proved uninhabitable. They were disassembled and moved to Lefortovo on the Yauza River, on the abandoned site of the Foreigners' Settlement. In the meantime Empress Anna lost interest in the entire project, and after less than two years in Moscow moved back to St. Petersburg. The palace complex lasted until 1746, when it suffered the seemingly inevitable fate of all Moscow's wooden buildings: it burned to the ground. For good measure, the gardens around it were severely damaged by a freak hurricane in 1905. The ghosts of the twin Annenhofs now hover over a public park.

By the early 1770s, Moscow's revival began in earnest. The architect Vasily Bazhenov was directed by the imperial court to reconstruct the Kremlin and to build a palace in classical style. This massive project would have entailed large-scale demolition, including its southern wall, facing the river. For two years he worked on his plans, which would have produced one of the largest palaces in Europe, the eighteenth-century equivalent of the Palace of Soviets. Like the Palace of Soviets, Bazhenov's project was abandoned in the midst of demolition, unrealized.

Bazhenov had to clean up after himself, including rebuilding the parts of the Kremlin wall he had destroyed. Like Empress Anna with her Annenhof, Catherine the Great had apparently lost interest in the Kremlin project for the same reason Stalin lost interest in the Palace of Soviets. War had intervened, in Catherine's case, war with Turkey. Her attention was also required to put down the Pugachev rebellion. Having lost favour with Catherine for the project, Bazhenov was sent to design an imperial estate near Moscow, Chernyi Gryaz, or Black Mud. He worked on the Black Mud project for ten years. When Catherine visited it in 1785, she objected to the fact that its design included corridors linking two equal parts of the palace, one for herself and the other for Grand Prince Paul, whom she detested, and ordered the whole thing destroyed. At the time of its destruction it carried the more elegant name of Tsaritsyno.

Bazhenov's most lasting achievement in Moscow remains the imposing Pashkov House, a large 'palace-estate' structure done in the late baroque style. It is now the Old Building of the Lenin Library, and despite its prominence on a hill overlooking the Kremlin's Borovitsky Gates, looks strangely out of place and ungainly in twenty-first-century Moscow, fenced in on two sides by heavy traffic and next to one of Moscow's main arterial bridges. Architectural historians still come to admire it.

Taking over Bazhenov's Kremlin project, Matvei Kazakov (1738-1823) succeeded in creating a harmonious, unified design incorporating the existing buildings around Cathedral Square with his commissioned works. The eighteenth-century buildings placed within the Kremlin walls are his work, together forming a kind of Acropolis. His crowning achievement was the Kremlin's Senate building, executed in transitional baroque–classical style. Construction started the same year as the American Declaration of Independence, 1776, and continued until completion in 1784. It was the largest building in Moscow. On New Year's Eve 1991, in a scene as emotive as the breaching of the Berlin Wall at the Brandenburg Gate, the red hammer-and-sickle flag of the Soviet Union was lowered for the last time from the flagstaff atop the Senate building, and replaced by the tricolour of Russia. This act was seen across the world.

Moscow revived in phases. The first phase belonged to the construction of imperial palaces and the reconstruction of the Kremlin itself. This was followed and in some cases accompanied by the construction of large villas for the nobility. The third, overlapping phase belonged to the reordering of Moscow as a whole. The first efforts were made to 'rationalize' the dilapidated city, first by Ivan Alexandrovich Mordvinov (the only city architect Moscow had at the time) whose work in drawing up a general plan for the city was completed in 1789 by his successor, Ivan Fyodorovich Michurin. Michurin also directed the repair of many public buildings, churches and palaces, and following Mordvinov's original plan, began the task of straightening the winding streets, often shifting buildings to a common sight-line by moving them on rails. Although the original plans were never fully realized, as other state priorities and a great fire intervened, Mordvinov is recognized as 'the true savior of Old Moscow'.[15] His work has survived Napoleon, Hitler, Stalin—and so far, the post-Soviet reconstruction of the city.

Along Mordvinov's roads, particularly the Tverskaya leading straight to the Kremlin (later travelled by Napoleon) and the road joining the Kremlin to the new court at Lefortovo, a new type of architecture appeared in the latter half of the eighteenth and early nineteenth centuries. Neoclassical in inspiration, these buildings resembled the great estate houses of the Russian countryside more than the formal palaces of St. Petersburg.

Moscow's revival began to accelerate as the aristocracy gravitated back to the city. Its members had been released from their military service obligations by Catherine the Great and many felt more comfortable either on their country estates or in Moscow than in artificial St. Petersburg. For them, Moscow was like a favourite childhood aunt, a sloppy, loving old lady in slippers in whose house one could be at home. Supported by revenue generated by their landholdings, some in effect brought their estates to Moscow, and in so doing created a new type of classicism in the city's architecture. Adding to the country look of the place was the growth of open areas and parks such as the Boulevard Ring, which wreathed the city in green. The nineteenth-century impression that Moscow was nothing but an overgrown village comes from the collective visual effect of *usadba,* or city estate houses, combined with the random growth of rough settlements housing first-generation urban peasantry. Architecturally, despite their superficial resemblance, the *usadba* differed radically from the French Empire style, for their owners were Russian aristocratic landowners, not the revolutionary bourgeoisie of the Napoleonic and post-Napoleonic periods.[16]

The conservative mentality, the Orthodox and countrified outlook and even the life-style of the owners of the city's villas of the eighteenth and nineteenth centuries were uniquely Muscovite. The *usadba* that their owners created conformed to a general pattern. They were all visibly country houses. The symmetrical central portico, which held the reception rooms and bedrooms, was surmounted by a dome. Wings containing drawing rooms and studies enclosed an inner courtyard with portals at the carriage entrance. The garden side of the *usadba* held the servants' quarters and stables.

The same group of talented architects who designed the *usadbas*, with their informal external decoration and pastel colours, also put their imprint on the face of Moscow in the form of the public buildings. Besides his work in the Kremlin, Matvei Kazakov was the chief architect of the House of Nobles (now the House of Unions) with its Hall of Columns, the scene of Stalin's purge trials, and the Residence of the Governor-General on Tverskaya Street, the first classical residential palace to be built in Moscow itself. It subsequently housed the Moscow Soviet, and after 1991 became Moscow City Hall—performing the same function in three guises. The great ensembles of Theatre Square, the Boulevard Ring and Manege Square belong to this period. Many of the lesser works of the great practitioners of Moscow classicism—besides Kazakov (1738-1812), Bazhenov (1737-99), Giacomo Quarenghi (1744-1817) and the architect who built the Bolshoi Theatre, Osip Bove/Beauvais (1784-1834)—are facing challenges to their survival as the pressures of commercial development and city economics bring their full weight to bear on the inner parts of the city.

Moscow, St. Petersburg and the Strategy of Empire

It is calculated that when Ivan III the Great ascended the throne in 1462, Muscovy covered some 24,000 square kilometres. In 1914 Nicholas II ruled over an empire of 13.5 million square kilometres. Territorial aggrandizement by the empire was supported by Russian (and to some extent, foreign) commercial interests, including those of the Romanovs themselves even before the nineteenth century. In that romantic age, economic pre-eminence was expressed culturally: Moscow the symbol of Rus', the 'original capital city', stood above all as the guardian and seat of Orthodoxy and hence the lodestone of national identity, the place where the emperor was crowned. As it revived, Moscow became the counterweight to the 'grimly

European capital on the Neva'.[17]

In the 1860s the technology of railways (in Russian, via French, 'roads of iron', *zhelezniye dorogie*) accelerated Russia's eastward expansion. Moscow, the commercial capital, not St. Petersburg, the imperial capital, was at the railway network's centre. The effect of Moscow becoming a railway hub had strategic implications, foreseen by Sir Henry Norman, who had travelled the Trans-Siberian Railway in 1901:

> Since the Great Wall of China the world has seen no material undertaking of equal magnitude. That Russia, singlehanded, should have conceived of it and carried it out makes imagination falter before her future influence on the course of events. Its strategical results are already easy to foresee.[18]

Sir Henry was thinking of the Eurasian landmass and China more than of Europe, but his insight implied that Moscow the city of commerce would also become Moscow the garrison city, and indeed it so became in the years before the First World War. Rails meant strategic mobility, an increasingly important military consideration in the early twentieth century as prospects of a generalized European conflict became more and more likely. Russian planners deliberately made the Russian gauge wider than the German rails so that in the event of attack they would be unusable. The planning of the Imperial Russian General Staff for the rapid deployment of troops by rail was inflexible and complex. The general mobilization called by the General Staff on instruction from Tsar Nicholas II on 30 July 1914 entailed the requisition of the country's rail system and the immediate deployment of masses of troops. In a chilling prefiguration of Cold War fail-safe nuclear scenarios, once the plan's machinery had been set in motion, it could not be reversed.

In the course of the two hundred years since its founding,

St. Petersburg was to come under threat of direct military attack in almost every major European war, but unlike Moscow, centred in the very heartland of Russia, this city located at its extreme fringes has never been occupied by an enemy.

Peter the Great's choice of location for his new city was strategic, and influenced by the Swedish encroachments in the eastern Baltic and Russia's involvement in the Great Northern War (1700-21). This conflict pitted a loose coalition of Russia, Denmark, Saxony and Poland against the victors of the Thirty Years' War (1618-48), Sweden and France. In eighteenth-century fashion, he intended to restore the balance of power in the Baltic by projecting Russian power there and beyond by establishing a military *point d'appui*, by founding a Baltic city from which a European-style navy would operate. Peter was earthily explicit: he could not 'moon the Swedes' unless he could meet them on equal terms. Narva, in present-day Estonia, was first considered, but after a disastrous land-battle with the Swedes in 1700, was judged too exposed for this project.

Peter followed the geopolitical thinking of his day, with the prime examples of France, Holland and England before him. Most major cities lay either on the coast or not far up navigable rivers. Peter's choice fell upon the mouth of the Neva, on land and associated islands occupied by the Swedes during the time of Ivan the Terrible. They had even tried to establish a fortress on the site, Landskrona. The territory and its surroundings is a land of bog and fen from which neighbouring Finland derives its English-language name, in summer a mosquito-ridden half-swamp, in winter an icy archipelago of frozen clumps of tangled grass and reeds. It would take a giant to transform it. But above all, its location gave access to the extensive river system of the Russian interior. Novgorod and Kiev were examples of successful riverine experience already gained, which the new city of St. Petersburg should emulate.

Despite a number of impressive victories against the

Swedes, Peter's navy and its successors were limited in their operations by the fact that the Baltic is a tightly-confined space, composed of many barriers and choke-points, both man-made and natural. This was the same problem faced by the German Kriegsmarine in both twentieth-century wars. In the First World War the Germans partially solved the problem by the construction of the Kiel Canal for their warships, thereby eliminating a narrow choke-point; and in the Second World War by basing major units of its navy including its submarines in occupied France, whose west coast allowed free access to the open Atlantic. The same set of factors applied to Russia's access to the Mediterranean, another confined space whose entry at the Bosporus was controlled by the rival empire of the Ottomans.

After the Second World War the Soviet solution to the Baltic problem was to establish a large naval base further west at Kaliningrad, built on the ruined East Prussian city of Königsberg, the first German city encountered by the Red Army in its long advance to Berlin. Terrible vengeance was wreaked for the 900-day siege and suffering of Leningrad. Even the bricks were destroyed. But the smoking ruins held one great strategic advantage: their location reduced the number of choke-points in the Baltic. Equidistant from both ends of the Baltic, the fortress city of Kaliningrad was built as a Soviet version of St. Petersburg's original military purposes, positioned to control the entire inland sea. The airspace above it is the outermost ring of the missile defence system of Moscow.

Storm-Warnings

Timothy Colton, the distinguished historian, succinctly states the causes of the Russian Revolution. Its ultimate cause was the unresponsiveness of the autocracy to urbanization and sundry demands of modernization. The proximate cause was its blundering into the First World War.[19]

Working-class conditions in Moscow in 1917 were intolerable, with long queues and little at the end of them. Already strained social conditions created by rapid industrialization and overcrowding reached crisis proportions. Under the pressure of war, the civilian railway lifeline for food and fuel collapsed. The autocracy, fearful of relinquishing its monopoly on power, had by a municipal statute in 1872 reduced the eligible voters to less than 1 per cent of Moscow's population, restricting suffrage to the elite, who by custom abstained from urban public affairs. The unequal burden of taxation, municipal indifference and incompetence remained festering sores. Whatever voice the city possessed bore no relationship to the voices on the streets. The same statute of 1872 compelled the city to cover the costs of billeting troops. The only way to do this was by reducing the city budget still further, at the expense of basic infrastructure. Public health was among the casualties through lack of adequate sanitation. Working-class districts of Moscow, already revolutionary since 1905, were scenes of increasingly violent strikes, all known to the authorities in St. Petersburg from reports by the city administration and corroborated by the Okhrana, the tsarist secret police.

The malaise in Moscow was merely an echo of storm-warnings in the country as a whole, heard but ignored, for the city possessed in microcosm all the features of a country with a dysfunctional autocracy ruling over a system whose pathology was terminal. According to the imperial census of 1897, the peasantry of 100 million accounted for 80 per cent of the population, but 130,000 landowners, classified as 'nobility', owned 95 per cent of all land. Across Russia, only 13 per cent of the population lived in cities, of which only half a million were classified as 'middle class' or bourgeois. Although the census did not collect data on income distribution, its statistics invite a picture of desperate poverty of the great majority living in the countryside, poverty which had already infected the industrialized cities of European Russia, with wealth concentrated in the hands of the very few. The masses of urban, *déraciné* peasants of late-nineteenth-century Moscow, existing on the edge of starvation and disease, were too deprived even to be called 'proletariat'. Like the bourgeoisie, real proletarians constituted an urban minority, confined to a few areas of Moscow, particularly the industrial centre of Zamoskvorechye and the unserviced outskirts. The economic and human burden of war, added to the stress of social dislocations caused by rapid industrialization, was sufficient to bring the whole edifice down.

Soviet historiography made much of the 'internal contradictions' of the tsarist system that precipitated the 1905 uprisings as well as that of November 1917 itself. That year, in the midst of a disastrous war and chaos on the streets, Nicholas II abdicated, and the Provisional Government that replaced his regime sought, ineffectively, to govern.

Soviet historiography also divided the Revolution into two phases: the historically necessary 'bourgeois–democratic' phase of April 1917, and then the historically inevitable 'socialist' phase, when the Bolsheviks first gained control over the Petrograd Councils of Workers and Soldiers' Deputies (the Soviets) and then wrested power from the government by armed insurrection. Governance was hijacked.

The role played by Empire in the gathering catastrophe is sometimes overlooked. Imperial Pan-Slavism, often in an Orthodox guise, was a pillar of imperial policy, and is directly implicated in Imperial Russia's support for Serbia against Austria in 1914, a link in the chain of events that led to the First World War. This policy also alienated many of the Empire's subject peoples, Catholic Poles and Lithuanians, and the Muslim and Turkic populations of Central Asia and the Caucasus. Moscow as much as St. Petersburg symbolized the oppression of the Empire, each as alien as the other. Even without the threat of war, and the social crisis of industrialization in its cities, the Empire was already under strain. Many of the leaders of the revolution-to-be were internal exiles, banished to Siberia or elsewhere within its boundaries, or were émigrés outside it. The leadership of the Bolshevik Party was disproportionately represented by the Empire's non-Russian subjects, including Joseph Viassiaronovich Dzhugashvili, Stalin. Few were native to Moscow.

In a sense, the Empire would eventually come home, but now with Moscow as its capital. It would take several years of chaos and civil war before it was so designated by resolution of the Pan-Russian Congress of Soviets in December 1922. Moscow would be governed by 'socialist principles of federalism and of proletarian internationalism'. Over time, the new Soviet empire, with Moscow now as its centre, would encounter many of the same challenges faced by the tsarist one.

With the establishment of Soviet power in Moscow in 1917, the city became an object of veneration for those who believed, some with religious intensity, that a new and hopeful era was at hand.

The Revolution represented the End of Days, the Second Coming in proletarian guise. That mixture of early hope and faith receded (but did not disappear) following revolutionary disasters in Germany and central Europe. By the early 1920s revolutions had failed in Germany and Hungary, and the Red Army had been thrown back from the gates of Warsaw.

Once he gained undisputed control, Stalin put to an abrupt halt any practical steps to promote world revolution. In

1936 he introduced his policy of 'Socialism in one Country', favouring the strengthening of the world's first socialist state over exporting revolution and, by implication, the creation of an empire beyond all empires. In the process, he destroyed the émigré elite of the original international revolutionary movement, many of them Old Bolsheviks, close comrades of Lenin and hence Stalin's potential rivals, among them Trotsky. Trotsky, a former Menshevik, had earlier opposed Stalin, and continued to oppose his policies. In 1940 Trotsky was murdered in Mexican exile. The assassin made an unusual choice of weapon, a mountaineering ice-axe.

Revolution transformed Moscow. Until Stalin's final ascendancy in the 1930s Moscow experienced many heady days of revolutionary socialism, unrestricted idealism and belief in the brotherhood of man—provided one was a worker or at least a peasant. Enthusiasm was sometimes limited by post-war crop failure, famine and the epidemics of the early 1920s as well as the exigencies of civil war, but none of this seemed to have much effect upon the idealists' revolutionary ardour, particularly if they lived outside the country. The honeymoon of revolution lasted only a couple of decades, but in the midst of hardship, it brought with it a starburst of artistic and cultural creativity.

Throughout the 1930s Moscow still remained, in the eyes of many, a revolutionary beacon, whatever the twists and turns of Soviet policy (or 'Party Line') of the day. The capital of the world communist movement was the invincible bastion against fascism, and the light of the future. The Molotov–Ribbentrop Pact was therefore the great betrayal, not only of countries and the international working class, but of the future itself. It is arguable that the pact, together with its secret clauses, did more damage to communism than all of the suffering visited upon the Soviet people by their own government, the artificially induced famines in Ukraine, the mass ethnic deportations, the purge trials, and the Gulag.

For some disillusioned believers, Moscow revealed itself as a city as venal as any other, not the City on the Hill, the Marxist New Jerusalem. Even so, Moscow remained the capital of world revolution until 1943, when, in deference to allied sensibilities, Stalin disbanded the Comintern. The Comintern was reinvented and renamed as the Cominform, a less revolutionary body, following the Soviet takeover of Eastern Europe. In due course Moscow became a kind of grotesque mirror-image of NATO Brussels as military headquarters of the Warsaw Pact, and also like Brussels, headquarters of a European trading bloc, the CMEA (Council of Mutual Economic Assistance or COMECON), the Eastern economic locus of power in a bipolar world.

The act of making Moscow the capital of a revolutionary state had given the city a global vocation lasting for 70 years of sacrifice and martyrdom until the economically and politically impossible system that sustained the Soviet Union finally collapsed under its own weight.

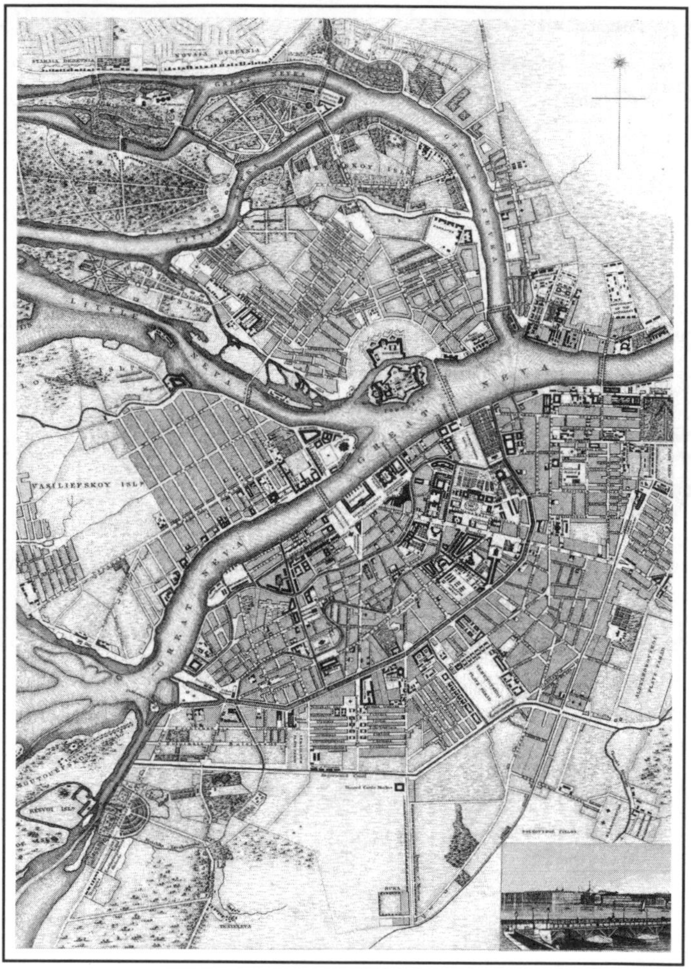

Eighteenth-century St. Petersburg, as shown in this map of 1834, was everything that Moscow was not: logical and planned, the product of the Enlightenment, its grid urban pattern the opposite of Moscow's historically determined layout.

Chapter Six
Anti-Cities

In 1904, an apocalyptical poem by Brusilov, 'The Pale Horse', inspired the symbolist poet Blok to write 'The Last Day', the first in a gloomy series called 'The City'. The modern city was 'a curse of the beast... the final curse of man, a labyrinth with many doors and no exits... populated by people with small, compressed, cubic souls'.

James Billington, *The Icon and the Axe*, 1970

Gorod is a word deeply rooted in most Slavic languages, including Russian, and indicates an enclosed space, by extension a walled city. Russian attitudes toward cities run from Alexander Blok's dreadful nightmare of an urban hell, the realm of the Antichrist—as many of the Old Believers thought of St. Petersburg—to a City on the Hill, a New Jerusalem. The thirteenth-century legend of the fortress monastery-city of Kitezh, which resisted the Tatar invasions and miraculously submerged beneath the waters of Lake Svetloyar, became the theme of Rimsky-Korsakov's opera, *The Tale of the Invisible City*. In a premonition of the trial at the hands of the Nazis that her home city of Leningrad would soon undergo, Anna Akhmatova wrote a tortured poem of suffering and redemption in the spring of 1940. It was entitled 'Passage to Kitezh'.

It is said that those pure of heart can just hear the sounds of the bells of Kitezh from beneath the lake at Svetloyar's edge. In the darkest days of fighting during the Second World War, mothers would come to the lake to pray on their knees for the lives of their sons.

Somewhere between 'the curse of the beast' and Kitezh lies Moscow, and its negations, Moscow's 'anti-cities'. They could be monasteries as well as alternative seats of government, and occasionally places of escape for Russia's rulers. Even before Ivan the Terrible established a state-within-a-state with its headquarters at Aleksandrovskaya Sloboda, he maintained a secluded country house at Ostrovka, outside Moscow, and undertook pilgrimages to the Troitska-Sergeev Monastery in expiation for his earthly sins. The Romanov tsars would later build Kolomenskoye, a gingerbread dream-palace of wood elaborately decorated with folkloric motifs and architectural styles found in the half-pagan north-east of European Russia.

Prefiguring Versailles by nearly two centuries, the complex at Kolomenskoye represented the imagery of national myth brought to life. The Palace of the Zhar-Ptitsa or Firebird, glittering in bright colours and gold, was a re-creation of a fairy tale, a kind of Kitezh for the tsars. It was demolished because of its advanced state of dilapidation on the instructions of Catherine II in 1768, but its memory lives on in the red-brick architecture of the Historical Museum (formerly the Lenin Museum) next to Red Square, and of the Residence of the French Embassy in downtown Moscow.

The great medieval city of Moscow 'of forty times forty' churches held a balance between the sacred and the profane that set it apart from the cities of the West. After the collapse of Constantinople in 1453, no other European city was at once a fortress, seat of government and seat of faith, a holy city that became, in Boris Godunov's inspiration, a 'New Jerusalem'. The establishment of the patriarchate in Moscow in 1589 was the ecclesiastical expression of Boris' vision, which found its material counterpart in his project to recreate the Church of the Resurrection in Jerusalem, whose rotunda housed the Holy Sepulchre. This grand project never came to pass, cut short by Boris' death in 1605. His idea endured, however, and New Jerusalem became a reality in the middle of the seventeenth century when Patriarch Nikon established a monastery of that name at Istra, on the outskirts of Moscow.

The same impulse that led to the New Jerusalem Monastery as an idealized, sacred place inspired secular equivalents in the twentieth century. The tomb of Lenin on Red Square amounts to a holy sepulchre. According to the architectural historian Andrey Ikonnikov, the combination mausoleum and tribunal that replaced the original wooden structure followed the medieval Russian tradition of constructing a building in memory of the dead , as opposed to a statue. In the face of the Tamurlane legend (p.54) there is also a persistent story that its architect was inspired by the tomb of Cyrus the Great. In any event, Moscow became a place of pilgrimage.

By way of contrast, some other Russian cities became non-destinations. Stalinist secrecy rendered many towns into places that did not exist, strange combinations of hidden Kitezh and monastery, known only by a number or a misleading postal code, if at all. They did not appear on maps. There, isolated from the rest of the world and its mundane problems, scientists led privileged lives designing weapons of massive destructive power.

Alternative Cities

With St. Petersburg, the ideal became real. At great human and material cost, it became Moscow's near-nemesis, in a sense Moscow's anti-city: rationally planned, neoclassical in design and (at least superficially) Western in spirit, the mirror-opposite of Moscow. Both parasitic upon Moscow as a source of state revenue and symbiotic with it, eighteenth- and nineteenth-century St. Petersburg housed the source of imperial authority that Moscow could not survive without. After 1812, Moscow recovered from the ruins in which the Napoleonic invasion had left it, largely because the imperial court at St. Petersburg ordered its reconstruction.

Both Moscow and St. Petersburg spawned their own anti-cities, idealized versions of themselves—Odessa for St. Petersburg in the eighteenth and nineteenth century, Magnitogorsk for Moscow in the twentieth, each alternative cities of their own times. These anti-cities repeated a pattern already well established in Moscow's history, echoing the contradictory role played by the great monasteries and convents of Romanov Russia. As alternatives to the urban model exemplified by Moscow, these protectors of the city and tax-exempt holders of vast estates were at once havens from the power of the state and its earthly authorities, and as servants to it, performing the role of prison, place of refuge and, upon occasion, burial-ground.

Moscow's ultimate anti-city came from the drawing-boards of architects of the 1920s. Moscow would become its own antithesis. In many plans, there would be a 'Moscow which is to come... a place where the Jacob's ladder rises leading to a higher reality'.[3] The ancient city would be razed, and in its place an urban complex would stand, the locus of a new socialist civilization. The same instincts that inspired Boris Godunov inspired the visionaries of the 1920s as they drew up plans for a radiant city expressing the ideals of socialism in the language of architecture. Moscow would become the beacon of world socialism, as medieval Moscow had been a beacon for the true faith.

It takes considerable historical imagination to recognize that the occupants of the Kremlin, its walls emanating permanence and solidity, were not permanently settled in it but transitory migrants. Even Russian rulers abandoned it. Together with his entire court Ivan the Terrible withdrew in 1564 to Aleksandrovskaya Sloboda after having successfully defended

Muscovy against a combined Polish–Lithuanian attack in the north and a Tatar attack from the south. His withdrawal was a transparently calculated act to induce his boyars (whom he suspected of insufficient loyalty) to beg for his return and to reaffirm their allegiance. When the anticipated results materialized, he returned to Moscow and the Kremlin to scenes of great rejoicing.

The implications of his withdrawal from Moscow were dire, for they were a prelude to his decision a year later to divide Muscovy into two parts: the *oprichnina*, the former territory of Novgorod over which he held total power and unrestricted authority; and the rest, the *zemshchina*, to be governed by his boyars. Certain districts of Moscow also belonged exclusively to the *oprichnina.*

Ivan's experiment in governance by appointing only those to run the *oprichinina* who were directly responsible to him, as opposed to the traditional boyars who had their own fiercely independent attitude to the Muscovite tsardom, turned out to be a disaster. Mounted on black horses and dressed in black with monk-like cowls, the *oprichniki* wore emblems of dogs' heads and brooms to signify that they bit like dogs and would sweep the superfluous from the land.[4] In their orgies of violence across the Russian countryside they were also responsible for the destruction of Novgorod in 1570, which in the light of the continuing threat that Muscovy faced from Lithuania was an open invitation to invasion. Reminiscent of the sack of Constantinople by the Fourth Crusade in April 1204, which 'surpassed even all its predecessors in faithlessness and duplicity, in brutality and greed',[5] the destruction of Novgorod was such that it never really recovered. Like the Crusaders, the *oprichniki* destroyed what they had come to protect. Ironically, the Crimean Tatar Devlet Girei led to their downfall, for the *oprichniki* proved incapable of defending Moscow against his defending Moscow against his exceptionally violent attack of 1571. After unbridled tortures, the still-living remains of the *oprichnina* leaders were put to merciful death, and the *oprichnina* disbanded.

The significance of Aleksandrovskaya Sloboda to Moscow however endured. It was here that Ivan sought refuge from wars and enemies to the north and south, as well as from plague and fire in Moscow. It was here that Ivan bludgeoned his son to death in 1581. It became the staging-base for the construction of a fortress at Vologda, coincidentally the main base of the English Muscovy Company, on the northern marches to the White Sea. Besides the fortress, integral to Ivan's strategic chain of northern defences was the Monastery of the Transfiguration on Solovetski Island. The monastery figured in Ivan's contingency plans as a departure-point for his escape to England should the need arise.

In the looting of Novgorod, the great wooden doors of St. Sophia Cathedral were removed and installed in Vologda's cathedral of the same name, modelled after Fiorovianti's Uspensky Sobor. Based as much as on legend as on fact, Ivan's project to create a new capital at Vologda never materialized, but the Cathedral of St. Sophia of Vologda, replica of the holy heart of Moscow, bears mute evidence of his intentions.

Attempts to abandon Moscow in one form or other began with Aleksandrovskaya Sloboda and Vologda, the first of Moscow's anti-cities. Ivan's example of an 'internal flight from Moscow' most likely provided the inspiration of Boris Godunov's walled compound of Borisov Gorodok, later to be copied in such tsarist estates on the fringes of Moscow as Kolomenskoe and Archangelskoe. Stalin's compound at Kuntsovo, 'a large but austere two-storey mansion painted a grim camouflage green... with a complex of guardhouses, two concentric fences, innumerable checkpoints and at least a hundred guards',[6] is their direct descendant.

Abandonment of Moscow was not always upon the

impulse of the ruler. On more than one occasion, plagues or conflagration were joined by invasion to drive the tsar out of the city. The abandonment of Moscow in 1812—the tsar and his government were in St. Petersburg, and for inexplicable reasons Napoleon had decided not to attack *that* capital—came close to repeating itself on 15 October 1941. As fighting approached the outskirts of Moscow, the State Defence Committee directed the relocation of the Soviet government to Kuybyshev.

Monasteries as Anti-Cities

The real anti-cities of Moscow, however, were not its historical alternatives chosen by the tsars, or places of temporary retreat, but the realms of the spirit, the monasteries. They were places of holy isolation, and if not rest (for monks worked hard in their assigned 'obediences', from agriculture to building walls) then for learning and, upon occasion, healing. Although this was the subject of an early debate, they were also in principle the antithesis of material glory, becoming nonetheless among the richest entities of tsardom, exempt from taxes, opulent recipients of bequests, receivers of paying pilgrims and owners of slaves and of vast estates holding the best and most fertile lands of the Muscovite state.

They were also places of imprisonment, arsenals for weapons and gunpowder, and fortresses in their own right, serving as a ring of defence around the fifteenth-century city-state. By the seventeenth century, as the monasteries spread outward, they became forward-bases in the expansion of the Russian empire.[7] At the beginning of the Soviet period, monasteries played a role contradictory to their original purposes. Red Moscow had the dubious honour of being the testing-ground of Soviet forced-labour camps. Appearing in 1918 under the wartime term, 'concentration camps', these camps acted as holding-pens for those held in detention for up to five years. The very first of such camps of Bolshevik Russia was established in Novospasski Monastery, whose burial vaults held the tombs of the Romanovs. By 1920 the NKVD and Cheka were operating two other camps in the closed-down monastery of Andronikov and Ivanovsky Convent.[8]

The intertwining of religious and secular history of Russian monasteries in service to the Muscovite state began early. As military strong points, the monasteries and military towns like Samara played the role of anchors in the *cherta* defensive lines that between the fourteenth and eighteenth centuries[9] spread out from Moscow, forming barriers to invasion. To the south of Moscow, three great defensive lines, extending over hundreds of kilometres each, were designed to break up attacks from Tatar cavalry. The monasteries in these lines later played a reverse role as staging-posts for imperial Russia's drive to the south. To the west, monasteries stood against Lithuanian and Polish invasion, bastions of Orthodoxy against the Catholic infidels. To the north, Ivan the Terrible's Monastery on Solovetski Island held out against Swedish invaders in 1611 when Moscow was under Polish occupation—and later against Moscow itself in 1673 when the monastery opposed reforms to the Orthodox liturgy introduced by Patriarch Nikon and the tsar. It would later become notorious as one of Stalin's earliest Gulag prisons.

Contrary to Western tradition, the monasteries encircling Moscow were not placed on the outer reaches of the city for seclusion but to protect it: the city developed behind the fortified ramparts of the monasteries. The pattern of monastic sites is obscured by the city's outward growth, now extending far beyond these defences, but is still visible if one follows the city's Boulevard Ring tracing the city's original perimeter. In today's Moscow these monasteries can have a slightly theme-park atmosphere as gawking, camera-laden visitors intermingle with the deeply devout. Some monks stoically accept tourism as a penance.[10]

Further out stand the purely military fortresses of Nizhnii Novgorod (1500-01), Tula (1507-20), Kolumna (1525-31), Zaraisk (1528-31) and Kashira (1531). It has been argued that Europe was saved the worst depredations of the Mongols and Tatars thanks to the strength of the fortress of Moscow and its outer defences, beginning with its monasteries, further out their five military counterparts and finally the three *cherta* lines.[11] Whatever the historical accuracy of this argument, it remains a persistent Russian belief that the monastic defences of Moscow, clad in white and enclosing and protecting their golden-domed churches, were the saviours of Europe from Eastern barbarism. President Gorbachev's vision of 'a common European home' extending from the Atlantic to the Urals was an indirect reflection of this belief. Gorbachev's grand idea fell apart in the aftermath of the collapse of the Soviet Union, and finally disappeared.

In their different ways three religious buildings, two monasteries and one convent, speak for all such places in Moscow. The first is Moscow's oldest monastery, St. Daniel, which was founded by Prince Daniel of Vladimir expressly to defend the city from the Tatars, a purpose shared with the later Donskoy, Simonov and Novospassky monasteries.

According to legend, St. Daniel Monastery is the progenitor of all of Moscow's monasteries, and has been rescued from disaster a number of times, each attributable to the heavenly intervention of its namesake, including its miraculous salvation from a Tatar attack in 1591, and its resurrection from its destruction in the Time of Troubles, and yet again from marauding French troops in 1812. Formally closed in the 1930s, the monastery underwent a further series of humiliations. Its cloisters were turned into barracks for orphans and juvenile delinquents, and into workshops. These humiliations descended into tragedy in 1937 with the 'St. Daniel Brotherhood Case' in which Bishop Feodor, the father superior of the monastery, and 50 of his monks were shot. Following the collapse of communism, St. Daniel Monastery was 'the first to be reborn after 50 years of desolation' with its consecration as spiritual and administrative centre of the Orthodox Church.

With the reconstruction of the Cathedral of Christ the Saviour and St. Daniel Monastery, the Moscow legacy of tsarism in its spiritual form has taken a physical shape. But even the martyrdom these buildings endured may not have prepared them for the assault of post-Soviet commercialism. The latter is as great a challenge to Moscow's religious buildings and their place in defining the city's identity as any they have faced in the past.

The second religious building is the Convent of Novodevichy, guarding the western approaches to Moscow, constructed in 1524 to celebrate the return of Smolensk to Russia after more than 100 years of Lithuanian domination. The convent became the symbol and in effect the protector of Smolensk, the outermost western defence of the Muscovite state, for from the west the road leads through Smolensk directly to Moscow—and at Moscow's gates stands the Convent of Novodevichy, Convent of the New Maidens.

If celebration and defence were the impulses for establishing the convent, its life was defined as refuge, house arrest and torture, and finally desecration at the hands of the Bolsheviks, who converted it into the Museum of Female Emancipation. Before that role was passed to St. Daniel Monastery, it was used as the official offices of the metropolitan in the 1980s.

One incident in the convent's history serves to identify it: the incarceration of Peter the Great's half-sister and rival to the throne, Sophia. She conspired in 1698 with the *streltsy*, the Kremlin's musketeer praetorian guard, to accede to the throne herself. Hearing of the conspiracy in Troitsa-Sergeev Monastery, Peter ruthlessly suppressed the incipient rebellion. Before the convent, 30 gibbets were constructed in a quadrangle, from which 230 of the conspirators were hung: 'The three principal ringleaders, who presented a petition to Sophia... were hanged close to the windows of the princess so near that Sophia could touch them... I believe this drove her to take the religious habit, in order to pass to a better life...'[12]

After Sophia's death Peter turned the convent into an orphanage, later to be restored by Empresses Anna and Catherine the Great. Today it survives as a museum. In Soviet times a foreign-currency shop was located nearby, and many gravestones were removed from its premises to stabilize the tunnels of the Moscow Metro, then under construction. Perhaps appropriately, its graveyard now holds the body of Khrushchev, denied a place in the Kremlin wall, his portrait sculpted by Nieizvestny giving him a curiously spiritual look. Among the other names found on Novodevichy's tombstones are those of Anastas Mikoyan, whose last position was chairman of the Presidium of the Supreme Soviet, and the only senior Soviet official to attend Khrushchev's funeral, held in the rain. In a gesture of respect and affection he gave the coffin a light tap as he passed by. Besides Stalin's wife Nadezhda Alliluyeva and the Soviet poet Vladimir Mayakovsky, Khrushchev was assigned a burial spot by resolution of the Party Central Committee.

Still resplendent in the beauty of its restored eighteenth-century spires and cupolas, the convent has thus become a city of the dead, perhaps the ultimate anti-city. It was at least spared the fate of some other monasteries, such as Novospassky which was turned into a necropolis where the mainly foreign communist victims of the Stalinist purges were secretly buried after their visit to the Lubyanka execution chambers. In a minor counterpoint to Novodevichy Convent's life story, Vladimir Tatlin, the visionary architect who designed the never-built Tower to the Third International in the 1920s, used as his offices the second floor of the convent's bell tower overlooking the graveyard.

The third monastery, Ivan the Terrible's object of pilgrimage, is the holiest place in Russia. The history of Troitsa-Sergeev (or Trinity-St. Sergius) Monastery and that of Moscow are as inseparable as are their places in Russian national identity. Echoing Moscow, it is a fortress of military and spiritual power. Above all, the monastery is of the spirit, a place of refuge and solitude, the very opposite of Moscow's Third Rome and the buildings that express that idea. It is therefore the antithesis of the Kremlin's Uspensky Sobor, yet its outward appearance shows a close family resemblance to buildings of the Kremlin itself.

The monastery is replete with legend and historical fact. Here, Ivan the Terrible's father forced his first wife to take the habit on account of her alleged barrenness. It provided shelter to Prince Pozharsky (whose statue stands on Red Square before St. Basil's with his comrade-in-arms Minin), wounded in a failed Moscow uprising in March 1611. A year later Pozharsky succeeded in expelling the Poles from the Kremlin. In this secular age, the monastery is a UNESCO World Heritage Site, joining the company of the temple complex of Angkor Wat, the pharaonic monuments at Abu Simbel and the City of Bath.

Situated some 90 kilometres north-east of Moscow, Troitsa-Sergeev Monastery was founded in 1345 by the monk Sergius of Radonezh as a small wooden hermitage in a forest clearing—'in the desert', meaning 'wilderness', a term derived from early Church experience in the sands of Egypt and the Sinai. He lived in harmony with nature, befriending a bear, and his saintliness attracted others, including the often-feuding Muscovy princes who sought his advice. In September 1380 the Grand Prince of Moscow Dmitry Donskoy sought his blessing in a military campaign, the outcome of which was the Battle of Kulikovo Field, the first significant Russian victory against the Tatars. Within its confines, Andrei Rublev painted his masterpiece *The Holy Trinity,* considered by many the perfect icon. The monastery became the object of princely patronage, although this did not prevent it from being destroyed by the Tatars in 1408; the rebuilt walls were strong enough to resist the Polish invaders 300 years later. By the sixteenth century its garrison numbered 20,000 men, and its walls at the base were 15 metres thick.

Declared the patron saint of the Russian state, Sergius was canonized in 1422. The monastery's subsequent history, including its use as a base of operations by Prince Pozharsky against the Poles and as Peter the Great's refuge in his struggle against the rebellious *streltsy*, confirmed the monastery's relationship to the power of the grand princes and tsars, the place of their baptism throughout the entire Romanov period. Over time, it became one of the wealthiest ecclesiastical estates in Russia, a centre of scholarship and learning next only to Kiev itself. Following the Crimean debacle of 1854-56, a company was formed to build a railway to the monastery from Moscow by private donation as an act of penance, but in the tradition of many of Moscow's other grand projects, it was never completed.

Troitska-Sergeev Monastery survived the Soviet period as the centre of Russian Orthodoxy. Amid the chaos of revolutionary Russia the mystical philosopher and writer Vasily Rozanov sought shelter in its solitude, and wrote *Apocalypse of Our Time,* declaring the Russian Revolution a disaster of biblical proportions for all civilization. Despite this inauspicious slur on the Soviet regime's possibilities, the monastery received the grudging forbearance of ex-seminarian Stalin, who in the midst of the Soviet Union's existential struggle with Nazi Germany made his own rough peace with the Orthodox Church in

1943. It suffered the indignity of having a Museum of Atheism erected within its walls, and in the post-Stalin period was the scene of anti-religious demonstrations culminating in the confrontations at the Easter Festival, when the celebrants—contrary to popular belief, they were by no means all old peasant women—walked in procession around the monastery's Uspensky Cathedral, a gesture representing the holy circle of eternal life, the symbol of the Resurrection. A Russian friend, Sergei, himself a member of the Moscow State University's Komsomol Executive Committee, took me to watch an Easter procession at the monastery in 1965, when the 'conservative communism' of the early Brezhnev period was just getting under way. Leaving the cathedral, the celebrants were taunted by drunken youths bussed in for the occasion. The police were also out in force, apparently tasked with keeping the two sides apart, but doing little to control the crowd. Sergei was quiet. Later he took me to his family dacha, where he offered me a piece of *kulich,* traditional Russian Easter cake.

The lingering Soviet suspicion that the Orthodox Church in general, and St. Sergius Monastery in particular, represented a potential alternative source of political legitimacy and therefore a challenge to the regime itself was matched by an equivalent belief in the West. This issue figured in a policy review of Soviet–British relations initiated by Prime Minister Thatcher in 1983.[13]

If disfigurement at the hands of the Soviet authorities did not take place within the monastery, disfigurement of a different kind occurred outside its walls. In the 1930s the town that surrounded it had its name changed from Sergeev Sloboda ('The Settlement of St. Sergei') to Zagorsk, after a Bolshevik revolutionary blown up by a terrorist bomb; in other words, it was an attempt to erase the place's memory. Traditionally the town was famous for its manufacture of *matryushki,* wooden nesting dolls, but in 1947 Zagorsk housed secret facilities for the Soviet effort to develop smallpox as a biological weapon. After the fall of communism, the town reverted to its original name.

The relationship the monasteries of Moscow had with their mother-city was both symbiotic and parasitic, in some respects similar to the relationship between the Kremlin and the city which surrounded it. Although the countryside was also taxed, like their urban counterparts the service nobility were generally tax-exempt, the city—or more accurately, the community of townsmen—being the major source of tax revenue. Tax exemption also applied to the monasteries, holders of vast estates in their own right. Moscow's jumble of contradictory tax laws encompassed a bewildering range of exceptions and concessions, including the tsar's personal monopolies and excises. The hugely profitable trade in vodka was the exclusive monopoly of the household of the tsar. Differentiation in tax status also had physical effects on the look of Moscow. There were districts set aside for the *gosti,* tax-exempt foreigners, and also for tax-exempt Cossacks in the tsar's military service. This had the effect of narrowing the tax base and increasing the tax burden on the townsman-taxpayer, who more often than not saw his contribution absorbed by the state for its own purposes of grandeur or war, while civic essentials such as adequate sewerage or clean water went wanting.

Monasteries and other ecclesiastical establishments were part of the problem. They were tax-exempt islands of fiscal refuge, living within the city, drawing supplies and services from it, but also existing apart from it. The archipelago of monasteries extending beyond Moscow lived in their own universes, dedicated to prayer and war, golden-domed and adorned with bells summoning monks to spiritual duties, or alternatively warning of impending attack, sending the message further up the line. Some were fabulously rich, isolated by God and tsar from the tax-collector.

The vibrancy of monastic communities contrasted with the struggling townsmen increasingly burdened with ordinary and extraordinary tax levies and other duties often to be paid in terms of *tiaglo* (or *corvée*), i.e. labour or personal service, for example by acting as tax-collectors for their own communities. The walls of Kitai-Gorod were built by the civic obligation of *tiaglo*. In sixteenth-century Russia the threat of urban collapse increased, the consequence not only of the Time of Troubles, famine and plague but also of the depopulation of Russian towns, including Moscow, as townsmen undertook an exodus to monastic estates to avoid the growing and remorseless burden of urban taxes.

It is estimated that in the fifteenth century Moscow's population was about 100,000. At the end of the Time of Troubles it had fallen by about 70 per cent. In the 1620s Moscow had a population of some 20,000, with many still-empty or burned-out houses, and its population continuing to drop. The early Romanov tsars recognized the problem of 'the flight from Russian cities' to the tax-exempt monastery lands and its implications for state and personal revenues,[14] but it took further reforms in the eighteenth century, including those of Peter the Great (who considered monks shirkers and wastrels) and his imposition of state control over monastic estates, before Moscow's population stabilized. Only then did it begin its rapid recovery followed by sustained, if uneven, growth.[15]

Moscow and Its Children

Novgorod, Borisov Gorodok, Aleksandrovskaya Posad/Vologda, Kolomenskoe and Kuntsevo represented alternatives to the city of Moscow or, for the select few, an escape from it.

St. Petersburg was the most dramatic case of all. In their own separate ways monasteries played a similar role. All had profound effects on Moscow's physical development and contributed to its character of place. There were exceptions. Stalin's Kuybyshev was not an alternative to Moscow; it was merely Moscow's provisional alter ego, created of necessity in time of war. There is, however, some historic poetry in Stalin's designation of Kuybyshev as Moscow's temporary administrative successor. In its pre-Bolshevik identity as Samara, it was constructed in the mid sixteenth century to be a military strongpoint in the *cherta* line expressly for the exercise of control over the entire Volga region, and hence ultimately over Moscow as well.

Moscow's evolution as a city was affected not only by the influences of these 'anti-cities' but also by the experience of replicating itself. The kremlin and town of Kazan, reconstructed after their conquest by Ivan the Terrible in the sixteenth century, show the distinctive urban characteristic of the expanding Muscovite state, complete with a fortress at the centre of a surrounding town. In the case of Kazan, much of its Asiatic character was retained with *souqs* or trading districts abutting its kremlin walls.

In belated recognition of the non-Russian ethnic composition of Kazan a mosque was built within the kremlin walls in the nineteenth century, making it unique in Russia. Still, the overall effect was Muscovite. Ivan the Terrible's architect, Postnik, was in charge of Kazan's reconstruction. He was later responsible for building St. Basil's. Mosques are still a rarity in Moscow. Perhaps the best-known is the mausoleum at Poklonnaya Gora, the site of Moscow's war memorial. It shares space with an Orthodox church and a synagogue.

Over time, 'Little Moscows' spread throughout Russia and the empire, inspired by the capital until its demotion in the eighteenth century and through the nineteenth, when the architectural style of St. Petersburg provided the model. Following the Revolution, after a period of hopeful experimentation Moscow again took the lead, this time through the instrumentalities of central planning and the Stalinist requirements of uniformity in substance as well as style. 'National in form, socialist in content' defined whatever regional variation was permitted in city planning or architecture, often expressed as a discrete ethnic frieze decorating a façade. The practical ramifications of this general line on Stalinist nationalities policy were elusive enough, and it was wiser to follow the lead of Moscow; and as the Moscow style changed, to change with it.

If the Party's line did not enforce conformity (often meaning uniformity), central planning organizations in Soviet Moscow did. Under Khrushchev and his successors in particular, a restricted number of building plans as modular, all-purpose templates were drawn up for use throughout the Soviet Union, from public office space to multi-block living complexes, all designed for maximum space at minimum cost, with only basic skill and material required for their erection. These plans were integral to the Gosplan planning system which controlled 'the commanding heights' of the Soviet economy, and to its subsidiary body, Gosstroi, the executive agency for construction throughout the USSR (that agency's subsidiary body for Moscow, logically enough, was Mosstroi). As a result, even today Soviet-era buildings from the Baltic Sea to Vladivostok, all cloned from Moscow, have a similar look and feel; some would add, 'and smell'.

Once the Muscovite 'socialist style' settled down into a rigid set of architectural canons during the Stalin and Khrushchev period, certain anomalies appeared, for the apartment-bloc complexes, designed for Moscow's high-density population and climatic conditions, were not universally appropriate. Solitary multi-storey blocks appeared on the steppe of Kazakhstan, alone and bereft of urban infrastructure.[16] In northern Siberia similar buildings were erected, duly insulated but still suffering enormous heat loss because of their height and surface exposure. In Norilsk, a Siberian nickel-mining town above the Arctic Circle, steel girders had to be driven into the frozen muskeg to stabilize the shifting of these buildings in the spring thaws.

Moscow's appearance was to undergo a dramatic change with the architectural revolution that took place in the latter half of the 1700s and the emergence of the so-called 'Empire Style'. It became a guiding architectural principle for over a century, and was replicated throughout the Russian provinces. Public buildings and private estates in the provinces owe their kinship to this style, perhaps in unconscious recognition of Moscow's relationship to them. Neoclassical in inspiration, the 'Empire Style' is sometimes named after its chief proponent, Matvei Kazakov, who had established his reputation in the construction of the colonnaded, symmetrical villas of Moscow. The style was inspired by the example of St. Petersburg, and by architectural fashion in the West. It was a complete break with Moscow's architectural tradition, but rapidly became a *sine qua non* for buildings across Russia and the provinces.

In a typical Russian town of the empire, close to the centre would be an Orthodox church sometimes with the onion-dome of northern Russia, but sometimes in the baroque style inherited from the time of Peter the Great. As in Moscow, the widespread use of baroque architecture for religious buildings was restrained because of its frequent association with Roman Catholicism, and hence the enemies, the Poles and Lithuanians. This, however, did not prevent the construction of baroque masterpieces in the Novodevichy Convent and in the Troitska-Sergeev Monastery, as well as other places in St. Petersburg and Moscow. They are rarer in the Baltic provinces of the Russian empire because of the influence of Lutheranism from East Prussia which favoured a more austere style. Baroque churches are more common west of the Urals than in Asia. Orthodox churches from Riga to Almaty generally bear a close resemblance to the Pre-Petrine churches of Moscow. The domes and layouts of traditional Russian Orthodox churches may have been inherited from Byzantium via Kiev, but the architectural inspiration comes from the wooden buildings of northern Russia, not from the brightly painted plaster, stucco and marble of the Catholic West. This leads to some 'cultural disconnects'. Dominating the Estonian capital of Tallinn is an Orthodox cathedral, done in the traditional, onion-dome style. At the time of Baltic independence it became an object of controversy as it symbolized Russian domination. In due course, the Estonian nationalist focus switched to a Soviet-era war memorial. The mostly-Russian congregation has been left in peace.

As the Russian Empire spread, Kazakov's style followed it. Any provincial town worthy of the name had a colonnaded public building. At the same time, wooden neoclassical villas typical of provincial estates appeared in Moscow. They often preserved in detail life in the countryside, including the serfs (who sometimes were dressed in Western-style livery and powdered wigs for great occasions) and the chickens. The aristocratic formality of St. Petersburg was far away.

There is some parallelism here. As the British Empire expanded, the housing of the colonialists from Simla in northern India to Cape Town in South Africa took on the look of rural Surrey. In New Delhi, high Victorian neoclassicism culminated in the Palace of the Viceroy, a huge arcaded pile of stone, complete with the obligatory Doric columns that made it heavily clear that India was indeed of empire. Even if the outposts of the Russian Empire were not overseas, and located on a contiguous landmass, the architectural impulse for replication was shared with other empires, as early as the Roman, but also the French, the Spanish, the Turkish (whose architectural styles the Russian Empire encountered in its expansion into the Balkans, the Caucasus and Central Asia) and even the Dutch—the three-storey buildings of Suriname are replicas of those of Amsterdam.

Emulation of Moscow architectural forms continued through Soviet times and beyond. Although not specifically Muscovite, the Soviet architectural style—which itself evolved, sometimes dramatically—spread throughout Soviet territory. For reasons not entirely clear, the great symbols of Moscow's High Stalinism, the monumental Seven Sisters, did not travel well, and replicas are found only in Kiev and in Warsaw, both cities which suffered horrifying war damage. The Kiev 'high building' lies just off its main street, the Kreschatik, and is bereft of the spire that Stalin insisted should replicate those of the Kremlin. In Soviet times the Warsaw 'high building' (called the 'Palace of Culture') was renowned for having in its basement the hottest strip-tease show in the Soviet Bloc.

East Berlin, the socialist showcase during the Cold War, was not graced with a Stalinist 'high building', even though the damage the city suffered was if anything even greater than what befell its two Eastern European counterparts; possibly this was because reconstruction of the city did not begin in earnest until Stalin's death in 1953. Instead, it received the full Soviet/Moscow treatment of pre-stressed, modular concrete construction of the late 1950s and early 1960s in Alexanderplatz, a huge square surrounded by uniform grey government buildings. Similar Soviet/Moscow architectural treatment was meted out to Kaliningrad, formerly Königsberg.

The Moscow Ideal Transported

It can be argued that secular emulation of Moscow began as early as the construction of the first kremlin along the first *cherta* line in the fourteenth century, and that in fact Moscow had borrowed much of its own urban style from Kiev, and from Pskov and Novgorod. Even in the mid eighteenth century Moscow was still a city of the Middle Ages, having expanded in successive concentric circles despite a number of near-death experiences, each one reflecting the challenges and events of the time. It was an enclosed city with high, narrow windows close together above dark twisting streets, often ending in *tupiks*, dead-ends. In cold weather it was covered in a smoky haze from thousands of house-fires and the burning of debris by the homeless. Above it all stood the Kremlin.

Emulation of Moscow belongs to tradition extending beyond isolated military outposts, secret scientific establishments and medieval monasteries. The walls of the great fortress of Smolensk, on the western road to Moscow, were built with hardened brick upon its reconquest by Russia in 1603. To construct them, a ban on the use of brick elsewhere was imposed throughout Russia, foretelling a similar ban on the use of stone anywhere but in St. Petersburg. The location of Smolensk destined it to the fate of many borderland cities of Russia, suffering first at the hands of the Tatars, then the Lithuanians and then the Poles. It was destroyed by the French in the nineteenth century and the Germans in the twentieth. Painfully evolved from means of defence to mere decoration, its parapets have continued to replicate the distinctive swallow-tail mullions of the Kremlin, themselves imported to Moscow in the designs of the Renaissance architects of northern Italy. The Kremlin walls sometimes took on a symbolic meaning as well. In Kazakhstan, Almaty's war memorial, loosely modelled after the memorial to the unknown soldier in Aleksandrovskii Gardens before the Kremlin, serves the same purpose as a place for newlyweds to lay their flowers. The monument depicts a Kazakh regiment wiped out in the defence of Moscow in 1941. As a backdrop to the figures of the soldiers stands a replica of the Kremlin walls, Moscow itself.

With a few notable exceptions, Soviet cities to the west of the Urals, particularly those badly damaged in wartime fighting, tended to follow in their reconstruction the layouts of their historic city-plans, since their underground infrastructure, including the water and sewerage systems built in the nineteenth and early twentieth centuries, generally remained intact. Often, however, the pattern of rehabilitation was from the outside in, with the new Moscow-designed apartment complexes and factories surrounding a centre left to its own devices. In the Baltic States, into the 1970s city centres were frequently left with burnt-out buildings, patrolled by packs of wild dogs and haunted by derelicts. On grounds of cost-effectiveness, state planning gave greater priority to new construction over reconstruction and repair, particularly for housing.[17]

East of the Urals the pattern was different in the towns that had sprung up during Russia's imperial expansion of the eighteenth and nineteenth centuries. Often reflecting their origins as military outposts, they retained their grid-like city plans (as in the case of Alma-Ata), a layout that made them particularly susceptible (as in the case of Tashkent) to the imposition of twentieth-century Moscow-based concepts of rectilinear city planning and wide boulevards. Consequently, much of their downtown areas could just as easily be mistaken for the suburban ring of the 1960s Soviet capital.

Whether east or west of the Urals, Soviet cities tended to share a number of common elements. There would be an Intourist hotel, often the tallest building of the town. In Moscow, the 3,200 room Rossiya Hotel, the largest hotel in Europe, was built on the foundations of a Stalinist 'eighth sister', a project cancelled by Khruschev in the 1960s. In its turn the hotel's destruction was mercifully ordered by Mayor Luzhkov in 2006. All Soviet cities contained a central square for public demonstrations, whether in favour of the regime and the local Communist Party leadership, or on the occasion of Soviet public holidays, such as 7 November, May Day, or the International Day of Democratic Women. Before Gorbachev's *perestroika,* rent-a-crowd demonstrations were also held for a variety of causes, against the Vietnam War and American imperialism or against Chinese big-power chauvinism, specifically military encroachments, along the Ussuri River.[18] Later, one of these squares, the Manezh in Moscow, was the scene of bitter demonstrations by mothers of soldiers lost in the Soviet intervention in Afghanistan.

These squares normally had a statue of Lenin, pointing onwards and upwards. Strangely, his likeness was missing from Red Square, possibly because his tomb beside a standing statue might look redundant and perhaps give the wrong impression. In the early Yeltsin years, when the Party had been declared illegal, pro-communist demonstrators had to resort to using a statue of Lenin on Oktyabrskaya Ploshchad as a rallying-point, across the river and several kilometres away from Red Square.

Following the collapse of communism, the location of Lenin's now-defunct statues and their implicit message of Moscow's pre-eminent role created a problem for the leaders of many newly independent states. Their first instinct was to distance themselves as quickly as possible from the failed Soviet regime, particularly if they themselves had been part of it. In 1991, just before the Soviet Union's final crisis, the imposing statue of Lenin overlooking Tbilisi was removed from the front of Party headquarters because, the Party first secretary told me, 'it interfered with the view'. The Lenin statue in the central square of Bishkek, capital of the Kyrgyz Republic, was allowed to remain for several years into the country's independence 'in recognition and respect for our own history', until it too was deemed a political embarrassment and replaced by a figure representing Ala Too, the mother of the Kyrgyz homeland.

The architectural tradition of emulating the capital (the distinction between Moscow and St. Petersburg was not always clear) is an old one. In the eighteenth and nineteenth centuries there was widespread copying of the 'St. Petersburg style' in the provinces. In many provincial towns, besides the obligatory statue of Lenin, or now possibly its replacement, there is more often than not a backdrop façade of ochre-coloured tsarist governmental buildings. Behind them loom high-rise apartment complexes inspired by Soviet-era Moscow.

Magnitogorsk: Soviet Moscow of the Future

The closest Soviet equivalent to the planned cities of the eighteenth century is Magnitogorsk, a Stalinist vision of urban development for the First Five-Year Plan of the early 1930s, but hardly a self-replication of Moscow. It represented in effect a socialist model city for which the means of production and its control were the ultimate arbiters of the new proletarian civilization. Magnitogorsk was Stalin's Odessa, a model city to be built according to the leading principles of its time, place and ideological fashion. Magnitogorsk, as Moscow's anti-city, is what the Soviet capital might have become had historical circumstance, economics and possibly even common sense not intervened.

Magnitogorsk is a heavily polluted city built to service

a vast iron and steel plant, already under construction in 1929. Its original design was inspired by the American steel town of Pittsburgh. The successful German architect Ernst May, who had played a leading role in the development of Frankfurt during the Weimar period, played the same role for Magnitogorsk as his Dutch predecessor Franz de Volan did for Odessa, responsible for overseeing the entire project. May's original plan, consisting of rows of superblock neighbourhoods running parallel to the massive plant but separated by a green belt, became a rope-like development with production and living quarters intertwined as the uncontrolled pace of factory construction outstripped that of housing. The result was an urban complex of troglodytic ugliness.

Stalin ordered Lazar Kaganovich, the senior Party member then responsible for rural collectivization, to transport some 20,000 peasants, themselves probably slave-labour kulaks,[19] to work on the project. At its height over 250,000 labourers, many living in tents, were engaged. As one observer noted, 'Soviet industry moved forward... with every manner of thunderous accident (collisions, explosions) with peasant boys twirling off frozen scaffolding, with many deaths, sudden or premature, in the usual atmosphere of myth and coercion, of error and terror—but it did move forward.'[20] Moscow still shows the scars of forced industrialization, but the experience it gained as the testing-ground for gigantic industrial projects made it the mother of Magnitogorsk, for the techniques in using forced labour in the construction of the city were the same.

The Stalinist vision of Moscow as a latter-day version of its own anti-city Magnitogorsk came only partially to fruition. The greatest similarity may have been the equivalent human costs in the building of the Moscow Metro and other mega-projects. The 'rope-like quality' of Magnitogorsk, caused by the unregulated intertwining of residential and industrial areas, was also characteristic of 1930s Moscow, without regard to the Moscow General Plan of 1935. The responsibility for implementation of the latter was given to the same Kaganovich, now Party chief of Moscow. Incompetent planning dogged them both. After playing a critical role in the production of steel for Soviet tanks in the Second World War, Magnitogorsk ran out of its own raw materials and now imports coal from the Kuznetsk Basin for its smelters, and its ore from Karaganda, Kazakhstan.

Soviet architecture and Soviet urban planning followed the same principles. In response to the arms race beginning in the 1950s, closed or secret cities, known as *zakrytiye administrativino-territoral'nye obrazovaniia* (ZATO) and often built by prisoners from the Gulags, were created to conduct research and technical development to support the Soviet military effort: sputniks, long-range missiles and warheads of grotesque explosive capacity, themselves deemed necessary to compensate for the relative inaccuracy of the missiles. According to one estimate,[21] there are about 40 ZATO, ranging from small individual facilities, such as the biological weapons dump on Vozrozhdenie Island[22] in the Aral Sea, to over a dozen full-blown cities with populations of over 20,000, each with restricted access and known only by their postcode identifiers, which are sometimes hidden or changed. Of the three with Moscow postcodes, Moscow-21, Moscow-300 and Moscow-400, the latter two are in fact located at Semipalatinsk, the nuclear testing facility in eastern Kazakhstan. Except for the very smallest, what they have in common is the street and building design of their parent-city, especially 1960s Moscow.

Moscow as *La Ville Radieuse*

In the early, heady days of NEP, following the Revolution and civil war, Moscow became a symbol for a better future for many of the exhausted and disillusioned. In the West they were survivors of the lost generation that had perished in the mud of Flanders; and in the East, survivors of entire armies lost on the plains and lakes of Mazuria. For many, Moscow's promise of progress and liberation, together with the prospect of the final triumph of the working classes over their capitalist exploiters, demanded a transformed Moscow.

Visionaries and architects set to work. At the time it was noted that architects were the most prominent among the professions that did *not* abandon Russia after the Revolution. Many were guided by their interpretation of Marxist concepts as applied to city planning and urban living. In one of his tracts, *Anti-Dühring*, Engels argued that in a socialist state the contradictions between cities and the countryside would disappear. By extension, the rural aspects of Moscow, under its many names still called the Peasant Metropolis, would be eliminated. The backward peasantry would be transformed into a socially conscious, red proletariat, and Moscow would become the engine-room of world revolution. A number of millennarian plans for the destruction of the city's inner core were drawn up, as plans were set in motion to make Moscow its own anti-city.

Ambitious plans for the renovation of cities are hardly the exclusive preserve of Moscow. By force of necessity, the reconstruction of London after the Great Fire of 1666, as well as Baron Haussmann's less urgent plans for Paris in the nineteenth century, are prime examples. Moscow itself was the subject of intensive city redevelopment after its Napoleonic destruction in 1812. Even earlier, in 1776, the Commission for the Arrangement of the Capital Cities of St. Petersburg and Moscow ordered a plan for the city which envisioned a reordering of the city centre to transform it into a place of tree-lined boulevards, squares and elegant parks. Bazhenov's plans for the Kremlin were part of this scheme. Like Franz de Volan's

Odessa, the needs of the middle and working classes—that is, those who gave texture (and, in fact, life) to the city, making it work—were not taken into account.

Before the First World War, however, some practical attempts were made to improve conditions in the cities, including Moscow, though falling short of the grand schemes of Paris or Berlin. Besides the cases of maladministration such as witnessed by Odessa, viable city planning was impeded by the generally obtuse attitude among officials about how a city should work and their responsibility for it. Reactionary statutes, restricted voting rights and lack of attention to essential city services were bad enough, but there was also the explosive growth of late-nineteenth-century Moscow, caused by uncontrolled industrialization and mismanagement of the destabilizing, long-term effects of thousands of ex-serfs, now freed from the land.

In the nineteenth century it was generally believed that peasant migrants to cities were uprooted, alienated and prone to irrational violence. This assessment permitted the authorities to dismiss the legitimacy of urban unrest and to use repressive measures against it.[23] Driven from impoverished and overtaxed land, it is estimated that after their emancipation peasants paid ten times as much tax to the state as the landed gentry, excluding indirect taxes on vodka, sugar, cotton and tea. In European Russia the overall death rate was almost 32 per thousand as compared to 20 in France and 16 in England. Consequently, the crop failures of 1891 in the country's Black Belt generated famine conditions that deepened already pestilential conditions in the Moscow slums. As if defying gravity, between 1890 and 1900 Moscow's population nevertheless continued its inexorable increase by 30 per cent, with the size of the workforce doubling to 500,000, half of whom were employed in the manufacturing sector. By the turn of the century, Moscow's overall population had tripled to about 1 million, almost doubling again by 1917, mostly by in-migration.

In 1885 the imperial Ministry of Internal Affairs established a technical committee to set building standards throughout the empire. It lacked the mandate to enforce its guidelines or to undertake city planning. Although there was a dim realization at the level of officials in St. Petersburg that 'something had to be done', Nicholas II and his immediate entourage, preoccupied with other problems, including the suppression of dissent and the maintenance of autocratic authority (as in the case of the failed Dumas following the 1905 disturbances), gave little sign of any awareness of the dimensions of the problem—or even that there was a problem at all. By the turn of the century the pressures of industrialization fell even on St. Petersburg, where the ban on wooden construction finally collapsed. In the latter days of the empire, city planning seemed a distant thought receding even further away.

This does not mean that in nineteenth-century Russia no attempt was made to found and construct latter-day versions of Kitezh, model communities in their own right. Some were indeed built, all of them representing an escape from noisome Moscow to a bucolic setting of never-never land Russia. This was an established tradition inherited from the monasteries, and with their distant retreats from Aleksandrovakaya Sloboda to Kolomenskoe, from the tsars themselves: in effect, anti-cities. In the early twentieth century a few satellite towns were created in the environs of Moscow, taking inspiration from the Garden City Movement of Ebenezer Howard, whose book *Tomorrow: a Peaceful Path to Real Reform*, published in 1898, advocated the founding of new towns as an alternative to the slums of industrial Europe. They would be separated from the metropolis by green belts, combining economy and tradition by the use of wood. The town of Nikolskoe (1908) was established in response to the Garden City Movement, but without an independent economic base, it rapidly became a gentrified bedroom community. The same fate befell Prozorovka (1912), originally built for workers on the Moscow–Kazan railway. In the face of the competing demands of the state and the administrative stasis that gripped the late-Romanov bureaucracy, the Garden City Movement withered because of the consequent failure of the civic authorities to provide the necessary infrastructure to make these communities viable, in particular an efficient transportation system to bring workers to the urban metropolis.

The Garden City Movement re-emerged in the 1920s as a solution to Moscow's urban dilemma. During the NEP period, there was an attempt to extend the Prozorovka model to take into account socialist principles. One result was Krasnyi Bogatyr, consisting of rural cottages of traditional design; a second was the town of Sokol, completed behind schedule in the 1930s when shifts in the Party Line towards collectivization and socialist realism had already doomed it. Romantic-looking satellite villages were simply too much for the urban Bolsheviks. With their individual wooden cottages, not only did the villages emphasize non-collectivist ideas, they also represented, in Engels' words, 'the idiocy of rural life'. Stalinism's anti-kulak campaigns, combined with the collectivization of the countryside, were the movement's nemesis. In 1931 the Association of Soviet Architects announced that as a proletarian building material, 'wood is barbaric'.[24] In the same stroke, ideology condemned wooden Moscow, accomplishing what centuries of fire could not.

If the garden city faltered as a solution to Moscow's urban dilemma, so did the early post-revolutionary plans for the redevelopment of Moscow. Many were inspired by the 1909 plans for Greater Berlin, as the triumphant capital of the unified German Reich. These called for broad axial boulevards lined with colonnaded public buildings interspersed with parks. The difference between the plans for Berlin and for Moscow was the difference between the vision and its realization. Berlin was the capital of an industrial state approaching its apogee of wealth and power in a time of peace. Moscow was the starving survivor[25] of a war that had destroyed the regime which had governed it for 400 years.

Radically altered but astonishing nonetheless, the garden city idea for Moscow re-emerged in the form of building not out, but up. Sometimes the fantasies of architects inspired by the social implications of Marx's writings reached fever pitch. One prominent architect, Melnikov, envisaged a garden city where orchestras in huge dormitories would drown out the snoring of fellow-workers and induce sleep. Another, Kuzmin, could contemplate the complete elimination of family life and the regulation of the day, including all bodily functions, strictly according to the clock.[26] Steel, glass and concrete, which allowed for high-density, multi-storey urban housing, were the officially approved materials for the socialist state.

The precepts of Marxism proved difficult to translate into urban design, but a valiant attempt was made when Le Corbusier was invited to produce a city plan by architects from the Moscow committee of the Communal Economy in the early 1930s (the competition went on for several years). Le Corbusier's proposal would transform Moscow into a '*ville radieuse*' of high-rise apartment complexes, each aligned for maximum exposure to the sun, surrounded by woodlands and parks. The entire city centre to the outer rings would be bulldozed (the fate he planned for the Kremlin was not clear). Like Ivan the Terrible's Vologda, and located on the same bend of the Moskva River, the '*ville radieuse*' would be Moscow's final anti-city, replacing Moscow itself. He even took the trouble to write the old city's epitaph: 'It is impossible to dream about combining the city of the past with the present or future. In the USSR more than anywhere the question is of back-to-back epochs, with no factors in common.'[27]

On 16 May 1930 the Central Committee of the Party, on the likely prompting of Moscow's newly appointed Party first secretary Lazar Kaganovich, issued a resolution awkwardly entitled 'On Work at the Reconstruction of the Way of Life', which put an end to such spectacular theorizing not only by Le Corbusier but by a number of Soviet planners as well. Weirdly reminiscent of Hitler's plans for Moscow, but without the human agency, the Soviet architects Moisei Ginzberg, co-founder of the Constructivist OSA School, and Mikhail Barshch published in *Contemporary Architecture* (1930) their own project for the city's transformation: 'Moscow should be turned into a vast green park for leisure and culture toward which the new zone lines will converge. This does not involve immediate demolition but rather waiting patiently for buildings to deteriorate naturally. In this way Moscow will progressively become an immense park...'[28]

In the event, Le Corbusier's plans for the city were no more successful than his plans for the Palace of Soviets, but as consolation he was given the responsibility for designing and building the Central Union of Cooperative Societies Building (Tsentrosoyuz), 1928-36, now housing the Russian State Committee for Statistics, considered as one of Moscow's best-preserved buildings of the inter-war architectural avant-garde.

Akademgorodok as Ivory Tower

Moscow has a history as a city of dreams, if not for itself, then for another place through which Moscow could attain its own self-actualization. In the 1930s Le Corbusier was only the most recent in the long line of foreign visionaries who joined Muscovite architects and others in building a Moscow of the Imagination. The secret cities of the Cold War were never intended to play the role of an idealized Moscow—their purposes were military and they became mini-Moscows only because of the pervading bureaucratic culture imposed on them from Moscow Centre, including their very architecture—in the way that Stalin's Magnitogorsk was envisioned as an appropriate urban setting for a proletarian state. Akademgorodok, a purpose-built city in the depths of the Siberian forests, was intended to be both a window on the future and the engine of leading-edge scientific research that would bring that future about.

Akademgorodok was not a new concept in Russian and Soviet architectural experience, and belongs to that tradition extending back to the early monasteries and the *cherta* defensive lines. In the twentieth century it was preceded by a Moscow residential cantonment of the Soviet Academy of Sciences, which held some 5,000 people by the late 1940s when the academy was transferred to Moscow. Even then, there were already single-industry research towns near Moscow: Troisk for applied physics and Pushchino for biology.

What set Akademgorodok apart, however, was the idea of an academic city devoted to pure research built on the highest socialist ideals and isolated from the mundane daily concerns of finance and politics. It was conceived in 1956 by Mikhail Alekseevich Lavrentev, a dynamic and well-connected mathematician. The choice of the Siberian location, where snow covered the ground for six months of the year and winter temperatures fell to minus 50°C, gave more than a passing reference to Kitezh itself, equally invisible and inaccessible beneath the waters of Lake Svetloyar. But in the triumphant atmosphere of post-*sputnik* Russia, the idea struck a chord with Khrushchev, who promoted it.

From the beginning the project ran into problems. Novosibirsk, the nearest city, opposed the draining-off of provincial (*oblast*) funds and resources for its construction, and funding had to be found elsewhere. Many scientists regarded Akademgorodok as another form of Siberian exile, a suspicion

Pembroke Library

Dublin City Library Service

Customer name: Ronan, Julie Anne

Title: Insane clown president : dispatches from the American circus / Matt Taibbi.
ID: DCPL2000004092
Due: 26 September 2020

Title: What's in the Queen's handbag : and other Royal secrets / Phil Dampier and Ashley Walton.
ID: DCPL0000011283?
Due: 26 September 2020

Title: At the Kremlin gates : a historical portrait of Moscow / Gerald R. Skinner.
ID: DCPL0000384777
Due: 26 September 2020

Total items: 3
05/09/2020 11:46
Checked out: 6
Overdue: 0
Hold requests: 0
Ready for pickup: 0

Thank you for visiting the Library

Thank you for visiting the Library

Pembroke Library

Dublin City Library Service

Customer name: McElligott, Mairead

Title: The wonder / Emma Donoghue.

ID: DCPL0000994248

Due: 18 February 2019

Title: Grace and truth / Jennifer Johnston.

ID: 184617158X8001

Due: 18 February 2019

Title: At the Kremlin gates : a historical portrait of Moscow / Gerald R. Skinner.

ID: DCPL0000384777

Due: 18 February 2019

Total items: 3

28/01/2019 15:25

Checked out: 4

Overdue: 0

Hold requests: 0

Ready for pickup: 0

Thank you for visiting the Library

reinforced by the lack of medical care, nurseries and basic infrastructure, creating isolation from the rest of the Soviet scientific community—and not incidentally from centres of promotion. Although some valuable work was done in theoretical physics, biology and sociology (the latter, conducted by Tatiana Zaslavskaya, destroyed the notion that workers' natural homes were factories, and that the proletarians liked living communally), the communist experiment foundered on human nature, as Zaslavskaya documented. Lavrentev had a private dacha built in the idyllic Golden Valley away from the muddy construction site, while other inhabitants were expected to live communally in order to 'demonstrate the material-technological basis of communism'. This they did in increasingly bad spirit. Despite the resources and priority given to the city, it too suffered from architectural *Khrushchevshchina,* and its buildings became a byword for the shoddy, crash-programme construction typical of Moscow itself. Khrushchev's Akademgorodok became an unintended replica of 1960s Moscow, of blank, identical ferro-concrete buildings facing unrelievedly straight streets under the leaden skies of Siberia.

If Akademgorodok failed as a model for the Moscow of the future, it also played a role in Khrushchev's removal from office. One of the accusations levelled against Khrushchev which led to his downfall was 'hair-brained scheming'. This was a reference primarily to his disastrous Virgin Lands project that turned vast areas of Kazakhstan into a dust bowl. Other offences included organizational changes that he introduced into the state and Party apparatus. They met stiff resistance from the bureaucracy, still set in their Stalinist ways. His support for the Akademgorodok project was added to the list of dissatisfaction, as concerns increased about the Soviet ability to maintain the leading, strategic edge of science as the Cold War deepened. Akademgorodok became regarded as a luxury attracting the best brains of the country in pursuit of nothing of use, who might be usefully employed otherwise.

Following the removal of Khrushchev and an ill-advised protest by Akademgorodok's inhabitants over the Soviet invasion of Czechoslovakia in 1968, the town went into a kind of receivership. Its relative independence and academic promise went into decline. Party and state officials were brought in to 'administer' the town, and with that, Akademgorodok became simply a privileged suburb of Moscow, thousands of kilometres away.

'Worker and Kolkhoz Woman' sculpted by Vera Mukhina. Created at the height of collectivization, the socialist realist statue emphasizes the Stalinist ideal of the unity of agriculture and industry, and of city and countryside under communism. During the collectivization campaigns, Moscow was supplied by forced requisitions. There was an artificially induced famine in Ukraine in 1932-3. The statues bear a striking resemblance to 'The Winged Victory of Samothrace', from which the sculptor appears to have drawn inspiration.

Chapter Seven
Soviet Moscow

> *...I raise my glass... to the fallen walls of the beautiful palaces and to the new precepts of a new aesthetic. And as an incorruptible sensualist I will express just one wish: may the impending battle not make life less aesthetic and may death be as radiantly beautiful as the resurrection...*
> Toast of cultural impresario Sergei Diaghilev at a dinner in his honour at the Hotel Metropol, Moscow, 1905

Moscow entered the twentieth century with the unfinished business of the nineteenth. Already suffering all the growing pains of a rapidly developing industrial city, it was about to endure its own self-immolation from which it would emerge from its tsarist past, rising phoenix-like from its own ashes. The new Soviet Moscow would be a place of both tragedy and hope.

In 1897 Moscow's population was just over 1 million; it had doubled by 1914, almost entirely through peasant in-migration. The central industrial region in Moscow and its surrounding districts accounted for over half of the new Russian industrial labour force. The causes of the 1905 insurrection went unaddressed in St. Petersburg, and as war approached, the imperial court took the unwise decision of burdening the city with an army garrison that would grow to over 100,000. By law, this garrison was to be maintained out of the city's already meagre resources. As the war progressed, the problem was exacerbated by the inflow of an estimated 150,000 refugees. During the war, inflation outpaced and finally rendered workers' wages meaningless. In 1915 there were 56 strikes involving almost 30,000 workers, and a year later 70 strikes broke out. A new word entered the vocabulary, *buntarstvo,* violent opposition to all authority.

Any hope of avoiding catastrophe through the introduction

of answerable city government disappeared in 1916 when the city governor, V. N. Shebko, banned the newly elected City Council from meeting, on the technical grounds that the new councillors were not drawn up from lists formally approved by the imperial court. With the memories of the 1905 uprising in mind, the imperial police developed a contingency plan to use the park-like Sadovoye Koltso, the Garden Ring, as a circular firebreak to protect the inner core of Moscow from insurrection. More than any other visible sign, Sadovoye Koltso marked the boundary between reaction and revolution.

In the event, the firebreak proved inconsequential. The bulk of workers supporting the Moscow City Soviet in 1917 lived on the inner side of the Garden Ring. The headquarters of the City Soviet was located at the entrance to Red Square, closer to the Kremlin than the governor's residence.

By the turn of the century, premonition lay heavily upon Moscow. Nicholas II's coronation in Uspensky Sobor in May 1895 brought a bad omen when the tsar's pendant fell to the ground during the ceremony. Tragedy followed on Khodinsky Field, where 2,000 people were trampled to death in a confined space as they gathered to celebrate the crowning of their new Little Father, the *tsar-batiushka.* Nicholas decided to continue with the ball scheduled for that evening. The city governor Grand Duke Sergei, morally corrupt, brutally reactionary and uncle of the tsar, was held responsible. He attended the ball.

In 1900 Moscow's urban profile was low, its centre dominated by the Kremlin's cathedrals and its great bell tower; further out, a forest of gold, green and blue onion-domes rose above a city still of wood. Over this scene presided the massive 'Great Samovar', as contemporaries called it, the Cathedral of Christ the Saviour, and to the south-west, the red bell tower of Novodevichy Convent. Here and there the skyline of the city was broken by the dissonance of factory chimneys, to the north-west and across the log-packed river to the south of the

Kremlin, reaching the city's outer limits in the industrial slums and factories of Zamoskvorechye. These limits were no longer defined by the needs of defence, and the encircling monasteries had lost their protective function, as had the city's inner walls. A further, outermost ring now redefined the city's boundaries, the Kamer-Kollezhsky Val originally constructed as a customs barrier on the approaches to the city, beyond which ran the circular railway, completed in 1908, which served as the main artery for provisioning and personal transport for all regions of the city.[1]

The elegance of this arrangement was thrown into discord as the city had already burst its perimeters. It now spread out in low-built wooden tenements inhabited by urban peasants, the raw material of imperial Russia's industrial revolution. Beyond the city limits, even the minimal attempts at civic administration were absent.[2] Auguries of change were sights of vast factory complexes alongside the onion-domes, the city partially obscured by a pall of smoke and airborne effluent from thousands of industrial and domestic fires in the dead-calm of freezing winter weather, itself welcomed as it reduced the stench of open sewers and the spread of infectious disease.

Within these boundaries, the north-western Presnaya district and the southern Zamoskvorechye district would rise in insurrection in 1905 and again in 1917. In the 1880s the new trading rows had been built opposite the Kremlin in reference to Russia's folkloric past, later to become GUM. But even here at the city's core lay the Khitrovo market, a crowded place of the *demi-monde*, of the dispossessed, of flop-houses and prostitutes. Cholera ravaged the district in 1910, and reappeared in 1917. On the eve of revolution it represented the worst of Moscow's past, a dark medieval vision of the Time of Troubles, impervious to change. It is estimated that in these districts the average working-class tenement held only 2 square metres of floor space and 3 cubic metres of air per inhabitant.

Dancing Before the Storm

By the turn of the century the great merchants and industrialists had created a stage-set on the approaches to the city more in keeping with the romantic notions of seventeenth-century Moscow as imagined in fairy-tales than with the new century. Protected by police barriers of the Sadovoye Koltso, radiating out from the Kremlin on the city's northern side, a neo-Russian architectural style informed the town houses and urban estates of the wealthy and the aristocratic. The generation living in these urban fantasies brought Moscow its Silver Age.

Privilege and decadence were not new to Moscow. The city's history is punctuated with the results, from the eighteenth-century transvestite balls of Empress Elisabeth to orgiastic feasts of unparalleled gluttony in the nineteenth century, complete with naked serving-boys. Yuri Shamarin sketched the prevailing attitude of the Moscow elite in the person of Prince Yusipov, a friend of Pushkin. Speaking of Yusipov's class, Shamarin wrote that 'above all they wished to be free of other people; free not only of obligations but of any ties whatsoever; to turn everything—the world, their fellow men—into adjuncts of a beautiful existence, into a means of satisfying their whims.' Yusipov was rumoured to have his apartment at his Moscow estate at Arkhangelskoye decorated with portraits of all the women with whom he had had a liaison. 'The walls were full, beyond number,' Shamarin concludes:

> Living for life itself, and retreating into cultural seclusion are the two things that characterized Moscow's aristocracy. Two separate worlds are in evidence: a corner of paradise where all is beauty, elegance and designed to serve the highest concerns; and beyond the boundaries, Russia—cold, grey and disorderly. There are no bridges linking the two, you can stay only on one side of the precipice.[3]

Yet for almost 40 years, almost two generations, from the last decades of the nineteenth century into the first of the twentieth, a slender bridge did in fact connect the two sides of the abyss. This was Moscow's Silver Age, a starburst of artistic creativity that overcame war, revolution and chaos to become a brilliant chapter in the city's history. Emblematic of the Silver Age in all its contradictions is the figure of Aleksei Shchusev, prolific architect of religious edifices, including the Martha and Maria Cloister in Moscow (1910) in the *style moderne,* and designer of the iconostasis for the corporate chapel in the Maltsev Glass Factory. The Bolsheviks turned to him to design the final version of Lenin's mausoleum, which in 1924 he did in an abrupt change of style, creating one of the world's best-known buildings, the low-lying constructivist ziggurat without God.

The Silver Age grew out of the Golden Age of Russian literature and art of the 1830s and 1840s, fostered by the intellectual ferment that followed the Napoleonic invasion and the ill-conceived rebellion of the idealistic young officers of St. Petersburg's aristocratic Preobrazhensky Regiment in 1825. The Golden Age found its gravitational centre in the refined salons of St. Petersburg and Moscow, and in the *usadbas* or country estates of Tolstoy and other great men of literature. By contrast, the natural habitat of the Silver Age was the urban club, attended by men who were neither aristocratic landowners nor of the traditional merchant class, but who accumulated great wealth as Russia's industrial revolution, fuelled largely by foreign capital, took hold and underwent a period of exponential growth. The railway magnate and patron of the arts Mamentov, sponsor of the artistic colony of Abramtsevo, and the industrialist Tretyakov, founder of the gallery which bears his name, belonged to this group.

The Silver Age belonged to the new urban middle class, in particular to a layer of wealthy entrepreneurs and the society that attended to them in the shops and services in the fashionable districts of Moscow—'bourgeois ghettoes' as they were called—running north-west from the Kremlin along Tverskaya Street and Miasnitskaya Street to Arbat Square. Other areas included Kalanchevskaya Street, the abode of wealthy Muscovites and their urban mansions, leading on to Kalanchev Square, now Komsomolskaya Square, location of three railway stations. In the revolutionary myths fostered after November 1917 these residences would be held against their owners as physical demonstrations of their arrogance and exploitation of the oppressed.

Bridging the two centuries, the Silver Age of Moscow encompassed all the arts, from literature to dance, from theatre to music. Igor Stravinsky's *Le Sacre du Printemps,* a ballet evoking primeval rites of fertility, was in perfect consonance with the discovery of the deep roots of human irrationality that Freud had introduced to the world: it had the unintended side-effect of throwing into doubt the logic and comfortable assumptions of nineteenth-century civilization. It caused a scandal when it was first performed at the Paris Théâtre des Champs-Elysées on 9 May 1913. The composer Saint-Saëns walked out in protest. Fights broke out in the audience. In its dissonance, it also put to music Freud's idea of a collective death-wish, revealing an intimation of the war that was to come and the social catastrophe that would follow in Europe generally, but in Russia in particular. If Stravinsky did not specifically anticipate the impending Apocalypse, others did. On the eve of the First World War Vasilii Chekrygin painted a series of paintings entitled *Beginning of the Resurrection*, evoking images reminiscent of Henry Moore's charcoal sketches of people huddling from the Blitz in the London Underground some fifty years later, except that Chekrygin's vision extended less than a decade, into the communist future of Russia.

Of all the arts it was probably painting that was the freest from the dead hand of imperial censorship, and visual experiments spanned from the works of Chagall to Kandinsky. But it was the work of the prolific artist Kazimir Malevich, straddling the Revolution, which best captured the mood of the time. Praised by art historians who admire the Futurist movement, like many of the Muscovite community he seemed obsessed with the theory of painterly techniques, but then unexpectedly produced a series of geometrical paintings culminating in *Black Square*. Four different versions exist, from 1905 to 1932, of a slightly irregular object painted on a neutral background, and first exhibited in St. Petersburg in 1915. Like *Le Sacre du Printemps*, it has provoked an avalanche of criticism ever since.[4] Formally, *Black Square* is a painting of the Supremacist School; that is, art as a geometrically-pure form. In fact, it is a four-sided Black Hole—the ultimate development of the icon, its perfect negation. Beyond it, there is nothing left to say or see, and it is deeply pessimistic. Malevich went on to make a successful traverse to post-revolutionary Russia, but in the context of its time and the upheaval about to take place, its prescience is unmatched. *Black Square* is the direct inheritor of the black Madonna icons of the medieval Muscovite state, not symbols of compassion and protection but of a blank void of despair which no prayer will ever reach.

Significantly, Silver Age Moscow and the people who inhabited it belonged to a borderless Western culture. The question of why *Le Sacre du Printemps* was first performed in Paris and not in St. Petersburg or Moscow, or why it had a French-language title, would not have occurred to them, any more than why in the fashionable emporia of the wealthy, merchandise was advertised only in French.[5] The bourgeois ghettos were islands of privilege looking out on a darkening urban sea of Russia and were as isolated from the country's realities as the imperial court itself. Following the eruption of Krakatoa in 1883 the sunsets over Moscow glowed brilliant red, at the time regarded as a grim forewarning of the fate that awaited Russia in the twentieth century. In turn-of-the-century Silver Age Moscow, the most fashionable dance was the tango; the most popular dancers scantily clad Isadora Duncan and her troupe, the Isadorables.

Revolution

On the eve of the First World War revolution loomed. The intelligentsia of Moscow, St. Petersburg and other imperial cities had in effect abandoned a system that had betrayed them and had actively persecuted them.[6] Without the support of the intelligentsia, who play a unique role in Russian history—they also destroyed the claims to legitimacy by the Soviet system—the tsarist regime lost its moral and intellectual underpinnings. One of the few enlightened imperial statesmen of early twentieth-century Russia, Prime Minister Pyotr Stolypin, was assassinated by a left-wing radical in the Kiev Opera House in 1911, expiring after giving the sign of the cross to the tsar.[7] Rumours persisted that the assassination was organized by conservatives with the possible collusion of the police. With a weak, short-sighted monarch and a reactionary, self-referential court in St. Petersburg, the regime was mired in a rigid autocracy whose prevailing culture allowed grotesque figures like Rasputin (who had foreseen Stolypin's death) to insinuate themselves into the highest levels of power. What was not inevitable was that the forthcoming revolution should be hijacked by the Bolsheviks.

When revolution came, it was the logical conclusion of an evolution having all the inevitability of a Greek tragedy. It began with the Russo-Japanese War, and the First Revolution of

1905, and culminated in the upheaval of 1917. Blindly, the past was seen by the imperial court as the way to the future. For the first time since Peter the Great, Tsar Nicholas II took to wearing the heavy coronation vestments of Byzantium in conscious evocation of tsardom's Orthodox legacy. The immediate cause of the Revolution, the regime's blundering into the First World War, came shrouded in the imperial court's (and many others') illusion of Russia's strength and steadfastness, based on a fatal misreading of Russia's Napoleonic experience.

The Bolsheviks were self-described inheritors of a Western revolutionary tradition established even before Marx devised a 'scientific rationale' for turning the world upside down. They were brilliant opportunists riding the crest of wartime chaos presided over by Kerensky's divided, inexperienced government of a dying state: the November Revolution of 1917 was in effect a coup against the Provisional Government successfully engineered by a conspiratorial party using their control of the city Soviets. This they gained by taking advantage of a walk-out of their other two partners in the Soviets, the Mensheviks and the Socialist Revolutionaries, in a dispute over tactics. The Bolsheviks did not cause imperial Russia's military and urban collapse any more than they precipitated the Russian Revolution, a claim they would in any event deny as un-Marxist. But they took full advantage of its consequences.[8]

The collective memory of the Russian Revolution owes as much to art as to history. Two of its greatest interpreters, John Reed and Sergei Eisenstein, continue to have an effect on how it is seen. Reed's sympathetic portrayal in *Ten Days that Shook the World* (1919) was criticized at the time and later as lacking factual accuracy; but as Bertram Wolfe, a historian of the Revolution himself, pointed out, as literature Reed's book was the finest piece of eyewitness reporting that the Revolution produced. In the 1927 film, *October,* Eisenstein's famous scene of the storming of St. Petersburg's Winter Palace offered a portrayal of the event with generous use of poetic licence. The eminent British historian Eric Hobsbawm noted that 'it has been said that more people were injured in the making of that film than in the actual takeover of the Palace on November 7, 1917'.[9] For his part, on that night, Reed was asked by his waiter to finish his meal in a back room of the hotel as it was only a few blocks away from the Winter Palace and the management anticipated gunfire. There was none.

Of the large armed force defending the palace and members of the Provisional Government sheltering there, only some 300 were left when the assault began; the rest had slipped away to have dinner.[10] The provisional government's Women's Battalion of Death had chosen to remain, but became hysterical when the cruiser *Aurora* opened fire with blank shot, and had to be confined to a basement room. Kerensky had escaped and was not present when members of his government were arrested and taken to the Peter-Paul Fortress. Once the palace's huge wine cellars were broken into, the insurrection degenerated into a drunken riot as wine was poured into the streets. Maxim Gorky wrote of his dismay at witnessing not a social revolution but a 'pogrom of greed, hatred and violence'.[11]

The real turning-point of the revolution in Petrograd, it could be argued, was not the storming of the Winter Palace, but the movement of crowds of demonstrators across the bridge separating the working-class districts of Petrograd from the fashionable areas along Nevsky Prospekt, until recently the off-limits area reserved for the nobility and officials of the imperial court. By this symbolic act, a 'forbidden zone' was breached, and despite Gorky's misgivings, social revolution would surely follow. A parallel event took place in Moscow a day later, as armed Red Guards moved through the fashionable districts bordering the Tverskaya area toward the Kremlin, the final symbol of the now-defunct tsarist state.

The violence in Moscow was a counterpoint to the relatively

bloodless upheaval in Petrograd. By Soviet estimates, of the 5-6,000 Red Guards engaged, over 1,000 were killed in the street battles with troops loyal to the Provisional Government's Moscow Committee of Public Safety. It had at its disposal some 15,000 troops in the Moscow garrison, in the two cadet schools and the six schools for junior officers. Soviet historians were later to condemn the efforts of the All-Russian Executive Committee of the Railwaymen's Union (VIKZHEL) to arrange a truce.[12] The failure of the union to do so marked the beginning of the Russian Civil War (1917-21) and the deaths of some 3 million people, the real cost of the November Revolution.[13]

In November 1917 Moscow had no equivalent of Petrograd's solidly working-class district of Vyborg, itself divided between supporting Soviet power and supporting the Bolshevik members of it. The same was true in Moscow, and despite later officially sponsored histories, the Moscow Soviets were by no means the automatic instruments of Bolshevik power. This complicated the work of the Soviets' Military Revolutionary Committee (MRC), still nominally a left-wing coalition responsible for securing Moscow from the forces of the Provisional Government and its Committee of Public Safety.

The heaviest fighting took place around the Kremlin. Initially, the local Red Guard contingents did not prove very effective, and were expelled by military cadets loyal to the Provisional Government who managed to get into the citadel through secret underground tunnels. The MRC had to call for reinforcements when the Moscow Red Guards were pushed back to their strongholds in the industrial suburbs. Fresh Red Guards from Petrograd arrived at Yaroslavl station to the north-east, and headed for the Kremlin, which changed hands twice. On 15 November the Committee of Public Safety capitulated. In all, there were about 1,000 casualties.

Shortly after the Red Guards had gained control of the

city, arrangements were made to construct two identical tombs by the Kremlin walls to hold the remains of 240 Red Guards killed in the fighting. When the time came, this gave birth to the idea of erecting a monument to Lenin on Red Square. With the construction of his mausoleum, the square was transformed from its traditional role as place of state ceremony and execution to a necropolis, adding yet another layer of symbolism to the citadel and fulfilling the role of medieval monasteries as places of burial.

According to official histories of the time, the decision of the Party Central Committee to move the capital to Moscow was based on strategic factors. Petrograd was too close to the German front lines, and the Whites were threatening from the north-east. Moscow was the centre of the rail communications network which put it at the strategic centre of the country.

The reality was more complicated. Petrograd was less secure in its support for the Bolsheviks than Moscow, and possessed no equivalent of the Kremlin to dominate the city. The Peter-Paul Fortress was poorly placed for this role, and served better as a prison. Bolsheviks' fears proved correct, for in 1921 the naval garrison of Kronstadt on Kotlin Island revolted against them, protesting against the rigours of War Communism and the arbitrary administration of the Bolsheviks. Ironically, many of the sailors had supported the Bolsheviks themselves, some of them serving on the *Aurora* when it fired at the Winter Palace with blank ammunition. An independent Soviet was set up on the island. Lenin condemned the rising as a plot against Soviet power instigated by the Whites in collusion with foreign reactionary forces. It took Trotsky, as Commissar of War, several months to organize its defeat. Several hundred were shot in the aftermath. From 1917 on, the Red Guards had a firmer grip on Moscow, and Petrograd–Leningrad was regarded in the minds of the authorities with suspicion that lasted throughout the Soviet period. This did not prevent official histories from making the most of the move. In an explanation intended for the general public, *Izvestia* gave the Soviet government's decision to move the capital global significance: 'Raising its flag in Moscow', the newspaper wrote, 'it graphically manifests the link between Russia's being and the fate of the whole world' (*Izvestia,* 17 March 1918).

Some were less sure. Maxim Gorky, already dismayed by the chaos the revolution had wrought in his home city, was appalled at the decision. Besides turning Petrograd into a ghost city, he wrote, the move of the capital to Moscow signified the end of civilization in Russia, and the turning of the country toward Asia.

For an entire decade after 1917 everything happened in Moscow at once. The Silver Age continued, and under appalling conditions many of its leading artists rode the wave of revolutionary idealism and, in direct contradiction to Gorky's dire misgivings, believed that they were acting as midwives to the birth of a new civilization. In thinking themselves the custodians of that birth, they gave it expression in art, literature and architecture. Perhaps gifted with a broader cosmic sense, musicians were more prescient, many having fled abroad in the early days of Soviet power. Diaghilev had already established himself in Paris; Rachmaninoff would emigrate to New York, never forgetting the deep strains of passionate Russianism which inform his music. Even Gorky chose to escape the heat of the revolution and its aftermath, seeking solace in Italy until Stalin lured him back to Moscow, where he allowed himself to be turned into a cultural artefact. In the end, many of the brightest lights of the Silver Age fell victim to the Revolution itself, and the fate of the Moscow intelligentsia was further confirmation of a bitter observation made at the time of the French Revolution, that revolutions devour their own children.

With Soviet power now firmly established in Moscow, fierce theoretical debates took place within the Party about whether historical conditions were ripe for the spread of the proletarian revolution beyond the borders of Russia, still engulfed in a civil war. The revolutionary logic of the left wing of the Bolshevik Party accepted the punitive Treaty of Brest-Litovsk, by which peace with Germany was obtained at the cost of the shrinking of Russia's territories in the west to the proportions of medieval Muscovy. The Red Army was in no position to oppose the imperial German army, and peace would allow the Bolsheviks to consolidate their power at home and to defeat the forces of counter-revolution, which by 1918 included Western interventionists.

It was anticipated—and fervently argued—by Trotsky and others both at home and abroad that the November Revolution would trigger other revolutions in the West, starting with Berlin. The dream of world revolution seemed about to be realized. The Treaty of Brest-Litovsk would be 'negated by history' and the class solidarity of the international proletariat would prevail over the internal contradictions inherent in capitalist states and their narrow, class-based national interests. In a series of brutal campaigns that became part of Soviet folklore, at home the Reds were gaining the upper hand in former imperial territories, and abroad Spartacist revolution in Berlin in 1918, the establishment of a communist government in Hungary in 1918 and the Red Army's advance as far as Warsaw in 1920 promised a new era. The failures of each were regarded as short-term setbacks.

During this phase of revolutionary idealism, Moscow, the seat of Soviet power and capital of world revolution, took on a global significance as the first truly international city in history. Marx's call for the international liberation of the oppressed in his *Communist Manifesto* (1848)—'Workers of the World Unite, You have Nothing to Lose but Your Chains'—appeared on the masthead of *Pravda*, the official organ of the Bolshevik Party. Moscow's revolutionary cosmopolitanism made it the twentieth-century's secular Third Rome. In March 1919 the First World Congress of the Communist International was held in Moscow, 'dedicated to the overthrow of the international bourgeoisie and ... the creation of an international Soviet republic as a transitional stage to the complete abolition of the State'. For the first decade of the Soviet state's existence, the left wing of the Bolshevik Party basked in this heady illusion. With their eyes fixed on the stars, they ignored the realities at their feet. This was to be their undoing.

Bolshevik Moscow

When Lenin arrived in Moscow on 11 March 1918 he did not go directly to the Kremlin (he had apparently not yet made up his mind about where to place his government) but stayed in the National Hotel, across from Red Square. Deciding on the Kremlin a few days later, he found it in a state of disrepair, having suffered from the bombardment in the recent fighting while its buildings were dilapidated from years of neglect by the imperial court in St. Petersburg. Roofs leaked, and wild dogs ran in packs in its open spaces. He chose a modest four-room flat for himself and Nadezhda Krupskaya on the third floor of the Senate building, formerly the offices and chambers of the imperial crown prosecutor, ensuring that all the furniture was properly enumerated and registered. The domestic staff was kept on, waiters carefully positioning the tsarist dinnerware with the double-headed imperial eagle correctly on the table. Other Bolshevik leaders scrambled for their own places in the Kremlin, or looked for choice locations elsewhere. This gave Moscow of the early Soviet period a slightly anomalous appearance with many of the architectural symbols of Soviet power housed in buildings constructed in contemporary Moscow baroque or even Art Nouveau style. Dark red plaques affixed to their entrances announced their new functions in gold lettering.

The Moscow of Lenin and its subsequent transformation into the capital of a socialist state with global significance present a profoundly ambivalent picture. It begins with the personality of Lenin himself. General Dmitri Volkogonov, who was charged by Gorbachev in the late 1980s to study the then-closed KGB archives in the name of *glasnost*, arrived at an unflattering portrait, much to his own disillusion: 'he was a humourless monomaniac, obsessed with power and its exercise'. In Volkogonov's portrait Lenin emerges as a slightly unsavoury revolutionary émigré on the boulevards of 1917 Zurich, but possessed with an uncanny ability to calculate, with the help of information supplied by his underground network in Russia, the probabilities of the collapse of imperial Russia under the strain of a war that it was clearly unfit to wage.

The Marxist tension between the impersonal 'forces of historical inevitability' and the voluntarism of individuals acting alone took second place to Lenin's overarching objective of gaining control. This began with the Russian Social Democratic Labour Party (whence his minority faction became known, inappropriately, as the Bolsheviks, a name implying that they were in the majority), then the Soviets, and ultimately the Russian state itself. He even sought to control life on the train bringing him from exile to Petrograd in 1917, dividing his fellow passengers into smokers and non-smokers, the latter having priority for the lavatory. The personal cost of this obsession would be enormous, for with his penchant for secrecy and intrigue he discarded allies and friends lightly and held grudges badly. His love-life was barren, and his association with the singularly unattractive Nadezhda Krupskaya seemed to have at its centre revolutionary comradeship, which in his case smothered any romantic impulse. But he also possessed brilliant insights, seeing that the spontaneous appearance of the Soviets in Russian cities closely resembled the *zemstvos,* traditional village institutions of the land, and the potential they held as an alternative source of legitimacy and power. His inspired slogan 'Peace, Land and Bread' could not be matched. Volkogonov's portrait goes further, describing Lenin as an 'unattractive, bald, stocky man with piercing eyes and the look of an intelligent craftsman',[14] who lost his bowler hat and fell into a ditch in an attempt to escape tsarist troops in 1905. Fearful of arrest in November 1917, he resorted to disguise as the Winter Palace was being stormed by others, 'bandaged, bewigged and bespectacled, fooling no-one'.[15]

The first years of Moscow under Soviet power were harsh. Many nevertheless believed the *Izvestia* editorial that Moscow had indeed become the headquarters of world revolution. The city and the Red Army had priority for confiscated or expropriated food, itself in short supply. There was little brotherly love in these confiscations, and the peasants, whom Lenin had only grudgingly accepted as partners in the Revolution, were on the receiving end of forced expropriations to feed the urban proletariat. 'The salvation of the Moscow workers from starvation,' Lenin wrote, 'is the salvation of the Revolution.' From 1919 into the early 1920s the winters were particularly hard, and many fences and even houses were destroyed for firewood. The city suffered outbreaks of cholera and tuberculosis. Starvation and the global influenza epidemic of 1918–19 affected the city as well. Even animals suffered, and twenty of the Kremlin horses died of hunger. Soviet officials working there were obliged to hire private cabs.

As conditions in Moscow worsened, the urban peasantry migrated back to their villages in order to survive, subsisting on food hidden from confiscatory raids. Despite the rural confiscations to feed the cities, the populations of all of Russia's northern cities, Moscow included, continued to decline. It is estimated that in Petrograd the number of Bolsheviks had fallen from the 1917 figure of 50,000 to 13,000; the Party could soon be 'the vanguard of a non-existent class'. Through Party discipline, organizational commitment and belief the Bolsheviks survived, but organized violence against the sources of real or imagined opposition, including the urban intelligentsia now frequently identified as 'class enemies', began early. Through it all, a new Moscow began to form in the minds of its new rulers.

The architectural historian Spiro Kostof classified two types of urbanism: as the City of the Dreadful Night and as the City of Monuments.[16] The main characteristics of the former were determined by the slums and, by the disease and violence that attended them; those of the latter, by the direct effects of the seizure of power by authoritarian regimes on the cities where they had become established. His examples, both drawn from the first half of the twentieth century, were Berlin and Moscow. Both cities suffered urban collapse as a result of the First World War, with the Russian case being the more severe because of Moscow's arrested development. Moscow's transition from the one classification to the other was accomplished with astonishing rapidity.

At first glance, Lenin's imprint upon the city's development is surprisingly light, and was restricted in Soviet times to the names of streets or public spaces like Lenin Stadium, banners containing slogans he had coined, or *znachki*, pins worn on lapels bearing his likeness. Unlike Stalin, his interest in works of art, architecture and culture was neither deep nor sustained. Before the end of the civil war he issued an appeal to overenthusiastic Bolsheviks bent on destruction to respect their national heritage and not to destroy any historic buildings or monuments, although he personally took part in pulling down a statue of Alexander II in the Kremlin. He followed this up through the creation of Soviet institutions such as the Department of Museum Affairs, as well as encouraging the Moscow City Council's Commission on the Preservation of Landmarks. Apparently on the advice of Maxim Gorky, who had brought to his attention Tommaso Campenella's monument-filled utopia of 1602, *City of the Sun,* Lenin sponsored a 'programme of sculptural propaganda' on the first anniversary of the Revolution. The wooden hoardings around newly commissioned monuments to the Revolution's heroes were soon covered with graffiti or stolen for firewood.

The revolutionary idealism of Marxist intellectuals (they were almost all Marxists) had fostered experimentation in the arts, but as they looked behind they saw that few followed. The public reaction to the post-modernist, abstract sculptures now occupying some of Moscow's most prominent public spaces was hostile, and many of the sculptures had to be hastily removed by the authorities to prevent them from being further vandalized. Some seventy years later there is a certain poetic justice in the fact that after the fall of communism abstract modernism in at least some monuments returned to Moscow with a vengeance. At one of the mass gravesites outside Moscow, a sculpture depicts a victim of Stalinism held in the grasp of an abstract, faceless monster, with the hammer-and-sickle mark of Cain upon its forehead.[17]

Lenin's approach to Moscow city planning and to the associated disciplines of architecture and design tended to be political-utilitarian. At the Eighth All-Russian Congress of Soviets in 1920, he stood before the model of Tatlin's Tower—the projected monument to the Third International—to confirm Russia's electrification programme. Electrification was Lenin's greatest contribution to the face of Moscow, not any architectural inspiration. The Tower, and other efforts of the Moscow constructivist school of architecture, which emphasized honesty of materials and clean lines as an expression of proletarianism, left him cold, even though its ideas and principles had received worldwide praise at the time—and even though his eventual mausoleum is an outstanding example of that school's work . Electrification and the social and industrial implications it carried in its sub-text were more in line with

Lenin's world-view.

The electrification of Moscow had in fact begun in 1887, when a private company was given the contract for the 'illumination of a passage' off fashionable Tverskaya Street. But it was Lenin's insight that identified electrification as the means by which technology could transform a backward society into a modern state. Anticipating the Five-Year Plans that would emerge beginning in 1928, the urgent priority given to this strategy is clear in the Bolsheviks' adoption of the State Plan for the Electrification of Russia precisely one month after they had seized power. Lenin's statement before the Tatlin Tower applied that priority to Moscow.

Carried out in appalling conditions of civil war, desperate shortages, famine and disease, the electrification of Moscow far surpassed in its achievement the projects of visionary architects whose grandiose schemes more often than not lay stillborn on the drafting boards. Typical of early, post-revolutionary urban planning were dreams of world revolution. The artist–architect El Lissitzky sought to apply Marxist principles to urban development, producing *Russia: an Architecture for World Revolution* which emphasized modernist structures within which workers would lead collective lives. Personal space and privacy would be at a minimum. Drawing on Lissitzky's pioneering work, another group of planners published *The Ideal Communist City,* which emphasized the need for urban planning 'to respond to the organic growth of the city and to replace the chaos inherent in the natural development of capitalist cities'.[18] Based on unproven and ultimately false assumptions about communal tendencies in human nature, both books were naïve.

On the more practical level, before the Revolution, whatever urban planning Moscow had was the preserve of the bureaucracy in imperial St. Petersburg. Following the Revolution, the first locally based head of urban planning for Moscow, Ivan Zholtovskii, was a specialist in Renaissance classical art, director of the Moscow Architectural Studio. He would come to the Kremlin to hear Lenin expound, and then go away to produce a practical series of recommendations based on Lenin's discourse dealing with traffic flows, public sanitation (including toilets) and other down-to-earth practical matters. His projects never got off the ground, and his efforts were shouldered aside by the extravagant designs of the architectural visionaries of the 1920s, including the famous avant-garde Higher Arts and Technical Studios (VKhUTEMAS), successor to Zholtovskii's studio. In its turn, VKhUTEMAS succumbed to the hard material realities of the consequences of the civil war and the priority the state placed on electrification and industrialization. Ultimately Stalin's General Plan for the City of Moscow ended its brief, brilliant life.

At the end of the civil war, War Communism had given way to the New Economic Policy (NEP), an economic and social pause in revolutionary development that allowed Moscow and the country a period of recovery. In a superhuman application of effort, the Bolsheviks had halted the city's decline and the flight of urban workers from Moscow. The 'commanding heights' of finance and industry remained under state control, but with the NEP there was a revival of Moscow's markets and even private housing. Agriculture began to recover, and a new class of relatively wealthy peasants emerged, the *kulaks*.[19] During those years, the city witnessed cabaret scenes, theatre, art and architecture strongly reminiscent of Weimar Berlin. The NEP saw the culmination of Moscow's Silver Age, and its denouement.

But yet another episode of darkness had already appeared early on the horizon. At the Mikhelson Factory in southern

Moscow on 20 August 1918, Fanny Kaplan, a disillusioned member of the Socialist Revolutionary Party, attempted to assassinate Lenin. Wounded in the neck, he lost spectacular amounts of blood, but recovered in a matter of weeks.

The incident had two profound effects upon the city's history. The first was that her torture and execution marks the beginning of the Red Terror in its civilian form, which became bureaucratized and legalized. Through its various transformations it reached its zenith during the great purge trials held in Moscow in the 1930s. From December 1918 to November 1920, the Moscow Cheka[20] alone is said to have hunted down and destroyed 59 'counter-revolutionary organizations', arrested more than 5,000 of their members and executed 52 of them.[21] A kind of early socialist decadence hung in the air even as the Cheka, under the direction of its Polish-born chief Felix Dzerzhinsky, hunted down enemies of the Revolution. They were later to be redefined as a class by Stalin with catastrophic effect on all those—the NEP-men, as they were called, in the cities, *kulaks* in the countryside—who had gained from the period of economic relaxation. Doing well economically was equated with exploitation, and an extra room or perhaps possessing a cow might make the difference between the exploited and the exploiter. As the Soviet mind-set developed, political assassins, peaceful opponents of the regime or its policies and unwelcome contestants for power within the Bolshevik Party itself were all lumped together with those of the wrong economic class or social background as 'enemies of the people', a term which was later to be given a precise legal meaning, often with fatal consequences.

The second effect was that Fanny Kaplan's shot (or perhaps more specifically, Lenin's rapid recovery) launched the Lenin cult, which even today is not completely extinguished. The Bolshevik press in 1918 declared his survival a miracle; Lenin himself was associated with the divine and blessed with supernatural powers.[22] In Soviet times, the figure of Lenin as Christ is based on the dead seriousness and devotion of his many believers, and can possibly be explained only by recourse to analysis of crowd hysteria. In his 1918 poem 'The Twelve', the Symbolist poet Alexander Blok portrayed the Red Guards of Petrograd as apostles with Christ himself at their head. Lenin died in 1924 following a series of strokes, and late photographs of him with his nurses show him as an uncomprehending human shell.

Lenin's legacy to the city is generally less certain than electrification but still visible. As we have seen the symbolism of the mausoleum holding his preserved (at least, officially) body has both a religious as well as a historical reference. By Orthodox tradition, many saints are interred with their uncorrupted remains exposed in underground vaults. The flags bearing his name and image, Lenin memorabilia and even his 24-volume *Collected Works* can now be bought for rock-bottom prices at the flea-market at Izmailovo and other semi-legal places around the city. A collection of his statues, along with those of Stalin, has been dumped behind the Museum of Contemporary Art, across from Gorky Park. On the Arbat, the pedestrian area in the centre of Moscow, he lives on as the innermost component of *matryushka* nesting dolls, now sometimes replaced by Nicholas II.

The NEP and its associated policies, including the relatively tolerant attitude of the state to political and artistic diversity, would survive for another four years following Lenin's death. Some analysts argue that this was the time it took for Stalin to ensure his own succession, and that this process took all his attention. Even so, the Bolshevik response to Fanny Kaplan's attempted murder of their leader by the rapid institutionalization of a vast political police apparatus at the heart of government—itself a creation of Lenin—created the preconditions for the tragedy that followed.[23]

The First Five-Year Plan was announced in 1928, accompanied by its foreign policy counterpart, 'socialism in one country'. In a period of capitalist encirclement the state would become stronger, not weaker. By extension, foreigners were not to be trusted, irrespective of their proletarian credentials or sympathies. Under Stalinism those unable to absorb this message, including the internationalists—for those of Moscow's Silver Age had as their first reference the culture of Europe—and the idealists in the Comintern who looked to promoting world revolution, went down together, both bewildered in their revolutionary idealism. Moscow may have been the capital of world revolution, but the Soviet state came first and Moscow was the capital of the Soviet state.

Failure to make this distinction, or to understand it, brought many to grief. Despite the continued enthusiasm amongst Western Marxists, and the continued existence of Comintern headquarters in Moscow, proletarian internationalism was already dead by the time of the Spanish Civil War. The Molotov–Ribbentrop Treaty buried it.

In retrospect, 'War Communism' was the actual precursor of Moscow's future development, not the NEP's tactical 'breathing space' allowed by Lenin. As a prototype of Stalin's Five-Year Plans, it called for the unrestricted deployment of force to secure the survival of the communist state. It also served the triple purpose of consolidating the regime itself, conducting class warfare (later to be perfected by Stalin who deployed the entire state apparatus as its instrument) and laying the foundations of a command economy where economic development was conducted in the form of a military campaign, with vocabulary and organization to match. Under the Five-Year Plans civil society became militarized, which led to the adoption of military vocabulary to civilian goals: 'the front of steel production' or 'mobilization of workers on the agricultural front'.

The Moscow Metro, the Moscow–Volga Canal and the great hydroelectric projects of central Russia were all to be built by means of militarily inspired organization. One of the most insidious effects was on the use of language, which became polluted with acronyms. Gulag, disguising the human misery beneath, is the best-known example, but this quasi-telegraphic practice extended into virtually all aspects of public life, from the highest, GOSPLAN and SOVNARKOM (Council of Peoples' Commissars, or government) to the most mundane, MOSOBSHCHEPIT, standing for Moscow General Food Enterprise, Moskovskoye Obshchestvennoye Pitaniye Predpriyatiye, printed on the back of every plate produced in the city. Similarly, the language of the Party newspaper *Pravda* and the government newspaper *Izvestiya* became simplified to the point of unreadability. People began looking between the lines for hidden meaning in the text, and perhaps for clues to shifts in policy that would help them in their own survival. Only in the post-Stalinist years did brave intellectual journals like *Novy Mir* attempt to rescue the language from the dead hand of socialist realism.

It was not only the unusually cold winters of the 1920s that prepared the ground for the transformation of Moscow in the 1930s. The defeat of the White Army had released many men from war, and they had already migrated to Moscow and other large Russian cities. The Russian architectural historian Vladimir Paperny observed, 'It was a time of dramatic explosion of population, the highest rate of urbanization ever achieved in human history.'[24] By the 1930s millions of peasants had moved to the city, he wrote, because of the vacuum left by purges and mass arrests, and hunger created by forced collectivization in the countryside. Another Russian author was moved to record that 'the movement of millions of people [into the city] ... resulted in that bright-eyed, high-cheekboned people filled the streets ... while in the barracks of the labour camps [were] sad

Petersburgers with their French-sounding 'r's.'[25] It was class war brought to the city with a vengeance.

As the Revolution became bureaucratized, Stalinism locked the system in a vice, effectively destroying the impersonal power of cash as a medium of exchange and, potentially, of social mobility and personal freedom. Money as the term is normally understood became for Gosplan merely a unit of account. The parallel, underground economy, already extant in tsarist times, became a standing feature of the entire Soviet era as arrangements *na levo* (on the side) perforce replaced the pivotal role of money as the 'cash nexus' of economic exchange. In the process Moscow became the crucible of Stalin's 'permanent revolution', now turned inward to Russia and its empire alone, now called the USSR. Building 'socialism' became synonymous with building Stalinism. The civil war of the early 1920s had become, under Stalin, the class war of the 1930s, 'Revolution from Above' conducted by the state against its own citizens. According to State Archives of the Soviet Economy, there were some 8 million 'excess deaths' in direct consequence of this process, which included those who perished in the Gulag in conditions of deportation.

Moscow became grey, the colour of uniformity of the streets as well as of the people, not only of appearance but also of the spirit. In strange contrast to the below-ground decorative effusions of the Moscow Metro, the above-ground buildings became grey. The famous Government House (or 'House on the Embankment'), built as living quarters for the elite, was originally designed by its architect Boris Iofan to be encased in white marble. On the orders of Lunacharsky, Gosplan allowed only dark grey stucco, also the shade of the Great Terror and the purges that swept through Moscow and other Soviet cities in the 1930s: grey NKVD uniforms in grey police vehicles; grey railway wagons transporting deportees to the grey Gulag barracks of Siberia.

Moscow and the Revolution Betrayed

Moscow's transition from the City of the Dreadful Night of the early post-war period to the City of Monuments of High Stalinism has its foundations in this period. In the process, and with the exception of the Kremlin, the look of the city changed almost beyond recognition. In the midst of massive in-migration, wooden Moscow was gone, burned for firewood, surviving only here and there in forlorn islands, last places of refuge of the unemployed *lumpenproletariat* who had no place in Marx's scheme of things. Soviet Moscow was to become a vertical city, its population as stratified as the multi-storey steel and concrete buildings that were to be built among the ashes. By the early 1920s the *nomenklatura* system was already well-established. Senior government officials and party members were classified according to their rank and responsibilities, from which derived their concomitant privileges as defined and administered by the state. They became effectively a new caste. The emergence of the new elite had an anomalous effect on Moscow's development, as they were largely exempted from the collectivist canon of the revolution, expropriating pre-revolutionary dachas for their own purposes at Serebryannyi Bor and elsewhere. The reality was that the dacha communities surrounding the city supplied the traditional means of escape from the noisomeness of Moscow before the Revolution, and after. The best-known is Peredelkino, the literary colony. Boris Pasternak is buried there.

Beginning with the move of the capital to Moscow, early communist city planning focused on the destruction of hierarchical (or 'feudal', as it was then called) aspects of the city, its concentric structure and its division into socially differentiated districts, the result of the accretion of centuries of natural growth. Even then, influence of the *nomenklatura* hierarchy could be seen in the construction of new six-and seven-storey luxury apartments in favoured areas of Moscow, such as the embankment of the Moskva River. The French intellectual and writer André Gide was shocked to discover 'the reappearance of social strata, a kind of aristocracy', and in many of the apartments of the *nomenklatura* the existence of maids' rooms. The new flats of the elite, which became increasingly in evidence in the late 1930s, held the potential of frustrating even the greatest of urban plans if they conflicted with the wishes of their occupants, for many had been hand-picked by Stalin himself. Consequently, man-made islands of the elite grew up in the midst of the Muscovite industrial site surrounding them. The neoclassical buildings of the late 1930s tended to be self-contained and autonomous, resembling in some respects the *slobodas* of Moscow's sixteenth and seventeenth centuries: homes of the privileged, guarded at the gates and under constant surveillance, within as well as without. For the elite, there was little talk of or attraction to the forced and cramped accommodation offered by the working-class *kommunalki.* In many elite homes comfort was provided by lace curtains and antimacassars, dainty doilies on the backs of heavy chairs. In the right-hand corner of the largest room there might by a portrait of Lenin or Stalin to replace the traditional icon and its candle. But just to be sure, the icon with its candle lit would often be found in its proper corner of the flat owner's dacha.

Trotsky's bitter anti-Stalinist tract, *The Revolution Betrayed*, written in exile in 1936, ascribed the 'degeneration of the Bolshevik Party into a bureaucracy' to two basic causes: following victory in the civil war, the demobilization of the Red Army of 5 million which released a huge number of officers for administrative activity; and the decision of the Tenth Congress of the Party in 1921 to forbid factions within it. This allowed Lenin's principle of 'democratic centralism', by which there should be unity of purpose following a Party decision, to become unanimity within the decision-making process itself. As a result, Trotsky wrote, 'revolutionaries had been replaced by *chinovniki,* bureaucrats'. This was the origin of the general atmosphere within subsequent Party Congresses beginning at the turn of the decade into the 1930s and beyond.

Held in the Bolshoi Theatre, the congresses' successive stenographic reports of Stalin's speeches are studded with the phrases like 'Heavy and sustained applause', culminating in 'Agitation in the hall, heavy and sustained applause, all rise'. In fact, as many observers have noted, in the late 1920s it is very unlikely that Stalin would ever have won an open election as successor to Lenin. Some go further, saying that of all the possible candidates he would have been the last.[26] This short, pockmarked man from the sticks of the Caucasus never managed to rid himself of his Georgian accent. Among the brilliant members of the Party, including Trotsky, he was permanently in the shade, holding unprestigious editorial jobs and later, as Party secretary, recording the decisions of others, ensuring their implementation and overseeing Party housekeeping, including the management of cadres or membership, for which he earned the nickname 'Comrade Filing-Cabinet'. His state function, as Commissar of Nationalities, seemed to condemn him to the periphery, dealing with inconsequential, historically irrelevant peoples far removed from the 'tide of history': the Uzbeks and the Kyrgyz as well as other distant nationalities like the occasional Kalmyk or Chechen. Some of his less astute opponents mockingly noted that his only claim to fame was shaving off Lenin's beard when the latter was in hiding. This assessment of Stalin proved a fatal mistake.

From the launching of the First Five-Year Plan into the mid-1930s Moscow's character underwent further transformation. Bolshevik doctrinal flexibility and the willingness to compromise, as exemplified by the NEP and the intellectual experimentation of the earlier post-revolutionary period, disappeared. Public debate and the competing ideas that underpinned it were replaced by enforced unanimity. Strict adherence to the 'Party line' became an iron rule. Under Stalin unanimity in politics translated into uniformity at all levels of public life, architecture included. Uniformity of concept and design was now enforced by unified, state-sponsored architectural organizations whose prime function was to enforce concepts of socialism in urban planning and construction. With the Stalinist urban revolution, the relative freedom of architectural innovation and experimentation ceased.

In Stalinist urban planning Moscow's centre took precedence over the periphery, and large projects and monumental expressions of state power took priority over more mundane aspects of urban development. Not that these were ignored. Stalin in his *incognito* nightly walks once returned to the Kremlin to order Khrushchev to open more public toilets in the city, and seemed fascinated with Moscow's sewerage system.

Social engineering was integral to the process. The growth and composition of Moscow's population reflected the priorities of the Five-Year Plans and its requirements in terms of the human raw material necessary to achieve set objectives. Amid explosive growth, elaborate systems for control of urban populations were established, including work permits and internal passports. Welfare, at least as the term came to be understood in the West, did not exist. During the early phases of 'socialist construction' Moscow's urban workers did not live under noticeably better living conditions than their nineteenth-century forebears.

Yet, 'building socialism' in Moscow would not have been possible without the idealism, dedication and self-sacrifice of those who earnestly believed that they were constructing a better future. This went beyond those who sacrificed themselves, wittingly or not, in the dark and pestilential bore-tunnels of the Moscow Metro. Not all the heavy work was done by ZEKs and forced labour on Stalin's grand projects, some was done by Komsomol Brigades—again, the military designation—and *subbotniki,* volunteers offering their free time. Perhaps even more astonishingly, within the Party many old Bolsheviks, dedicated first-generation revolutionaries whom Stalin regarded as potential challenges to his power, were invited to practise extreme forms of self-abnegation, which required confession before execution. Criticism and self-criticism, *kritika i samokritika*, became expected, and indeed codified, operational procedure in the Great Purge Trials of the 1930s as well as on the shop floor, in the latter case for shortcomings in production activity or of 'incorrect attitudes towards work', usually drunkenness. Arthur Koestler's *Darkness at Noon* is a fictionalized account of the actual trial of the old Bolshevik Nikolai Bukharin, who admitted guilt he did not deserve for the sake of Party unity.[27] Explaining himself before his execution, Bukharin said that the thought of 'going out alone unforgiven, apart from the Party ... which to me is life itself, was a prospect I could not face'. Richard Crossman, writing in *The God That Failed*, noted the same religious quality of martyrdom in communism, 'a belief that offered nothing, and demanded everything'.[28]

The same level of self-denying sacrifice was expected at the rock-face and the building site. Aleksei Stakhanov's achievement of producing 102 tons of coal in a six-hour shift, four times the norm in 1935, set a standard that invited suicidal emulation. Lionized at the time, it turned out that he dug the coal from an already prepared vein, and with a large team supporting him. Stakhanov's 'overfulment of the norm' was a pioneering example of the temptation to distort planning and to report false statistics. This practice bedevilled Soviet planners thereafter, including those involved in housing construction in Stalinist Moscow. In the interests of exceeding the norm in record time, apartments were half-completed with the job declared done, for that was where the rewards lay in terms of promotion and bonuses. Lower-status maintenance workers were left to pick up the pieces.

These blemishes on rapid industrialization notwithstanding, socialist emulation, encouraging workers to overreach their norms, became as much a slogan for the country's—and Moscow's—development as electrification. Sponsored by Sergo Ordzhonikidze, the Minister of Industry and fellow-Georgian of Stalin's inner circle, the slogan for the 1928 First Five-Year Plan was 'Five in Four', achieving the goal of the plan ahead of schedule.

Many welcomed the bloodletting and purges of the 1930s, as it opened up career prospects for the second generation of Party cadres who saw their path to promotion blocked by the old Bolsheviks. These Party elders upheld their claims to superior legitimacy and hence authority because of their association with the early days of the struggle.

Stalin's reading of human nature was deadly accurate. His control of Party cadres ended in checkmate for any of the old Bolsheviks who stood against him, and for that matter any whom he judged to have even the remotest potential of doing so. Technically, Stalin was an old Bolshevik himself and a close associate of Lenin at that. He was later disowned by his master, a fact he was at pains to keep secret. By 'delegitimizing' and in a number of instances physically eliminating his opponents he opened the way for the next generation whose career prospects depended exclusively on him.

Both within the Party and in Soviet society as a whole, Stalin's dictum, that under socialism the class struggle intensifies, provided a means for the zealous and ambitious to eliminate human obstructions to their advancement. To the dialectically inclined there was no contradiction between the Stalin constitution of 1936, 'the freest constitution in the world', guaranteeing the entire range of freedoms and human rights, abolishing discrimination and even announcing the right of secession of each Soviet Republic, and the final annihilation of the remaining old Bolsheviks, Bukharin included, in the Great Terror beginning in 1936.

The atmosphere generated by the Five-Year Plans prevailed in Moscow, affecting the city directly. The demands of industrialization had increased its population of 2.2 million in 1929 to 3.6 million in 1936. One of the lesser reasons why early post-revolutionary plans for the destruction of the old and the creation of the new Moscow never got off the ground is that city planners expected an urban population of a million and a half by 1935 or 1940. Like the visionary plans of the1920s, the plan for New Moscow called for the razing of the city's core and concentrating functions according to district, but it died before it was born. Even before the execution in January 1937 of Lev Kamemev, the Plan's principal sponsor, the project was doomed to failure.

At the time of Kamenev's death, the General Plan for the Reconstruction of Moscow had been adopted by the Plenum of the Party Central Committee, and simultaneously by the Soviet government at the level of the Council of Ministers (SOVNARKOM). Earlier, in the summer of 1932, the tendency of architects to assert their artistic independence had been brought under firm control by a resolution of the Central Committee applying to all the arts. Entitled 'On Restructuring of Literary-Creative Organizations', it replaced autonomous writers' organizations with the single Union of Soviet Writers. The Central Committee's resolution stipulated that 'analogous changes be made in the other arts'. The Union of Soviet Architects was established the same year. Originally scheduled for 1 March 1936, its first congress was held on 15 June after the meeting had been delayed six times because of the Party's insistence that each speech and document be vetted and approved.

The General Plan for the Reconstruction of Moscow held

little space for the contribution of architects and dreamers. It was a document out of the Party's Central Committee headed by the omnipotent Stalin himself and implemented by Lazar Kaganovich, the Moscow Party first secretary, and his energetic subordinate Nikita Khrushchev. Under Stalin, Moscow, like the country itself, would become a place of mammoth construction and of wanton destruction, both human and material.

Beginning with Stalin, for over a generation aesthetics became the preserve of the Party. Socialist realism—positive, understandable and future-oriented—governed architecture as much as all the other arts. In a 1939 publication entitled *A New Moscow in Construction,* Dmitry Chechulin, the head of the planning department of the executive committee of the Moscow City Soviet, and one of the founders of the Soviet mass-culture monumentalist school of architecture, inadvertently presents the mindset expected of pre-war architects under Stalinism. As Party members became bureaucrats, so architects became engineers:

> All of the capital's pipes and wires will be tucked away in a subterranean collector system which will run alongside the tunnels of the subway. The gas mains will supply the factories, laboratories, offices and homes with over 20,000,000,000 cubic feet of gas a year, the water mains with 486,000,000 gallons of pure liquid every day, in contrast with 129,000,000 gallons in 1934. Telephone wires and electric cables, sewage pipes and distance heating tubes, conveying hot water, steam and heated air from central heat-and-power plants will also be enclosed in these collectors.[29]

Stalin's own aesthetic, summed up as 'socialist realism', has a vague and tortured history, but even in today's Moscow its presence is immediately recognizable in public spaces, from sculptures in Metro stations to paintings in galleries. The term, as adopted at the First Congress of Soviet Writers, was intended to encompass an overall philosophy for all the arts—that all Soviet cultural production should reflect and advance socialist ideals of organization and economic development. Above all, the message should be positive and forward-looking. When applied to architecture, it ended the experimentation of the constructivist school, now condemned as 'formalism', that is, being suspiciously internationalist and susceptible to foreign influences.

A larger-than-life 1937 work by Alexander Samokhvalov represents the effect of socialist realism in the visual arts. Entitled *Metrostroyevka* (Builder of the Metro), it depicts a powerfully built young woman in a formal pose grasping an industrial drill. The play of light on her worker's overalls transforms them into the sensuous linen folds of Greek statuary. The walls of the pit in which she works hint at the columns of classical architecture. As a symbol, she has become a caryatid, the bearer of a new civilization, successor to her effete male cousins bearing the weight of the portico of the Winter Palace upon their shoulders.

Moscow's glorification of worker and peasant reached its climax with Vera Mukhina's 27-metre stainless steel monument *Worker and Kolkhoz Woman* holding aloft a hammer and sickle. It has 'branded' Soviet Russia as much as the Statue of Liberty stands for the United States. The comparison is deliberate. With their respective bases included, the Soviet statue is 19 metres taller (112 as opposed to 93 metres). Created the same year as the *Metrostroyevka* painting and displayed on top of the Soviet pavilion at the 1937 Paris Exhibition, it now stands at the entrance to the Park of Economic Achievements. In Stalin's time the park was known as the All-Union Agricultural Exhibition and was intended to demonstrate the successes of collectivization.[30]

In 1948 a painting of the same genre, bearing the title *The Morning of Our Motherland,* depicts Stalin in early morning light gazing across wheat fields to distant high-tension electric pylons.[31] It won that year's Stalin Prize. Once it was safe to do so, the socialist realist style and its close brush with kitsch were parodied, particularly when the subject was Stalin, himself the object of a pervasive, un-Marxist cult.[32] One composition, *The Origin of Socialist Realism* (1982-3), painted by two collaborating artists Komar and Melamid in the officially approved style, depicts Stalin sitting bolt upright in his marshal's uniform, staring straight ahead while accosted by a naked Muse about to climb on for a lap-dance. The background has all the neoclassical clichés, complete with heavy draped curtains and Doric columns. For this genre of satirical painting (another was called, *I Once Saw Stalin as a Child*) the two artists were expelled from the Soviet Artists' Union in 1973.

Contradictions persisted in the physical look of Moscow of the 1930s. Socialist realism in the arts, including architecture, conflicted with physical reality. At great human cost, Moscow had become a palatial workers' paradise below ground, combining in its architecture the proletarian image with the Greek ideal; above ground, it was a different story. In some of the stations the conflation was explicit. The Dynamo Station, leading to the Stadium and sports complex—itself eerily reminiscent of the Nuremberg Stadium where Nazi rallies were held—has the appearance of a Greek temple, complete with a sculpted frieze of athletes on its upper walls, a clear reference to the Parthenon.

Moscow's crash industrialization of the 1930s created a new generation of slums, rivalling their nineteenth-century predecessors. In the First Five-Year Plan, Moscow housing, even after dividing existing housing yet again, was unable to absorb the 800,000 new workers and their families who had been commandeered to work on the new construction projects. The short-term expedient took the form of estates of open-bay, roughly built bunkhouses or *baraki,* put up by the state enterprises where the workers were assigned. In the early 1930s one such building, attached to the electronics enterprise Elektrozavod, held 550 men and women, each of whom had an average of 2.2 square metres of floor space. Many of them were obliged to 'hot-bed', sleeping in the same bed in shifts, or on the floor.[33] Although *baraki* were officially banned in the later 1930s, state enterprises continued to build similar bunkhouses on Moscow's unregulated vacant land. The quality of construction and density were about the same, but the name, *standartnyye doma* or 'standardized houses', sounded less ominous.

Even under these awful conditions there were exceptions. Workers' palaces were not always confined to below ground. One of the greatest constructivist monuments, the Rusakov Club for Transport Workers, was completed one year before the First Five-Year Plan, in 1927. Even after constructivism had fallen out of favour, its modernist/cubist design became a pilgrimage site for architectural historians, since the Rusakov Club represented a style linked to the left-wing ideas of the Bauhaus school of inter-war Germany. The building's many architectural innovations are in support of its ostensible function as a meeting-place for workers in conditions of comfort and ease. In practice, it was also designed to perform another function, now largely forgotten: to replace the Church as an atheistic meeting-place for the now liberated victors of revolution and focusing undivided loyalty on the socialist state. The building is also intolerably ugly.

Moscow in the Aftermath of High Stalinism

On the eve of the Great Patriotic War the Moscow of the late 1930s presented a muddy, uneven landscape, giving the impression of being two cities in one. The first was horizontal Moscow, the big urban village, domain of the first- and second-generation working classes whose underground Metro palaces were works in progress; and the second, the vertical, along the main approaches to the Kremlin, the six- and seven-storey neoclassical buildings of the ruling elite. The ring of wooden structures temporarily erected to accommodate the influx of workers now replaced the industrial shantytowns of an earlier generation. With massive projects to widen roads and to create vast public spaces, the planners were designing a new Moscow to be the showpiece of a new civilization, overshadowing Berlin and New York.

The Kremlin bells now chimed the opening bars of the *Internationale.* Replayed on Radio Moscow as a call-signal, they rivalled in familiarity the BBC's Big Ben striking the hours. The purges of the 1930s and the Great Terror generally left the workers untouched. Their lot had in fact improved. If housing remained a problem, programmes of universal education and a rough-and-ready health care system, combined with the installation of municipal sanitation and other measures, brought a modicum of comfort. In the Stalinist hunting-grounds of the Great Terror, the prey were the professional classes and the politically active, not generally the workers, referred to in Soviet guide-books for political activists as 'the masses'.[34] Provided one belonged to the right social class and had the right ethnic credentials, there was a reasonable chance of having a relatively normal existence.

The Second World War put most of Moscow's projects on hold. Already in trouble because of engineering and other problems, the Palace of Soviets had its steel structure dismantled to build the defences around Moscow, but even at the height of the Battle of Moscow construction of the Metro continued. Following the war, in the period known as High Stalinism, the reconstruction of Moscow resumed. The Seven Sisters gave architectural expression to the High Stalinism of 1950s Moscow, and gave final shape to the profile of the city until the fall of communism. At last street-talk of post-war Moscow would refer to them as *neboscreby*, literally 'skyscrapers' in reference to their American cousins (and not the officially approved 'high buildings', the term deliberately intended to distance them from their capitalist competitors). With some cynicism, Moscow street-talk also referred to the makeshift dwellings of the workers as 'groundscrapers'.

The change in the 'feel' of Moscow and in Soviet life in general after Stalin's death at the age of 73 in March 1953 was surprisingly abrupt. His funeral and lying in state in the Hall of Columns generated scenes of genuine emotion for the loss of a leader whom many believed immortal. But the mood and the politics had changed. Formerly untouchable, Stalin's own place in Soviet history came increasingly under scrutiny. By resolution of the Twenty-Second Party Congress in October 1961 Stalin's body was removed from the Lenin mausoleum and buried in a deep pit behind. The slab on top simply reads, 'J. V. Stalin'.[35] Of his interment, the poet Yevgeny Yevtushenko was later to write: 'He was scheming. Had merely dozed off. And I, appealing to our government, petition them to double, and treble, the sentries guarding his slab, and stop Stalin from ever rising again, and with Stalin, the past...'[36]

Less than a year after Stalin's death, Ilya Eherenberg's novel *The Thaw* appeared in *Novy Mir*. Reflecting the new mood, the novel portrayed a self-seeking, three-dimensional figure who happened to be a communist. It caused a sensation among a war-experienced and newly literate population, for in a single book the official image of life on the collective farm and in the workplace was destroyed. Stalinist monumentalism in Moscow architecture was out of sync with the times.

By the mid-1950s *stilyagi*, zoot-suited teenage children of the elite complete with pegged trousers and jazzy shirts, appeared on the streets of Moscow in sartorial protest against their parents' grey and frightened generation. Complaints about the Stalinist legacy in film-making, where all the talk on screen was of bulldozers and tractors, became more assertive and frequent. There were the first, hesitant steps toward the shrinking of the Gulag, and former *Zeks* found ready employment in post-war construction projects in Moscow and other Russian cities. The Great Fatherland War had prepared the ground for the liberation of Soviet citizens from Stalinism, but in ways unimagined by the country's new leaders as they struggled to redefine their roles. In the process, Moscow would never be the same again.

Even as the *stilyagi* lounged about the streets of Moscow and the reverberations of *The Thaw* were in the air, Nikita Khrushchev, still only a member among others in the Party's Central Committee, addressed a 'Builders' Conference' in the Kremlin Great Palace on 30 November 1954. His interest, besides being responsible under Kaganovich for the early phases of the Metro's construction in the early 1930s, was his experience as first secretary of the Moscow City Party from 1938. It was a remarkable performance, for it signalled the end of Stalinism in architecture well before Stalinism itself was discredited in politics; in the arts, too, it was only just being challenged, and then with great hesitation.

Ignoring his own role in the creative destruction of Moscow, Khrushchev denounced the 'extravagances and superfluities' of the massive apartment blocks built along Moscow's main arteries for the elite. He announced, in the name of the Party, that the days of the construction of 'high buildings' were over,[37] and accused the cream of the Soviet architectural community gathered in the hall of 'wanting pretty silhouettes' for Moscow when people wanted apartments. Inevitably, the Second Congress of Soviet Architects held shortly thereafter unanimously endorsed this radical change in direction. With Khrushchev's direct interest and prompting, a new functionalist style of buildings and city planning spread out side by side with the creations of High Stalinism, but never replaced them.

As the outward appearance of Moscow moved away from its jumble of Stalinist-heroic buildings and makeshift dwellings to the urban practicalities of infrastructure and accommodation, the *kommunalki,* residences of communal living, disappeared. Khrushchev's interest was not above ordering plastic toilet seats for the mass-produced apartment blocks he promoted. At one blow he put paid to almost a half-century of theorizing about how to give architectural expression to the communal ideal. Khrushchev had tacitly acknowledged that the wish for privacy was integral to the human condition.

In 1961 Yuri Gagarin became the first man in space, while Moscow grew outwards as well as upwards. The close association of Moscow with communism and its inextricable links with the triumphant Soviet experiment (or so it was thought by many at the time), demonstrated by victory in the war and now by triumph in space, was symbolized by the location of Moscow city's Party headquarters just two doors away from the Party's Central Committee headquarters on Staraya Ploshchad in central Moscow.[38] The Supreme Soviet decreed a larger Moscow, more than doubling its size from 35,000 hectares to 88,600, making its surface area larger than New York and over four times the size of Paris.[39] Khrushchev's no-nonsense, utilitarian approach, and his insistence that the needs of urban housing be met by 'type plans', i.e. modular construction, led to a housing boom and the development of 'micro-regions'; in turn, these developed into the 'housing massifs' of the Brezhnev era of the 1970s that encircled Moscow from the south-west. The first was Novye Cheremushki, a demonstration estate of several hectares, but Khrushchev's suburban sprawl of high-density apartment estates rapidly spread in the form of huge projects like Tuparevo, completed in the late 1970s. By the early 1980s, almost two decades after Khrushchev had been forced from office (he was removed in a coup in 1964), his legacy continued in the construction of further apartment complexes around Moscow. One such project of the 1980s, Strogino, contained a population of 150,000. Over 70 per cent of Moscow's present housing is in the high-density estates typical of the micro-regions.

Beginning with Khrushchev, the basis of Moscow's housing boom (from the 1950s to the 1980s average flat sizes increased from 28-square-metre one-room dwellings to three or four rooms with over double the area) was the belief that pre-cast ferro-concrete slabs erected on a steel framework provided the most rapid and cost-effective solution to the city's urgent housing problems. This building technique permitted an entire five-storey block to be built by semi-skilled labour in a single season. This construction technique gave the new 'micro-regions' of Moscow the look of a dense field of upright matchboxes. The simplicity of their construction did not allow for some of the more architecturally imaginative and sophisticated building methods, including the use of reinforced concrete. The huge complexes of Novye Cheremushki and Khoroshevo-Mnevniky, however, were originally intended as a short-term expedient and not the final answer to the socialist dream of good housing for all. By the 1980s Khrushchev's five-storey rule (calculated as the maximum number of storeys that could be climbed without inviting a health risk) had been superseded by taller buildings, usually of nine or twelve storeys. Some were built as high as twenty storeys once lifts were deemed a justifiable expense.

Soviet-produced lifts tended to be cramped and dark and

liable to breakdown, even well into the 1980s. Their jolting stops eliminated any possibility of their use as places of assignation. Even now, I have some queasiness at the thought of visiting a Russian acquaintance's apartment for the first time if there is an unknown lift; there are always two threatening possibilities: either that the lift will balk and stall between floors; or that it will take a dive to the basement.

The ferro-concrete slabs used in Khrushchev-era construction programmes suffered from numerous problems. They did not always fit together accurately, and shoddy construction techniques combined with inferior materials made them the perennial butt of jokes. The satirical magazine *Krokodil* made much of the ageing of new apartment blocks even before they were finished. Problems were exacerbated by extensive pilfering on the shop floor and on the worksite. Many dachas were built of expropriated materials, technically designated as state property. The spontaneous, opportunistic nature of the dachas' construction gave them a happy, slap-dash look. As a result, there were frequent unplanned shortages on the housing estates, and there were many complaints about new flats without sinks or doors without doorknobs. The 'parallel economy' did a roaring business in making up the difference, participation reaching into the highest levels of the Party.

On the larger scale, some Western critics celebrated the new apartment complexes. One observer eulogized the entire Khrushchev construction programme as producing buildings of 'lyrical plainness, transparency and expression of economy at its best'.[40] Only with the turn of the millennium are these buildings of 'lyrical plainness' being replaced by Western-style apartment blocks of higher quality with at least some regard for aesthetics.

But even in these complexes, now that privacy was an accepted part of Soviet Moscow, the Law of Unintended Consequences prevailed. The privacy now offered by the kitchen table was supplemented by the introduction of the photocopy machine. If the public entrances to the apartment blocks still remained open to all, locks were now routinely installed on apartment doors. These created the conditions where discussions were now possible among a circle of trusted friends. With the advent of privacy and the means to enjoy it, in the absence of surveillance an entire culture of foreign broadcasts and *samizdat* (underground publishing) material would eventually develop. In turn, this would set the stage for the human rights and reform movements of the 1980s.

Khrushchev was also the initiator of an architectural sea-change to Moscow's public buildings, although the ingrained habit of giganticism lingered. In public buildings his 'new functionalism' was a reinterpretation of Stalinist monumentalism, but appropriate to the sputnik era with its emphasis on a modernist approach to Moscow's public face. The setting for Khrushchev's apotheosis was the Party's Twenty-Second Congress held in the Kremlin Palace of Congresses. Besides his final denunciation of Stalin, Khrushchev announced the Party Programme for the completion of the transition from socialism to communism, to be completed in twenty years' time: the USSR would surpass the United States in per capita production, and the distinction between town and country would disappear.

Begun in 1959 under the direction of an architectural team headed by Mikhail Posokhin, the building was rushed to completion against the deadline of the Congress opening, and was inaugurated on the same day, 18 October 1961, a few months after Yuri Gagarin's historic flight. Half of the building was underground, and with its reflective glass and neutral marble facing, it was specifically designed not to disturb the ensemble of the other Kremlin buildings. There were some complaints that its construction was illegal as a number of historic buildings were destroyed to make way for it, but the complaints were suppressed. Its practicality was strikingly anti-Stalinist, and in its poetic justice matches the removal of Stalin's body from the Lenin's mausoleum, decided at the same Congress. The Kremlin Palace of Congresses also put a formal end to the inhumanly vast project of the Palace of Soviets, replacing it with a low-profiled building holding some 6,000 delegates. The 'Little Hall' of the Palace of Soviets would have held that number; the Main Hall, 21,000.

Khrushchev's sense of monumentalism stayed with him. Inspired by his initiative, the 100-metre Monument to the Conquest of Space carries the inscription:

I nashi tem nagrazhdenye usil'ya
Chto poborov bespravie i t'mu
My otkovali plamennye kryl'ya
Svoei
Strane
I veku svoiemu

And thus our strivings are rewarded
For triumph over oppression and darkness
We forged wings of fire
For our country
And for our century

Less reverential Muscovites, true to their city's rough character, were prompted by the suggestive angle of the monument's rocket plume to dub it 'the impotent man's dream'.

After the exuberant energy of Khrushchev, things slowed down under his successor, Leonid Brezhnev,[41] whose period one historian described as 'less of the same'. Mikhail Posokhin was put in charge of the remaking of Moscow. He devised a new General Plan which was approved by the Central Committee and the Council of Ministers in 1971. Prospekt Kalinina, or 'the New Arbat' in the centre of Moscow, a product of the Brezhnev era, is built in a modernist style that would not be out of place in Stockholm. Under the 1971 Plan, the city's outer regions and massive apartment complexes took final shape. New sports complexes graced the skyline in preparation for the 1980 Olympics, and in a major technical and construction achievement Ostankino Television Tower reached 385 metres into the sky on a 4-metre base. By its height it dominates the city, rather like the Berlin television tower dominating both sides of 1970s and 1980s Berlin. Besides modernizing the city's skyline, the Brezhnev era of *zastoi*, or stagnation as it was called, produced one building which would be the stage-set upon which key acts in the drama of the fall of communism and its aftermath would be enacted—the White House. In its symbolic role, it was to become Moscow's equivalent of the Brandenburg Gate, where people stood triumphant over a disintegrating East German regime and a collapsed Berlin Wall.

USSR postage stamp of the White House, issued in October 1991. President Yeltsin faced down the coup leaders from this building.

Chapter Eight
The Turbulent Passage

The moral conviction, the sense of unity, the optimism, the belief in themselves, the devotion to public work, the enthusiasm for the common cause—all these are beyond the power of description. The flavour and the atmosphere of the social environment of the building up of Moscow that is taking place can only be captured by the personal experience of a visit. The impact of these forces almost takes away one's breath by its tremendous strength.

Sir E. D. Simon, 1935

In a short period of time, this lieutenant colonel of the KGB [Putin] carried out what amounted to a coup d'état. Power was seized by a clique of bitter, rancorous and greedy KGB officers. Democracy was demolished, along with the freedom of the media. Russia became a typical authoritarian country, with a corrupt and repressive government...

Oleg Gordievsky, 2009

Muscovites appear to be more concerned with the latest restaurant openings than the latest legislative debate... The optimism is pervasive. It is evident in the construction of skyscrapers, shopping malls, theme parks and theatres, in the 'world premieres' and 'grand openings'; and on the faces of shoppers, strollers, diners and drinkers on the crowded Moscow streets.

Lonely Planet, 2009

Clad in marble, the White House, or the Building of the Council of Ministers of the Russian Federation as it is now called, stands on a bend of the Moskva River to the west of the city centre. Over the bridge is the massive Ukraina Hotel. Nearby is the former headquarters of the Council of Mutual Economic Assistance (CMEA), the defunct organization intended as the Soviet answer to the European Economic Community. In 1991 it was taken over as a command post by the KGB's Alpha Group for a possible assault on the White House.[1] The ensemble of the three buildings and the bridge that joins them form the gates of the route to Mozhaisk, the traditional path of invaders from the west, and now one of the great triumphal ways into the centre of the city.

The White House belongs to the same generation as the Kremlin's Palace of Congresses, both having monumental vastness of scale, but minus the elaborate decoration of 1950s Stalinist Moscow. Its streamlined shape, however, does not belong to the 1960s when it was built but to the 1930s, its inspiration coming from the exploits of a Soviet aircrew which rescued the men of the icebreaker *Chelyuskin* from an ice floe in 1934. It was originally designed as headquarters for Aeroflot, and was to have pillars at its entrance in honour of each of the airmen-heroes.

Significantly, the White House, and not the Kremlin, was the main public setting for the failed coup of 1991. After four generations of communism, the Kremlin had become inextricably identified with Soviet power, the historical memory of the place almost extinguished. The outward manifestation of that power was the procession of curtained ZIL limousines driving through the Spassky Gate, their occupants hidden from public gaze, a practice followed by Gorbachev himself. Gorbachev's public walkabouts, reaching out to miners in the Donbass or in the oilfields of Siberia, did not change his sometimes remote and vaguely foreign image in Moscow, contrasting with Gorbymania abroad and Raisa Gorbacheva well dressed in Western haute couture at home. The White House represented Russia as well as the former Moscow Party chief and now democratically elected Russian President Boris Yeltsin, who rode public transport and checked on services and products at the local *gastronom*. Yeltsin was a hard drinker, 'a real Russian'; Gorbachev had launched an anti-alcohol campaign which included tearing up vineyards in the Caucasus and banishing drinks at state occasions. As the complicated tug-of-war between Gorbachev and Yeltsin unfolded over the fate of the country, Moscow's mayor, Gavriil Popov, also the first elected to office by democratic vote, had already thrown in his lot with Yeltsin. The MosSoviet building, formerly the Moscow governor's mansion, was within walking distance of the White House, and would become the second place of resistance to the coup.

In the spring of 1991, rumours and warnings of a right-wing revolt were in the air. Some reformers, including Mayor Popov, had considered using Red Square as a 'place of showdown' with the conservatives. The logic was riding on the crest of an idea: the successful mass demonstrations in Eastern Europe, particularly the Velvet Revolution in Prague's Wenceslas Square, and the 'Leipzig Factor'—the demonstrations that fatally weakened the regime in the GDR—to hasten reform. In retrospect we know that some of the Kremlin hard-liners were considering 'a Chinese solution' of zero tolerance: to put down any further demonstrations by force. At tragic human cost, this is what befell the demonstrators on Tiananmen Square on 4 June 1989.

What exact reform the demonstrators were demanding was by no means clear. Leaders of the reform movement, Yeltsin and Gorbachev, were reformers but with competing agendas at cross-purposes. In any event, Mayor Popov's project for a popular showdown by mass demonstrations was dropped when it was concluded that demonstrations around the Kremlin could give a pretext for the imposition of a state of emergency by the old guard, and perhaps even of martial law.

As it was, the White House as a setting for resistance to the coup was laden with symbolism, and its open, retro-futuristic appearance, juxtaposed against the impassive medieval walls of the Kremlin, provided the perfect backdrop for the events that followed. Ironically, the White House was chosen in August

1991 as a place of confrontation not by the reformers, but by the plotters themselves.

Mayor Popov was among a number of leading public figures, including the Soviet Foreign Minister Edvard Shevardnadze and one of Gorbachev's closest advisers on *perestroika*, Alexander Yakovlev, who at different times had caught wind of the impending coup and had spoken out.[2] Already at loggerheads with the city's *gorkom,* the Moscow Party organization, Popov had written an article in *The New York Review of Books* entitled 'The Dangers of Democracy' which foresaw a right-wing reaction against uncontrolled reform. Throughout the spring of 1991 Moscow developed an advanced case of the jitters. Bread and other staples suddenly became scarce, and the queues lengthened. There were rumours that the countryside had revolted against 'parasitic Moscow' and that farmers were no longer willing to subsidize the capital with artificially low prices for their products. Other rumours suggested that the conservatives within the Party were deliberately creating shortages by holding supplies in warehouses in order to discredit *perestroika* and to weaken Gorbachev's leadership. The tension increased when unusual military manoeuvres took place around Moscow, unconvincingly explained by military commanders as deploying troops 'to assist in the potato harvest'.

In the midst of this gathering, poisonous atmosphere, Moscow's economic problems deepened when Prime Minister Valentin Pavlov, a recent Gorbachev appointee (he laboured under the nickname 'hedgehog-bum' because of his peasant-style haircut) announced that 50- and 100-ruble notes would no longer be legal tender. Nominally aimed at speculators, this had a devastating effect. In one blow it wiped out the savings of people who were traditionally mistrustful of banks, hiding their cash under mattresses.

Interrupted Holiday

As the evidence continued to accumulate, Western assessments of the possibility of a conservative reaction against Gorbachev's policies were turning into calculations of probability. As early as 1987 the CIA judged that if it suspected that the process of reform was getting out of hand, the Party, instead of supporting Gorbachev, 'could well execute an abrupt about-face, discarding Gorbachev along the way'.[3] In 1991 Moscow, the secrecy of preparations for a conservative takeover was only relative, but even Gorbachev himself did not take the odds of a move against him seriously enough to cancel his vacation in the luxurious presidential villa at Foros on the Crimean Black Sea coast.

The coup leaders drew on a precedent. Acting in the name of 'national salvation', the Polish communist leader, General Jaruzelski had launched a military crackdown in December 1981, and arrested thousands of Solidarity members and sympathizers, dividing up Warsaw into districts under military control. A similar tactic was followed by the Moscow coup planners, who split Moscow into eighteen regions, each with a senior officer directly answerable to the leaders. By sealing Poland's borders and placing the entire country under martial law with a show of armed force, Jaruzelski and his colleagues had effectively invaded their own country. In theory, at least, the Moscow coup would follow the same pattern. Besides lack of attention to detail and of resolve, a crucial difference was that the Moscow plotters did not look to a simultaneous, country-wide operation. Although they had made arrangements for their takeover in a number of key Soviet cities, their strategy was to launch a narrowly focused, surgical strike at the centre of power, and to present the country with a *fait accompli.* This meant Moscow.

Moscow learned of the coup in the early morning of 19 August, when as customary on such occasions, Chopin and Tchaikovsky played non-stop on the radio and all channels of Moscow television presented unscheduled transmissions of *Swan Lake.* Newsreaders were ordered to announce that the awkwardly named State Committee for the State of Emergency in the USSR (GKChP)[4] had declared at 4:00 a.m. the imposition of 'a state of emergency ... to obviate society from sliding into a national catastrophe'.[5] Already there was a hint of future trouble for the plotters. Acting under duress, some newscasters still dared to read their message with undisguised sarcasm. Half an hour later, on the orders of the Minister of Defence Marshal Yazov, the Taman Guards and the Dzerzhinsky and Kantemirovsky Mechanized Divisions, in company with the Ryazan Airborne Division, occupied Moscow.

The elevated status of the coup leaders was not matched by their competence. The curfew imposed on Moscow proved spotty at best. Yeltsin was not arrested and managed to drive from his dacha to the White House. Gorbachev, still at Foros, refused to cooperate. Communications within the city remained intact. Fatally, the chain of command proved unreliable, and many KGB officers sabotaged or ignored commands of their senior officers, some of whom actively or passively undermined orders from Kryuchkov, chairman of the KGB, who within the service was considered an unprofessional political outsider. In Leningrad the chief of the KGB openly sided with Mayor Sobchak against the putschists.[6] Columns of military vehicles moving into the centre of Moscow observed the city's traffic signals, which continued to operate. Units of the army, including a number of tanks, went over to the defenders of the White House. Air Force General Shaposhnikov threatened to bomb the Kremlin and to shoot down any helicopters attempting to land there.

Some of the episodes related to the coup had an unreal aspect. The curfew announced by the State Emergency Committee was only partially observed. Sheremetyevo Airport remained open. Arriving at the airport's immigration control in the midst of the crisis, I was waved through by an unsmiling officer of the Ministry of Internal Affairs as if all were routine. I was subsequently driven into the centre of night-time Moscow in the only car on the road, a main artery which had become a kind of no-man's land. Through the gloom, makeshift barriers could be made out at a number of crossroads. Opposite them were arrayed columns of tanks. My route was down the middle. No attempt was made to stop the car: the *militsia* had simply disappeared.

The area in which the drama took place was surprisingly small, bounded by the Kremlin, the White House, the KGB headquarters on Lubyanka Square and the Party Central Committee building on Staraya Ploschad, all within walking distance of each other. The main scene of action was in front of the White House, where the barricades were set up and crowds gathered, reckoned at the height of the standoff to be some fifty to a hundred thousand. Lesser scenes took place before the City Hall (MosSoviet) where impromptu leaflets denouncing the coup were printed and distributed to the waiting crowds. Manezhnaya Square, the traditional place of demonstrations, and Red Square itself had been closed off by Ministry of Internal Affairs police and tanks, manned by crews who were apparently unsure of their orders. They were given food and flowers by the crowds.

The Emergency Committee's nerve-centre was Vice-President's Yanayev's office in the Kremlin's eighteenth-century administration building and the Senate building which housed the Council of Ministers. After the coup's failure, Lubyanka

Square briefly held the spotlight when Dzerzhinsky's 40-ton statue was pulled down by five cranes operated by the MosSoviet, concerned that if it were pushed it could collapse into the Metro tunnels underneath the square. The large semi-secret Ministry of Defence building close to the Arbat (a plaque in front identified it) was ignored by the crowds, who passed directly by it on their way to the White House. At the time some observers noted that the crowds represented less than 10 per cent of Moscow's population. Later, cynics claimed that if all who maintained that they had stood on the barricades and faced down the tanks had actually been there, their numbers would have counted in the millions.

In drawing on the Polish precedent, the coup leaders chose to discount another experience closer to home in terms of both time and distance than Jaruzelski's Poland. In June 1991 elite troops for special tasks (OMON) had surrounded the central administration buildings housing the offices of Lithuanian President Landsbergis in downtown Vilnius in an operation to arrest the country's rapid advance toward independence, awaiting orders for an assault. For reasons still unclear, those orders never materialized. But the siege of the Lithuanian government buildings became a dress-rehearsal for the siege of the White House some three months later. Even the deaths at the Vilnius television tower were a forewarning of the violence that under greatly different circumstances would take place before the Ostankino TV station in 1993.

Replicating the defence of the Vilnius government buildings, Yeltsin's supporters were directed by monitors, *starski*, who divided the defenders into sections, each responsible for a given area and instructed to link arms in the event of an attack. Many Lithuanians had, in fact, come to Moscow to participate in the defence. Less remarked on at the time was the astonishing similarity of the 'installation art' that decorated the barricades: heavy earth-moving equipment, buses, rubble from nearby building sites and concrete slabs still used in Khrushchevite crash-construction projects. In the cold, mid-August drizzle even the braziers, fashioned out of oil-drums were the same. Their glow at night, with figures huddled around them, could have come straight from Vilnius.[7]

The course of events in Moscow was closely linked to the city's identification with Russia and with its former communist boss, Boris Yeltsin, now the Russian president. Shaking his fist in defiance atop a tank—he had first shaken hands with the driver, who had gone over to the White House side—he used the word 'usurpers' to condemn the putschists. In its old Russian form, it carries a deep resonance, referring to the Time of Troubles and its illegitimate tsar, the False Dmitry, a story known by all Russians since childhood.

The solemnity of those standing on the barricades in the coup's first hours, and of the volunteers distributing soup and bread, bore parallels to the Orthodox ritual of the Eucharist before battle, a sacrament offered to those prepared to face death.[8]

The meaning behind these gestures became strikingly clear when Gorbachev returned from Foros after his release from house arrest in a Russian (not Soviet) TU-134 aircraft. The larger IL-62, reserved for the Soviet president, came separately, carrying a dispirited group representing the now-defeated Emergency Committee. The group had gone to Foros 'to plead for understanding' from Gorbachev. In the Russian aircraft, Gorbachev was accompanied by Russian Vice-President Rutskoi and Russian Prime Minister Silayev. On their arrival at Vnukovo Airport, crowds waved the Russian tricolour. The red hammer and sickle flag of the Soviet state was barely in evidence.[9] Looking slightly out of place with his open shirt and tan, Gorbachev commented that he had returned to 'another country'. Although his nominal position as head of the Soviet state remained unchanged, Gorbachev had in effect become Yeltsin's guest.

Moscow Liberated

Well before the attempted conservative takeover, Mayor Popov and his team of advisers and senior bureaucrats had already taken a number of steps to release the city from the faltering efforts of *perestroika* to reshape the economy and the foundations of the Soviet state, including the one-size-fits-all confines of centralized planning. The latter had already given many Soviet cities the look of mini-Moscows, sometimes appropriately, but in many cases, as in the far north or in Central Asia, not. The converse was that Moscow was not in control of key areas of its own budget, planning or even architecture. As central control weakened in the late 1980s, for the first time in its history Moscow City Council was moving towards gaining full control of its own affairs—and with that, independence from the city Party organization (*Gorkom*) headed by Yuri Prokofiev. Prokofiev, successor to Kaganovich, Khrushchev and indeed Yeltsin himself as Moscow Party chief, was deeply implicated in the coup attempt, but fearing a split within the Party declined to call a *Gorkom* emergency session. Consequently the *Gorkom* took no position on the coup.

Popov had already sided with Yeltsin, and his anti-party moves were relentless. Out of the city when the coup took place, he returned to announce on 23 August that the Party's brooding Central Committee headquarters on Staraya Ploshchad had been confiscated and its doors sealed in the name of the city. Prokofiev (he was *ex officio* member of the Central Committee) ignominiously made his escape to a waiting taxi, protected by a tight police cordon. The following day Gorbachev announced his resignation as General Secretary of the Communist Party of the Soviet Union.

Standing beside the Muscovites' defence of the White House, Moscow City Council's takeover of the Central

Committee building represents in symbol and in fact the final humiliation and defeat not only of the plotters but of the organization that had ruled Russia and the rest of the country for seventy years.[10] It is one of the defining moments in the city's history.

Uncertainty and confusion marked the period between August and Christmas Day. On 25 December 1991, Gorbachev resigned as Soviet president. In that period, the Central Committee building, now in the hands of the Russian government, had been converted into the Russian Ministry of Foreign Affairs, competing with the Stalinist edifice on Smolenskaya Square, still housing the Soviet Foreign Ministry. The latter was now run by Boris Pankin, who feared that the building might be taken over by street mobs intent on destroying the dying remains of the Soviet presence in Moscow, but carried on, business as usual.[11] High on the agenda was the decision of whether to proceed with a previously scheduled international human rights conference, an event that would have been unheard of in Stalinist or even in Brezhnevite Moscow, but was in line with Gorbachev's policies of *glasnost*. This was likely to open up dark areas of the Soviet past. The decision was taken to go ahead, and the conference was held in the same Hall of Columns of the House of Soviets where State Prosecutor Vyshinski conducted the infamous purge trials of the 1930s, Stalin watching in a secret room from behind a curtain.

August versus October

As the human rights conference proceeded in the autumn of 1991, a Russian 50-kopek stamp pictured the White House, and its implicit message of an independent Russia. This message was compromised in October 1993 as a political struggle between the Russian legislators and the presidency over the extent of executive power came to a head. The White House now housed the legislature. In a cruel parody of the events of 1991, standards of the Romanov family and Soviet flags appeared side by side on the same steps that the pro-democracy defenders of the White House, full of resolution and hope, had stood on barely two years before. In the space of a few days, the White House's image changed from a citadel of Russian freedom against the power of the Soviet state to that of a burnt-out shell housing a lost generation of defeated Communists and their unlikely allies.

A festering dispute over constitutional authority culminated in a strange mirror-image of the August 1991 events. Conforming to an established pattern, the leader of the Russian Congress of Peoples' Deputies, Ruslan Khazbulatov, and Yeltsin's own vice-president, Alexander Rutskoi, protesting against Yeltsin's increasingly autocratic methods of rule, became involved in an attack on Moscow City Hall, considered a Yeltsin stronghold, and on Ostankino Television Station. Their followers briefly occupied the former and stormed the latter. Declaring a state of emergency on 21 September 1993, Yeltsin prorogued the legislature, deliberately choosing a date to avoid any association with 19 August 1991. The deputies resisted and sequestered themselves inside. In the White House shelling of 4 October, over one hundred were killed and nearly a thousand were wounded. A number of the same military units that encircled the White House in 1991 were deployed and did not flinch. This time, the streets remained quiet, perhaps even indifferent.

Yeltsin's shelling of the White House, with its renegade parliamentarians huddled inside, was the worst case of public violence since tsarist troops fired at point-blank range into the workers' barricades in the Presnya district in 1905. Only the Red Guards' assault on the city in November 1917 was comparable. Then, the target was the Kremlin itself.

Surrealism mixed with farce: in the midst of the shelling of the White House the Metro continued to function normally, and crowds on the streets went about their business. Some gathered to watch the shelling, but as onlookers at a display or spectacle, fireworks perhaps. The commitment and the conviction of 1991 had gone—and with them, the symbolism of the White House as the touchstone of Russian freedom. Yeltsin's office, furthermore, was now located in the Kremlin. He had moved in even before Gorbachev had left.

The events of August 1991 and October 1993 generated competing narratives, each offering a different image of the White House. Its ambivalent legacy was tacitly recognized by Yeltsin in 1994. A group of veterans of the August 1991 [illegible] Ring, petitioned him to name the White [illegible] he issued a [illegible] blic holiday. [illegible] ise were too [illegible] fiance at an [illegible] e underlying [illegible] ne other, the [illegible] by force. In [illegible] illusion.

[illegible] nfusion of the [illegible]. Mayor Popov [illegible] n the municipal [illegible] nable. He was [illegible] can take credit [illegible] early post-Soviet [illegible] ed democracy', a hallmark of Putin's political style and of Luzhkov's own version of post-Soviet capitalism. Luzhkov was Mayor of Moscow through three presidential administrations: those of Yeltsin, Putin and now Medvedev, a remarkable achievement. He was voted into office several times. Putin appointed Luzhkov to a fifth term in 2002. This made him one of the longest-serving mayors Moscow has ever had, and was a tribute to his adaptability, and to his sheer *chutzpah* - at least until 2010.[12]

In his makeover of the administration of post-Soviet Moscow, Luzhkov faced a double challenge. First, the political–administrative infrastructure left over from the Soviet era had collapsed, and with it the old parallel system whereby the city administration was in effect governed by policies laid down by the Communist Party's City Executive Committee. By default, the City Council became the city's sole policy-making body and had to adapt to this new role as well as conducting the day-to-day business of municipal administration. Second, the city's resource-allocation mechanism in the form of Gosplan had disappeared, leaving a vacuum. Although Moscow and some other Soviet cities had their own architectural and planning bureaux attached to their city councils, Gosplan tightly controlled budgets and building standards across the Soviet Union.

Now, in straightened circumstances, Moscow had to fall back on its own resources. The recent past had not been kind to the city. One of the bitterest criticisms that Yeltsin aimed at Gorbachev on his return from Foros was that in his pursuit of *glasnost* and *perestroika* he failed to take any interest in the city and its development, clearly one of his primary responsibilities as Party general secretary. Moscow was simply run down.

As legal title to Soviet and Party assets in Moscow was redistributed, there was inevitably some pushing and pulling, but with the exception of a few state dachas and Moscow landmarks, like the Central Committee building, the process went remarkably well. The fact that Yeltsin and Moscow City Council were 'on the same side' during the coup attempt did much to smooth the process. The result was that if Gorbachev had indeed returned from Foros 'to a different country', he had also returned to a different city.

Yeltsin and Luzhkov soon fell out. In the confused period between August 1991 and the White House siege of October 1993, Luzhkov, riding high on his popularity and as ambitious and driving as Yeltsin himself, moved beyond the city to enter Russian national politics, and in September 1997 launched his candidacy for election as Russian president with a $60-million celebration of the 850th anniversary of the founding of Moscow. Yeltsin regarded Luzhkov's Russian ambitions as a betrayal, accusing him of getting too big for his boots with the Stalinist phrase, 'dizzy with success'.[13] The issue was further complicated by Luzhkov's role in founding the national political party, Fatherland, with Yevgeny Primakov, which was to be his political engine on the national level.

Rancour deepened when Yeltsin saw his name blackened as Moscow-controlled NTV reported his relationship with a growing circle of cronies who were to gain millions in the Soviet sell-off (his successor Putin was later to solve the problem of uncontrolled media by taking them over). But even as he continued his attacks on Luzhkov (he had derided Luzhkov's Moscow anniversary celebration as 'an incredibly pompous and overblown affair') he grudgingly recognized Luzhkov's dynamism in transforming Moscow into a city 'with clean streets, gleaming storefronts and a modern infrastructure'.[14]

Luzhkov bore some resemblance to Yeltsin, and their shared temperament and the generation to which they both belonged may have exacerbated their differences in politics. Like Yeltsin, Luzhkov was a hands-on politician, visiting building sites in hard-hat, a practice shunned by Brezhnev, observed by Khrushchev[15] and undertaken by Stalin accompanied by armed guards and only in the dead of night. Anatoly Sobchak, then Mayor of St. Petersburg, once criticized Luzhkov for his populist style, when 'he should have been in his office attending to more important city matters'.

Sobchak lost the 1996 municipal elections; Luzhkov was returned with an increased majority. The key to Luzhkov's success in running the city lay hidden in Yeltsin's accusations, specifically in the way the mayor made money for his city: 'Moscow's treasury had managed to collect a large amount of money from banks and companies... that were forced to pay the city of Moscow... enough for excessive anniversary festivities, the incredible architecture, and his own political ambitions...'[16]

Yeltsin's laissez-faire style of management had in fact created opportunities for Luzhkov and his city. Yeltsin and Popov had earlier cut a deal that Luzhkov should succeed Popov as mayor, and despite a number of attempts by the Moscow City Council to hold mayoral elections, Luzhkov was appointed mayor by presidential decree in June 1992. Yeltsin had feared that elections could bring unrest in the capital, as indeed materialized a year later. He therefore resorted to the mechanism of presidential appointment. In 1993 the newly promulgated Russian constitution accorded Moscow and St. Petersburg 'special status' within the Russian Federation, giving the two cities the power to develop their own independent legislative and economic programmes.

The 1993 constitution also fixed Moscow's administrative boundaries at the outer-ring circular motorway (MKAD). This has had the effect of focusing the city's development on obsolete, under-used or derelict parts of the city.[17] It also concentrated the administration's attention on practical issues of city management and infrastructure. These seemingly innocuous administrative adjustments have determined that the city's future direction will be not out, but up, in the form of 'vertical cities', the skyscrapers of the twenty-first century.

With 128 municipal districts regulating and planning land use and allocation, the management and control Moscow City Council holds over its own budget are without reference to the usual requirements of transparency and accountability to any independent body. Through the creation of unaccountable holding companies and the use of secret funds, the city administration rapidly gained control over its most profitable economic sectors and, in due course, over the 'commanding heights' of the capital's economy.[18] According to the Russian–American Chamber of Commerce, Moscow City Financial Management (MCFM) holds a stake in more than 500 companies on behalf of the city government. Already by 2000, over $60 million was allocated to city-owned industrial enterprises. By retaining control over city privatization arrangements, the City Council is able to select private investors, and tops up the city budget by selling city-owned real estate at high prices.[19]

The city's constitutional authority to set its own rules is a dramatic reversal of the situation of nineteenth-century Moscow, when all was decided by St. Petersburg, virtually the sole recipient of the city's taxes, and the final authority for the municipal budget. In practical terms this means that Moscow City Council has the legislative competence to regulate land law, including land use and town planning, as well as determining areas of municipal jurisdiction. Yeltsin's huge sell-off of Soviet state assets at rock-bottom prices, moreover, was not followed by Moscow City Council, which resisted pressures to dispose of those assets, calculating that land and real estate prices would multiply as the economy recovered. This has led to contention between Moscow and the federal authorities as the precise amount of revenue the city gains is obscured by the its numerous legal entities and holding companies, including city-owned or controlled enterprises. The City Council's power to make its own laws has led to the proliferation of business acquisitions.[20]

In the end, Luzhkov's freewheeling style proved his undoing. In September 2010 he 'lost the confidence' of President Medvedev and was sacked. Grounds for his dismissal included his cavalier attitude to suppressing the fires that encircled and shrouded Moscow in a cloud of toxic mist that summer (he did not return from his holiday in Austria), his inattention to the city's growing traffic congestion, and his wilful destruction of many of the city's historic buildings. Like Yeltsin, President Medvedev evidently felt that Luzhkov was getting too big for his boots.

Moscow, the engine of post-Soviet state capitalism[21] with its strategy of monopoly, legal flexibility and budgetary opaqueness, reflects the culture of the new Russian elite, its manner of doing business and its driving ambition. This culture will no doubt survive the departure of its long-term Mayor.

The New Moscow

In the New Moscow memory of the city's past and the artefacts evoking it—the citadel, buildings and monuments—intrude upon the present, giving it depth and meaning. Some fear that much of the evidence could disappear without a trace, leaving little more than a small collection of tourist attractions, turning the centre of Moscow into little more than a quaint Slavic theme park. Organizations such as the Moscow Association for the Preservation of Monuments (MAPS) seek to protect the physical remains of the city's history from the ambitions of developers and projects of city planners. Ironically, foreigners are heavily represented in the organization.

The collective memory of Moscow, however, is selective: the recent past uncomfortable, the more distant past terrible to contemplate. New Moscow therefore lives in the existential present. Even the city's 850th anniversary celebrations in

1997 were more of an event dedicated to its revival than a commemoration of its turbulent past and how life was actually lived.

New Moscow bears some parallels with twentieth-century New York and Chicago, both rough around the edges and the products of an explosive period of growth and unequally shared wealth. Moscow city administration is reminiscent of Mayor Daley's Chicago, but in fact the 'municipal culture' is rooted in the Brezhnevite managerial style of deal-making among tightly-knit groups; and the grand vision of the City Council for the New Moscow compares closely to that of urban planner Robert Moses, who did much to influence the final outline of twentieth-century New York City.

Other comparisons are with Lazar Kaganovich, to whom the shape of Soviet Moscow largely belongs, the counterpart of Baron Haussmann, the designer of the grand boulevards and apartment buildings of Paris, or perhaps with the producer of unrealized dreams for Berlin, Albert Speer. But with the exception of Mayor Luzhkov himself, the planners of New Moscow are relatively little known.

Side by side with huge building sites, new multi-storey buildings of indifferent, globalized design and massed traffic, New Moscow also offers a combination of glitz and *gadost*, tacky junk. In the days immediately following the Soviet collapse the city sought to redefine itself, and as the new rules had not yet been set, it experienced an unbridled form of capitalism, where business had its special Russian translation, *bizness*, with its underlying meaning of dealing under the table, and a hint of strong-arm methods on the side. In Soviet times fast practices existed just below the surface in the unofficial 'parallel economy', combined with influence and 'connections', *blat*, which filled in the gaps left by Gosplan's lumbering machine. For urban residents, including those of Moscow, *babushkas*' village gardens and their produce often figured in strategies of survival: it is estimated that into the 1990s about one-third of Moscow's diet came from home-grown sources.

With the collapse of the Soviet state the parallel economy, in particular the practices that went with it, in effect took over. In addition, Moscow City also received the same questionable advice given at the federal level by outside consultants about selling off/giving away its assets to private interests in the name of establishing a free-market economy.[22] Luzhkov and his team of advisers were prescient enough to resist, and the city continued to hold on to its strategic assets, mainly real estate and land. In the early post-Soviet days, GUM on Red Square was among the first institutions to be transformed into a capitalist emporium. The first steps in Moscow's transformation to capitalism took two main forms: private restaurants and casinos. For some well-established restaurants such as the Aragvi, specializing in Georgian cuisine, the Soviet collapse brought a bonanza of new customers, many with bulging leather jackets and swarthy complexions sitting in dark corners. Newer establishments, some with frisky names like Razgulyaem ('let's have a ball'), got in on the ground-floor catering to the new rich. Chicago-style, many restaurants started off with locked doors, peepholes and rough-looking bouncers.

From personal recollection I can attest that, in the early post-Soviet days, restaurants took matters of security very seriously indeed. In one instance, my host offered a credit card which failed to clear the account. He was then in effect held hostage by two back-room types who came to sit stolidly on either side of him while one of us was delegated to rush home to collect the necessary cash. Garish, neon-lit casinos followed the same pattern, absorbing the excess cash of the over-wealthy, while alongside them the depressed proletarian architecture of Soviet Moscow continued to disintegrate. In the early days of the transition the split between new wealth and the collapse of the old Soviet social-safety net of social services and pensions prompted many ambitious young women to aspire to become 'party girls' for the clothes, the cash and the good life. Many found their calling in the lobbies of international hotels, their numbers threatening over-supply and creating downward pressure on prices for services, paid for in foreign currency of course.

Already faced with economic challenges elsewhere, many Western firms have pulled out while others have been deterred from entering the Moscow market because of its rough business practices, which in extreme cases have included murder. An American businessman, Paul Tatum, involved in a dispute with a city agency over a hotel property, was on the receiving end of an apparent contract killing in 1994. Other foreign businessmen, like their Russian counterparts, have been exposed to criminal protection rackets in attempts to bring them *pod kryshkoi*, 'under the roof'. This may account for a general tendency among Western businesses to invest in projects not requiring heavy capital commitment, particularly banks, accounting or legal firms and merchandizing. As some Western firms have discovered to their cost, extensive capital commitment to such projects as pipelines and refineries can sometimes expose them to various attempts at 'shakedown' where there is little room for manoeuvre. These can take the form of sudden tax audits or similar ploys.

If New Moscow held from its early post-Soviet past a shadow of violence and life lived on the edge of the rules, this seemed to accord well with the city's ethos. Former Mayor Luzhkov had a reputation as a man who produced results made him genuinely popular. He won the municipal election of June 1996 with a huge majority and his subsequent withdrawal as candidate in the Russian presidential race had no discernable effect on his popular appeal. His high-profile opposition to the coup of 1991, and even to the controlling hand of Yeltsin, attracted wide support, as did his attention to the details of

Moscow's daily life. He presided over the financial arrangements for new apartments for the wealthy, using the balance of their elevated prices to assist in the relocation of families still living in Khrushchev-era mass tenaments, or on waiting lists. Ever since Luzhkov, Moscow City Council has been scrupulous in ensuring that pensions to the aged and infirm, and benefits to war veterans are paid on time. As in Renaissance Venice, this beneficence is not extended to the street-rabble and the homeless who, if they refuse municipal shelter and the supervision that comes with it, are unceremoniously dumped outside city limits.[23]

Sometimes Luzhkov's ambition transcended the merely political and financial to encompass the intellectual and perhaps even the stupendous as well. Already holder of the Order of the Red Banner for Labour and Order of Lenin, both from previous times, in 2003 Luzhkov published a book with the not particularly modest title, *The Renewal of History: Mankind in the Twenty-First Century and the Future of Russia*.[24] In his acknowledgments Luzhkov wrote that the list of authors 'who assisted in his reflections' included Jeremy Bentham, Thomas Hobbes, Erasmus of Rotterdam and 'Mark [*sic*] Weber'.

This larger-than-life image acquired by the new Russian elite was shared by Luzhkov's wife, Yelena Baturina, who had amassed a fortune as head of one of the city's largest construction groups, Inteko. In 2004 a special edition of *Forbes* magazine named her as one of the richest people in Russia. Highlighted by the publicity, her billionaire status became a factor in Moscow's complex relationship with the federal government. In June 2004 the Moscow editor-in-chief of *Forbes* was murdered. There were many suspects, but no one was ever charged.

Sergei Sobyanin, nominated to replace Luzhkov by President Medvedev in October 2010 is described by the *Economist* as a graduate of the school of Putin. And indeed he is. Among other things, he is Putin's former chief of staff, and belongs to a bureaucratic class which is eclipsing the Yeltsin-era oligarchy and its hangers-on. Now without Luzhkov, and with a diminishing number of regionalists within Moscow City Council, Moscow is no longer governed exclusively by its own inhabitants (Sobyanin is from Siberia) and despite the constitutional deal once worked out by Luzhkov and Yeltsin, Moscow continues to lose whatever urban autonomy it once possessed.

Control of real estate is as much a test of municipal success as a military challenge, and has been at the core of the city's history. This has spanned the residential conflagrations of wooden Moscow in the Middle Ages to the palaces of the privileged of the eighteenth century, the hovels and barracks of industrial Moscow to the expropriated properties of War Communism of the early 1920s, reaching the wrecking-teams and dynamite of Kaganovich a decade later. In the mid 1950s Stalin's seven huge architectural tombstones dominated the city, challenging even the Kremlin. Before the final Soviet collapse, there were the massed urban walls of Khrushchev- and Brezhnev-era apartment complexes.

Architecture reflected the shifting social stratification of the city. Ivan the Terrible's *oprichniki* had their own reserved areas of the city, and the *posady* of seventeenth- and eighteenth-century Moscow harboured recognized trades or crafts within a single district. Along the city's main thoroughfares the elaborate apartments of the pre-war Stalin era were for the *nomenklatura,* not the workers, many of whom were still confined to *baraki* with their families or were unhappy forced residents of *kommunalki,* each with a few square metres of space and common dining areas. The Khrushchev architectural revolution recognized that even under socialism, the workers, in whose name the state existed, needed privacy, a place to hang lace curtains and to have a chair and table where the vodka could be placed without being filched by someone else. In the late 1950s Moscow's difficult housing situation was still at its pre-war levels, fluctuating between one room per person and one room per family. Rebuilding the country's industrial strength, Gosplan had other priorities. As the 1950s gave way to the 1960s, the explanation that sacrifice was necessary because of the war began to wear thin as it became common knowledge that Russia's defeated and devastated enemy Germany (or at least its western part) was roaring ahead with its *Wirtschaftswunder* and the good life it promised for all. In ways unthinkable under Stalin, housing became a yardstick by which the success of competing social systems would be measured.

Under Khrushchev's reinterpretation of Marxism–Leninism, 'peaceful coexistence', East Berlin, the socialist showcase to the west, was rebuilt from the rubble as a city consecrated to the triumph of socialism, not only in its public buildings but also in the complexes of workers' flats. Moscow had not benefited from wartime destruction, and behind the architect Zholtovsky's 1930s buildings for the elite, the drab dwellings of early industrial Moscow survived and festered amongst clapped-out factories, some barely changed since the Revolution.

The residential complexes that ringed Moscow under Khrushchev were designed to change all that. A one-room flat was a standard 30 square metres, complete with waiting list. By the 1980s flats had increased to three or four rooms at twice the size, 60 square metres or more. At the height of *perestroika* in the late 1980s, 70 per cent of Moscow's housing was located in these complexes, and would remain so well into the Yeltsin period. Change to this pattern was triggered with the deal Yeltsin had struck with the city that gave it control over its real estate, and hence prices. In downtown Moscow it is now possible to buy and own a flat on the basis of a 50-year leasehold. The city holds title for the land that the apartment building rests on. Like the city plan itself, prices are arranged concentrically around the Kremlin. Before the economic downturn, and at the height of the oil boom, flats in the inner-core areas of Ostozhenka and Prechistenka sold for about $25 per square metre; in the next price-ring, the Arbat and Tverskaya districts, only a few hundred metres away, prices ranged from $17 to $20 per square metre.[25] Within a few months in 2008/9, oil prices dropped from $148 per barrel to less than $50 per barrel, and residential property prices in downtown Moscow have suffered severe downward pressure.

Moscow's commercial property development has also been affected. In some cases completion schedules have been set back and projects downsized. According to the Moscow Chamber of Commerce, commercial property rents dropped by 35-50 per cent, to less than $600 per square metre per year, 'still more costly than equivalent property in Paris or Frankfurt at $500 per square metre per year'.

These growing pains and the accompanying pains of adjusting to capitalist economic reality were inevitable. Even with city-subsidized housing, the Moscow property market is still out of reach for most Muscovites who traditionally still gravitate to the centre. Mortgages are a new phenomenon and remain difficult to obtain. Wages and salaries remain low by Western standards, and prices for a variety of reasons are inflated. Still high prices for the city's downtown flats have left many vacant. For the first time in the city's history, living quarters are unfilled for reasons not associated with the plague.

The hidden consumption and structure of privileges for the elite under communism has been replaced by the conspicuous consumption of the 'new Russians', some of whom display the same vulgarity and attraction to kitsch that was common among the nouveaux riches of nineteenth-century America and England. Hardship seems to bring out the best in Russian humour, but there are few jokes about the new Russians:

> Ivan: Look, Kolya, I bought this silk tie in Paris for $200.
> Kolya: Ivan, you fool. I could have got it for you in New York for $400!

The middle class in tsarist Russia was politically negligible, and in this century it has yet to have a commanding influence on city government. As chronic problems of fraud and corruption persist, and as opposition to them mount, there will be increasing pressure for Moscow's administration to be more open and transparent. In May 2006 a protest by defrauded home buyers threatened to turn violent and had to be broken up by police. The issue was defused only when Moscow City Council promised compensation. As growing legal controversies surrounding former Mayor Luzhkov demonstrate, there is increased willingness of businessmen and others to use the Russian justice system to press claims against the improper exercise of municipal authority. This trend will no doubt continue under his successor

There is also a largely ignored section of the Moscow population, the rough equivalent of German *Gastarbeiter,* unregistered workers from Central Asia on the roughly 4,000 building sites existing largely outside the city's remit.[26] They live in on-site conditions comparable to the worker tenements of tsarist Russia or the *baraki* of the 1930s. In relation to the street-people and derelicts, social improvement in the city is relative.

New patterns of growth are taking place. Gentrification has reached Moscow. A case in point is one of the 'high buildings' of the Stalinist era, as described by one of its foreign inhabitants:

> The *vysotka* in the Taganka—my *vysotka*—has been officially classified as a historic landmark and is finally being preserved...

> My neighbours personify the full length of Russia's geographical political, social and historical spectrum. Some are prospering, some are just coping, and others are struggling, either against the 'new Russia' or to hang on desperately as it passes them by... Here are the witnesses to the past and the leaders of the future.[27]

Some of the flats in the *vysotka* have been enlarged by combining them with adjacent flats and knocking out the walls in between, but reminders of the Soviet past persist. Without individual thermostats, the flats overheat in the winter and windows must be left open. As in the Moscow State University building on Sparrow Hills, the wiring is often better than in the buildings of Khrushchev's time with their pre-programmed lifespan. Many of the older buildings have wiring installed by German war prisoners and are known to be more reliable and safer, even today. The locks and bolts that decorated the entrance of each flat in Soviet times have largely disappeared, as have the heavy steel doors on the ground floor, now replaced by a full-time concierge and electronic surveillance equipment.

Occasionally retro-renovation reaches Disney-like dimensions. The Hotel Ukraine, one of the Taganka apartment block's sisters opposite the White House, has been remodelled in art-deco style. It no longer offers select accommodation for official visitors to the capital of world socialism. With hammer-and-sickle detail still in place, it has become an attraction for the casual tourist.

Perhaps the most significant new monument to Moscow's twentieth-century past lies not in the renovations of post-Soviet Moscow, but in a new eighth sister, the Triumph Palace, the secular equivalent of the resurrected cathedral of Christ the Saviour. Its inspiration is unapologetically Stalinist, or more precisely taken from the design studios of Lev Rudnev and Boris Iofan, leading architects of that period. Standing at over 260 metres and holding 1,000 luxury apartments over

57 floors, its giganticism makes the high buildings of Stalin look suddenly in proportion. Until the inauguration of Tower Block C on the Naberezhnaya development in 2007, it was the tallest building in Europe. The Triumph Palace is merely one of the many buildings changing the face, and ultimately the character, of Moscow.

The gentrification of Moscow has also created a new phenomenon in the city's history: suburbs. Moscow is no stranger to outside settlements, many of which are closely tied to the city's history, from Ivan the Terrible's *oprichnik* base at Aleksandrovskoe Sloboda to Kolomenskoe and other suburban estates of the tsars. Even semi-villages like Peredelkino, the literary and artistic colony, have their own Moscow cachet. In the nineteenth and early twentieth centuries, working under radically different regimes, city planners and visionaries investigated the idea of relieving urban population pressures by creating satellite towns, but not with particular success. Both Moscow's strong urban-oriented culture and weak or nonexistent infrastructure, particularly transportation networks and services, worked against them. Often close together, as in Serebryanni Bor, or at Kuntsevo where Stalin spent his last days, the dachas of the elite outside Moscow are deeply rooted in the Russian tradition. Even so, peasant villages in the Moscow region, the *podmoskovie,* remain exactly that: villages.

It is now a matter of interpretation and debate whether the clusters of new housing springing up on both sides of the Moscow Circular, the MKAD, are in fact miniature versions of the anti-cities that form such an integral part of the Moscow experience, or merely a straight transplant on the soil of Muskovy of Western suburbia, complete with two-car garages and barbecues. The weight of history suggests the former; the economics and rationalities of city planning suggest the latter.[28] In the first decade of the new century the largest project was Kurkino, to the north of the centre, with homes and cottages housing some 40,000 families. Some more up-market gated communities have also appeared, including Pokrovsky Hills, a project of 260 town houses specifically aimed at Russian yuppies and Petrine-style foreigners living in the isolated, modern equivalent of the Lefortovo settlement of the eighteenth century. Pokrovsky Hills even has its own Anglo–American school nearby.

The Darkness of the Past and of the Present

The past haunts the present, and recognizable traditions, 'continuities', persist. The raffish quality of the Lower Trading Rows of sixteenth-century Moscow re-emerges in the low-life of street-hawkers, vagrants and petty criminals around railway stations and other areas of transitory Moscow, the impromptu flea markets and cheap digs of migrant workers from Central Asia and the Caucasus. The intimidating brown or black leather jackets, signature outfits of *mafiosi* foot-soldiers, give them an uncanny resemblance to the Bolshevik thugs who swaggered through the city in the 1920s. Along with the leather jacket, also worn by employees of Moscow's many private security firms, the mobile phone clamped to the ear is part of the contemporary dress-code. In the immediate post-1991 days, authentic phones were difficult and expensive to obtain, and before they became commonplace, ersatz phones imported from Hong Kong that would ring convincingly were much in demand as they gave their owner an air of importance, particularly in a crowded restaurant.

There is still no exact Moscow equivalent of the urban bourgeoisie which drove forward the industrial revolution of nineteenth-century Europe. To some extent the new Russians fill their place. At the same time, Moscow's dark side is in some respects the direct inheritor of the city's Soviet past, not only that of Stalin and of Lenin, but also that of the long years of Brezhnevite social and economic stagnation. Gorbachev's *perestroika* was too short-lived, too weak and too uncertain to make much of a difference.

Techniques of survival, sharply honed during the long Brezhnev years, came to the surface seemingly to become part of the fabric of everyday existence. In the process, the *modus operandi* of Brezhnev's *nomenklatura* found its way into the subculture of Yeltsin's oligarchs. It is said that the blue flashing lights on vehicles reserved for high state officials, intended to clear traffic, can be had for the right private buyer on the black market for US$50,000.

Moscow's dark traditions continue elsewhere as well, occasionally with lethal effect. With a few well publicized exceptions,[29] state-sponsored murder common in Stalin's Moscow has now been largely eliminated. In both quality and quantity, homicide has changed. In Soviet Moscow most privately motivated murders[30] were the result of drunken brawls, at about 2-300 a year. Then as now the most common weapon of choice was the kitchen knife, followed by various means of garroting, from rope to leather belts (in the countryside the axe continues to be the preferred instrument). As in other cities, handguns with silencers are considered up-market; and semi-automatic weapons or assault rifles, such as Kalashnikovs or AK-47s, are reserved either for the army or, the tax police or for terrorists.

Moscow's murder rate compares unfavourably with Western cities. New York, with a population comparable to that of Moscow at 9 million, had 643 murders in 2001. Over the same year almost 3,000 Muscovites were killed. The Moscow murder rate is more than nine times London's rate. In fairness to Moscow, however, it should be pointed out that in terms of all reported crime in Russian cities, Moscow ranks 111th, with an average of 200 cases per 10,000 population per year. First is the depressed mining town of Surgut with 500 cases on the same scale.[31]

The long acquaintance Moscow has had with 'letting loose the red rooster' of terrorism, traditional acts of arson and sabotage, has acquired the more recent meaning with the bombings the city has endured. The consequences of modern sabotage are recorded in an entire room in the Museum of the History of the Reconstruction of Moscow. The room records the effects of the Second Chechen war on Moscow. In August 1999 explosions in Moscow and in other Russian cities killed over 300, and continued with a bombing at Pushkin Square in 2000. In February 2003 an attack in the centre of the Metro's interchange under Manezhnaya Square left 39 dead and hundreds wounded, an operation repeated at the Rizhskaya Metro Station in July of the same year, killing 10 and wounding 50.

Other attacks included by the destruction of two aircraft in September 2004. The hostage-taking of an entire audience of 700 attending the musical *Nord-Ost* at the House of Culture of the State Ball-Bearing Plant Number One in October 2002 and the subsequent siege ended in the deaths of 33 terrorists and 129 hostages, mostly by a still-unidentified gas used by the putative rescuers. Perhaps unconsciously borrowing the phrase from his predecessor, Mayor Luzhkov referred to this event as 'Black October' in his memoirs, but through scruple or painful memory does not elaborate.

Although the Second Chechen War has now ground down to what passes for a halt, the after-effects of attacks on Moscow hang like a pall over the city, uniting it with 9/11 New York and Washington, the London Underground, Tokyo and Madrid. Varying degrees of anti-terrorist measures undertaken by the authorities are strikingly familiar, although Chechens above all of Moscow's many ethnic groups remain the primary objects of watchfulness. In the Soviet period the number of Chechens in Moscow was estimated at around 20,000. By 2002 that number might have quadrupled,[32] but the exact figure is unknown. In several cases investigations into the bombings have been inconclusive, and not necessarily all of them can be attributed to the Islambouli, the Chechen Islamic group that has often claimed responsibility.

Even now, the Chechen women of Moscow, along with their sisters from other parts of Central Asia and the Caucasus, with their Islamic ways and dress, evoke memories of 'the black widows of Moscow' who came from the killing-fields of Chechnya to avenge the deaths of their husbands and children, wearing explosive vests under their loose, flowing robes.

The passing of the Soviet Union has had a direct effect on the development of the city, and not only by the constitutional provisions relating to its budgetary independence and boundaries. The political basis of city government, as exercised through the Party, has vanished. Moscow's loss of its 'political' character—the slogans, statues and red-bannered parades have all disappeared—has also influenced city planning in very practical ways. The last Soviet-era refashioning of the city was Brezhnev's General Plan of 1971, which carried on the communist tradition of urban destruction. The Plan called for the bulldozing of a large swathe through the old Arbat district in central Moscow to create the New Arbat, a domino-like complex of ferro-concrete buildings lining a new main street, Prospekt Kalinina.

Less than a year after the attempted putsch, the Moscow Structure Plan of 1992 aimed at stabilizing the city's population through zoning and housing policies. Four years later, the Plan was reviewed. In belated recognition of the city's neglected state, greater emphasis was put on refurbishment. Economic activity was shifted away from industry to the service sector. With an oil-fuelled boom in the real estate market also intervening, the semi-rural character of Moscow's industrial back streets finally disappeared.

The 1996 Plan is now replaced by the 2020 Plan, aimed at 'a basic restructuring of the city... with priority given to ecological requirements in the city's development'; that is, the goal is to turn the city green. It is the most ambitious undertaking since Stalin's General Plan of 1935, so greatly admired by Sir E. D. Simon, and is proceeding on track despite economic and other challenges.

Among the latter are so far intractable issues such as the urban degradation caused by the 3 million plus cars jamming the city streets, turning Stalin's triumphal thoroughfares into a kind of Los Angeles at rush hour, minus the discipline. European Union pollution standards will not be met until 2020. Meanwhile, in the absence of adequate parking facilities, cars invade public spaces, pavements, pedestrian walkways and even green areas in front of apartment buildings, churning the grass into mud. This has given rise to a new term: *avtomobilnoye guliganstvo,* car hooliganism.

For the first time since the great influenza epidemic of 1918-19, Moscow's population is dropping, with deaths outnumbering births, the difference only partly compensated by in-migration. [33]

New Moscow is profoundly affected by its past. Physically, the city has a still-identifiable medieval ground-plan, the cliff where the first citadel was built rises above the city's meandering river. Viewed from the same spot opposite the Kremlin a number of Stalinist edifices can be seen in the distance, not clustered, as in Western cities, but spread, forming landmarks like navigation points on medieval maps. From them, lines of bearing converge on the site of the Palace of Soviets where the Cathedral of Christ the Saviour now stands.

In the further distance, some five kilometres from the Kremlin's western wall, rise the towers of New Moscow (officially Moscow-City, now Moscow International Business Centre) still under construction, its general aspect drawing the same inspiration as is found in the globalized architecture of Dubai, Singapore or Frankfurt. Even the land where this $12-billion megaproject (at last count) is located cannot escape its history. As it straddles the Moskva River, on one side it is anchored in the revolutionary district of Red Presnya; and on the other, Zamoskvorechye, where the Mongols first set their encampments.

Lord Foster, one of the principal architects engaged in the construction of New Moscow's International Business Centre, follows a tradition begun by the Italian architects who built the Kremlin walls in the fifteenth century. As one in an ensemble of super-buildings, Lord Foster's project, described as 'a vertical city', is the 118-storey Moscow City Tower. It is twice as high as the Empire State Building, and at 600 metres a third again as tall as the gargantuan dream of the Palace of Soviets. It is planned that the entire project will accommodate 25,000 people. A witness to Moscow's new internationalism is the Moscow City Tower's prototype and lesser twin, also designed by Lord Foster, the Tokyo Millennium Tower.

If Moscow has had more than its share of city planning, each successive plan has reflected the spirit of the age. In the twentieth century alone, Moscow has had three distinct personalities—Orthodox seat of the coronation of the tsars; Red Moscow of world revolution, later to become Moscow of socialist construction; and New Moscow, rising phoenix-like out of its own charred past. Twentieth-century city plans for each of these personalities have been radically different from each other: amid its tsarist splendour Moscow smothered under its own industrialization; Soviet planning envisaged Moscow as a city where building socialism would be made manifest; and the planning for the city of passage, New Moscow, is still not yet settled in its own identity, but aspires to a global role.

The complex of super-buildings rising on the banks of the Moskva, a city within a city, is designed to give substance to this aspiration, Moscow's Canary Wharf. The destruction of New York's Twin Towers has not affected the confidence of New Moscow any more than its own experiences with terrorism. New Moscow's emerging skyline still carries the shape of the original city, but on a vastly different scale and purpose. It remains a work in progress.

The Triumph Tower is emblematic of architectural continuity in post-Soviet Moscow. In the 'capitalist realist' architecture of new Moscow, the Tower's reference to its Stalinist past is unashamedly front-stage centre, and is only partially balanced by the huge complex of the International Business Centre's international style.

Chapter Nine
The Meaning of Place

You yourselves are the town, wherever you choose to settle... it is men that make the city, not the walls and ships without them.
Nicias to Athenian soldiers, on a beach at Syracuse, Thucydides vii, 63

Many have tried to better Thucydides' forthright statement of what cities are about, but the Greek notion that at the heart of the *polis* or city is a sense of community has proved remarkably durable. With a sense of community come collective memory and a shared identity, often taking the form of founding myths. The history of Moscow is replete with the latter, from Yuri Dolgoruky, the legendary founder of the Muscovite state, to the myth of Moscow's religious and temporal calling as the Third Rome.

Geographers have emphasized the strategic advantages the city's site enjoyed in its long evolution from a hillside fort at the confluence of an extensive net of water-courses from the Baltic to the Black Sea, the relative protection afforded by vast distances and forests, and natural resources—even sometimes the lack of them. One theory of Moscow's expansionist tendencies is that its relatively poor soil drove it outwards to richer agricultural areas.

By contrast, historians have tended to focus on the single-mindedness of Moscow's successive rulers, chronicling in detail the step-by-step transformation of a medieval city-state and its adjoining hinterland into a unified whole. Even in the seventeenth century, the Russian historian Solov'ev noted, the words 'Moscovite state... usually meant just the chief city'. [1] Some would argue that Moscow's 'imperial calling' was founded on the struggle for survival in those early days, and the need for a strong, centralized authority that came with it. Even with Thucydides' definition of city as a community, it is the meaning of place that informs Moscow of its own identity.

Sometimes this seems larger than reality, with the borderline between life and art finely drawn. One can, for example, attend the historical opera *A Life for the Tsar* at the Bolshoi and then see the exact stage-set of the final act in real life. Uspensky Sobor on Cathedral Square is only a fifteen-minute walk away.

Some writers have argued that cities can be categorized according to a number of basic types: the normative, the 'prime motivator of cities' which exists because of the multiplier effect of people living and working together for mutual benefit; the 'cosmic model', so constructed as to be a collective temple to the gods (in temporal form 'articulated expressions of power'); and monumental cities, typified by a walled enclosure with protective gates and a dominant landmark at its centre.[2] Others have suggested additions to these basic types, for example the 'practical city', often pre-planned and laid out in a grid, machine-like and functional. Le Corbusier's plans for Moscow in the 1930s fell into this category. His scheme of turning Moscow into a '*ville radieuse*' was developed on the basis of logical principles, even at the cost of the destruction of the city itself. Yet others have suggested that cities are 'organic', i.e. having definite boundaries and clearly-defined areas of control by a centralized urban authority, 'constantly seeking a balanced state, always evolving like a collective living thing'. The distinguished critic of cities Lewis Mumford once described cities as 'humanity's greatest artifact'. They are also the physical expression of their people and the social system that created them.

In support of these categorizations, one analysis[3] identifies three basic 'organizing principles' that are common to any city: sacredness, security and commerce. Sacredness is often linked to founding myths and collective memory, not the same thing as actual history. Security is a necessary prerequisite for the long-term survival of the community, and without a collective 'will to survive' a city is threatened with extinction. In its various forms, commerce—economic activity might be a better term—is also an integral part of city life. Security and sacredness have ranked higher in Moscow's history than commerce. In the nineteenth century, when commerce in the form of industrialization struck, it brought social upheaval.

Triggered by an ill-advised war, the result was the Revolution of 1917. It was essentially an urban phenomenon, and under the Bolsheviks industrialization became equated with *permanent* revolution, as much a political and social phenomenon as an economic one. Following the civil war, and the 'breather' of NEP, collectivization brought revolution to the countryside. This took on aspects of class war, the urban against the rural. Moscow's famous statue of the Worker and Kolkhoz Woman was produced during this period, representing a unity of purpose between city and countryside that never existed. Under communism Moscow acquired a further characteristic: an instrument of urban-based coercion.

What to make of Moscow? To visitors, it is opaque. The introductory pages of tourist guides struggle to describe its character. To Muscovites, it is many cities, each with a layer of meaning and myth. To both visitors and natives, the homogenizing effects of globalization place Moscow firmly within a worldwide pattern, positioning itself to be a strategic centre of a global economy. Yet Moscow is apart, and its tightly-woven past and present suggest a number of constants—continuities—that define the city's 'meaning of place'.

The first of these relates to the city's security and survival. Moscow has undergone a number of near-death experiences, from destruction at the hands of the Tatars to the designs of the Third Reich, which planned to create a lake where the city stood. A key, indefinable element in its survival lay in a belief in the city itself. Neither the 200 years of Mongol overlordship nor, several centuries later, the 200 years of eclipse by St. Petersburg and Moscow's immolation in 1812 were able to extinguish the city's inner vitality. The myth of the Third Rome alone is clearly inadequate as an explanation of the city's 'will to survive', but survive it did. Its two most prominent monuments, the Cathedral of Christ the Saviour and St. Basil's Cathedral, were erected to commemorate victory, the one against Napoleon's *Grande Armée*, the other against the Kazan Khanate. With those victories, Moscow survived. The two monuments can be interpreted as being dedicated as much to Moscow, bringer of victory, as to divine intercession.

The blessing and curse of Moscow have been its leaders. Their single-minded ruthlessness was instrumental in the city's survival and ultimate domination of huge tracts of territory. They have defended the city but on more than one occasion have also abandoned it. With fearful consequences, the Romanov tsars set the state apart from the urban community which supported it, and only with the advent of Soviet power did the one become more closely identified with the other. Even so, the legitimization of Russia's leadership has rested with the cities, in particular Moscow. Uspensky Cathedral, the place of coronation of the tsars, suggests that this role is deeply rooted in collective memory. It also hints at the traditional conflation of political power and belief. Along with the close association of Moscow with Russian national identity, this fusion in its various expressions lies near the heart of the city's 'will to survive'.

The tradition of legitimization began early, and by the eighteenth century had a fully developed religious connotation. In 1688 Simeon Ushakov completed an icon entitled *The Tree of the Muscovite State,* a powerful representation of the 'symphony of Church and state'. At the centre of the icon is a reproduction of the Vladimir Mother of God. Tradition has it that it had been brought to Moscow in 1395 from Vladimir to save the city from the armies of Tamerlane.[4] Vladimir had acquired the icon from Byzantium. In Ushakov's icon, the divine favour accorded to Moscow by the Vladimir Mother of God was extended to the rulers of the Muscovite state, thus adding an aura of divine legitimization. The swallow-tail crenelations of the Kremlin walls are clearly visible in the icon, as is Uspensky Cathedral, the holiest place in Moscow. The icon within the icon is depicted as being venerated by prominent members of the Romanov family, their legitimacy and sacred link to Moscow thereby made explicit.[5] One of the charges whispered against Peter the Great by the Old Believers was that, besides being a secret German, in having forsaken the Mother of God by building St. Petersburg as his new capital he was indeed the Antichrist.

That the icon has had an uncertain history as a talismanic insurance policy is counterbalanced by the traditional belief that, in the end, citadel Moscow has prevailed against a long succession of enemies. Even in atheistic twentieth-century Moscow that belief persisted. On 31 October 1941 a breach in the outer ring of Moscow's defensive line at Mozhaisk was finally closed by Marshal Zhukov's forces. That day happened to coincide with the Feast of the Protection of the Mother of God, whose name had been invoked by Metropolitan Sergei. The Vladimir Mother of God had in fact already been reinterpreted for Soviet purposes in the wartime poster created by I. M. Toidze. In it, the radiant streams of sanctity of the original are replaced by a halo of bayonets. Draped in holy red, she had become Mother Russia, calling her sons to battle.

The strength and persistence of Russian Orthodox tradition in contemporary Muscovite politics was dramatically revealed fifty years later. On 26 August 1991, in an unconscious act of legitimization, the first Russian parliament not held under Party control was preceded by a liturgy in Uspensky Cathedral. This would have been unthinkable only a few weeks before. As is customary among Orthodox believers, President Yeltsin had earlier asked for forgiveness from the parents of the three young men who died during the coup attempt. Coincidentally one was Jewish. This same gesture of holy closure is witnessed in the final passages of the librettos of two of Russia's greatest operas, Mussorgsky's *Boris Godunov* and Tchaikovsky's *Mazepa,* both set in the Kremlin.

In the Muscovite mythology, victory also figures in the narratives relating to legitimacy of place and of its rulers, whatever distress the latter may have caused the city in real life. Another icon demonstrates *Blessed is the Host of the Heavenly Tsar*, which celebrates Ivan the Terrible's conquest of the Kazan Khanate in 1552. As a painting, it is the equivalent of St. Basil's in architecture. The huge, two-metre icon depicts the Archangel Michael leading Ivan's victorious troops back from a burning Kazan. The visual biblical reference suggests that Ivan is Joshua to Kazan's Jericho, the victor of good over evil. The placing of the icon in Uspensky Cathedral, the sacred heart of the Muscovite state, underscored its symbolism.[6] In a not-too-distant process, Stalin directed the defeat of the Nazi evil from the Kremlin and took Berlin.

Complementing its founding myths, military influences in the shaping of the city give physical expression to its 'will to survive'. These begin with the *cherta* lines of defence against the Mongol horsemen who could be ambushed as they passed through barriers of felled trees, to the Kremlin walls and the fortress monasteries and strategic settlements of the seventeenth and eighteenth centuries. These included the great fortress town of Smolensk on Moscow's western approaches. In its modern expression, the ABM defence system ringing Moscow conforms to a pattern established centuries past where space is traded for time.

The First Congress of Soviet Architects in 1937 confirmed socialist realism as the governing philosophy in architecture. It held one closed session. In it, 'a war engineer of the first category'[7] made it clear that architectural and planning activities begun in Moscow in 1931 and formalized in the General Plan of 1935 were designed with military considerations as a priority. His no-nonsense exposition put to an abrupt close some of the more grandiose but militarily untenable schemes for the city. In this, the First Congress also marked the death knell of Moscow's 'paper architects' whose plans lost all hope of realization but who continued in their visionary work into the 1930s.

The impact of the military dimension on a range of Moscow projects, either in progress or planned, was long-lasting. Besides their ceremonial function, the wide boulevards built in that decade also had the purpose of firebreaks (imitating similar widening and straightening of the streets in wooden Moscow centuries before) and allowed rapid defensive movement within the city. Water supply, necessary for the suppression of incendiary attack, was assured by the construction of the Moscow–Volga Canal. All Moscow streets were laid with asphalt, to assist in decontamination in the event of a chemical attack, and the Metro underground stations were dug particularly deep as shelters against bombardment. After the war, the placement of Stalin's 'high buildings' took into account military as well as other considerations. Each held a secret radar installation.

This historic pattern of Moscow's almost uninterrupted preparations for its defence contains one great anomaly. Even with the sacredness of its centre, Moscow has never been a final line of defence, and its rulers and citizens have abandoned the city on numerous occasions, most famously when Ivan the Terrible established his capital at Aleksandrovskoe Selo, and

Peter the Great established his imperial capital on the Baltic. Citizens have fled the city in flames in medieval times, and the governor, Rostopchin, set fire to the city before joining others fleeing the city in 1812. Napoleon found this act of arson incomprehensible. In 1941 Kazan railway station was the scene of chaos as people tried to escape the advancing Wehrmacht armies. Stalin was a day away from leaving Moscow for Kuybyshev, already designated as the Soviet Union's provisional 'administrative capital' and new centre for the diplomatic community. Fleeing with the living, Lenin's corpse had already been secretly transported away. In 1991, Yeltsin had made contingency plans to establish a base in Sverdlovsk, his old political base, in the event that his opposition to the coup failed.

Of all the abandonments of Moscow, Peter's was the most traumatic. It lasted 200 years and symbolized the schizophrenia in Russian national identity, between 'Westernizers' and Slavophiles. The echoes of that debate continue to this day. Moscow remained 'Asiatic, anti-Western, heavy-handed, vulgar and oppressive',[8] everything that St. Petersburg was not. The vast project to Westernize Russia, epitomized by St. Petersburg, created a wave of Western architectural emulation which reached across the entire country. Like St. Petersburg (and emphatically unlike Moscow) new towns laid out during the years of Russia's imperial expansion had a logical grid-plan. Each town of any size possessed public buildings with identifiable architectural references to St. Petersburg and its Western inspiration. Building standards were laid down by the imperial court. A parallel process occurred in Soviet times as Gosplan and Gosstroi, the state architectural and planning agencies, enforced the observance of an architectural template for all buildings across the whole of the Soviet Union, creating mini-Moscows as they went.

Before the Revolution, Russian cities, St. Petersburg and

Moscow included, stood outside the agrarian social order upon which the tsarist autocracy rested. After 1917 the Bolshevik regime inverted this order, and Moscow became the principal agent for an urban-based industrialized civilization. Paradoxically, even before the Bolshevik seizure of power, industrializing 'calico Moscow', nodal point of the country's extensive and growing network of railways, proved more suited to meeting the challenges of industrialization than aristocratic, service-oriented St. Petersburg. But it was the 'artificial city' (as its critics called it) of St. Petersburg/Leningrad that successfully endured a 1,000-day siege in the Second World War; and at great human cost, its citizens never abandoned it.

Stalin's antipathy to St. Petersburg/Leningrad was deep-seated. In the 1930s his potential rival to power, the popular Party chief Sergei Kirov, had his base there. His assassination put an end to a story before it had begun but triggered the Great Terror, culminating in the Purge Trials. Stalin grudgingly accepted that the city should be designated 'Hero-City' for its record of resistance only long after a similar designation had been conferred upon Moscow. In one of those ironies of history, Prime Minister Putin, President Medvedev and Foreign Minister Ivanov and a group of others from St. Petersburg belong to the inner core of Russia's current leadership. As a direct result of the constitutional arrangements established during Yeltsin's presidency, however, Moscow belonged to the Muscovites, or at least to a closed circle of them. With a new mayor, this may well change.

The Symbolic Landscape

In common with other cities, Moscow has an array of monuments, each contributing to the city's self-image. In addition, these symbolic structures can change in meaning over time and circumstance. For example, the reverence once accorded to Dzerzhinsky's statue[9] in front of the Lubyanka is now reserved for the Solovetsky Stone, placed on the same square by the Memorial organization in honour of victims of the Gulag.[10] The stone itself is from the monastery of that name, one of the Gulag's first prisons. Stones and monuments, statues and buildings are all part of Moscow's symbolic landscape. Cemeteries evoke their own collective memories.

In contrary fashion, the famous statue of the revolutionary poet Mayakovsky on the square which bears his name in downtown Moscow (popularly known as 'big pants Mayakovsky', from the statue's voluminous proletarian trousers) still rests on its pedestal with its name and place intact even though in New Moscow the poet's modernist, revolutionary writings are largely forgotten. One of the first acts of the Moscow City Council in its early post-Soviet phase was to restore or rename many of the streets, eliminating their communist flavour. Statues of Lenin went as well, beginning with the huge idealized head behind the podium in the Congress of Soviets building. Just as the Bolsheviks had removed a statue of Alexander II from the Kremlin grounds, so a seated statue of Lenin was taken away. Moscow's largest Lenin statue, on Kaluga (formerly Oktyabryaskaya) Square, however, remains standing, with its coat blowing in the breeze and its arm now gesturing to nowhere in particular. The satirists Komar and Melamid suggested that statues of Lenin be left in peace, but with huge sculptured pigeons, presumably complete with the requisite droppings, perched on his head. This, arrangement, they suggested, would 'be an instructive history lesson'.[11]

Officially sponsored historical amnesia was a characteristic feature of the Soviet period, associated mostly with the 'non-persons' who had disappeared in Stalin's various machinations against his enemies, but also with Khrushchev's anti-Stalin campaigns. Besides the removal of his name from cities like

Stalingrad, Khrushchev saw to the wholesale removal of Stalin's statues from Moscow and other Soviet cities, although he allowed one to remain standing in Tbilisi. Khrushchev went further than eliminating names and statues. He also abolished the Stalinist school of 'monumental propaganda', the Moscow Institute of Architectural Design, and put an abrupt halt to any further construction of Stalinist buildings, including one whose foundations had been laid next to the Kremlin. The Khrushchevite Hotel Rossiya was built in its place, until, in its turn, it was torn down.[12]

Until the creation of Victory Park on Poklonnaya Gora, a project undertaken by Mayor Luzhkov, Moscow had no monument commemorating the Second World War. His was exclusively a Moscow and not a Russian project. Despite some muted opposition, buildings representing Russia's three principal religious faiths—an Orthodox chapel, a synagogue and the previously mentioned mosque—figure in the grounds. One monument, designed by Zurab Tsereteli and entitled *Tragedy of the Peoples,* has been removed. Its depiction of falling figures, representing suffering and loss disturbed some mothers and their children visiting the park. Both mothers and children also wanted reinstated the ice-cream kiosks that had been taken down to make way for the monument. In their own way, the new kiosks also carry a subliminal, perhaps even hopeful, message about the New Moscow.

Despite the support Tsereteli has received from Mayor Luzhkov, his work is not universally admired as symbolic of Moscow's identity. His monument representing Peter the Great as founder of the Russian navy is a case in point. Some objected that Moscow had nothing to do with the founding of the Russian navy, while others dispensed rumours that the statue was originally of Christopher Columbus to celebrate the 500th anniversary of the discovery of the New World, but that an American buyer had backed out at the last moment. Many dislike the statue on aesthetic grounds. An initiative to have it taken away foundered because of the prohibitive costs, but with Luzhkov's dismissal its removal is again an active issue.

More conventional statues and their placement also define modern Moscow. An equestrian statue to the hero of the defence of Moscow and victor of the Battle for Berlin, Marshal Zhukov, sits astride his horse in conventional pose at the entrance to Red Square. The frisky horse which he rode on Victory Day in May 1945 into the square is most likely the same one that Stalin had earlier fallen off. The statue's creator Viacheslav Klykov, a strong nationalist, sought unsuccessfully to have another of his works, this one of Nicholas II, erected within the grounds of the Kremlin. In the end he settled for the statue's location being in the town of Tainskoe, a tsarist way-station in the emperor's travel to Moscow. A second version of the statue, in Podolsk, was destroyed by vandals.

In its variety, Moscow's symbolic landscape ranges from the deeply tragic to the trivial. Monuments like Victory Park and the Cathedral of Christ the Saviour occupy a sort of middle ground. The cathedral, in the view of many of its critics, has betrayed its founding purpose through the use of air-conditioning and the construction of a three-storey parking garage complete with ecclesiastical offices below its main floor. Holiness in collective memory, they say, has migrated to other places. The burial-pits of Butovo, holding victims of Stalinist executions, have been consecrated by the Church. An unadorned tablet now marks the spot above the underpass where the three young men died in August 1991; on the day of their deaths it was the place where an impromptu memorial of heaped flowers and candles appeared. In contrast, Aleksandrovsky Gardens, a few paces away from the Monument to the Unknown Soldier, has an array of fairy-tale sculptures to delight the children. Further on, there is a McDonald's restaurant. In May 2003 Paul McCartney became the first Beatle to sing inside the Kremlin walls before an estimated 100,000 people gathered on Red Square. In those brief hours, Moscow became the New Jerusalem of Rock.

Some critics despair of Moscow's new monumentalism, saying that it presents a face of Moscow that never existed. The Hotel Moskva just off Red Square has been replaced by a building virtually identical in outward appearance, and the reconstruction of Kazan Cathedral on Red Square, as well as the restoration of the Iverskie Gates at the entrance to the square, has given the heart of the city a contemporary retro-look. These criticisms have not deterred city planners who continue in their efforts to create a positive architectural narrative of the city. They are trying to emulate Berlin, a city with a comparable dark past, which has demonstrably succeeded in coming to terms with its own history through two iconic new buildings: Foster's Reichstag and Libeskind's Jewish Museum. But the architectural reinterpretation of Moscow's monuments in a contemporary idiom, critics fear, carries the risk that the heart of the city is 'turned into a heritage theme park'.

Stadtkrone

Facing the devastation caused by the First World War, the German architect and planner Bruno Taut developed the idea of a *Stadtkrone,* the crown of a modern city that would supersede the anomie and chaos of the industrial city which, in Taut's view, 'had lost its centre'. By 'centre' he meant the cultural core with its cumulative symbolic content around which the old city had grown.[13] He believed that the loss of centre was a driving factor in urban alienation, which in turn contributed to the outbreak and disastrous course of the war. The need was therefore to restore the centre through the creation of a focal point for the modern city. This could take the form of a monumental structure, rich in symbolism and folk-memory.

Taut's vision was bent to Nazi ends, and had it materialized, the huge domed *Stadtkrone* designed by Albert Speer would have been at the heart of Hitler's New Berlin, where 'tens of thousands would enter into a solemn, mystic union with the Leader of the German Nation'.[14]

In Moscow, the Palace of Soviets would have played precisely such a role—but also as a beacon for world revolution. What Taut left out of account was that such a building, rather than bringing peace and harmony in a vast ritual setting, would require the imposition of an unprecedented level of social discipline and organization, the ideal of all authoritarian, centralizing regimes. Nevertheless, Taut's communitarian vision carries a particular resonance in Moscow, for the Kremlin as *Stadtkrone* and focal point goes beyond its own physical boundaries to become at one with the identity of the city itself.

Moscow, expanding outward from a single, seminal core, the Kremlin, has replicated itself over vast distances, and has also experienced decline and threat of extinction. Moscow's 'will to survive' has taken many forms, from icons invested with a belief in holy protection to practical matters to ensure the city's continued existence in the event of a nuclear attack. At the same time, Moscow culture contains hints of transcendence. In 1947, at the 800th anniversary of the founding of Moscow, Stalin declared that Moscow was the 'model city of the world', favoured by the forces of history to be the forebear of a new civilization.

That vision was not realized, and is now replaced by a postmodernist image of New Moscow, its silhouette of modern skyscrapers reiterating the outline of the old. Above all presides the Kremlin, diminished by some of the huge structures rising less than five kilometres along the embankment to the west. Even with them the Kremlin remains the focal point of this complex city: it is the Kremlin that gives Moscow its meaning of place.

Endnotes

Chapter 1

1. V. I. Lenin, *Collected Works,* 4th English Edition (Moscow: Progress Publishers, 1972), Vol. 29, pp. 240-41.
2. *Istoriya Moskvy* (Moscow: Izdatel'stvo Akademii Nauk SSSR, 1952-9), p.709, quoted in Timothy J. Colton, *Moscow: Governing the Socialist Metropolis* (Cambridge, MA: Belknap Press, 1995), p. 57.
3. M. N. Tikhomirov, 'O proizkhozhdenii nazvaniia' Rossii' (Voprosi *Istorii,* 1953 no. 11), pp. 93-6.
4. By name they are the Andronikov, Novospassky, Simonov, Danilov, Donskoy and Novodevichy monasteries.
5. This was not the first time Germans had flown over the Kremlin and Red Square. In May 1941, a Luftwaffe Ju-52 observation aircraft flew over the city unopposed by Soviet air defence.
6. Kathleen Berton, *Moscow: An Architectural History* (London: I.B. Tauris, 1990), p. 230.
7. Berton, p. 222.
8. Serge Fauchereau, ed., *Moscow 1900-1930* (Paris: Seuil, 1988), p. 21.
9. The Great Terror is a term coined by Robert Conquest, from a book by the same name. It derives from the French, *la grande terreur,* describing the excesses of the French Revolution during its Jacobin phase.
10. Konstantin Akinsha, *The Holy Place* (London: Yale University Press, 2007), p. 126.
11. Richard Pipes, *Russia under the Old Regime,* 2nd Edition (London: Penguin, 1993), p. 199.

Chapter 2

1. Reported by BBC, 28 February 2008. The e-war was apparently brought about by an Estonian decision to remove a Soviet war memorial in downtown Tallinn. The Russian youth organization was held to be responsible for this attack on Estonian computers, which threatened to bring all Estonian business to a halt.

2. Nicholas Riasonovsky, *A History of Russia, Vol.1,* p. 75.
3. Boris Kagarlitsky, *Empire of the Periphery,* p. 70.
4. Historians dispute the various names of the empire as much as its influence on the future development of Muscovite political institutions and civic culture. The Mongols called themselves the khanate; the term Golden Horde did not appear until the seventeenth century, and this in Russian (not Mongol) sources. By the same token, Rus' sources, including those of the Orthodox Church, refer to all steppe peoples as the Tatars, a term the Mongols did not like themselves since the actual Tatars, a Chinese borderland people, had killed Genghis Khan's father Yisyegu. Western European sources did not make the distinction, however, and used the term indiscriminately, sometimes adding a superfluous 'r', as in Tartar, apparently confusing it with a region of Hell in Greek mythology. Early on, some European travellers pointed out this error, but to little effect.
5. John Keegan (Toronto: Key Porter Books, 1993), p. 213.
6. Quoted in Laurence Kelly (London: Constable Robinson Ltd, 2004), p. 32.
7. The British Embassy Chancery was located here, just opposite the Kremlin, and was said to have one of the best views in the whole of Moscow from the Ambassador's residence. Stalin hated the building's location, and made several half-hearted attempts to have it relocated. A new structure was eventually built further up-river after 1991.
8. Karl Wittfogel (New York: Vintage, 1981), p. 225.
9. Tibor Szamuely (London: Secker & Warburg, 1974).
10. Szamuely, p. 20. Tibor Szamuely is a nephew of a prominent Hungarian communist of the same name. He taught at the Kwame Nkrumah Ideological Institute and emigrated to Britain in 1964.
11. Ostrowski, p. 19.
12. The Old Believers were opposed to reforms of Metropolitan Nikon, who in the 1650s correctly sought to bring the traditional Russian Orthodox Church ritual and text, both of which had developed a heavy accretion of home-bred elements, into line with those of the Greek Byzantine church. Particularly bitter was the issue of whether two fingers (God the Father and God the Son) or three (to include God the Holy Spirit,

believed to be a Western theological invention) should be used for genuflection. A famous painting by Vasily Surikov of Boyarina Morozova (1884) being transported out of Moscow to torture and exile for her beliefs illustrates the emotion and depth of an issue so closely connected with the question of Russian national identity.

13. The Russian historian Karamazin wrote that St. Petersburg had been built on 'tears and bones'. Contemporary estimates put the death toll at between 60,000 to 100,000. About 5 per cent per annum of state revenue was devoted to its construction. Some believe that these figures are exaggerated.
14. At the outbreak of the First World War in 1914, St. Petersburg's name was changed to Petrograd to make it sound more authentically Russian. It was changed to Leningrad at Lenin's death in 1924. Following the collapse of the Soviet Union in 1991, it reverted to its original name of St. Petersburg by popular vote under Mayor Sobchak.
15. Yu. P. Malinovskii, *Voprosy Istorii*, No.11 (Noyabr 1968), pp. 99-103.
16. Colton, p. 193.

Chapter 3

1. *Izvestia* TsK KPSS, no.12 1990, p. 217 in Acton, p. 102.
2. John T. Alexander, *Bubonic Plague in Early Modern Russia: Public Health and Urban Disaster* (Oxford: Oxford University Press 2003).
3. It is believed that venereal disease came to Moscow in the 1490s from Cracow, which had contracted the disease through Italian trade routes. A second wave of the disease hit Moscow apparently carried by discharged mercenaries from the Thirty Years' War. Venereal disease was known in Russia as 'the Latin Sickness', a possible back-reference to the Muscovites' Polish Catholic enemies during the Time of Troubles (1598-1613).
4. Kelly, pp. 4 and 5. The cathedrals date from 1326, and the particular merchants' house from 1471.
5. De Larrey, quoted in *Zamoyski*, p. 301.
6. Braithwaite, p. 187.
7. Official Soviet figures report 2,000 deaths and 6,000 injured during the campaign. Comparable figures for the London Blitz are 30,000 killed and 50,000 wounded. Braithwaite, p. 186.

The bombing of Rotterdam began in the afternoon of 14 May 1940 and lasted fifteen minutes; 800 died, and 78,000 were left homeless. The Dutch surrendered the day after.

8. The author Andrew Nagorski quotes a figure of 2 million, based on his reading of the Russian word, *pogibli*, roughly meaning 'perished'. This figure is accounted for by the larger number of Red Army troops captured during the early stages of Operation Typhoon. They did indeed perish, either in Nazi POW camps, where they froze to death, or at the hands of Stalin, who suspected that the survivors were unreliable and so were sent to Siberia. They simply perished later.
9. The plan was drawn up by Alfred Rosenberg, author of *The Myth of the Twentieth Century*, an influential book framing Nazi racial policies.
10. Joachim C. Fest, *Hitler,* Richard and Clara Winston, trans. (New York: Vintage, 1975), p. 652.
11. *Izdatel'stvo 'Nauka', Istoriya Moskvy* (Moscow: 'Nauka', 1976), p. 253. This official history does not mention total casualties at the battle of Moscow.
12. *Bulletin of the Atomic Scientists*, March/April 2004. Hans Kristenson, Matthew G. McKinzie and Robert S. Norris, *'The Protection Paradox'.* Http://www.the bulletin.org. issues/2004/mao4kristenson.html
13. Op. cit.
14. A dark vision of Moscow surrounded by fire came close to realization in August 2010, when some 500 fires from peat-bogs and forests ignited before the summer heat finally abated. Carbon monoxide levels rose to over four times the normal and airports were closed as smog enveloped the city. Having miraculously escaped fallout from the Chernobyl explosion Moscow was suddenly at risk from radioactive contamination from the burning forests. Emergency defences were first priority for the Nuclear Research Facility at Sarov, three hundred miles east of Moscow. Moscow still lives under the shadow of nuclear fire.

Chapter 4

1. The phrase is Karl Schloegel's: *Terror und Traum* (Moscow: Hanser, 1937), p. 297.
2. Technically, the 'oligarchy' refers to the group of financiers

who gained their huge wealth by buying up state property at rock-bottom prices in the economic chaos following the Soviet collapse. Some, such as Boris Berezovsky and Vladimir Gusinsky, became members of President Yeltsin's 'family' and deployed their wealth and influence to help him win the June 1996 election. Many became implicated in various financial scandals in the Yeltsin period and were then brought to book under President Putin. Some, including Berezovsky, sought refuge abroad; others were prosecuted. Mikhael Khodorkovsky, founder of the Yukos oil conglomerate, was convicted of fraud and tax evasion in 2004; he is serving an eight-year sentence in Chita prison, 3,700 miles east of Moscow. His supporters claim he was jailed for funding opponents of Putin's government in the 2003 Duma elections; his opponents say he was attempting to buy MPs. Putin and the surviving oligarchs apparently reached a deal whereby they stay out of politics, including foreign policy, in return for not being prosecuted.

3. Jean-Louis Cohen, *Le Corbusier and the Mystique of the USSR: Plans and Projects for Moscow 1928-1936* (New York: Princeton University Press, 1991).
4. These historians follow the analysis established by the great anti-Mongol Russian historian, Kliuchevsky. Other modern revisionist historians dispute the case, arguing that the *Pax Mongolica* brought more good than harm. It also brought the plague to all of Europe.
5. Cf. David Hoffmann, *Peasant Metropolis* (Ithaca, NY: Cornell University Press), p. 15.
6. He was appointed to replace the Grand Duke Sergei, who had been assassinated. This may have had something to do with his subsequent behaviour.
7. The idealistic, liberal officers leading the revolt had instructed their troops to call for Konstantin i Konstitutsiya (Constantine and Constitution), i.e. for the establishment of a constitutional monarchy under Grand Duke Constantine. Subsequent investigations by the tsarist police revealed that many of the troops believed that Konstitutsiya was Constantine's wife.
8. The Westernizers, as they were called, and their opponents, the Slavophiles, were the dramatis personae in a debate that had its origins with Peter the Great. The debate still continues over the

calling of Russia and the identity of the Russians.
In the nineteenth century, the issue of Russian identity was often referred to as the unsolvable 'cursed question'. The matter was solved at least temporarily, when Soviet citizenship was substituted for nationality. Soviet internal travel documents however continued to use 'nationality' as a reference criterion. Under this arrangement, some Jews objected to their being singled out by background, insisting that they were Russian by nationality. On the identity debate, see Nicholas Riasonovsky, *Russian Identities: A Historical Survey* (Oxford: Oxford University Press 2005).

9. *'The First Letter on the Philosophy of History'* in M. Gershenzon, ed., *Socheneniya i Pisma P.Ya. Chaadayeva*, Vol. I (Moscow, 1913), p. 79, in Pipes, *Russia under the Old Regime,* 2nd edition (London: Penguin, 1993), p. 266.
10. Troyat, p. 216.
11. Isaiah Berlin, *The Soviet Mind: Russian Culture under Communism* (Washington, DC: Brookings Institution Press, 2004), p. 132.
12. Henri J. M. Nouwen, *Behold the Beauty of the Lord* (Notre Dame, IN: Ave Maria Press, 2007), p. 22.
13. The influence of religion on civic culture was by no means confined to turn-of-the-century Moscow. The relative peace of Cairo's Shubra district, which stands some comparison to Presnya in terms of first-generation peasant composition, poverty and high population density, is attributed to the prohibition in Islam against violence within the community of Believers, the Umma. Conditions accepted and indeed tolerated in Shubra were a fundamental cause of the riots that destroyed the Watts inner-city district of Los Angeles in 1965.
14. BBC World Service, 30 October 2009.
15. 'Gulag' is a Russian-language acronym standing for *Glavnoye Upravleniye Ispravitel'no-Trudovykh Lagery i Kolonyi* – Chief Administration of Corrective Labour Camps and Colonies.
16. Robert Conquest, Preface to the Fortieth Anniversary Edition, *The Great Terror: A Reassessment* (Oxford: Oxford University Press, 1990). When his editor asked Conquest to suggest a new title, mindful of some of the questioning his first pre-glasnost edition had provoked, he came up with, 'I Told You So, You Fucking Fools'. *Guardian*, 15 February 2003. At the time, some

Western observers who attended the trials reported that they were run fairly.

17. Roy Medvedev, *Stalin and Stalinism*, quoting his previous book, *Let History Judge*.
18. Anatoli Rybakov, *Children of the Arbat* (London: Little, Brown & Co., 1988), p. 320.
19. Ibid., p. 272.
20. Alexander Solzhenitsyn, *The Gulag Archipeligo* (New York: Harper and Row, 1973), p. 181.
21. *International Herald Tribune*, 27 June 2007.
22. Catherine Cook, *Modernity and Realism in Russian Art and the West* (Chicago: Northern Illinois University Press, 2009), p. 184.
23. Dominic Lieven, *Empire, The Russian Empire and its Rivals* (London: Yale University Press, 2001), p. 209.
24. A. N. Pankratova, ed., *History of the USSR* (Moscow: Foreign Languages Publishing House, 1948), p. 33.
25. Arkady Timiriazev, *'Moscow University' in Moscow: Sketches on the Russian Capital* (London: Hutchinson & Co., 1947), p. 41.
26. Reasons for apparent student passivity are not hard to guess. At Moscow University, through a system of preferred entry (the same was practised in tsarist times, but with different criteria), students were the offspring of the *nomenklatura*. A parent's advantageous position in the system was hostage to the good behaviour of the child. Individual control was exercised by Komsomol members in every faculty, who were required to prepare a report on each student. Even the physical configuration of the *obshscezhytie*—living quarters of the University—played a part. The University's four wings could be sealed off, and each floor searched as students were confined to their rooms.
27. In the 1960s and 1970s, Western journalists were impressed with the intensity and seriousness which passengers on the Metro and other public places displayed as they read their books. Reading seemed ubiquitous. Some journalists drew the mistaken conclusion that the Russian attitude to learning was putting the Soviet Union ahead in the space race and was responsible for the (non-existent) 'missile gap'. In fact, most of the stuff the passengers were reading was rubbish. Later, the same intensity and seriousness were evident when bootleg copies of *Playboy* magazine appeared.

28. The best work in English on Gorbachev and the development of *perestroika* is Archie Brown, *The Gorbachev Factor* (Oxford: Oxford University Press, 1996).

Chapter 5

1. Michael J. Hittle, *The Service City: State and Townsmen in Russia, 1600-1800* (Cambridge, MA: Harvard University Press, 1979), p. 10.
2. Exceptions include the last tsar, Nicholas II, whose remains are interred in the Peter and Paul Fortress, across from the Winter Palace in St. Petersburg. Nikita Khrushchev is buried in Novodevichy Monastery, as is Stalin's second wife, Nadezhda.
3. Brumfield, p. 98.
4. Mitropolit Moskovskii Makarii, *Istoriia russkoi tserkvi (*St. Petersburg, *1886)* V Book II, pp. 480-88, quoted in Richard Pipes, *Russia under the Old Regime* (London: Penguin, 1993) p. 225.
5. Cf. S. N. Bratus' et al., eds., *Slovar' Pravovykh Znanii (Moskva: Izdatel'stvo Sovyetskoya Entsiklopediya, 1965).*
6. Catherine the Great also founded Odessa in 1794 with the double purpose of promoting commerce on and out of the Black Sea and of protecting Russian imperial possessions against encroachments by the Ottomans, following the Russo-Turkish War (1787-91). After 1801, the same Alexander I who had shown such interest in the reconstruction of Moscow took up Catherine's imperial project; it was never completed.
7. Frederick W. Skinner, *'Trends in Planning Practices: the Building of Odessa, 1794-1917'* in Michael F. Hamm, ed., *The City in Russian History* (Lexington, KY: University of Kentucky Press, 1976), p. 141.
8. At the beginning of the nineteenth century, large sections of the trading rows had been roofed over, creating a proto-arcade; and in their turn, in 1886, the middle and lower trading rows were demolished by order of the government. Russian architects and designers, inspired by the design of Victorian train stations, rebuilt the upper trading rows as a three-storey European-style gallery. Its huge glass roof was unique at the time, and until the 1920s retained the name Upper Trading Rows. It reopened in 1953 as GUM (Gostydarstvennyi

Universal'nyi Magazin); now stocked with the international brands of Benetton and Gucci, it presides over the east side of Red Square. Following the suicide in 1932 of Stalin's wife Nadezhda, her body was displayed in the building, then an office complex.

9. Dmitri Volkogonov, *The Rise and Fall of the Soviet Empire* (London: HarperCollins, 1998).
10. There may be some danger of confusion here. Elizabeth was crowned in 1742, and the triumphal gates were originally built in wood for the occasion. They were subsequently rebuilt in stone in 1753-7.
11. Boris Kagarlitsky, *Empire of the Periphery* (London: Pluto Press, 2004), p. 171.
12. V. K. Rukovsky, quoted in Voyce, p.168.
13. The emancipation of the serfs was one of the initiators of these changes, which gathered momentum as the century progressed. By 1853, some fourteen artists of the St. Petersburg Academy broke away from its formalized strictures and became known as the *Peredvizhniki* (roughly, secessionists, sometimes translated as 'wanderers') who emphasized 'authenticity' and social commentary in their work. They are regarded by some art historians as the forebears of socialist realism in the arts, which reached its height as official artistic dogma—art in the service of the working class—in the high Soviet period.
14. Douglas Smith, 'Count Zakhar Chernyshev's Snuffbox' in Valerie Kievelson and Joan Neuburger, *Picturing Russia* (New Haven: Yale University Press, 2008), p. 67.
15. Berton, p. 118.
16. Schloegel, p. 106.
17. Geoffrey Hosking, *Russia: People and Empire 1552-1917* (Cambridge MA.: Harvard University Press, 1997), p. 259.
18. Sir Herbert Norman, *'The Strategic Dream'* in Deborah Manley, *The Trans-Siberian Railway: a Traveller's Anthology* (London: Century Books, 1988; Signal Books, 2009), p. 41.
19. Colton, p. 72.

Chapter 6

1. Andrey Ikonnikov, *Arkhitektura Sovietskoi Rossii* (Moscow: Raduga, 1990), p. 183.

2. A website on Moscow entertainment, element moscow.ru at http://elementmoscow.ru/top-7.php?i=174000, states this categorically in an article on the 'top seven' constructivist buildings of Moscow.
3. Quoted from an unattributed source, in Colton, *Metropolis*, p. 285.
4. Hosking, p. 53.
5. John Julius Norwich, *A Short History of Byzantium* (London: Penguin, 1997), p. 306.
6. Simon Sebag Montefiore, *Stalin: In the Court of the Red Tsar* (London: Weidenfeld & Nicolson, 2003), p. 119.
7. Billington, p. 47.
8. Colton, p. 90.
9. Extending progressively outwards, the three cherta lines were the Bereg Line (fourteenth century), the Zasechnaya Cherta (fifteenth–sixteenth centuries) and the Belgorodskaya Cherta (seventeenth century). These lines straddled the main routes of the Tatar raids, and with a few notable exceptions were effective in reducing their impact. Bereg Line forts were made of wood; the Zasechnaya Cherta reinforced the strongpoints with long lines of felled trees, pointed in the direction of expected attack and impassible to horses. The Belgorodskaya Cherta's forts and monasteries were of stone, impervious to the horse raiders. Vast distances and the relatively backward state of nomadic technology precluded the Tatars' use of cannon against their walls. The trenches dug to the west of Moscow in 1941 are the direct descendants of the *cherta* lines of 600 years before.
10. Tourism as a scourge of monasteries is an international phenomenon. An Orthodox monk at the monastery of St. Catherine, originally isolated in the middle of the Sinai desert, made the same observation to me.
11. Schloegel, p. 300.
12. Johann Georg Korb, *Diary of an Austrian Secretary of Legation*, 'Seventh Execution 27 October 1698' in Kelly, Moscow, p. 149.
13. Archie Brown, 'The Change to Engagement in Britain's Cold War Policy: the Origins of the Thatcher–Gorbachev Relationship', *Journal of Cold War Studies*, Vol. 10, No.3, Summer 2008, pp. 3-47.
14. A systematic update and revision of Moscow's contradictory medieval laws, the *Ulozhenie* of 1649, approved through a semi-democratic process, was one immediate response to the

gathering urban crisis. The *Ulozhenie* would remain in effect until further legal reforms in 1835. Cf. Riasonovsky, p. 165ff.

15. The plague of 1771, as well as the construction of St. Petersburg which attracted Muscovite craftsmen and merchants, also had serious effects; but by the end of the eighteenth century Moscow had reached a population of nearly 300,000.
16. Soviet planners were not entirely without logic. In the Kazakh case, the rationale for erecting such buildings reflected shifting Soviet policies. During the Stalinist period, there was a concerted effort to urbanize the still-nomadic populations, and therefore to 'proletarianize' them. Moscow-style apartment blocks were part of this strategy, as can be seen in the outskirts of Karaganda, a mining centre. Later, Khrushchev's plan to erase the distinction between town and country led to the creation of *'agro-gorods'*, dense housing projects for collective farms. They were not successful.
17. Andrei Ikonnikov, *L'architecture russe de la période Soviétique* (Moscow: Raguda, 1990), p. 344.
18. A wry joke at the time said that Lenin statues had their hands up because Lenin wished to use the loo. Often misunderstood by foreigners in 1991, hand-painted signs sometimes appeared below the statues, *'Da, Mozhno, Pozhaluista'*, meaning roughly, 'yes, you may ', as teachers say at school. It was commonly observed that the attire of his statues, a three-piece suit complete with tie, were more typical of the upwardly-aspiring bourgeoisie than of a horny-handed revolutionary proletarian leader. The only concessions to proletarianism by the sculptors were heavy workers' boots, and much less frequently a worker's hat. The cap he frequently wore in life was in fact French, often worn by artists.
19. Montefiore, p. 94.
20. Martin Amis, *Koba the Dread* (London: Jonathan Cape, 2002), p. 146.
21. Website GlobalSecurity.org at http:// www.globalsecutiry.org/ wmd/world/russia/secret-cities./htm
22. Under international agreement, this facility is now closed. As the Aral Sea continues to dry up, a causeway is forming between the island and the mainland. There were reports of outbreaks of anthrax in local sheep, possibly exaggerated as the result of an anthrax scare in Sverdlovsk in 1979, where a research facility was located.

23. Hoffmann, *Peasant Metropolis*, p. 5.
24. Ya. Lakin, *Zhilische i byt'* (Moscow: Izdatel'stvo Nauka, 1931), p. 5.
25. There was famine in Russia in 1918-19, caused by the Great War and the Civil War. This and malnutrition in Moscow made the city particularly vulnerable to the global influenza of 1919.
26. Berton, p. 210.
27. Colton, p. 243.
28. Quoted by Andrzei Turowski, 'Town Planning and Architecture' in Serge Fauchereau, ed., *Moscou 1900-1930* (Paris: Seuil, 1988), p. 213.

Chapter 7

1. This description is taken from Baedeker's *Russia*: a *Handbook for Travellers,* 1900.
2. The outer limits of the city are now defined by the MKAD, the circular autoroute (see Chapter One) which now performs the same function as the Circular Railway did previously. Within the space defined by the MKAD, Soviet-style restrictions, including internal passports, have now disappeared. They are replaced by other measures of urban population control, including zoning and standards of residential construction. Cost is also a factor.
3. Yuri Shamarin, *Podmoskovnaya Kulturnaya Sokrovishcha Rossii,* in *Kelly*, p. 210.
4. Jane A. Sharp, *After Malevich: Variations on the Return of the Black Square* in Kievelson and Neuberger, p. 233.
5. The reasons were in fact mundane. Diaghilev's Ballets Russes had relocated to Paris and he had contracted Stravinsky to produce the piece for the Ballet Company there.
6. In 1915 the penalty for opposition to tsarist policies or those of the imperial court was compulsory enlistment in the army, effectively a death sentence.
7. Amongst Stolypin's reforms was an initiative to accelerate court proceedings against terrorists. Gallows became known as 'Stolypin's neckties', a play on words as the Russian word for necktie is *galstuk*, from the German for neckpiece.
8. At the time of the Revolution, the Bolsheviks were called the Russian Social Democratic Labour Party (Bolshevik)—RSDLP (B)—to distinguish themselves from the Menshevik wing of the

Social Democratic Party. The Bolsheviks renamed themselves communists in the 1920s to emphasize their continuity with the Paris commune of 1871, and the worldwide significance of the movement, following the establishment of the Comintern. In 1917, many preferred the Socialist Revolutionaries to the Bolsheviks because the SRs' name suggested their purpose. Others associated the Bolsheviks with the peasant term for 'bigwigs', *bolshaki*.

9. Eric Hobsbawm, *The Age of Extremes* (London: Abacus, 2008), p. 62.
10. Orlando Figes, *A People's Tragedy* (London: Penguin, 1998), p. 487.
11. Figes, op. cit., p. 495.
12. Ya. A. Polyakov, ed.et.al., *Moskva: Illustrirovannaya Istoriya (Moskva: Mysl'*, 1986),p. 41.
13. Of this number, an estimated 50-200,000 were executed during the Red Terror, well before Stalin, and some 500,000 perished in prison or were killed in various uprisings against Bolshevik power. Combat deaths were followed by further deaths caused by famine, as a result of the war and forced expropriations of grain and livestock. Many peasants slaughtered and then burnt their animals rather than hand them over to the Bolsheviks. Under war communism, the total number of civilian deaths in the famine of 1921-2 amounted to about 5 million.
14. Volkogonov, p. 1.
15. Volkogonov, quoted in Pipes, p. 30.
16. Spiro Kostof, *The City Shaped* (London: Thames & Hudson, 1991).
17. Catherine Merridale, *Night of Stone* (London: Granta Books, 2001), p. 357.
18. Lazur Markevich and El Lissitzky, Russland, *Die Rekonstruktion der Architetur in der Sowjetunion* (Wien, 1930; Cambridge, Mass.; MIT Press, 1970); Gutnov, Alexei, et al., *The Ideal Communist City,* Renee Watkins trans. (New York: George Braziller, 1970).
19. *Kulak* is the Russian word for fist; by implication, people who grasp. A pre-revolutionary term for a rich peasant, by Stalin's time it came to mean a peasant who had sufficient means to hire labour or to lease land; therefore petit bourgeois class enemies. Stalin's collectivization campaigns of the 1930s were

conducted through the 'intensification of the class struggle' and the 'liquidation of the kulaks as a class'. These followed a grain procurement crisis in 1927-8 and coincided with the inauguration of the First Five-Year Plan, culminating in 1930-31. It is estimated that 'about 5 million people were dekulakized, that is, driven from their homes, locked in prisons transported to the remotest parts of the taiga, shot or starved to death'. Some historians put the number of deaths at 1 million, others at twice that level. Katherine Merridale, *Night of Stone,* p. 212.

20. Russian acronym for Extraordinary Commission for Struggle Against Speculation and Counterrevolution. In the 1930s, and after a number of organizational changes and a revised mandate, it became the domestic wing of the KGB.
21. Colton, p. 90.
22. Figes, p. 627.
23. The term 'tragedy' is used advisedly. It is taken from the title of Orlando Figes' book, *A People's Tragedy: The Russian Revolution 1891-1924.*
24. Vladimir Paperny, *Moscow in 1937: Faith, Truth and Reality.* (http://www.univ.edu/centers/cdclv/archives/paperny_moscow.html)
25. Vasilii Grossman, loc.cit.
26. Roy Medvedev et al., *On Stalin and Stalinism*, Ellen de Kadt, trans. (Oxford: Oxford University Press, 1979), p. 38.
27. The real-life Bukharin, author of the Marxist primer ABC of Communism, and Chairman of the Comintern in the late 1920s, was accused of the political crime of belonging to a clique of 'Right Opportunists' opposed to Stalin's radical collectivization policies. He was found guilty of treason and executed on 15 March1938.
28. Richard Crossman, ed., *The God That Failed: Six Studies in Communism* (London: Hamish Hamilton, 1950).
29. D. Chechulin, *A New Moscow in Construction* (Moscow: Foreign Languages Publishing House, 1939), p. 15. In contemporary Moscow, telephone and power lines are still exposed in the outer areas, and the city heating pipes, wrapped in reflective aluminium cladding, snake through many residential suburbs, arching over roads.
30. After its opening was postponed several times, the chief architect

of the Exhibition, V. Oltarzhevski, was unmasked as a saboteur, and he was arrested. One of the charges against him was that he was secretly broadcasting a message about the conflict between workers and peasants by juxtaposing the hammer-and-sickle emblem in such a way that it looked as if the hammer was about to smash the sickle. In 2005 it was planned to put the monument on a new pedestal containing a very capitalist shopping mall.

31. Mark Bassin, 'The Morning of our Motherland' in Valerie A. Kievelson and Joan Neuberger, ed., *Picturing Russia* (New Haven: Yale University Press, 2008), p. 214.
32. Occasionally the adulation reached levels of unbelief. An early Soviet attempt at consumerism in the 1950s produced a perfume with the name 'Stalin's Breath'.
33. Colton, p. 342.
34. *Spravochnik Obshchestvennogo Agitatora* (Moscow, 1960) is a manual running through several editions instructing Party functionaries how to organize public rallies and to create awareness and enthusiasm for various Party programmes. In its lexicon, 'the masses' appears to mean passive and undifferentiated urban workers.
35. An account of Stalin's reburial is given in Medvedev's *On Stalin and Stalinism.*
36. George Reavy, trans., *The Poetry of Yevgeny Yevtushenko* (New York: October House Inc., 1965), p. 161. Quoted in Medvedev, p. 174.
37. The practical effect of this was that work on an eighth 'high building' located to the east of the Kremlin was halted. In its place rose the immense Rossiya Hotel, as described previously.
38. After Yeltsin's 1991 decree expropriating all Party property in the name of the Russian Federation, the now-vacant Central Committee building on Starya Ploshchad' would briefly house the Russian Foreign Ministry with the Soviet Foreign Ministry still operating several blocks away, on Sverdlov Square. Following the Soviet collapse, Russia took over the existing Foreign Ministry building.
39. S. S. Khromov, *Istoriya Moskvy* (Moscow: Izdatel'stvo Nauka, 1976) p. 314.
40. Quoted in Catherine Cooke and Susan E. Reid, *'Modernity and Realism' in Russian Art and the West*, Rosalind P. Blakesley and

Susan E. Reid, eds. (Chicago: Northern Illinois University Press, 2004) p. 181.

41. It was widely believed that Brezhnev's interest in the city was limited to ensuring that there were high-speed lanes out of the city for him to make a fast getaway to his dacha, and to exercise his collection of powerful foreign cars. He drove them badly, and his many accidents were hushed up.

Chapter 8

1. The Alpha Group never did attack. There are conflicting accounts as to why. One version is that the coup leaders lost their nerve. According to later testimony, Soviet Vice-President Yanayev, who was nominally in charge, declined to sanction the attack. Another version, also given in testimony, was that 'the middle and upper ranks of the KGB refused to launch the attack and had in fact provided Yeltsin and his advisors with the Emergency Committee's plans'.
2. Archie Brown, in *Seven Years that Changed the World* (Oxford: Oxford University Press, 2007), p. 19 notes that Shevardnadze resigned in December 1990, apparently because of Gorbachev's lack of support for his policies. His resignation speech warned of a right-wing takeover. Yakovlev was more specific. On Friday 16 August, he handed in his Party card, announcing that an influential Stalinist group had formed within the Party's leadership core who were 'planning social revenge, a Party and state coup'. The coup took place the following Monday.
3. *Gorbachev: Steering the USSR into the 1990s* (CIA Intelligence Assessment SOV-8710036X), July 1987.
4. The eight main plotters, a kind of Praetorian Guard of Soviet Power, were: Oleg Baklanov, Party Central Committee Secretary in charge of the Soviet military-industrial complex; Vladimir Kryuchkov, Chairman of the KGB; Prime Minister Pavlov; Boris Pugo, Minister of the Interior and formerly Chairman of the Latvian KGB; Vasily Starodubtsev, Chairman of the Soviet Peasants' Union; Alexander Tizyakov, president of the Association of State-Owned Enterprises; Gennady Yanayev, Soviet Vice-President who was in charge during Gorbachev's absence; and Dmitry Yazov, Defence Minister, appointed by Gorbachev to reform the military following the humiliating

Rust landing on Red Square four years earlier. In 1994, most of the plotters were amnestied by the State Duma. Pugo committed suicide once the coup was on its way to failure.

5. *Pravda*, 20 August 1991.
6. Following the defeat of the coup, Mayor Popov publicly thanked the Moscow Directorate of the KGB, headed by General Prulikov, 'for its non-participation in the putsch'. He never went into details about what exactly he meant. Many KGB officers were in fact Russian nationalists, and their attitude put Russian interests before those of the Soviet Union.
7. There were however some differences. Defenders of the White House gained access to its armouries and seized 400 AK47s plus ammunition. The Lithuanians facing the OMON troops had to raid a nearby museum, and were armed with a motley collection of World War Two weapons. Others had managed to smuggle shotguns into the building from home. Private possession of semi-automatic weapons in the Soviet Union was prohibited.
8. The Russian commentator Lilia Shevtsova was later to write that in 1991 the Russian people as a whole 'had not really been united—the democrats and Muscovites supported Yeltsin, but the rest of the country calmly watched the events as onlookers at their nation's crisis'. Lilia Shevtsova, *Putin's Russia,* p. 115.
9. It should be noted however that in a referendum before the putsch, a vast majority of the population of the Soviet Union (the three Baltic states did not participate) voted in favour of some kind of continuation of the Union. This was one of the justifications of the coup leaders for their actions.
   In August 1991, the tricolour was by no means a universally accepted national emblem of Russia. Some associated it with pre-revolutionary tsarist oppression. Others remembered it as the flag carried by General Vlasov's troops who fought on the side of the Wehrmacht in the Second World War.
10. After some dispute, Moscow City Council eventually turned over the Central Committee building to the Russian government.
11. Details are recounted in Boris Pankin, *The Last Hundred Days of the Soviet Union* (London: I.B. Tauris, 1996).
12. Yury Mikhailovich Luzhkov became mayor on 26 April 1990 His full title was Premier of the Moscow city Government, or more formally, President of the Executive Committee of

the Moscow Council of Deputies. When Putin replaced elections by appointment for regional heads of government in 2002, he was appointed from his formerly-elected position. He was dismissed by President Medvedev in September 2010.

13. Boris Yeltsin, Catherine A. Fitzpatrick trans., *Midnight Diaries* (New York: Public Affairs, 2000), p. 289ff.
14. Yeltsin, loc. cit.
15. Khrushchev's forays into Moscow tended to have a didactic flavour. His famous judgment of post-modernist art in the Manezh exhibition hall was that it was 'dog shit'. The organizers got the message and quickly closed it down.
16. Yeltsin, op. cit., p. 292.
17. This has included imaginative 'co-partnerships' with foreign organizations. Moscow's 'reference city' Berlin, for example, is the home of a scheme entitled 'ArchXchange: Berlin and Moscow, Cultural Identity Through Architecture' which undertook a number of renovation projects in obsolete parts of the city. Lara Eichwe et al., *ArchXchange* (Berlin: Jovis Verlag, 2006).
18. Virginie Coulloudon, 'Moscow City Management: a New Form of Russian Capitalism?' in *Business and State in Contemporary Russia,* Peter Rutland, ed. (Boulder, CO: Westview Press, 2001), pp. 89-200.
19. Coulloudon, op. cit.
20. In the late 1990s, for example, the City Council gained control of its 63 cemeteries and three crematoria by introducing regulatory legislation that only one company, Ritual Services, could meet. Ritual Services' main shareholder was the city itself, and with a monthly mortality rate of over 12,000, Moscow's potential revenue was over $1 million for the same period. The Monopoly Committee abandoned its investigation into the case when the city produced legislation to authorize the monopoly.
21. 'Post Soviet state capitalism' is the description given to Moscow's management strategy in the *Encyclopedia Britannica*, 2009 edition.
22. On the federal level, privatization was one of the main strategies in Russian Prime Minister Yegor Gaidar's shock therapy, aimed at making a rapid transition from a public-owned to a free-market economy in the shortest possible time, whatever the short-term pain. The rationale was provided by Jeffrey Sacks and the Chicago School of economists, who argued that the

free-market economy was the most effective and efficient way to ensure economic growth. Based on the same philosophy, the 'Washington consensus' led to a wave of deregulation during the George W. Bush presidency. Relatively successful in Poland, shock therapy led to the amassing of huge assets by a handful of private individuals in Russia, now known as oligarchs. With the global economic downturn, the weaknesses of a philosophy of unregulated free markets have been exposed and have fallen out of fashion. A sophisticated and authoritative analysis of Russia's economic transition is given in Yegor Gaidar (Antonina W. Bouis, trans.), *Collapse of Empire: Lessons for Modern Russia* (Washington, DC: Brookings Institution Press, 2007).

23. Moscow city authorities say that the presumption that these are war veterans suffering from drug abuse can be misplaced. Many are frostbite victims, having lain drunk overnight in the deep Russian winter.
24. Yuri Luzhkov, *The Renewal of History: Mankind in the Twenty-First Century and the Future of Russia* (London: Stacey International, 2003).
25. Prices are quoted from Knight Frank, February 2009. www.knightfrank.ru.
26. *The Economist*, 20 August 2006.
27. Anne Nivat, *La maison haute: Des russes d'aujourd'hui* (Paris: Fayard, 2002), p. xxvii.
28. The Deputy Head of the Moscow Planning Department has argued for the development of suburbia on economic as well as environmental grounds. Sergei Ambartsumjana, Presentation at the 39th ECCE Meeting, Moscow, 21 May 2004: 'The Policy of a Building Complex in Moscow: Environmental Protection within a large City'.
29. Presumed political murders include that of Anna Politkovskaya, bitter opponent of President Putin and his style of government and the Second Chechen War. She was gunned down in the lift to her flat on 7 October 2006. More recently, in February 2009, two young activists, Anastasia Barburova, a journalist for *Novaya Gazeta*, and Stanislav Marlekov, a human rights lawyer, were shot to death in downtown Moscow. Perhaps the most bizarre case is that of Aleksandr Litvinenko, who died in London of polonium-210 poisoning in November 2006. The origins of the radioactive substance

were traced to Moscow.

30. Mosiurizdat, *Osmotr Mesta Proishestvia* (Moscow, 1965).
31. *Kommersant*, 16 February 2009. The magazine *Prism*, Vol. 8, Issue 2, February 2002, quoting statistics issued by the Moscow Bureau of Forensic Medicine, reports Moscow suicide rates at some 2,000 a year, four times the US national average.
32. BBC News, 26 October 2002.
33. The British medical journal *The Lancet* (Spring 2009) attributed the decline of Moscow's population directly to the disappearance of the Soviet social safety net, including universal medical care. Difficult post-Soviet economic conditions also play a role (the Russian economy suffered a near-collapse in 1998) affecting the birth-rate. The actual population of Moscow is difficult to estimate because of the great number of unregistered in-migrants who exist outside the city's purview, often receiving pay below the minimum wage. United Nations sources quote the population of the city at 9 million; Moscow City reports it as 10.4 million. If Greater Moscow (i.e. Moscow Oblast') is included the figure rises to 15 million, twice the size of Greater London.

Chapter 9

1. S.M. Solov'ev, *Istoriia Rossii c drevneishikh vremen*, 15 vols. (Moscow: Izdatel'stvo Sotsialno-ekonomicheskoi Literatury, 1959-66), Vol. 7, p. 263.
2. Kevin Lynch, *Theory of Good City Form* (Cambridge, MA.: MIT Press, 1981).
3. Joel Kotkin, *The City: A Global History* (London: Weidenfeld & Nicolson, 2005).
4. According to tradition, the icon was brought first to Kiev from Byzantium to offer that city the same protection it had afforded the Greeks. As disaster after disaster befell the Eastern Slavs, including the destruction of Kiev by the Mongols in the thirteenth century, the icon was transported to Vladimir, the then seat of the Orthodox Patriarch, whence it was brought to Moscow.
5. The icon's visual narrative is in fact more complex. Some prominent figures are missing, including Metropolitan Nikon, the originator of the Great Schism, and Boris Godunov.
6. Some scholars interpret the icon as a visual representation

of Chapter Nine of the Book of Revelation where Christ on a white horse leads an army of the just against the forces of evil in the last days. Daniel Rowland, 'Blessed is the Host of the Heavenly Tsar' in *Picturing Russia*, Valerie A. Kivelson and Joan Neuberger, eds. (London: Yale University Press, 2005), pp. 23-37.

7. Vladimir Paperny, *Architecture in the Age of Stalin: Culture Two* (Cambridge: Cambridge University Press, 2002), p. 249. Given the nature of the secret session, the name was not published, but was most likely Major General Petr Vasilevich Utkin of the Army Quartermaster Service. In 1941, he was Chief of Staff for Rear Organization and Defence.
8. Kotkin, *The City: A Global History*, p. 15.
9. Dzerzhinsky's statue was removed to the Park of the Central House of Artists, 'the Statues Graveyard', near Gorky Park. The pedestal on which it stands was originally the base for a tsarist statue. When Dzerzhinsky's statue was pulled down in 1991, there were several unsuccessful attempts to erect a cross in its place atop its plinth. With a few exceptions, most statues of prominent Soviet figures were placed on pedestals well out of reach of vandals, a practice also common in the West.
10. In Russian, statues are named in the dative case; that is, erected to the person.
11. Kathleen E. Smith, *Mythmaking in the New Russia: Politics and Memory during the Yeltsin Era* (Ithaca, NY: Cornell University Press, 2003), p. 106.
12. The resolution of the Central Committee of the CPSU and the Soviet Council of Ministers of 23 August 1955 was precise in bringing the anti-Stalin campaign into architecture. It was entitled 'Eliminate the Academy of Architecture, Transferring all its Institutions and Organizations to the Academy of Construction and Architecture, Prohibit the Introduction of Changes into Standardized Projects'.
13. Taut's definition is given in *Spiro Kostof, The City Shaped: Urban Patterns and Meanings Through History* (London: Thames & Hudson, 1991), p. 322.
14. Kostof, p. 323.

Chronology

1147 First mention of Moscow in the chronicles: traditional date of the founding of Moscow by Yuri Dolgoruki, Prince of Suzdal, who is believed to have fortified an already existing settlement with a stockade.

1177 Second mention of Moscow. Gleb, prince of Ryazan, 'burns Moscow to the ground'.

1155 Prince Andrei Bogoliubsky takes an icon produced in Constantinople from Kiev to Vladimir, his new capital. In 1395, the icon is transported to Moscow where its presence is reputed to have saved the city several times from catastrophe; it is now known as the Vladimir Mother of God, protectress of Moscow.

1223 First appearance of Mongols in southern Russia

1237-40 Under Ghenghis Khan's grandson, Batu Khan, the Golden Horde overwhelms Russia. Moscow is taken in 1237. Kiev is levelled and its population exterminated in 1240.

1240-1380 Mongols retain effective control over Russia.

1252 Batu Khan founds Sarai on the lower Volga as headquarters of his khanate and centre of Mongol authority in Russia.

1276 Moscow's first monastery, the Danielov.

1328 Grand Prince Ivan Kalita (1328-40), so called for his role as bagman for the Mongols, makes Moscow the seat of his principality of Vladimir-Suzdal. Begins consolidating territories next to the Muscovite principality. Peter, Metropolitan of Kiev and all Russia, transfers his chair from Vladimir to Moscow the same year.

1331 Moscow destroyed by fire.

1339-40 With permission from Sarai, the Moscow Kremlin's pine log walls replaced with oak.

1360 Kremlin becomes 'a white stone fortress' as its walls are now constructed with limestone.
1364 Black Death in Moscow.
1380 Dmitri Ivanovich 'Donskoi' (1362-92), grandson of Ivan Kalita, leads a coalition of Russian princes to defeat the Mongols for the first time at the Battle of Kulikovo Field. Moscow becomes champion of Russia against the Mongols.
1382 In retaliation, the Golden Horde under Khan Kokhtamysh attacks Moscow principality. Massacres in Moscow as order collapses and the city is incinerated by the Mongols. Mongol power begins its decline as the Golden Horde divides into separate khanates of Crimea, Kazan and Astrakhan.
1400 Moscow population reaches c.40,000.
1453 Constantinople falls to the Turks.
1461 The Metropolitan of Kiev and all Russia changes his title to 'Metropolitan of Moscow and all Russia'.
1471 The first domestic stone buildings appear in Moscow.
1472 Ivan III ('the Great', 1462-1505) marries Zoe/Sofia Paleologue, niece of the last Byzantine emperor, reinforcing his claim to the Byzantine succession.
1475 Over several years Ivan III rebuilds the Kremlin. Limestone walls are replaced by stone ones, completed in 1479 under the direction of Aristotle Fieravanti. Uspensky Sobor (Cathedral of the Dormition), together with the Cathedral of Archangel Michael and the Cathedral of the Annunciation, form the sacred heart of the Moscow Kremlin.
1478 Ivan incorporates Novgorod into the Russian state, followed by Tver and other Russian principalities, including Riazan and Pskov. The 'gathering in of Russian lands' accelerates.
1480 Ivan III renounces allegiance to the Khan. In alliance

with Lithuanian and Polish forces, Khan Ahmad invades Muscovite territory, but is checkmated in a bloodless stand-off on the opposite banks of the Ugra River.

1480s Moscow gives the impression of two cities: the stone buildings and brick walls of the Kremlin, and wooden Moscow surrounding it. Long after the physical distinction loses its prominence, the psychological distinction remains. Moscow develops in concentric rings around the Kremlin, with an outer ring composed of noble estates and small holdings.The approaches to Moscow are defended by fortified monasteries.

1492 Metropolitan Zosima names Moscow 'the new Constantinople'.

1500 Moscow population reaches c.100,000.

1521 Sigizmund Herberstein, ambassador of the Holy Roman Empire, produces a plan of Moscow showing double-sloped wooden houses of two stories typical of its domestic architecture.

1533-84 Reign of Ivan IV ('the Terrible'), as Grand Prince of Moscow (1533-1547) and then as Russia's first tsar (1547-84).

1547 Conflagration in Moscow. Hysterical mobs attack the Kremlin, killing Ivan's uncle.

1555-61 Construction of St. Basil's to celebrate Ivan's victory over the Kazan khanate in 1552.

1564 Ivan abandons Moscow for Aleksandrov; returns a year later.

1565 Ivan establishes the *oprichnina*, a huge separate jurisdiction comprising a third of the Muscovite state and large sections of Moscow. Precursors of the political police of the 20th century, *oprichniki*, answerable only to Ivan, run amok. Ivan destroys Novgorod 1570 and massacres the population.

1571 The Crimean Tatar Devlet Girei puts Moscow to

the torch but fails to seize the Kremlin. Famine and plague follow. Holding the *oprichniki* responsible for not preventing the Tatar attack, Ivan disbands the organization and executes its leaders, although parts of the *oprichnina* continue for several years.

1572 Muscovite forces annihilate a second Crimean Tatar invasion.

1589 During the reign of Ivan's eldest surviving son Fedor (1584-98), Constantinople recognizes the Muscovite Church as autocephalous, with its head, Metropolitan Job, designated its first patriarch.

1598 Boris Godunov (1598-1605) named tsar as tensions gather over Fedor's succession.

1600 Moscow population reaches c.180,000.

1600 At the turn of the century, Moscow's earliest industrial enterprise is established near the Kremlin on the Neglennaya River. The Pushchenny Dvor (Cannon Yard) casts bells and produces 100 cannon a year.

1604-13 Time of Troubles. In 1601-2 bad weather brings crop failure and famine. Epidemics decimate Moscow's population. Mobs take to the streets; in the countryside, Bolotnikov launches a rebellion and marches on the city, but is finally defeated. Foreign interventionists, sometimes in concert with competing princely Muscovite factions, sponsor a succession of pretenders. Interregnum (1610-13) coincides with Polish occupation of Moscow.

1612 A Russian army, by tradition composed of all classes, is raised in Nizhny Novgorod by a commoner, Kuzma Minin, and Prince Dmitry Pozharsky. It storms Moscow, and after a second attempt evicts the Polish garrison from the Kremlin. Poles capitulate and burn Moscow as they retreat. Last observed before the revolution of 1917, from 2005 National Unity Day

(*Den' Narodnogo Edinstva*) is celebrated on 4th November, in effect replacing the Soviet holiday of 7th November.

1613 Michael Fedorovich Romanov (1613-45) elected tsar by the Zemsky Sobor and acclaimed by the crowds on Red Square. His direct descendants reign until 1762; the Romanov dynasty lasts until 1917.

1643 First stone paving appears in Moscow, replacing logs and dirt roads.

1645-76 Tsar Michael's son, Alexey Mikhailovich, reigns over the 'time of riots' in Moscow: the Salt Riot (1648), the Copper Riot (1662), as well as Stenka Razin's rebellion of Cossacks, farmers and the dispossessed in southern Russia.(1670-71). Razin is executed on Red Square.

1649 Against the background of unrest in Moscow and elsewhere, the Zemsky Sobor approves a universal legal code, the *Ulozhenie*.

1652 Nemetskaya Sloboda is established as an obligatory foreign quarter.

1661 After several years of famine, the plague returns and reaches its height in Moscow.

1666-7 Patriarch Nikon introduces textual and other reforms to Orthodox ritual, splitting the Church. Between 1672 and 1691, over 20,000 Old Believers burn themselves to death rather than accept the reforms. With their traditions of austerity and hard work, Old Believers become one of the most dynamic elements of the entrepreneurial classes in nineteenth-century Moscow.

1682 Khovanshchina, a succession struggle named after a leading conspirator and involving the Kremlin guard, destabilizes Moscow. It is given an operatic reinterpretation by Modest Mussorgsky, first performed in 1886.

1698 Peter the Great (1689-1725) orders the public execution of 1,000 *streltsy*, an elite guard of musketeers planning to depose him. The executions 'symbolize the death of the old order and the beginning of the new'.

1700 Moscow's population is about 200,000, but fluctuates according to seasonal influx of agricultural workers. The Julian calendar is adopted, changing the Byzantine reckoning of time from the beginning of the universe to the Western calculation from the birth of Christ. Street lighting in Moscow is not introduced until 1730, and mobility within the city after dark is restricted and dangerous.

1703 St. Petersburg founded and Moscow loses its status as capital in 1712. With the exception of the new capital, building in stone is banned 1714-28. Moscow's first newspaper, *Moskovskii Vedomosti*, begins publication.

1712 Decline of Moscow, eclipsed by St. Petersburg, whose population by 1780 exceeds that of Moscow, briefly reinstated as capital 1730-32. Public buildings including the Kremlin fall into disrepair. City administration is neglected.

1737 Ivan Michurin, city architect of Moscow, directs the rebuilding of Moscow's palaces after a serious fire. In 1739 Michurin completes the first plan of Moscow using scientific surveying techniques. By mid century, Prince Dmitry Ukhtomsky and others further elaborate baroque architectural forms in Moscow. They evolve into 'Moscow Baroque' or 'Naryshkin Style' by the end of the century.

1755 Lomonosov founds Moscow University.

1763 As part of her aim to create 'a new race of men' based on Enlightenment principles of citizenship,

Catherine II ('the Great', 1762-99) undertakes an 'Imperial Project' to Europeanize Russia. Unified town planning would emphasize monumental effects and integrated design for public buildings. Moscow would become 'an enlightened city' and 'beacon for Empire'.

1770 Beginning of Moscow's 'Kazakov period' of architecture (named after Matvei Fedorovich Kazakov (1738-1823), or 'Empire style' of neoclassicial building, lasting until about 1860.

1771 Bubonic plague strikes Moscow in September. An estimated 50,000 die. Forced quarantines, burning property without compensation and food shortages provoke 'plague riots' on Red Square. The plague subsides with the onset of colder weather.

1772 Catherine II instructs Vasily Bazhenov (1737-99) to reconstruct the Kremlin along baroque lines, but two years later is obliged to restore dismantled towers and walls when she loses interest. Pugachev rebellion of Don Cossacks, Old Believers and others. He is executed on Red Square.

1800 Moscow population reaches 250,000; by mid century, 380,000. The Kamer-Kollezhny Val, customs ramparts with 18 *zastavas*, or gates, define city limits from 1806, doubling the size of the city to over 7,000 hectares. Only 20% of the city is built of stone or brick.

1801-25 Reign of Alexander I.

1812 Napoleon and his Grande Armée invade Russia, making Moscow (not St. Petersburg) the target. Muscovites desert the city, and Moscow's burning forces a retreat under constant attack. Napoleon abandons his army. Alexander is hailed as 'the liberator of Europe'.

1813 The Moscow Planning Commission draws up ambitious plans to reconstruct Moscow along neoclassical lines, but leavcs the entire project unfinished. Completed work includes the Alexandrovsky Gardens, the 180-metre long imperial stables (the Manezh) and the replacement of the city's two outer defensive rings by the Boulevard Ring and the Garden Ring. The Garden Ring marks the *de facto* boundary separating middle-class and working-class districts of nineteenth-century Moscow.

1812-25 Inspired by European liberalism of the early nineteenth century, ideas coalesce in secret societies working for reform, including abolition of serfdom, and the establishment of a constitutional monarchy.

1825 Decembrist revolt in St. Petersburg crushed by Nicholas I (1825-55). Its participants are executed or exiled. Monitored by informers, double agents and the police, secret societies continue to grow, particularly in Moscow. The same year, the Bolshoi Theatre opens in Moscow.

1830-70 Moscow doubles in size from 350,000 to over 700,000 population.

1839 Architect K. A. Ton supervises the construction of the Great Kremlin Palace. Ton also builds the Cathedral of Christ the Saviour, commemorating the Russian victory over Napoleon. Consecrated in 1883 in the presence of Alexander III, it combines Byzantine and Russian traditions.

1848 Revolutionary events in Europe prompt Nicholas to appoint the reactionary Count Arseny Andreevich Zakrevsky as Moscow Governor General. He imposes severe restrictions on political activity and funnels the greater portion of city taxes to St. Petersburg. Already overburdened and obsolete, civic infrastructure is severely strained. Defying authority, and inspired by the French example, disparate groups continue to organize, seeking radical reform. The Black Hundreds retaliate by violence and persecutions, including against Jews.

1850 Industry overtakes commerce as Moscow's economic driving force. St. Petersburg's industrial development is financed mainly by foreign capital. 'Calico Moscow', so-named because of the dominance of the textile industry in the city, draws from its own resources.

1851 Moscow–St. Petersburg rail link completed.

1861 Manifesto by Alexander II (1855-81) on liberation of the serfs. Freed serfs provide the raw human material for Moscow's industrial expansion. The underground version of Alexander Herzen's novel, *Fathers and Sons*, a turning-point in the development of revolutionary ideas in Russia, is circulated. Marx and Engels' *Das Kapital* (1867) appears in Russian in 1882. Earlier, the *Communist Manifesto* (1848) is translated and smuggled into Russia in 1852.

1870-92 Period begins with hesitant experiments in reform of Moscow city administration and ends with retreat into autocracy. The City Code of 1870 provides for a Duma (legislative assembly) of 190 deputies elected for a four-year term to replace class-based appointees. In 1876 Sergei Tretyakov, entrepreneur and art collector, becomes Moscow's first mayor without a noble lineage. The City Code is overhauled by an 'anti-reform' City Code of 1892 which reduces the powers of the Duma, the number of deputies and eligibility to vote.

1881 Alexander II assassinated in St. Petersburg. The Okhrana (political police) is established.

1883 Electric street lighting appears in Moscow.

1885 Typhus outbreak in Moscow.

1885 In response to worsening conditions, Moscow

administration under Mayor N.A. Alexeev, a wealthy manufacturer, undertakes major infrastructural projects including underground piping for water. Construction of a municipal sewage system is not begun before the 1890s. Student unrest breaks out in Moscow over restrictive laws on subjects of study and travel.

1891-1905 Construction of the Trans-Siberian Railway. Its railhead is Moscow.

1892 A new City Code further restricts effective representative government, assigning executive power to the Governor-General, Grand Duke Sergei Alexandrovich, brother of Alexander III (1881-94). Nascent labour organizations in Moscow are placed under the direct control of the secret police.

1894 Nicholas II (1894-1918) crowned tsar in Uspensky Cathedral. Grand Duke Sergei is held responsible for the deaths in a stampede of 1,500 people gathered in Khodynka Field to celebrate. Sergei is assassinated in 1905.

1900-20 Moscow's population grows from over 1 million to 1.5 million in 1914, becoming the ninth largest city in the world. Between 1900 and mid 1920s Moscow enjoys a 'Silver Age' of extraordinary artistic creativity.

1900 *Iskra*, 'The Spark', the Russian émigré revolutionary newspaper edited by Lenin (1870-1924), is smuggled into Russia. In 1902 Lenin writes *What is to be Done*, advocating the creation of a professional and tightly knit conspiratorial party to seize power.

1905-7 The 'First Russian Revolution', begun in St. Petersburg, spreads to Moscow and becomes more violent. In December 1905 the workers' district of Presnaya is the epicentre of the fighting. Over 1,000 are killed before the insurrection is finally put down by the Semyonovsky Guards Regiment, transferred from

St. Petersburg. Between 1905 and 1917, limited experiments in constitutionalism, including creation of State Dumas. None are successful.

1913 Lavish celebrations on the 300th anniversary of the accession of the Romanov Dynasty take place in Moscow, featuring a huge military parade and the unveiling of a statue of Alexander III before the Cathedral of Christ the Saviour.

1914 August. Beginning of World War One.

1917 Under pressure of war, and the chaotic return of demoralized troops, urban administration breaks down. Bread riots and strikes in Petrograd are supported by a general strike in Moscow in February 1917. Imperial authority collapses. Nicholas II abdicates 15 March. Having gained control of the workers' councils (soviets) Bolsheviks seize power in Petrograd on 7th November. In Moscow, troops loyal to the Provisional Government fight on until they are finally suppressed by Red Guards brought in from Petrograd.

1917-21 War Communism. Period of forced expropriations and confiscations. Communal housing. In March 1918, capital of Russia is transferred to Moscow. In July, Left Socialist Revolutionaries attempt to overthrow the Bolsheviks; in August, one of the SRs seriously wounds Lenin. An elaborate state security organization is created under Felix Dzherzinsky. In October the Whites are defeated as they approach Moscow, by Trotsky and the Red Army. By 1920, the Whites are effectively defeated.

1919 Founding in Moscow of the Communist International. Moscow becomes 'Capital of World Revolution'.

1921-2 Moscow population drops to 1 million after reaching 2 million in 1917. Factories operate at 10%

capacity. Worldwide influenza outbreak, beginning in 1919, affects Moscow, now threatened with starvation. In December 1922 the USSR is created, with Moscow as its capital.

1921-8 'New Economic Policy': Its breathing space signals a tactical retreat from pure communist principles. Moscow begins to revive. The Constructivist school dominates Moscow architecture. Era of 'paper architecture'. Lenin dies in 1924.

1928 Stalin (1879-1953) achieves supreme power. Five Year Plan 1928-31 for rapid industrialization employs administrative techniques based on military principles. Moscow's 'silver age' ends. Collectivization campaigns and the 'elimination of the kulaks as a class'. Requisitions bring food to Moscow.

1930 Introduction of Moscow time as offset to GMT. Destruction of large areas of Moscow to build 'the first communist city', including in 1931 The Cathedral of Christ the Saviour. In the 1930s Moscow becomes 'a dark star, sucking everything in'.

1934 Headquarters of the Academy of Sciences transfers from Leningrad to Moscow, which becomes the scientific centre of the USSR.

1935 General Plan for the Reconstruction of Moscow introduced. Described as the expression in stone of centralization of power. First line of the Moscow Metro opened. Further destruction of many districts and their replacement along main arteries by monumental buildings with neoclassical motifs for the *nomenklatura*.

1936-8 Height of the Great Terror and *Yezhovshchina*, named after the head of the NKVD. Purge trials in the Hall of Columns. The Red Army leadership is decapitated.

1937 First Congress of Soviet Architects confirms Socialist

Realism as the governing philosophy in architecture.

1941 22nd June: Operation Barbarossa and Nazi invasion of USSR. State of Siege 16-20th October. Moscow panic. Kuybyshev is 'the capital in exile', but Stalin stays in Moscow. By November, the tide has turned.

1951 Second Plan for the Reconstruction of Moscow. Period of High Stalinism and construction of the monumental 'Seven Sisters'.

1953 Stalin dies and is entombed next to Lenin. Nikita Khrushchev (1894-1971) becomes First Secretary of the Party, but leadership struggles continue until 1956.

1954 Khrushchev announces at the All-Union Conference of Builders the end of Stalinism in architecture, replaced by 'simplicity and standardization' and emphasis on cheap public housing.

1955 The Kremlin is opened to the public for the first time since 1918.

1956 Khrushchev's secret anti-Stalin speech before the XX Party Congress. Official policy calls for priority to be given to pre-stressed concrete apartment blocks to relieve the housing crisis. They are replicated across the USSR, and change the face of Moscow as huge housing complexes (*micro-rayons*) encircle the city and old buildings are destroyed.

1960 The building site of the Palace of Soviets is converted into the world's largest outdoor swimming pool.

1964-82 Leonid Brezhnev (1906-82) succeeds Khrushchev in a Party coup, ushering in an era of *zastoi*, stagnation. Moscow is run by Party Chief V. V. Grishin and President of the Mossoviet Executive Committee V. F. Promyslov. Construction of the New Arbat in central Moscow razes the artistic centre of the city.

1968 Demonstrators on Red Square are arrested for protesting against the invasion of Czechoslovakia.

1971 The Moscow General Plan replaces the master plan of 1935 and its successor of 1951. Emphasis is on industrialization and infrastructural development. The latter does not keep pace with the continuing growth of *micro-rayons*.

1979 Soviet invasion of Afghanistan in December. As casualties rise, mothers demonstrate on Manezh Square.

1980 Moscow holds the XXII Olympic Games. Boycotted by USA and others.

1982 The 'Luzhniki disaster': several dozen are crushed to death at a football match.

1983 Able Archer 83, a 10-day NATO command post exercise involving nuclear release, is taken for the real thing. Air defences around Moscow go on high alert.

1985 Mikhail Gorbachev (b.1931) follows a succession of aged and ailing leaders. Policies of *glasnost* and *perestroika* are elaborated with unforeseeable consequences. Preoccupied with these great projects, Gorbachev devotes little attention to Moscow.

1987 Mattias Rust lands his Cessna near Red Square, exposing the military leadership to ridicule. Gorbachev uses the occasion to sack military opponents of his policies, including the Defence Minister.

1989 First open elections since 1917.

1990 In Kremlin Palace of Soviets, XXVIII Party Congress renounces its monopoly on power.

1991 19th August: Moscow coup attempt. Former Moscow Party chief and now Russian President Boris Yeltsin (1931-2007) denounces it as illegal, making the White House the focal point of resistance. He is assisted by Muscovites on the barricades, Moscow City Council and elements of the army and KGB who ignore orders. The coup collapses three days later. Dissolution of the Soviet Union. Gorbachev resigns as Soviet President

25th December.

1992 Moscow's first popularly elected Mayor, G. Kh. Popov, declares Moscow 'ungovernable'. Yuri Luzhkov succeeds him and is elected in June. A new Moscow City General Plan envisages more effective use of urban space and relocating heavy industry beyond city limits. Inner ring roads are built and restoration projects are undertaken for some historic buildings. Work begins on the $12 billion Moscow International Business Centre ('Moscow City').

1992-5 Oligarchs gain prominence in the Russian economy and in politics. Appearance of 'New Russians' as a post-Soviet social phenomenon. Creation of North American-style gated communities.

1993 The new Russian Constitution gives Moscow and St. Petersburg 'special status' as autonomous cities within the Federation. As the result of a conflict between the legislative and executive branches of government, Yeltsin orders the shelling of the White House, now the Supreme Soviet of the Russian Federation. The City Duma replaces the Mossoviet. The Mayor is given full powers.

1994-6 First Chechen War: Suicide bombings in Moscow.

1994 Reconstruction of Cathedral of Christ the Saviour.

1995 Victory Park, the city war memorial, opens on the 50th anniversary of the end of the Second World War.

1996 Patriarch Alexis II attends the first service in the restored Cathedral of Christ the Saviour.

1997 Mayor Luzhkov organizes elaborate celebrations for the 850th anniversary of the founding of Moscow. Critics charge that he is turning Moscow centre into 'a Disneyland theme-park'.

1997 Sculptor Zurab Tsereteli creates 96 m tall Monument to the Russian Navy. This statue of Peter the Great is heavily criticized, but still stands on the Embankment. With Mayor Luzkhov's removal the monument's future is uncertain.

1998 1,000th anniversary of the Christianization of Russia. Danilov Monastery is returned to the Orthodox Church and becomes the official residence of the Patriarch.

1998 Completion of reconstruction of the Moscow Outer Ring Road (MKAD). Russian financial crisis and de valuation of the ruble severely affect Moscow. Fuelled by petrodollars, economic recovery begins.

1999 Yeltsin resigns from office in December, naming Vladimir Putin (b. 1952) as Acting President. On 26 March 2000 Putin is elected President.

1999 Second Chechen War begins in August. Retaliatory bombings of civilian targets, including the Moscow Metro shopping arcades, aircraft and rail networks. Between 2000 and 2010 there are over 30 separate bombing or terrorist incidents in Moscow. Modernization of Moscow begins with the General Plan, superseded in 2004 by the Development Plan until 2020.

2002 Chechen rebels hold over 700 people hostage in a Moscow theatre.

2004 Putin re-elected President. He reacts to the Beslan massacre of over 180 schoolchildren on 1st September by an overhaul of state security laws and the adoption of authoritarian measures. Despite some concerns about the erosion of civil liberties, they receive broad public support in Moscow and elsewhere.

2004 General Plan for the Development of Moscow until 2020 calls for phased projects to decentralize the city's structure according to 'market-oriented principles', called by cynics 'capitalist realism'. The Plan marks a fundamental change away from the historical ring-radial pattern of Moscow's urban development. By 2020, Moscow will have the ten tallest buildings in Europe.

2007 Mayor Luzhkov sworn in for a fifth term.

2008 Putin's term as President ends. Dmitry Medvedev succeeds him in March. Putin is elected Prime Minister by the Russian Parliament.

2010 28th March: Suicide bombs kill 37 people at two separate stations of the Moscow Metro. The 'counter-terrorism operation in Chechnya' had officially ended on 6th April 2009.

2010 9th May: Parade on Red Square celebrates 65th anniversary of the defeat of Nazi Germany. For the first time, troops of the wartime alliance participate in a military parade on Red Square.

2010 Moscow population exceeds 11 million. The General Plan is modified and extended until 2025 to allow for a 60% increase in residential housing and improvements in traffic infrastructure. Protesters claim it legitimizes illegal property confiscations by developers, and call it a 'death penalty' for the city. Demolition and reconstruction is to cost an estimated $1 trillion.

2010 In intense summer heat, peat and forest fires pollute Moscow with dense smoke.

2010 September: Mayor Luzhkov is dismissed by President Medvedev on grounds of 'losing the confidence of the Presidency'. In October Medvedev names Sergei Sobyanin to succeed him.

Bibliography

Acton, Edward and Tom Stableford, *The Soviet Union: A Documentary History*, 2 vols. (Exeter: Exeter University Press, 2007).

Akinsha, Konstantin et al., *The Holy Place: Architecture, Ideology and History in Russia* (London: Yale University Press, 2007).

Aleksandrov, Yu., *Krasnaya Ploshchad': Liudi, Sobitiya, Pamyatniki* (Moscow: Moskovskii Rabochii, 1983).

Alexander, John T, *Bubonic Plague in Early Modern Russia: Public Health and Urban Disaster* (Oxford: Oxford University Press, 2003).

Amis, Martin, *Koba the Dread* (London: Jonathan Cape, 2002).

Benjamin, Walter, *Moscow Diary* (Cambridge, MA: Harvard University Press, 1986).

Berlin, Isaiah, *The Soviet Mind: Russian Culture under Communism* (Washington, DC: Brookings Institution Press, 2004).

Berton, Kathleen, *Moscow: An Architectural History* (London: I.B. Tauris & Co. Ltd, 1990).

Billington, James H., *Russia in Search of Itself* (Baltimore, MD: The Johns Hopkins University Press, 2004).

Billington, James H., *The Face of Russia: Anguish, Aspiration and Achievement in Russian Culture* (New York: TV Books, 1998).

Billington, James H., *The Icon and the Axe* (New York: Random House, 1970).

Blakesley, Rosalind and Susan E. Reid, eds., *Russian Art and the West* (Chicago: Northern Illinois University Press, 2004).

Bonavia, David, *Fat Sasha and the Urban Guerrilla*

(London: Hamish Hamilton, 1973).
Bowit, John E., *Moscow and St. Petersburg in Russia's Silver Age* (Thames and Hudson, 2008).
Braithwaite, Roderick, *Moscow 1941: A City and its People at War* (London: Profile Books, new edition, 2007).
Bratus, A. N. et al. eds., *Slovar' Pravovykh Znanii* (Moscow: Izdatel'stvo Sovyetskaya Entsiklopediya, 1965).
Brown, Archie, *The Rise and Fall of Communism* (London: The Bodley Head, 2009).
Brown, Archie, *Seven Years that Changed the World* (Oxford: Oxford University Press, 2007).
Brown, Archie, *The Gorbachev Factor* (Oxford: Oxford University Press, 1996).
Brumfield, William Craft, *A History of Russian Architecture* (Seattle, WA: University of Washington Press, 2004).
Bukharin, Nikolai and E. Preobrazhinsky (1924), *The ABC of Communism* (London: Merlin Press, 2009).
Carr, Francis, *Ivan the Terrible* (Newton Abbot: David & Charles, 1981).
Central Intelligence Agency, *Gorbachev: Steering the USSR into the 1990s* (Washington, DC, 1989).
Chechulin, D., *A New Moscow in Construction* (Moscow: Foreign Languages Publishing House, 1939).
Cohen, Jean-Louis, *Le Corbusier and the Mystique of the USSR: Plans and Projects for Moscow 1928-1936* (New York: Princeton University Press, 1991).
Colton, Timothy, *Moscow: Governing the Soviet Metropolis* (Cambridge, MA: The Belknap Press of Harvard University Press, 1995).
Conquest, Robert, *The Great Terror: A Reassessment* (Oxford: Oxford University Press, 1990).
Cook, Catherine, *Modernity and Realism in Russian Art and the West* (Chicago: Northern Illinois University Press, 2009).
Custine, Marquis de, *Empire of the Czar: Journey through*

Eternal Russia (New York: Bantam Doubleday, reprint 1990).
Derrida, Jacques, *Jacques Derrida v Moskve: dekonstruktsia puteshestvia* (Moscow: Izdatel'stvo Progress, 1933).
Fauchereau, Serge, ed., *Moscow 1900-1930* (Paris: Seuil, 1988).
Fennell, John Lister Illingworth, *The Emergence of Moscow, 1304-1359* (Berkeley: University of California Press, 1968).
Fest, Joachim C., *Hitler* (New York: Vintage, 1975).
Figes, Orlando, *A People's Tragedy: The Russian Revolution 1891-1924* (London: Penguin, 1998).
Figes, Orlando, *Natasha's Dance: A Cultural History of Russia* (London: Penguin, 2008).
Gaidar, Yegor, *Collapse of the Soviet Empire: Lessons for Modern Russia* (Washington: Brookings Institution Press, 2007).
Gilbert, Martin, *The Routledge Atlas of Russian History*, 3rd edition (London: Routledge, 2002).
Grachev, Andrei, *Gorbachev's Gamble* (Cambridge: Polity, 2008).
Gutnov, Aleksei et al., *The Ideal Communist City* (New York: George Braziller, 1970).
Hamm, Michael F., ed., *The City in Russian History* (Lexington, KY: University of Kentucky Press, 1976).
Harris, Chauncy D., *Cities of the Soviet Union: Studies in their Functions, Density and Growth* (Chicago: Rand McNally and Company, 1970).
Haxthausen, Baron von, *The Russian Empire: Its People, Institutions and Resources,* 2 vols. (London: Frank Cass, 1968).
Herzen, Aleksandr, *My Past and Thoughts,* 2 vols. (Berkeley: University of California Press, 1992).
Hittle, Michael J., *The Service State and Townsmen in Russia*

1600-1800 (Cambridge, MA: Harvard University Press, 1979).
Hobsbawm, Eric, *The Age of Extremes 1914-1991* (London: Abacus, 2008).
Hoffmann, David, *Peasant Metropolis: Social Identities in Moscow 1929-1941* (Ithaca, NY: Cornell University Press, 2000).
Hosking, Geoffrey, *Russia and the Russians* (London: Penguin, 2001).
Hosking, Geoffrey, *Russia: People and Empire 1552-1917* (Cambridge, MA: Harvard University Press, 1997).
Ikonnikov, Andrei, *Architektura Sovietskoi Rossii* (Moscow: Raguda, 1990).
Izdatel'stvo Nauka, *Istoria Moskvy* (Moscow: Nauka, 1976).
Josephson, Paul R., *New Atlantis Revisited: Akademgorodok, the Siberian City of Science* (Princeton: Princeton University Press, 1997).
Kagarlitsky, Boris, *Empire of the Periphery: Russia and the World System* (London: Pluto Press, 2008).
Karamazin, N. M., *Izbrann'ie Socheneniia* (Izdatel'stvo Moskva-Leningrad, 1964).
Keegan, John, *History of Warfare (*Toronto): Key Porter Books, 1993).
Kelly, Laurence, *A Traveller's Companion to Moscow* (London: Constable & Robinson, 1983).
Khromov, S. S., *Istoria Moskvy* (Moscow: Izdatel'stvo Nauka, 1976).
Kivelson, Valerie A. and Joan Neuberger, eds., *Picturing Russia: Explorations in Visual Culture* (London: Yale University Press, 2008).
Kliuchevskii, V.O., *Sochinenia v Vosmi Tomkh – Kurs Russkoi Istorii* (Moscow: Gosudarstvennoe Izdatel'stvo Politicheskoe Literatury, 1956).
Koestler, Arthur, *Darkness at Noon* (London: Vintage

Books, 2005).
Kostof, Spiro, *The City Shaped: Urban Patterns and Meanings Through History* (London: Thames & Hudson, 1991).
Kotkin, Joel, *The City: A Global History* (London: Weidenfeld & Nicolson, 2005).
Kotkin, Stephen, *Magnetic Mountain: Stalinism as a Civilization* (Berkeley: University of California Press, 1995).
Kristenson, Hans et al., 'The Protection Paradox', *Bulletin of Atomic Scientists* (Washington, DC, March/April 2004).
Lakin, Ya., *Zhilische i byt'* (Moscow: Izdatel'stvo Nauka, 1931).
Lenin, V. I., *Collected Works, Vol. XX-XXII: The Revolution of 1917* (New York: International Publishers Co. Inc., 1929).
Lenin, V. I., *Collected Works*, 4th English Edition (Moscow: Progress Publishers, 1972).
Lieven, Dominic, *The Russian Empire and its Rivals* (London: Yale University Press, 2001).
Longworth, Philip, *Russia's Empires: Their Rise and Fall from Prehistory to Putin* (London: John Murray, 2005).
Louis, Victor and Jennifer, *The Complete Guide to the Soviet Union* (New York: St. Martin's Press, 1976).
Luzhkov, Yuri, *The Renewal of History: Mankind in the Twenty-First Century and the Future of Russia* (London: Stacey International, 2003).
Lynch, Kevin, *Theory of Good City Form* (Cambridge, MA: MIT Press, 1981).
Madariaga, Isabel de, *Ivan the Terrible* (New Haven: Yale University Press, 2006).
Mahan, Alfred Thayer, *The Influence of Sea Power upon History* (New York: Dover Publications Inc., 1988).
Malinovsky, Yu. P., 'Sozdanie Moskvy kak Stolitsa Revolyutsii', *Voprosy Istorii, No. 11* (Moscow: Noyabr,

1968).
Manley, Deborah, ed., *The Trans-Siberian Railway: A Traveller's Anthology* (London: Century Books, 1988; Oxford: Signal Books, 2009).
Markovich, Lazar and El Lissitzky, *Russland, der Rekonstruktion der Architektur in der Sowietunion* (Vienna, 1930; Cambridge, MA: The MIT Press, 1970).
Merridale, Catherine, *Night of Stone* (London: Granta Books, 2001).
Medvedev, Roy A., *On Stalin and Stalinism* (Oxford: Oxford University Press, 1979).
Mironov, B. N., *Russkii gorod v 1740-1860 gody* (Leningrad: Nauka, 1990).
Montefiore, Simon Sebag, *Stalin: In the Court of the Red Tsar* (London: Weidenfeld & Nicolson, 2003).
Nagorsky, Andrew, *The Greatest Battle: The Fight for Moscow 1941-42* (London: Aurum Press, 2007).
Nivat, Anne, *La maison haute: Des russes d'aujourd'hui* (Paris: Fayard, 2002).
Norwich, John Julius, *A Short History of Byzantium* (London: Penguin, 1997).
Nouwen, Henri J., *Behold the Beauty of the Lord* (Notre Dame, IN: Ave Maria Press, 2007).
Osetrov, Yevgeny, *Moe Otkrytie Moskvy: Rasskazy o* (Moscow: Moskovskii Rabochii,1987).
Ostrowski, Donald, *Muscovy and the Mongols: Cross-cultural Influences on the Steppe Frontier* (Cambridge: Cambridge University Press, 2002).
Pankin, Boris, *The Last Hundred Days of the Soviet Union* (London: I. B. Tauris, 1996).
Pankratova, A. N. et al., *History of the USSR* (Moscow: Foreign Languages Publishing House, 1948).
Paperny, Vladimir, *Architecture in the Age of Stalin: Culture Two* (Cambridge: Cambridge University Press, 2002).

Pipes, Richard, *Russia under the Old Regime*, 2nd edition (London: Penguin, 1993).
Piskarskaya, I. and I, Romicheva, *Moskovskii Kreml'* (Moscow: Moskovskii Rabochii, 1979).
Polonsky, Rachel, *Molotov's Magic Lantern: A Journey in Russian History* (London: Faber & Faber, 2010).
Polyakov, Ya. A. et al. *Moskva: Illustriurovannaya Istoriya* (Moscow: Mysl', 1986).
Preobrazhensky, Alexander, Chief Editor, *The Russian Orthodox Church: 10th to 20th Centuries* (Moscow: Progress, 1988).
Prozorov, Sergei, *The Ethics of Post-Communism: History and Social Praxis in Russia* (London: Palgrave Macmillan, 2009).
Reavy, George, trans., *The Poetry of Yevgeny Yevtushenko* (New York: October House Inc., 1965).
Remnick, David, *Lenin's Tomb: The Last Days of the Soviet Empire* (New York: Vintage, 1994).
Riasonovsky, Nicholas V., *Russian Identities: A Historical Survey* (Oxford: Oxford University Press, 2005).
Riasonovsky, Nicholas V., *A History of Russia,* 2 vols. (Oxford: Oxford University Press, 2005).
Robson, Roy R., *Solovki* (New Haven: Yale University Press, 2004).
Royal Academy of Arts, *From Russia* (London: Royal Academy of Arts catalogue, 2008).
Rutland, Peter, ed., *Business and State in Contemporary Russia* (Boulder, CO: Westview Press, 2001).
Rybakov, Anatoly, *Children of the Arbat* (London: Little, Brown & Co., 1988).
Rybakov, B.A., *Russkie Karty Moskovii XV-Nachala XVI veka* (Moscow: Nauka, 1974).
Schapiro, Leonard et al., *The Soviet Worker: Illusions and Realities* (London: Macmillan, 1981).
Schloegel, Karl, *Moskau* (Munich: Reaktion Books, 1984).

Service, Robert, *Comrades: Communism in World History* (London: Macmillan, 2007).

Service, Robert, *A History of Modern Russia from Nicholas II to Putin* (London: Penguin, 2003).

Shevardnadze, Edvard, *Moi Vybor (*Moscow: Novisti, 1991).

Simon, Sir E. D., *Moscow in the Making: the Simon Report on Moscow, 1932* (Longman, Green & Co., 1936).

Smirnova, Zh. E., *Uspenskiii Sobor Moskovskii Kremlya* (Moscow: Nauka, 1985).

Smith, Douglas, 'Count Zakhar Chernyshev's Snuffbox' in Knievelson and Neuburger, *Picturing Russia* (New Haven: Yale University Press, 2008).

Smith, Kathleen E., *Mythmaking in the New Russia: Politics and Memory in the Yeltsin Era* (Ithaca, NY: Cornell University Press, 2002).

Solov'ev, S. M., *Istoriia Rossiii s drevneishikh vremen (*Moscow: Izdatel'stvo sotsialno-ekonomicheskoi literatury, 1959-66).

Solzhenitsyn, Alexander, *The Gulag Archipelago* (New York: Harper and Row, 1973).

Stalin, J. V. (pseud. CPSU), *History of the Communist Party of the Soviet Union, Short Course* (Moscow: Foreign Languages Publishing House, 1941).

Szamuely, Tibor, *The Saddled Cow* (London: Secker & Warburg, 1974).

Taubman, William, *Khrushchev* (London: The Free Press, 2005).

Tikhomirov, M. N., 'O proizkhodzhenii nazvanii Rossi', *Voprosi Istorii* (Moscow, 1953).

Timiriazev, Arkady, 'Moscow University' in *Moscow: Sketches on the Russian Capital* (London: Hutchinson & Co., 1947).

Tolz, Vera, *Russia* (London: Hodder Arnold, 2001).

Troyat, Henri, *Ivan the Terrible* (London: Phoenix Press,

1984).
Tucker, Robert C., and Stephen F. Cohen, *The Great Purge Trial* (New York: Grossel & Dunlap, 1965).
Tung, Anthony M., *Preserving the World's Great Cities: The Destruction and Renewal of the Historic Metropolis* (New York: Clarkson Porter, 2001).
Vipper, B.R., *Architektura russkogo Barokko* (Moscow: Nauka, 1978).
Volkogonov, Dmitri, *The Rise and Fall of the Soviet Empire* (London: HarperCollins, 1998).
Voyce, Arthur, *Moscow and the Roots of Russian Culture* (Newton Abbot: David & Charles, 1972).
Wilson, Edmund, *To the Finland Station* (New York: Anchor Books, 1953).
Wittfogel, Karl, *Oriental Despotism: A Comparative Study of Total Power* (New York: Vintage, 1981).
Yeltsin, Boris, *The Struggle for Russia* (New York: Times Books, 1994).
Yeltsin, Boris, *Midnight Diaries* (New York: Public Affairs, 2000).
Zabel, Eugen, *Moskau* (Leipzig and Berlin: Seemann, 1902).
Zamoysky, Adam, *1812: Napoleon's Fatal March on Moscow* (London: HarperCollins, 2004).

Glossary

ABM: Anti-Ballistic Missile (System and Treaty). The ballistic missile defence shield around Moscow. The ABM Treaty signed between the USSR and the USA in 1972 was abrogated by the second Bush Administration in 2002. Western nuclear theorists regarded the ABM Treaty as evidence that the Soviet side played by 'the same nuclear rules'.

***agitprop*:** short for *agitation and propaganda.* A technique practised by the communist parties to engage the masses and to enlist their active support of a given policy. Besides ubiquitous posters and slogans, Komsomol and trade union organizations were the main vehicles for *agitprop,* which also included demonstrations on Red Square.

Alpha Group: also known as *Spetsnaz,* short in Russian for 'special operations'. A commando unit of the KGB established in 1974. In 1991, it refused orders from the coup leaders to storm the White House and capture (other sources say kill) Russian President Boris Yeltsin and his associates. Sometimes confused with regional police commando organizations (OMON).

Anti-Duehring: a tract written by Engels in 1878 in which he argued that in a fully developed socialist state the 'social contradictions' between countryside and cities would disappear.

Arbat: pedestrian street in central Moscow, originally a district of artists, now largely destroyed and replaced by the Brezhnev-era Novyi Arbat of high-rise office buildings and apartment blocks. In 1812 Napoleon led his army down the Arbat on his way to the Kremlin.

art nouveau: also known as Jugendstil. An international

movement and style of art, design and architecture which peaked in popularity at the turn of the twentieth century. Gustav Klimt, Charles Rennie Mackintosh, Alphonse Mucha and Louis Comfort Tiffany were leading exponents. The art nouveau period coincided with the Russian Silver Age, and thus straddled the Russian revolution. In the 1920s it was overtaken by modernism.

***babushka*:** literally, grandmother. Generally, an old woman, sometimes a gently mocked figure. Many were war-widows, and left to fend for themselves, or delegated to stand in queues on behalf of their working children. They were a common sight on Moscow street-corners after the Second World War, and made their reappearance selling personal possessions in the economic turmoil of the 1990s.

***baraki*:** rough-built communal huts for industrial workers and their families in Moscow and other Soviet cities, beginning with War Communism and continuing into the first Five-Year Plans. Succeeded by *standartnyie doma*, which had the same look and function, but a better name.

Bauhaus: from German, *bau* (building) + *haus* (house), denoting a school of art and architecture founded by Walter Gropius in 1919. The teaching of the Bauhaus school was based on the principles of guild or fraternity. These principles passed into its work, which had a heavy left-wing flavour, emphasizing the community over the individual, and industrial shapes and design over natural ones. The Bauhaus school was represented by many early post-revolutionary buildings in Moscow until socialist realism was imposed upon Soviet architecture in the 1930s.

***'bizness'*:** Russified English-language term for 'business'.

Carries a secondary meaning of under-the-counter dealings and possible mafia connections.

***bogatyr*:** legendary Russian folk-hero or warrior whose calling was to protect the Russian land from the Tatars. The *bogatyry* are the main characters in Russian sagas or *bylny*.

Bolshevik: from *bolshoi/bolshe* (big/bigger) + v*ik* (one of): an adherent to the more radical wing of the Russian Social Democratic Labour Party which split in 1903 over issues of policy and power. Led by Lenin, the Bolsheviks or majority faction seized power in 1917. Thereafter the Bolsheviks collectively became known simply as 'the Party'. After a series of name-changes, in 1952 it was formally designated the Communist Party of the Soviet Union (CPSU). The term Bolshevik became identified with Stalin and his policies. In the early Soviet period, Bolshevik was sometimes confused by the peasants with a related term, *bolshak,* meaning 'bigwig'.

boyar: a Russian landowning aristocrat belonging to a closed upper stratum of medieval society, consisting of some 200 families. Often occupying high positions in state administration, the boyars were a dominant political force from the fifteenth to the seventeenth centuries, and bore a complex power relationship to the tsar. The boyar system of heredity and precedence was abolished by Peter the Great.

***buntarstvo*:** from *bunt* (revolt, mutiny) + *stvo* (ness) a word denoting the rebellious mood of industrial workers in Moscow and Petrograd before the November Revolution.

***Bürgerstadt*:** from German, 'a city of citizens' as opposed to aristocratic cities such as Odessa and St. Petersburg. Exemplified by Novgorod before it was destroyed by

Ivan the Terrible. In urban developmental theory, the 'city of citizens' is the direct descendant of the Hanseatic cities of northern Europe, and ultimately of the Greek *polis* in which all its citizens participated. Moscow never achieved this status.

Byzantine: refers to the empire of Byzantium, with Constantinople as its chief city. The medieval Muscovite principality inherited many Byzantine practices and beliefs from Kiev, the original capital city of ancient Rus'. Whether justified or not, 'Byzantine' also acquired the meaning of intrigue and pointless religious obscurantism. It became a term of opprobrium, particularly when applied to methods of Soviet and Russian rule.

capitalist realism: a 'take' on socialist realism, describing international and post-modernist architectural styles and tastes in Russian cities after communism.

Centre: during the Soviet period, variously used to describe Moscow and its leading organs and institutions: the CPSU Central Committee, Warsaw Treaty Headquarters, COMECON headquarters and the Soviet (now Russian) government itself. The latter in Western terminology is often referred to as 'the Kremlin'. In contemporary Russian usage the term is confined to KGB/FSB headquarters or to its directorates. Amongst Orthodox circles it sometimes refers to the Moscow Patriarchate.

***Cheka*:** from Russian initials *Ch+Ka,* 'Extraordinary Commission', *Chrezvychaynaia Kommissia,* precursor of the KGB. Lenin appointed Felix Dzerzhinsky as its first head.

***cherta*:** one of four defensive lines south of Moscow in the sixteenth and seventeenth centuries constructed to ward off Tatar attacks.

Comecon (CMEA): Council of Mutual Economic Assistance. Established in Moscow in 1947 in reply to the Marshall Plan. By the 1970s it aimed at economic integration of the socialist *sotrudnichestvo* or commonwealth, thereby mirroring in Eastern Europe the organization and ostensible purpose of the EEC's Treaty of Rome. Its effectiveness was undermined by its use as an instrument of control, including the manipulation of exchange rates in Soviet favour. Alpha Group forces occupied the Comecon building in downtown Moscow in preparation for an attack on the White House in 1991.

Comintern (Third or Communist International): established in 1919 and disbanded in 1943. The international communist organization whose aim was 'the overthrow of the international bourgeoisie'. As its headquarters, Moscow became the centre of the world revolutionary movement. In 1947 it was succeeded by the less ambitious Cominform which lasted until 1956.

Constructivism or 'machine art': a revolutionary art movement established in Russia in 1919 and put 'at the service of the Revolution'. Its main exponent was the Moscow Higher Art and Technical School (VkhUTEMAS). Constructivist aesthetics were inspired by the industrial landscape and industrialized means of production. In architecture, the distinction between workplace and home would be eliminated, and other art-forms would emphasize industrial shapes. In theatre, acting was to be 'bio-mechanical', on the theory that the proletarian audience would find resonance in mechanical, production-related movement. In 1920, a Constructivist International was formed, based on a 'Moscow–Berlin Axis' which was to complement in the art world the Communist International of the political world. Constructivism was superseded by socialist realism, and VkhUTEMAS was abolished in 1930. Constructivism's best-known example is the Lenin Mausoleum on Red Square.

CPSU: Communist Party of the Soviet Union.

***derzhavnik*:** from *derzhava,* state, by extension, 'men of the state', now signifying those at the top of the 'power minis tries', regional governors or senior officials in state organs such as the FSB. Mayor Sobyanin is a *derzhavnik;* Mayor Luzkhov was not.

***diamat*:** Acronym for dialectical materialism, a Marxist philosophical concept adapted from Hegel describing the process of change in the physical world. *Diamat* became a much-hated but compulsory university subject, and its untested propositions were the source of derision amongst many students. In the late Soviet period it was dropped from the academic curriculum, but by then the damage had been done to the ideological underpinnings of the Party.

***gadost'*:** tasteless junk. Supposedly a speciality of New Russians.

GKChP: State Committee for the State of Emergency in the USSR, *Gostvennyi Komitet po Chrezvychainomy Polozheniyu v CCCR.* Composed of the 'Gang of Eight', right-wing conspirators and senior Soviet officials who sought to overthrow Gorbachev in August 1991.

***glasnost*:** 'openness'. Fundamental to Gorbachev's policy of *perestroika,* it was originally intended as a technique to bring reforms to the Soviet economic (and later, political) system by means of open discussion. One of its unintended consequences was an outburst of regional nationalisms, particularly in the Baltic States and in the Caucasus.

Gorkom: acronym for City Executive Committee, or

City Council.

***gorod*:** city. Originally denoting an enclosed, walled space.

Gosplan: acronym for 'State Planning Commission', responsible for drawing up the Five-Year Plans (or *Pyatiletki),* of Soviet economic development, beginning in 1928. Gosplan oversaw thirteen Plans, although the last (1991-5) went uncompleted because of the collapse of the Soviet Union.

Gosstroi: acronym for the State Construction Committee, *Gostudarstvennoe Stroitel'stvo.* Under Gosplan, it was responsible for all construction in the Soviet Union with the exception of nuclear and military projects. As such it was the driving force for the spread of Moscow 'clones' across the USSR, irrespective of climate or local architectural tradition.

***gosudar*:** normally translated as 'lord', but carrying the meaning of both ruler and proprietor. This lack of distinction in early modern Russia was fundamental to the subsequent political and economic development of the Muscovite state, and of Moscow itself.

Gulag: acronym for Main Administration for Corrective Labour Camps. First established in 1919, the forced-labour camps held dissidents, political opponents and 'class enemies' as well as common criminals. The Gulag system eventually counted prisoners in the millions and was finally shut down as the result of Gorbachev's reforms. In the 1990s the rapid emptying of the camps brought an upsurge of communicable diseases, particularly tuberculosis, to Moscow and other cities. Some penal colonies still exist.

GUM: initials for *Gostudarstvennyi Universal'nyi Magazin,* State Department Store. Built on the eastern side of Red Square in 1893, it replaced the small shops of the Upper Trading Rows. GUM is now the premier up-market shopping address for Moscow's 'New Russians'.

'high buildings': *vysotniye zdaniye.* Soviet term used to distinguish them from capitalist skyscrapers, *neboskreby.*

icon: from Greek, meaning image. Object of veneration by Orthodox believers.

intelligentsia: precise meaning disputed. Generally, the articulate, educated layer of tsarist (and later, Soviet) Russia: roughly, the Russian equivalent of the French intellectual class. The Soviet authorities co-opted the term to describe white-collar workers, although it persisted in a parallel definition as critics of the Soviet system.

***Iskra*:** 'spark', name of the newspaper of the émigré Russian Social Democratic Labour Party, first published in Stuttgart in 1900. Lenin was chief editor.

***Izvestia*:** 'News'. Official organ of the Soviet government, as opposed to *Pravda,* 'Truth', the newspaper of the CPSU.

***Jacquerie*:** French, from *Jacques Bonhomme* or everyman: after late-medieval popular insurrections in northern France. Used to describe the seventeenth-century rebellions of Pugachev, Bolotnikov and Razin.

***khrushchoby*:** pejorative word combining *trushchoba* (slum) with Khrushchev's name to describe his housing projects of the 1960s.

Kitezh: mythic Russian city hidden beneath Lake Sevetloyar. Legendary, final citadel against the Mongols.

***kommunalki*:** communal living quarters of the early Soviet period, typified by shared facilities in divided apartments or houses. See also *baraki* and *standartnyie doma.*

Komsomol: acronym for Communist Youth League, the youth wing of the CPSU. Many former Komsomol members have achieved high political office, while others have become successful business leaders. Critics say that it has been succeeded in spirit by *Nashi,* 'Ours', a youth organization which supports the present Russian government.

kreml' **:** English, kremlin. Citadel; the Kremlin.

Kriegsmarine: German navy of the Nazi era.

kritika i samokritika**:** 'criticism and self-criticism'. A technique of public confession practised by the Bolsheviks designed to maintain and enforce discipline within the Party. It is the background to Arthur Koestler's anti-communist novel, *Darkness at Noon.*

kulak**:** 'fist', meant to describe peasants who became rich and by definition exploitative during the NEP. They were 'eliminated as a class' as a prelude to Stalin's collectivization campaigns.

Luftwaffe: German air force during Nazi era.

MAPS: Moscow Association for the Preservation of Monuments.

matryushka**:** Russian nesting doll.

MGB: Ministry of State Security, one of the forerunners of the KGB.

MGU: Moscow State University, *Moskvoskii Gostudarstvennyi Universitet Imeni Lomonosova.*

MID: Foreign Ministry, *Ministerstvo Inostrannykh Del.*

mikro-raion**:** 'micro-region'. Soviet equivalent of 'satellite communities', composed of large housing estates.

MKAD: Moscow Automobile Ring Road, *Moskovskaya Koltsevaya Avtomobil'naya Doroga.* A 10-lane, 108.9 kilometre bypass encircling Moscow, built in 1961 to relieve traffic congestion in the centre; originally Moscow's outer boundary. Comparable to Paris' *Périphérique*, London's M 25 and Washington's Beltway.

Mongols: a loose federation of Central Asian tribes which conquered Russia in the thirteenth century, beginning an occupation that lasted for almost one hundred and fifty years. Russian sources refer to them as Tatars, an ethnically Turkic people, originally enemies of the Mongols but often united with them in their campaigns.

***muzhik*:** Russian peasant. Also boor. Occasionally, husband.

***na levo*:** colloquial Russian, 'on the left', meaning under the table or illegal.

***narod* :** people, pl. *narodny*, peoples. Originally closely identified with Russian ethnicity. *Narodniks* were nineteenth-century idealists who sought political reform by 'going to the land', mixing with peasants and promoting their forms of rural democracy. *Narodniks* were met with incomprehension. *Narod/narodny* entered Soviet jargon to signal 'the broad masses of workers and peasants'. Soviet state institutions routinely incorporated *narodny* into their formal titles. The word later took on an additional meaning, as in *Peoples' Democracies*, which signalled that a state in question was on its way to the full development of socialism but still contained 'non-antagonistic contradictions' amongst its classes.

NEP: New Economic Policy. Styled 'a temporary retreat' from socialism by Lenin, the NEP was a breathing space that allowed the Russian economy to recover after the rigours of War Communism and the starvation period of the early 1920s. The Party retained full control throughout, and the Soviet government held 'the commanding heights' of the economy. Some believed that NEP offered an alternative route to socialism. It gave rise to 'Nepmen', small businessmen and entrepreneurs, and to *kulaks*, their peasant counterparts. NEP was abandoned with Stalin's accession to power and the launch of the First Five-Year Plan in 1928.

'New Class': a term coined by Milovan Djilas who became disillusioned with communism as he witnessed the emergence of a privileged elite within the state bureaucracies of the Soviet Union and Eastern Europe in the 1950s.

New Russians: nouveaux riches. Wealthy Russians who emerged out of the post-Soviet chaos of the Yeltsin years. Described by one historian as 'a class defined not only by their rapid acquisition of wealth but also by their presumed dishonesty, selfish greed, links with political privilege and underground crime, showy consumerism, and low cultural level'.

New Soviet Man: the theoretical product of a worker's complete integration into the productive process, his sole source of spiritual fulfilment, and matched by the disappearance of the distinction between life and work. The New Soviet Man was idealized in many socialist realist novels. However, weaknesses in the concept soon became clear when workers resisted communal living and persisted in drinking on the job.

NKVD: Peoples' Commisariat for Internal Affairs, *Narodny Kommisariat Vnutrennikh Del.* An umbrella internal security organization formed at the All-Union level in 1934. It has had a number of organizational and name changes throughout its lifetime. It was responsible for the mass executions of the 1930s, and for enforcing military discipline in World War II. When Commissariats were renamed Ministries in 1946, the NKVD was renamed MVD (Ministry of Internal Affairs). It shared headquarters in the Lubyanka with the KGB (Committee of State Security) of which Beria was Chairman as well as head (Minister) of the MVD. The KGB was disbanded after the August coup attempt, and its functions split between foreign intelligence and domestic security organizations.

***nomenklatura* :** Soviet-era elite identified by rank and concomitant privileges. In principle, the greater the contribution an official within the *nomenklatura* gave to the state, the greater the reward, for example holidays abroad or access to special shops. In practice, the system was subject to widescale abuse.

***oblast'*:** administrative district of the USSR; also region or province.

***oblomovshchina*:** named after Oblomov, the brilliant but slothful hero in a novel by Goncharov. Oblomov developed elaborate rationalizations for never moving out of bed. Russians use the word to describe an underlying condition in their national character.

***obshchezhitiye*:** common living quarters; student expression for the main building of MGU, one of Moscow's 'seven sisters'. One can live one's entire life in this Stalinist edifice, although it is against University rules to be born or to die there.

Old Believers: or Old Ritualists, Orthodox believers who rejected the Nikonian reforms of the 1660s as 'Anti-Christ'. They were particularly successful in business and were amongst the leading commercial figures of Moscow and other Russian cities up to the Revolution of 1917.

oligarchy: collective name of the group of financiers and businessmen who gained great wealth, influence and power by the purchase of state property at discounted prices or who financed projects of the Yeltsin government, including the funding of electoral candidates. Rightly (and sometimes wrongly) they have been accused of being involved in a variety of illegal activities. A number have been convicted of tax evasion.

***oprichniki/oprichnina*:** armed servitors of Ivan the Terrible, appointed by and responsible only to him. They controlled and terrorized the *oprichnina,* roughly half the territory of the Muscovite state, including property within Moscow itself, all designated as the personal possession of the tsar. The *oprichnina* was abolished in 1572, and the word banned on pain of death. Some historians have compared Ivan's experiment to the Stalinist excesses of the NKVD in the 1930s.

***Pax Mongolica*:** 'the Mongolian Peace', roughly between the late thirteenth and fifteenth centuries, when Mongol domination permitted a secure land route between Europe and Asia, sometimes known as 'the Silk Road'. *Pax Mongolica* followed the terrifying Mongol invasions of the thirteenth century and rested on the complete subservience of Russian principalities, including Muscovy.

peaceful coexistence: Soviet policy line towards the West during the Khrushchev years, but falling out of use thereafter. It postulated that nuclear weapons made military confrontation between socialism and capitalism suicidal. The superiority of socialism would be expressed by winning on the 'ideological front', by overtaking capitalism economically, and by victories of 'progressive forces' in the Third World. The policy led to a relatively stable nuclear stalemate, but also to an increase in 'proxy wars'. In Moscow and other Soviet cities, 'peaceful coexistence' was a principal theme at public rallies.

***perestroika*:** 'restructuring', identified with Gorbachev's reform programmes for the political and economic makeover of the Soviet Union.

***pod kryshkoi*:** colloquial Russian, 'under the roof', meaning victim of a protection racket.

posad: technically, a settlement of craftsmen and traders outside the Kremlin, each established according to its economic specialization. By tradition, Moscow had designated areas for various *posady* which were accorded a variety of privileges or concessions and were taxed at different rates. Some historians argue that the *posad* system was a factor contributing to the slowness of Moscow to develop an integrated civic culture.

Potemkin village: named after Catherine the Great's statesman, lover and later procurer Grigory Potemkin, who devised stage decor villages for the admiration of visiting potentates. Later used to describe Soviet model factories, collective farms and housing estates designed to impress foreigners.

Pravda**:** official organ of the CPSU. Kremlinologists sought to discern shifts in Party policy by analysis of its contents. As with *Izvestia,* Russians learned to read it between the lines.

rasputitsa**:** annual spring thaw when roads turn into churned bogs, and thin river ice makes crossing impossible. A major factor for any military operation in Russia.

'red rooster': colloquial for arson.

riady**:** trading rows; in Moscow, located on the eastern side of Red Square until removed in the late nineteenth century to make way for a shopping emporium that later became GUM.

samizdat: 'self-publishing'. DIY publishing of banned or forbidden material became a major underground activity of the intelligentsia from the 1970s onward. Much of *samizdat* material focused on human rights issues, although when picture technology improved, Western-sourced pornography enjoyed a large readership. State organizations unsuccessfully attempted to suppress *samizdat* by arrests and fines, and by the control of duplicating machines.

Sarai: capital of the Crimean Tatar Golden Horde from the thirteenth to fifteenth centuries.

***silniki*:** post-Soviet bureaucrats, military and state security officials occupying the upper levels of the 'power ministries'.

Silver Age: period of great artistic creativity, particularly in Moscow and St. Petersburg, which straddled both sides of the Revolution of 1917.

Sobornoe Ulozhenie : Muscovite legal code of 1649, and the first systematic treatment of Muscovite laws, superseding earlier codes. In addressing property rights and other issues of importance to Muscovite urban and land-owning communities, it had the legal effect of turning peasants into serfs. It was not replaced until 1835. Serfdom was theoretically abolished in 1861, but indentured ex-serfs were the principal human capital that fuelled Moscow's industrialization of the late nineteenth century.

socialist realism: official Soviet policy for all the arts. In 1934, it was defined as 'the truthful, historically-concrete depiction of reality in its revolutionary development'. In practice, socialist realism meant Stalinism, with the arts becoming instruments for the development of the New Soviet Man. Its most lasting results are found in Moscow architecture.

socialist reconstruction: umbrella term for the rebuilding of Russian infrastructure and industry following the Second World War. It was used to justify continued economic austerity and hardship in the immediate post-war period.

***Sotrudnichestvo*:** 'socialist commonwealth'; Eastern European members of the Soviet Bloc.

***sotsart*:** short for socialist art. Coined by dissident artists Komar and Melamid to parody socialist realist paintings. Their works included *Stalin Visited by the Muse* and *I saw Lenin as a Child.*

***souq*:** A pre-Isamic Arabic word derived from the verb 'to drive cattle', by extension, market. Oriental-style markets are found in districts of Moscow inhabited by Muslims or people from Central Asia. The first *souq* established under Russian auspices may have been in Kazan after its conquest by Ivan the Terrible.

***Sovnarkom*:** acronym for Council of People's Commissars, *Soviet Narodnykh Kommissarov.* First established in 1918 by the Second All-Russian Congress, it was effectively the Russian Government or Cabinet, becoming the USSR Council of Ministers in 1946. Of its original sixteen members, only five died by natural causes, including Lenin and Stalin.

***Sputnik*:** 'fellow-traveller'; also Soviet term for an artificial satellite.

***Stadtkrone*:** from German, 'Crown of the City'. An architectural concept that a city should have a dominant focal-point that would give definition to its entire public space. The projected Palace of Soviets would have fulfilled this role in Moscow, and the Church of Christ the Saviour was demolished to make way for it. The Kremlin remains Moscow's *Stadtkrone.*

***standartnyye doma*:** 'standard housing'; cheap, communal workers' living quarters, resembling military barracks, but replacing the latter which were considered inferior. Most were demolished as the result of Khrushchev's urban housing programmes.

***Stepnnaya Kniga Tsarskogo Rodoslovia*:** the Book of Degrees, the first narrative history of Russia, tracing tsarist genealogy back to Roman Emperor Augustus.

Worked out by monks under supervision of Archbishop Makarius between 1556 and 1563, its purpose was to give divine historical sanction and therefore legitimacy to the tsar.

stilyagi: from *'stil'*, or 'style'. A generation of zoot-suited youth who hung out in Moscow streets; the Russian equivalent of the British 'Mods' of the 1960s. They were often the offspring of senior Party officials having access to Western fashions, and were thus a source of embarrassment.

***streltsy*:** an elite Russian military unit of musketeers created by Ivan the Terrible in the sixteenth century and disbanded by Peter the Great in 1698 for rebellion. Numbering about 25,000 at their height, the *streltsy* acted as a kind of Praetorian Guard, having amongst their functions assuring the security and the policing of Moscow.

***subbotnik*:** literally, 'Sunday-worker', a communist ideal; i.e. volunteers who work on their days off without pay for the common good. *Subbotniki* were often called out on emergency work, such as bringing in the potato harvest. Alongside miners and convicts, many were also deployed in the construction of the Volga–Don canal and in the building of the Moscow Metro.

Sudebniki: legal codes of 1497 and 1550.

supremacism: Russian art movement of the 1920s which emphasized basic, primordial shapes. Its major exponent was Gregory Malevich, and his best-known work, *Black Square.* Some art historians have noted that its simplicity and shape recall the veil covering the Kaaba in Mecca, hence representing a deeply religious object. Obsessed with *Black Square,* Malevich had it hung above his death-bed in place of an icon.

Tatar: a Turkic ethnic group, now representing a variety of racial types owing to assimilation. Crimean and Volga Tatars migrated westwards from the Gobi region after their defeat by the Mongols in the thirteenth century, one branch becoming the Golden Horde in Crimea; another founded Kazan on the Volga. They and the Mongols, with whom they sometimes cooperated but sometimes fought, subjugated Russia. Contemporary Russian sources refer to Mongols as Tatars.

Tatlin Tower: a huge structure designed by the architect Vladimir Tatlin in 1920 as headquarters of the Third International, first planned for St. Petersburg but possibly for Moscow. Although never built, it is considered the supreme expression of constructivism in architecture.

***tiaglo*:** a complex and changing system of taxation whereby dues to the state were paid in currency, labour or in kind; later used on country estates as a unit of serf labour consisting of the serf, his wife and a horse. The *tiaglo* system allocated collective responsibility to each rural and urban community for its collection. It provided the manpower to build the successive walls of Moscow, and often, the troops to man them. Peter the Great abolished it in 1724, replacing it with a 'soul tax', but it continued in various forms, including as a source for the supply of manpower for early industrialization. Prior to its abolition, various exemptions from the *tiaglo* were a major source of social friction in Moscow.

TsKKPSS: Central Committee of the Communist Party of the Soviet Union, *Tsentral'nyi Komitet Kommunichestkoi Partii Sovietskogo Soyuza.* Highest decision-making body of the Communist Party and scene of leadership struggles.

***usadba*:** country house with outbuildings and garden. Many were built in Moscow in the eighteenth and early nineteenth centuries.

'***ville radieuse***'**:** an urban concept by the Swiss architect Le Corbusier, which would replace urban agglomerations with planned multi-storey complexes suffused with light. To achieve this in Moscow, he would have destroyed it and put a large park in its place.

VKhUTEMAS: Higher Arts and Technical Studios, *Vysshiye Khudozhestvenno-Technicheskiye Masterskiye.* Opened by Lenin in 1920, this avant-garde institution paralleled closely the German Bauhaus school in aesthetics and modernist philosophy. Post-war economic and social conditions confined it to producing 'paper architecture' of grand designs that would never be realized. Stalin had it closed in 1930.

War Communism: between 1918 and 1921, the Russian Civil War period of austerity, confiscations and expropriations. Private property was abolished and the state took controlof all labour activity. War Communism unsuccessfully attempted to eliminate money as a medium of exchange. It was succeeded by NEP.

White House: building in central Moscow of the Supreme Soviet of the Russian Federation, and scene of President Yeltsin's public defiance of the coup leaders in August 1991. Following a constitutional crisis and its bombardment in 1993, it was renamed House of the Government of the Russian Federation.

Wirtschaftswunder**:** German 'economic miracle' of the 1950s which brought about dramatic industrial growth and established the Federal Republic as a leading industrialized economy.It was triggered by the currency reform of 1948 which replaced the Reichsmark with the Deutschmark, thereby halting inflation and ensuring economic stability in West Germany.

Zamoskvorechie: 'beyond the Moscow river', on its southern bank of the river facing the Kremlin. Originally a marshy area used by the Mongols as an encampment site, by the late nineteenth century it had become a densely populated working-class district. It played a major role in the Revolution of 1917.

***zastoi*:** political and economic stagnation during the Brezhnev years.

zek: slang for *zaklyuchyennye,* 'locked', abbreviated in prison records as *z/k*. Refers to prison inmates or former inhabitants of the Gulag.

Index